... Within Reach

... Within Reach

A Guide to Successful Writing

Anna Ingalls
Southwestern College

Dan Moody
Southwestern College

Allyn and Bacon

Boston   London   Toronto   Sydney   Tokyo   Singapore

Vice President and Editor-in-Chief, Humanities: Joe Opiela
Editorial Assistant: Kate Tolini
Editorial-Production Administrator: Rob Lawson
Editorial-Production Service: Ruttle, Shaw & Wetherill
Design and Electronic Composition: Denise Hoffman
Composition Buyer: Linda Cox
Manufacturing Buyer: Suzanne Lareau
Cover Administrator: Suzanne Harbison

Copyright © 1997 by Allyn & Bacon
A Viacom Company
Needham Heights, MA 02194
Internet: www.abacon.com
America Online: keyword: College Online

Library of Congress Cataloging-in-Publication Data

Ingalls, Anna.
    Within Reach: A Guide to Successful Writing / Anna Ingalls, Dan Moody.
      p.   cm.
    Includes bibliographical references and index.
    ISBN 0–205–16085–9
     1. English language—Rhetoric.   2. English language—Grammar.
  I. Moody, Dan.   II. Title.
  PE1408.I46   1997
  808'.042—dc20   96–2381
                                         CIP

Printed in the United States of America

10 9 8 7 6 5 4 3 2 1   00 99 98 97 96

■ ■ ■ Contents

....2

Writing That Tells a Story   35

■■■3

Writing That Explains
How to Do Something   87

....4

Writing That Describes Something 141

...5

Writing That Explains Similarities and Differences   205

Enrichment Section: Writing an Imaginative Comparison   258

Section Two: Sentence and Grammar Skills   291

Enrichment Section: Conducting a Survey   311

▪▪▪ 7

Writing That Analyzes
Why and How   317

Enrichment Section: Writing a Book Review   437

Reference Section   441

Index   457

■ ■ ■ Thematic Contents

All writing examples, sentence combining paragraphs (identified by SC), proofreading paragraphs (identified by PR), and other continuous discourse class practices (identified by CP), are grouped thematically in the following list.

■ ■ ■ Preface

Within Reach: A Guide to Successful Writing is a developmental writing textbook/workbook designed to appeal to and meet the needs of a wide range of students in basic writing courses. Written for students from many different backgrounds, it incorporates both mainstream and multicultural viewpoints and experiences. Varied learning styles are also accommodated, with exercises and activities ranging from discovery learning, oral prewriting, and group workshops to more traditional explanations, examples, exercises, and checklists. These varied activities lend themselves to both traditional and progressive teaching approaches.

Organization of *Within Reach: A Guide to Successful Writing*

The eight chapters in *Within Reach: A Guide to Successful Writing* are arranged to provide a smooth, step-by-step transition from writing informal paragraphs in Chapter 1 to writing a short essay in Chapter 8. Organizational patterns as well as critical thinking skills progress in sophistication throughout the book. The writing focus begins with students writing about themselves in Chapter 1, continues with the writer's own life experiences in Chapter 2, where narration is featured, moves to the writer's own abilities with instructions in Chapter 3, and then to the writer's observations in Chapter 4, highlighting description. Chapter 5 focuses on comparison/contrast, followed by progressively more demanding critical thinking and organizational skills with classification in Chapter 6 and cause and effect analysis in Chapter 7. By Chapter 8, students are choosing and combining rhetorical styles and organizational patterns to fit their topics.

Each chapter includes a writing section and a sentence structure and grammar section, with both sections integrated, that is, with students encouraged to apply each sentence structure and grammar element to their own writing. Each chapter also includes an optional enrichment section for those who want a more challenging and/or more imaginative writing assignment.

The writing sections walk students through the steps of the writing process, from prewriting through revising and proofreading. Students are encouraged to work collaboratively during the various stages of the writing process with oral prewriting activities, workshop questions, and various other opportunities for group work. Critical points are not only explained but also illustrated, and students are asked to make judgments as to what techniques work best in specific cases; for example, which type of topic sentence or conclusion is most effective. There are forty-five student-written examples, mostly single paragraphs in the first four chapters and mostly multi-paragraph examples in the second half of the book, and the writing process presented in each chapter is applicable to either single paragraph assignments or multi-paragraph papers.

The sentence structure and grammar sections present the basic patterns of English sentences and high-frequency grammar items, emphasizing how to use a variety of correct sentence structure and grammar forms rather than teaching the forms in isolation. Beginning with simple sentences in Chapter 1, each chapter presents a new group of connectors and new sentence patterns, culminating in Chapters 6 and 7, where students learn how to put everything together in order to create a variety of longer sentences with three or more clauses, and Chapter 8, where students develop a sense of style, using a variety of sentence lengths and types. Exercises range from discrete to contextualized, and students are repeatedly guided toward incorporating these structural tools in their own writing. Sentence combining paragraphs in each chapter also provide a more intuitive approach to writing fluency and mastery of target structures.

Features of *Within Reach: A Guide to Successful Writing*

- **Step-by-Step Explanations** are clear and easy for students at a basic writing level to understand.

- **Exploring Topics Worksheets** help students generate interesting topics with audience appeal.

- **Prewriting Worksheets and Oral Prewriting Activities** enable students to discover details about their topics.

- **Cooperative Learning Activities** encourage students to use feedback from workshop groups as they plan, develop, and edit their papers.

- **Authentic Student-Written Examples** representing a wide range of ages, backgrounds, and ethnicities provide easily accessible models for basic writers.

- **Writing Checklists** at the end of each chapter help students check the content and organization of their writing, as well as sentence structure and grammar.

- **Sentence Patterns** enable students to master a variety of different sentence structures without complicated terminology.

- **Sentence Structure Errors,** such as comma splices, run-ons, and fragments, are taught in conjunction with sentence patterns, giving students an understanding of how these errors occur, as well as how to correct them.

- **Looking at Sentences in Context** leads students to recognize target structures and to use them in their own writing.

- **Proofreading Paragraphs** provide practice in editing and revising continuous discourse.

- **Sentence Combining Paragraphs** help both native speakers and non-native speakers develop greater writing fluency.

- **Selected Grammar Topics** in each chapter include items most often needed by basic writing students, such as subject–verb agreement, past tense verbs, and perfect tenses.

- **Gender Issues** are addressed with pronoun usage, and every effort has been made to portray both genders on an equal basis in professional, academic, and recreational situations.

- **Enrichment Sections** offer additional writing options for classes or individuals who may be at a somewhat higher level or whose experience will be enriched by a more creative assignment.

- **The Reference Section** contains four useful appendices that students may consult during the process of writing and revising: extra prewriting worksheets, a list and examples of the main English sentence patterns, a list of irregular verb forms, and spelling rules for -ed, -ing, -er, and -est suffixes.

Acknowledgments

Anna would like to express her appreciation to her daughter and son, Joy and Todd, for their patience and understanding during the many months that writing this text absorbed her time and attention. She wants to thank her parents, Louis and Margaret Diedrich, for encouraging her to grow up to become a teacher and a writer and for giving her some of the life experiences that found their way into this text. Special thanks also go to her friends Marisol Samaras and Steve Flick, who reviewed portions of the manuscript, made creative suggestions, and helped to keep her writing. Professionally, Anna owes a debt of gratitude to Sheridan Baker, of the University of Michigan, who taught her well, and whose teaching strategies have influenced her own.

Dan would especially like to thank his wife Kathleen, without whose love and support *Within Reach: A Guide to Successful Writing* would not have been possible; his children Rachel, Sarah, and Hannah; and his parents, brothers, sister, and friends for encouraging and supporting him emotionally during the long process of writing this book. He also wishes to thank the many teachers and mentors who have taught, inspired, and advised him, especially Dr. Jean Zukowski/Faust, at Northern Arizona University, and Sally Berke, Gary Jensen, and Deborah Phillips, at the American Language Institute at San Diego State University.

Numerous friends and colleagues have also contributed to making this book possible. Jane Tassi, more than anyone else, helped our book find its way to the publisher. Cristina Chiriboga, formerly Dean of Language Arts at Southwestern College, first suggested that we work together as a writing team and encouraged us as our project grew into a textbook. Dagmar Fields, Frank Giardina, Joe Leonard, Phil López, Glenda McGee, Kathy Parrish, Marsha Rutter, Bobbe Tatreau, and Eileen Zamora offered us their comments and insights, as well as some of their students' well-written papers. Steve Kowit encouraged us by sharing his own experience as an author. Elvira Córdova, Ron Vess, and Art Stone helped provide us with facts and information. David Shepherd, Jo Ann Forbes, and Bill Alexander provided technical support when we needed it. Patti Larkin, at the Southwestern College bookstore, efficiently facilitated publication of preliminary versions for classroom use. These are just a few of the many friends and colleagues at Southwestern College and elsewhere who helped in so many ways by giving us a word of advice here, a suggestion there, and a sympathetic ear at times when our project threatened to overwhelm us.

Our students have been of great help to us in writing this book by telling us what they needed, showing us what worked and what didn't, and classroom testing everything that we wrote. We are especially grateful to the following students who gave us permission to use their paragraphs and papers in this text: Arturo Alcantara, Cassandra Dorsey, Mayra Donado, Kumiko Inman, Mark Albarran, Mark Field, Steven E. Wiggs, Deanna Hernandez, Jason Cross, Todd Louis, Liza Torres, Denver Greiner, Richard D. Munholand, Karmina Charfauros, Pilar Guerrero, Maria Theresa B. Barron, Sadie Sullivan-Greiner, William S. White, Todd Tenbrook, Shawn McPherren, Yanina Swiderski, Danny Banda, Estel Manito-Stokholm, Armando Barcelon, Trent Parker, Carla Garcia, Ray Jensen, Toshiko Williams, Damon Aikens, Aurora Alvarez, Cynthia Uribe, Steven Tanciatco, Tiffany Turner, Mary Miller, Joy Snyder, Zachary Reiff, Nancy Gutierrez, Rosa Hammar, Angelique St. Jacques, Ann E. Pietrzak.

At Allyn and Bacon, we wish to thank Katrina Kohanowich, Regional Sales Representative, and Joe Opiela, Vice President and Editor-in-Chief, Humanities, for discovering our book and believing in us, and Kate Tolini, Editorial Assistant, for her helpfulness and efficiency. We would also like to acknowledge the following reviewers for taking the time to read our manuscript and providing valuable feedback: Eric Hibbison of J. Sargeant Reynolds Community College, Eileen Schwartz of Purdue University, and Audry Roth of Miami–Dade Community College.

■ ■ ■ Introduction

Welcome to *Within Reach: A Guide to Successful Writing*. Whether you are a fairly experienced writer or a beginning writer, this book can help you learn to express your ideas more clearly and effectively. In each chapter you will learn a variety of writing skills and techniques, as well as useful sentence and grammar skills, that will help you progress as a writer.

Because different people learn in different ways, this book teaches writing in more than one way. Some people learn best by reading or hearing explanations, others learn best by studying an example, and some learn best by doing—by practicing writing and learning from their own errors. *Within Reach: A Guide to Successful Writing* uses all of these methods of teaching. There are explanations and step-by-step instructions *telling* how to write, there are numerous example paragraphs and short papers *showing* how to write, and there are many worksheets and class practice exercises to help you learn to write by *doing*.

The rest of the introduction will give you a preview of the writing process and will tell you what *Within Reach: A Guide to Successful Writing* has to offer.

Preview of the Writing Process

Writing paragraphs and short papers can seem like a difficult and complex process, but you can learn to write well by taking things one step at a time. This book will take you through all the necessary steps, from start to finish, that will enable you to write a good paper. Each chapter will show you how to develop a different kind of paragraph or short paper by following these steps:

The Writing Process

- **Prewriting:** exploring topics, discovering details, and planning what to write
- **Writing:** organizing your ideas and making a rough draft
- **Rewriting:** using feedback and revising
- **Proofreading:** checking your paper for good sentence structure, grammar, spelling, punctuation, and completeness

Using this step-by-step writing process will help make writing easier and less stressful. It is the method that most good writers use, even professional writers.

The first step, *prewriting,* begins as soon as you start to think about writing something. Have you ever been assigned a paper and didn't know how to begin or what to write about? Maybe you sat down with a pen and paper, but the words just wouldn't come. For many people, this is the hardest part of writing. In this book you will learn and practice a number of ways to come up with ideas, organize them, and get them on paper. These spoken and written prewriting activities are not difficult to learn, and they will help you get ready to write so that your writing experience will be successful. By the end of this book you will have practiced a number of different methods of prewriting so that you can choose the ones that work best for you.

After you have figured out what you want to write about and have a pretty good idea of what you want to say, the next step is *writing.* Sometimes, especially for a paper written in class or a short informal paragraph (like the assignment in Chapter 1), the writing process may stop here. However, in most cases, the first version of your paper is simply a *rough draft.* This is where you get all the information you have into roughly the form and style you want.

The next step is *rewriting* the rough draft to make it as complete, interesting, and well-organized as you can. An important part of rewriting is getting feedback from other people by asking for their opinions and suggestions, so each chapter includes cooperative learning activities in which you will work with others to improve your writing. These supportive activities will help reduce the stress experienced by many writers, especially during this part of the writing process.

The final step is *proofreading* your paper to make sure that your sentence structure, grammar, spelling, and punctuation are correct and that you have not forgotten anything. Section Two of each chapter, which focuses on Sentence and Grammar Skills, will help you learn how to proofread for the most common types of sentence structure and grammar problems. At the end of each chapter, there is a checklist to help you put the finishing touches on the final draft of your paper before you turn it in.

By following this step-by-step process of *prewriting, writing, rewriting,* and *proofreading,* you will be able to complete each writing assignment successfully, and you will feel better about your writing as you develop stronger writing skills.

Writing Objectives

Part of learning to write well is understanding how to organize and develop different kinds of paragraphs and short papers effectively. Here is a list of important writing skills that you will learn:

Writing Objectives

- How to write a good topic sentence and short introduction
- How to present and organize the information in the body of a paragraph or short paper
- How to end a paragraph or short paper effectively
- How to use a variety of different types of writing for different purposes
- How to make your writing interesting so that it appeals to your audience
- How to combine different types of writing in a short essay

A good paragraph or short paper should be organized so that the writer's ideas are clear and easy to follow. A *topic sentence* expresses the main point of the paper in one clear sentence, usually at the beginning. Next comes the main part of the paragraph or paper, also called the *body*, which explains the major points the writer wants to make, including details about each point. At the end, the *conclusion* ties everything together. Each chapter will take you step by step through the process of writing a paragraph or short paper with a topic sentence, body, and conclusion. Although the first few chapters focus primarily on paragraph-length assignments, you will also learn how papers that are longer than one paragraph can be organized and developed using the same techniques. As soon as you are ready, you may move from writing paragraphs to writing papers that are more than a page in length.

You will also learn about a number of ways to write for different purposes, beginning with the types of writing that are most natural and easiest to organize: writing about yourself, telling a story, and explaining how to do something. Later in the book, you will learn various methods of planning and organizing other kinds of writing, including writing that describes something, writing that classifies things into groups, writing that analyzes why and how, and writing that explains similarities and differences. For each type of writing, you will learn special techniques to make your paper interesting and effective so that it will appeal to your audience. In the final chapter of the book, you will learn how to combine various types of writing in a short essay.

Sentence and Grammar Objectives

Sentence structure and grammar skills are also an important part of writing an effective paper. Poorly written sentences and incorrect grammar can cause readers to focus on the mistakes rather than on the ideas you want to communicate. To help you improve your sentence structure and grammar, each chapter has a Sentence and Grammar Skills section that will review and allow you to practice the following skills:

> ## Sentence and Grammar Objectives
>
> - How to use a variety of sentence types to make your writing interesting
> - How to recognize and correct common sentence errors
> - How to combine sentences to develop an intuitive mastery of sentence structure
> - How to apply useful grammar points to your writing and avoid common grammar errors

Just as a mechanic or a carpenter has a large number of tools to get the job done more effectively, a writer also must be able to use a wide variety of writing tools in order to communicate effectively. By learning to use a variety of sentence structures, a writer can select the one that feels right to express a particular idea. In each chapter you will learn about and practice sentence patterns, starting with basic sentences and progressing to more advanced sentence structures that can help you express your ideas more clearly and effectively. You will also learn how to recognize and correct common sentence errors, such as fragments, run-ons, and comma splices. After practicing with proofreading paragraphs in the text, you will be able to avoid these kinds of sentence errors in your own writing.

For many students, grammar seems like one of the biggest obstacles to writing confidently, and for that reason each chapter of *Within Reach: A Guide to Successful Writing* includes a grammar review section. The grammar topics have been chosen with attention to the needs of both native English speakers and students for whom English is a second language. They include areas where writers most often have problems or questions, such as subject/verb agreement, irregular verbs, and pronoun usage.

A special feature included in the Sentence and Grammar Skills section of each chapter of *Within Reach: A Guide to Successful Writing* is sentence combining. Using the sentence and grammar elements presented in the chapter, as well as your own intuitive knowledge of the language, you will combine groups of short, basic sentences into longer, more effective sentences. For many people, sentence combining is an ideal way to develop greater fluency in their writing because the focus is on putting the elements together smoothly and naturally rather than on analyzing grammar and structure.

Another special feature of *Within Reach: A Guide to Successful Writing* is that the sentence and grammar topics for each chapter have been selected to coordinate with the type of writing used in that chapter. For that reason, several of the exercises and proofreading paragraphs, as well as the sentence combining paragraphs, provide additional examples of the type of writing featured in the Writing Section. However, the Sentence and Grammar Skills sections can also be done separately if you prefer, for example if you want to learn about a certain grammar topic before you get to the rest of that chapter.

Becoming a Successful Writer

When you finish this book, you should understand the steps of writing a paragraph or short paper, be familiar with different types of writing, know how to use a wide variety of sentence types correctly and effectively, and be able to avoid common grammar errors. This book is based on the belief that, with the right kind of help and support, every student can become a better writer. We wish you success as you work to accomplish this goal.

Getting Started

SECTION ONE:
Writing an Informal Paragraph

Goals

In this section of the chapter you will learn how to do the following:

- Recognize the basic form of a paragraph
- Use an oral prewriting activity to help you get ready to write
- Write an informal paragraph about yourself
- Become more comfortable with the writing process

Learning about Paragraphs

What Is a Paragraph?

A paragraph consists of *a group of sentences that all relate to the same specific topic*. Some paragraphs are only a few sentences long, while others may be as long as a page. A paragraph can be part of a longer paper, or it can stand alone as a separate writing assignment. The first sentence of every paragraph should be indented about half an inch, and each new paragraph must start on a new line. Indenting each paragraph is important because it is a signal to the reader that the sentences to follow all relate to the same topic and belong together. Unless your teacher tells you otherwise, you should also leave about one inch blank (a *margin*) on each side of the page and write on only one side of each piece of paper.

All of the sentences in a paragraph must be about the same topic. For example, if you are writing a paragraph about your interests and activities, everything you say in that paragraph has to relate to one of your interests or activities. Your paragraph could include a sentence or two about each activity, or perhaps several sentences about the most important ones. If the topic of your paragraph is only one specific activity, such as bicycling or restoring old cars, then all of the sentences in the paragraph would have to be about that activity. A paragraph on the topic of bicycling, for instance, could include information such as where you like to ride, how often and how far you ride, what kind of bike you have, how bicycling improves your muscle tone and relieves stress, and so on.

The following paragraphs were written by two students telling about themselves as an introductory assignment on the first day of a writing course. They show the basic form of a paragraph. Since the topic for the paragraph was themselves, the writers included a variety of things about themselves, such as their interests and activities, their jobs, their family life, their goals for the future, and so on. Notice that these two writers did not include exactly the same kinds of information in their paragraphs because different things were important to each of them, but they both stayed focused on the specific topic of the paragraph—themselves.

Me

Hi! My name is Arturo Alcantara. I'm twenty-six years old and getting older. I used to work for Holiday Inn at the Embarcadero as a waiter. It wasn't a bad job, but I quit and got hands-on training to get a better life. My trade is solar installation now. I like sports, especially football, baseball, and basketball on T.V. In my free time I often go mountain bicycling or road cycling. I enjoy listening to rock-and-roll like Metallica, Megadeth, and Slayer. I drive a Z-28 Camaro that I bought with my own money. During most of my life I want to be rich because life is boring without money. If I had just one wish I would wish to live in a place where time would never run out.

About Myself

My name is Cassandra Dorsey. I was born in Pachuta, Mississippi, but I was raised in San Jose, California. After I got married, my husband and I moved to Los Angeles. He was in the Navy, so his job transferred him there. Later we moved to San Diego. Now I'm in the process of going through a divorce because of spousal abuse. In my spare time I enjoy having quiet moments reading, sewing, walking, meditating, or just listening to soft, quiet jazz. When I'm not studying, I make sure I spend at least an hour and a half a day of quality time with my daughter. I love to travel and take small mini-vacations at least once a month with my new boyfriend and my daughter. When times get stressful, we take off and forget our troubles and just have a wonderful time in a new environment. I'm reentering college and hoping to become a physical therapist when I graduate. I would love to help people rehabilitate themselves and regain their strength.

Writing Objective: An Informal Paragraph

Your objective for this chapter is to write a paragraph about yourself. It should have the basic form of a paragraph, like the examples above, but it does not need to have any particular kind of organization or structure, as many other kinds of writing do. Therefore, it is an *informal paragraph*.

One purpose of this writing assignment is to help you become familiar with the steps in the writing process and start to get comfortable with writing. Writing about yourself is a good place to begin because you are very familiar with your topic. In fact, writing an informal paragraph about yourself is almost like talking to someone about yourself except that you are doing it on paper. You can include many of the same kinds of things that you would talk about if you were getting acquainted with someone or introducing yourself to a group.

The two paragraphs above, by Arturo Alcantara and Cassandra Dorsey, are both informal paragraphs. These writers simply explained some of the most important or most interesting things about themselves, such as their jobs, the things they enjoy doing, their hopes and plans for the future, and a little bit about their life histories. They wrote down the information in whatever order seemed natural and tried to include some interesting details so that readers would get to know them better.

Your own informal paragraph may also include a variety of different kinds of information about yourself. However, you do not have to write about exactly the same kinds of things as Arturo and Cassandra did. It is all right to include whatever you want to say about yourself. If you prefer, you may narrow down your topic to only one or two aspects of your life, such as your career goals or some special talent that you have, rather than writing about a variety of different things.

It is always important to have a clear understanding of your writing objective before you begin to write a paper. That's why each chapter, like this one, begins by explaining the type of writing that you will be doing, with details about the specific writing assignment for the chapter. At this point, you are ready to begin the actual writing process with *Prewriting Activities*.

Prewriting Activities

The first step in writing an informal paragraph about yourself is *prewriting*, or getting ready to write. Before you start writing this or any other paper, you should have a general idea of what you are going to say. Knowing what you are going to write about will help you feel more at ease when you are writing, and therefore you will be able to do a better job.

The first prewriting activity in every chapter is called *Exploring Topics* because it will help you think of a variety of topics and find one that you like. In this case, you already have a general topic—yourself. Therefore, the *Exploring Topics Worksheet* will give you several options to help make your topic a little more specific and clear in your mind.

After you have finished the *Exploring Topics Worksheet*, the next part of prewriting is *Discovering Details*. This activity, which you will do with other classmates, will help you think of details to make your paper interesting. Each chapter in the book will have these same two types of prewriting activities: *Exploring Topics* and *Discovering Details*.

Exploring Topics

Do you already have some ideas for what you want to write about yourself, or are you worried that you won't have anything to say? Either way, doing the following *Exploring Topics Worksheet* will help you come up with several ideas that you may want to include in your informal paragraph about yourself.

■ **WORKSHEET I** | ### Exploring Topics for an Informal Paragraph about Yourself

Directions: Briefly answer at least seven of the following questions about yourself. It is not necessary to write complete sentences.

1. What are some of the things that you like to do in your free time? (sports, recreational activities, etc.)

2. What type of job do you have or want to have?

3. What are your goals and ambitions?

4. What are you studying, and which classes do you enjoy the most?

5. What are some of your special skills or talents?

6. Who are the most important people in your life, and why are they important to you?

7. What are some of your best qualities or characteristics?

8. What makes you feel happy or proud?

9. What special or interesting things have you done?

10. What else would you like to tell readers about yourself?

Discovering Details

Answering Interview Questions

It is usually helpful to talk about a topic before you write about it. Talking with someone else helps you think of interesting ideas and express them in words, and you will be able to use some of these ideas when you write. For this activity, you and one of your classmates will interview each other. In addition to getting acquainted, you will be talking about things that you can include in your informal paragraph.

Before you begin, look over the following list of interview questions. They are based on the questions on the *Exploring Topics Worksheet* that you just completed. However, they ask for more detailed answers than you wrote on the worksheet. There are blanks at the end of the list so that you can add some additional questions of your own. You may want to discuss ideas for questions with the entire class, or you and your partner can come up with your own questions. Try to think of some of the same kinds of questions that you normally ask when you are getting acquainted with new people.

Interview Questions

1. What sports, recreational activities, or other things do you enjoy doing in your free time? What do you especially like about each one?

2. Describe your present job or a job that you hope to have in the future.

3. What are your goals and ambitions? Which ones are most important to you? How do you plan to achieve them?

4. What are you studying, and which classes do you enjoy the most? Why do you like these classes?

5. What are some of your special skills or talents? Are you involved in any activities that use these skills or talents?

6. Who are the most important people in your life, and why are they important to you?

7. Describe your personality. What are some of your best qualities or characteristics?

8. What makes you feel happy or proud? Can you tell about some specific experiences that have made you feel happy or proud?

9. What special or interesting things have you done? Tell about some of your experiences.

10. Is there anything else that you would like to say about yourself?

11. _____

12. _____

After you have added your questions to the list, you and your partner can begin interviewing each other. First one person should be the interviewer and ask questions for about five minutes. Then you should switch roles so that the other person can be the interviewer. When you are answering questions, include details and explanations to make your answers interesting. The interviewer can also ask additional questions in order to find out more information. If you run out of questions before the interview time is up, you can simply talk about yourself for the remaining time, telling your partner anything that you would like to.

Writing

Putting Your Ideas on Paper

Now that you have completed the prewriting activities, you are ready to write an informal paragraph about yourself. You may choose several ideas from the *Exploring Topics Worksheet* that you would like to include, or, if you prefer, you may narrow down the topic to only one or two things from the worksheet. In order to come up with interesting details, try to recall your answers to some of the interview questions. You may also add anything else about yourself that you would like to.

Here are two more examples of informal paragraphs. Both writers included a variety of topics from the *Exploring Topics Worksheet*. In the first paragraph, Mayra Donado introduces herself by telling about her family, where she lived and went to school, the courses she is taking, her major, and her goals.

My Life

My name is Mayra Donado. I was born in Guatemala. I'm nineteen years old. I have one sister who is twenty years old, and one brother who is eighteen. I'm the middle child in my family. When I was younger, I went to school in Guatemala from first to tenth grade. I lived there with my grandmother until I was seventeen. After that, I came to the United States because my mother was working here and she wanted me to live with her. I came with my sister to live here in Chula Vista because we wanted to learn English. Chula Vista has been my home for almost three years, and I graduated from Chula Vista High School one year ago. Now, I'm studying here at Southwestern College. I'm taking just general classes, like English, because I want to increase my knowledge of English. The next semester, I will take some classes in my major, which is International Business. After I have a career, I would like to get married and have two children. I think that if I study hard and have a career, I am going to be someone who doesn't have to depend on other people.

The next informal paragraph, by Kumiko Inman, also includes why she came to the United States, her career goals, and her plans to have a family. In addition, she talks about her present job and her favorite activities.

Myself

I am Kumiko Inman, and I have been in the States for a year now. When my husband had to transfer to San Diego from Japan, I was glad and also a little bit scared. But when I started life with him in San Diego, I really felt glad we had come to the United States. One reason is that I got a job as a wait-ress, so I can meet people and get used to speaking with many Americans to improve my English. Also, I started going to college. My goal is to transfer to a four-year college eventually. After I get a degree in accounting or business, I would like to get a job in a Japanese company in the States or an American company in Japan because that way I can help both nations in some ways. At the same time, I would like to have a family since I am already twenty-nine years old. I would like to have a child within a year if we can. I know it is going to be difficult to go to school and raise a child, but with my husband's help, I think I can do it. In my spare time, I go to see movies or do exercises to keep in shape. I still have to lose weight, and I like the feeling that I have accom-plished something after I exercise or run. I am not sure how long we will stay in the States, but I would like to make the best of it while I am here.

Your own paragraph may include some of the same kinds of topics that Mayra and Kumiko wrote about, or you may want to explain different kinds of things about yourself. You may also want to look again at the example paragraphs by Arturo and Cassandra earlier in this chapter on page 8 to see how they introduced themselves. Try to give your readers (your *audience*) some idea of who you are and what is important in your life.

As you are writing your paragraph, remember to indent the first line, and leave a one-inch margin on each side of the page. Don't worry too much about your spelling and punctuation in this first paragraph, especially if you are writing in class, but do your best to express your ideas clearly. Try to write at least half a page, but feel free to write as much as you want.

How Did You Feel about Writing?

After you have finished writing your informal paragraph, in a small group, discuss how you felt when you were writing. Did it seem easier than you thought it would be? Were you nervous about it or fairly relaxed? One of the goals of this textbook is to help you feel comfortable with writing. If you like, share your feelings with your group or with the class.

Completing the Writing Process

Usually the next step in the writing process is *rewriting*, that is, revising and improving what you have written, followed by *proofreading*, to make sure that everything is written accurately and correctly. However, since this first paragraph is informal, it is not necessary to do these additional steps, unless your teacher tells you otherwise. The goal of this writing assignment was to introduce you to the first two steps in the process, *prewriting* and *writing*. All of the other chapters will take you step by step through the entire process.

Before you go on to writing a paragraph that tells a story in Chapter 2, your teacher may ask you to complete Section 2 of this chapter, Sentence and Grammar Skills. In Section 2, you will learn the essential elements of basic sentence structure and guidelines for choosing verbs that agree with their subjects. In addition, you will have an opportunity to try sentence combining, which will help you become a more fluent writer.

SECTION TWO:
Sentence and Grammar Skills

Goals

In this section of the chapter, you will learn how to do the following:

- Recognize subjects and verbs
- Recognize and write complete sentences
- Use correct subject–verb agreement
- Combine short sentences for greater sentence variety

Learning about Sentences

Recognizing Subjects and Action Verbs

In order to be able to write a variety of correct sentence types, you must learn how to recognize *subjects* and *verbs*. In everyday English, *subject* means about the same thing as *topic*. However, when we are talking about sentence structure, the word *subject* has another meaning altogether. In most sentences, the *subject* is the word or words that tell who or what performs the action of the sentence. Let's take a look at the subjects in the following sentences:

EXAMPLE 1 ➤ *Dave* supervises the microcomputer lab at Southwestern College.

Dave is the subject of this sentence because he is the one that does the supervising.

EXAMPLE 2 ➤ *Students and instructors* work in the lab.

The subject of the sentence is *students and instructors* because they perform the action: they do the work. As this sentence shows, sometimes more than one person may be the subject of a sentence.

Most subjects are *nouns*—that is, words that name people, places, things, or ideas. However, sometimes other kinds of words can also be used as subjects, as in the next two sentences:

EXAMPLE 3 ➤   *We* attended the graduation ceremony last Friday.

EXAMPLE 4 ➤   At the end of the game, *everyone* ran onto the playing field.

The subjects *we* and *everyone* are *pronouns,* that is, words that can be used in the place of nouns. Pronouns are generally used when it isn't necessary or practical to name the people involved. Some other pronouns that can be used as subjects are *I, you, he, she, it, they, everybody, someone,* and *somebody.* (For more information about pronouns, see Chapter 7.)

In addition to having a *subject,* sentences also need to have a *verb.* An *action verb* is the word or words that express the action in the sentence. In the four sentences above, the action verbs are *supervises, work, attended,* and *ran.* Notice that the subject comes before the verb in all of these sentences. This is the normal word order for most English sentences. Just as there can be more than one word used as the subject of a sentence, there can also be more than one verb in a sentence.

Look for the subjects and action verbs in each of the following sentences. Try finding the verb (or verbs) first, and then locate the subject by figuring out who or what did the action.

EXAMPLE 5 ➤   Javier's ancestors came from Bolivia.

EXAMPLE 6 ➤   During the storm, lightning flashed across the sky and struck a tree.

Did you find the action verb *came* in Example 5 and the two action verbs *flashed* and *struck* in Example 6? These verbs tell us the actions that took place. To figure out the subject of each sentence, we need to identify who or what did these actions. In Example 5, Javier's *ancestors* are the ones who came from Bolivia, not Javier, so *ancestors* is the subject. In Example 6, *lightning* is the thing that flashed and struck something, so *lightning* is the subject. "During the storm" is an introductory phrase that tells us when the action happened (like "at the end of the game" in Example 4). In sentences with an introductory phrase, remember to look for the subject and verb *after* the introductory phrase.

Recognizing Auxiliary Verbs

Sometimes a verb consists of more than one word. We often use *auxiliary verbs* (or helping verbs) to put the action into a different time period or modify the meaning of the main verb. Some of the words that are most commonly used as auxiliary verbs are *has, have, had, do, does, did, am, is, are, was,* and *were.* A special group of auxiliary verbs called *modal auxiliaries* add other meanings to the main verb, such as possibility or obligation. Some of the most common modal auxiliaries include *can, could, may, might, should, would,* and *must.*

Look for the subjects and verbs in the following sentences. Remember that the verb may consist of two words (or sometimes more) if it includes an auxiliary verb.

EXAMPLE 7 ➤   Jake might work as a lifeguard at Myrtle Beach this summer.

EXAMPLE 8 ➤   Two helicopters are flying over the area now.

The subject and verb in Example 7 are *Jake* (subject) and *might work* (verb). The modal auxiliary *might* adds the idea of possibility to the main verb *work,* so both words should be identified as the verb. In Example 8, the verb consists of two words, *are flying,* and the subject is *helicopters.* (If you identified "two helicopters" as the subject, your answer could also be considered correct. Words like *two* that help to identify or describe the subject may be included as part of what we call the *complete subject.* However, in this book, we will normally use the word *subject* to refer to the *simple subject,* the main word or words that identify who or what performs the action.)

Recognizing Imperative Verbs

All sentences in written English must have both a subject and a verb, with one important exception. Sentences with *imperative verbs,* which are used to express a command or request or to give instructions, do not have a subject stated in the sentence. The subject of an imperative verb is understood to be "you," the person who is being asked or told to do something. Here is an example of a sentence with an imperative verb (V) and the understood subject (S) "you":

                    S = [You]   *V*
EXAMPLE 9 ➤   *Write* at least a page in your journal every week.

Distinguishing Subjects from Other Nouns in a Sentence

Sentences often contain nouns that are not part of the subject but are used in other ways. Therefore, it is important to be able to distinguish the subject from these other nouns in the sentence. Two of the other ways that nouns can be used are as *objects following verbs* and as *nouns in prepositional phrases.*

The most common type of *object* (also called a *direct object*) is a person or thing that is acted upon or receives the action of the verb, like *short stories* in this example:

                        S   *V*   *O*
EXAMPLE 10 ➤   Deborah and Joel submitted their *short stories* for the scholarship competition.

If there is an *object* (*O*) in a sentence, be careful not to confuse it with the *subject,* which *performs* the action, like *Deborah* and *Joel* in this sentence.

Nouns also frequently appear in *prepositional phrases*. A *prepositional phrase* is a group of words that begins with a special word called a preposition and ends with a noun (or sometimes a pronoun). A few of the most common prepositions are *about, across, after, at, by, during, for, from, in, of, on, onto, to,* and *with.* (A more complete list of prepositions can be found later in this chapter on page 27.) Sometimes a writer may add important information with a prepositional phrase right after the subject. In this case, be careful not to mistake the noun in the prepositional phrase for the subject of the sentence. Notice the prepositional phrases in italics in the following sentence:

EXAMPLE 11 ➤
$\quad$ *S* $\qquad$ *Prep Phrase* $\qquad$ *V* $\qquad\qquad\qquad$ *Prep Phrase*
Stories *of the Old West* have a certain appeal *for many people.*

The subject in this sentence is *stories,* not *the Old West.*

Prepositional phrases can appear after the subject, after the verb, after the object, as introductory phrases at the beginning, or almost anywhere else in a sentence. Example sentences 4 and 6, for instance, both had introductory prepositional phrases, as well as prepositional phrases in other places:

$\quad$ *Prep Phrase* $\qquad\qquad$ *S* $\quad$ *V* $\qquad$ *Prep Phrase*
At the end of the game, everyone ran *onto the playing field.*

$\quad$ *Prep Phrase* $\qquad\qquad$ *S* $\qquad$ *V* $\qquad$ *Prep Phrase* $\qquad\qquad$ *V*
During the storm, lightning flashed *across the sky* and struck a tree.

As a general rule, if a noun is part of a prepositional phrase, it cannot also be the subject of a sentence.

■ CLASS PRACTICE 1

Recognizing Subjects and Action Verbs

PART A

Directions: The following sentences are from the informal paragraph *Me* by Arturo Alcantara. (The complete paragraph is on page 8.) Mark each subject with an *S* and each verb with a *V.*

(1) I like sports, especially football, baseball, and basketball on T.V. *(2)* In my free time I often go mountain bicycling or road cycling. *(3)* I also enjoy listening to rock-and-roll like Metallica, Megadeth, and Slayer.

PART B

Directions: Mark each subject with an *S* and each verb with a *V*.

EXAMPLE ➤
         S   *V*

The *glider soared* on the rising air currents.

1. Few people live north of the Arctic Circle.

2. The veterinarian from the zoo examined the injured mountain lion.

3. Some manufacturers are building bicycle frames from a strong new plastic material.

4. With Irma's help, Elvira will translate the lab manual into Spanish.

5. Breathe deeply and relax.

6. Todd and Jason have been studying at the New School of Architecture.

7. A deer ran across the road and disappeared among the trees.

8. At the graduation ceremony, Lorenzo sang *The Star Spangled Banner*.

9. The Red Cross helps people in other countries as well as in the United States.

10. Should we get an alarm system for the Jeep?

Recognizing Subjects and Linking Verbs

Although most verbs are action verbs, many of the most common verbs do not show action. Instead, they connect (or link) the subject with words that describe or identify it, so they are called *linking verbs*. These verbs show a condition or state rather than an action. The *subject* of a linking verb is the person or thing that is in that condition or state. Look at the subjects and linking verbs in the following sentences:

EXAMPLE 1 ➤
    S *V*

Steve is a professional jazz musician.

EXAMPLE 2 ➤
    S   *V*

Some *people might feel* uncomfortable about speaking in front of a group.

In Example 1, the verb *is* links the subject with the words "a professional jazz musician," which describe the subject *Steve*. Other forms of the verb *"to be,"* including *am, are, was, were, has been, have been,* and *will be,* can also be used as linking verbs. In Example 2, the linking verb *feel* is followed by the word "uncomfortable," which describes the subject. Other linking verbs include *appear, become, look, seem, sound, smell,* and *taste*.

Look for the subject and linking verb in each of these sentences:

EXAMPLE 3 ➤   Vincent Van Gogh became famous after his death.

EXAMPLE 4 ➤   Van Gogh's paintings look intriguing.

Did you identify *Vincent Van Gogh* as the subject and *became* as the linking verb in Example 3? The verb in Example 4 is *look,* and the subject is *paintings* because the paintings are the things that look intriguing. Notice that both linking verbs lead to words that describe the subjects—"famous" and "intriguing."

■ CLASS PRACTICE 2

Recognizing Subjects and Linking Verbs

PART A

Directions: The following sentences are taken from the informal paragraph *My Life*. (The complete paragraph is on page 12.) Mark each subject with an *S* and each verb with a *V*.

(1) My name is Mayra Donado. *(2)* I'm the middle child in my family. *(3)* Chula Vista has been my home for almost three years.

PART B

Directions: Mark each subject with an *S* and each verb with a *V*.

          S   *V*
EXAMPLE ➤   The *Mississippi River is* the longest river in the United States.

1. After the rain, the air smelled fresh and clean.

2. Arnel's special talent is interpretive dancing.

3. Paul became the first person from Grosse Pointe to win the lottery.

4. So far the astronomy course seems interesting.

5. Does the warm sand feel good on your bare feet?

6. According to the mechanic, the engine doesn't sound right.

7. Dinosaurs were the largest creatures to ever exist.

8. A hot dog at the ball park tastes better than one at home.

9. Summer concerts in the park have become popular.

10. The defendant might not be guilty.

Recognizing and Correcting Fragments

In order for a sentence to be complete, it must have at least one subject and one verb, that is, one *clause*. A *clause* is a group of words that contains a subject and a verb, either an action verb or a linking verb. In this book we will use the symbol *SV* to represent a clause.

A sentence with only one clause, or *SV*, is called a *simple sentence*. In Chapter 2 we will begin to look at sentences that have more than one *SV*, but in Chapter 1 we will concentrate on simple sentences.

Here are some examples of complete simple sentences with the subjects and verbs in italics:

EXAMPLE 1 ➤ *Computers connect* us to information networks.

EXAMPLE 2 ➤ *High surf and heavy rains caused* flooding along the coast.

All of the sentences that we have looked at so far in Chapter 1 have also been complete simple sentences.

A sentence that does not have both a subject and a verb is incomplete. If an incomplete sentence is used in writing, it is a type of sentence structure error called a *fragment*. Usually fragments do not make complete sense by themselves (except perhaps in casual conversation), so it is important to learn how to recognize and correct them.

Let's look at some examples of common fragment errors and see how they can be corrected:

EXAMPLE 3A ➤ *(Incorrect):* You can have your blood pressure checked at the nurse's office. Across from the library.

In this example, the second word group, "Across from the library," doesn't contain either a subject or a verb, so it is a fragment. To correct it, we could add a subject and a verb, or we could simply join the fragment to the previous sentence:

EXAMPLE 3B ➤ *(Correct):* You can have your blood pressure checked at the
$$S \qquad V$$
nurse's office. The nurse's office is located across from the library.

EXAMPLE 3C ➤ *(Correct):* You can have your blood pressure checked at the nurse's office across from the library.

Most fragments are simply pieces of sentences that have been accidentally separated from the sentence where they belong. Therefore, the best way to correct a fragment is usually to connect it to the previous sentence (or sometimes to the following sentence).

Here is another example:

EXAMPLE 4A ➤ *(Incorrect):* By running three miles every day. Art stays in shape.

The first word group in Example 4A has no subject or verb, so it is a fragment. Although "running" may look like a verb, *an -ing word cannot be a verb by itself; it always needs a form of "to be" as an auxiliary verb with it in order to function as the verb in a sentence.* The easiest way to correct this fragment is to join it to the next sentence, like this:

$$S \qquad V$$
EXAMPLE 4B ➤ *(Correct):* By running three miles every day, Art stays in shape.

EXAMPLE 5A ➤ *(Incorrect):* Michelle has studied for weeks. To pass the admissions test for the Sheriffs Academy.

Both the subject and the verb are missing from the second group of words in Example 5A. "To pass" is an *infinitive,* that is, "to" plus the simple form of the verb. *Even though it names an action, an infinitive cannot be used as the verb in a sentence.* To make a complete sentence with one *SV*, we can join the fragment to the previous sentence:

$$S \qquad V$$
EXAMPLE 5B ➤ *(Correct):* Michelle has studied for weeks to pass the admissions test for the Sheriffs Academy.

When you are writing, it is important to make sure that all of your sentences are complete, with both a subject and a verb. In Chapter 3, you will learn more about writing complete sentences, including how to recognize and correct other kinds of fragments.

■ **CLASS PRACTICE** **3**

Proofreading for Fragments

Directions: As you read the following paragraphs, look for fragments (incomplete sentences that do not contain at least one subject and verb). Underline each fragment and correct it by joining it to the appropriate complete sentence. (You may want to recopy this exercise on your own paper.)

Becoming a Writer

Unfortunately, not everyone is born. Knowing how to write well. In order to become good writers. Most people have to learn and practice writing skills. Some people dislike or even fear writing assignments. A blank piece of paper can be a scary thing for them. In some cases, they may have had bad experiences. With writing in the past. In other cases, they may never have had an opportunity. To learn effective writing skills. These fears and problems can be overcome. By starting at the beginning and learning to follow a step-by-step writing process.

This book will show you how to use prewriting activities. To find a topic and get some ideas down on paper. Your first draft does not have to be perfect. With help from your teacher and your workshop group. You can revise and improve it. Don't be afraid to ask questions. About organization, sentence structure, grammar, or word choices. Each step in the writing process. Will help you write a better paper. Gradually writing will become easier.

■ **CLASS PRACTICE** **4**

Writing Complete Sentences

Directions: Now write your own complete sentences. You may write about anything that you want to. When you finish, mark each subject and verb with *SV* and be sure that each sentence contains a complete clause.

1. _____

2. _____

3. _____

4. _____

5. _____

Learning about Subject–Verb Agreement

Almost all verbs in English have two forms in the present tense, depending on the subject. The following sentences show how this works:

Subject	*Verb*	
I	enjoy	hiking.
We	enjoy	hiking.
You	enjoy	hiking.
Matthew	enjoys	hiking.
Patricia	enjoys	hiking.
Patricia's dog	enjoys	hiking
Many people	enjoy	hiking.

> ### Subject–Verb Agreement
>
> When the subject is *I, we, you,* or *they* (like *many people* above), don't use an *-s* on the verb.
>
> Use the *-s* ending on the verb only when the subject is *he, she,* or *it* (like *Matthew, Patricia,* or *Patricia's dog* in the examples above).

Although almost all verbs follow this rule in the present tense, there are a few spelling variations. Certain verbs that end with an *-o*, like *go* (*goes*) and *do* (*does*), need an *-es* for *he, she,* or *it* subjects. Also use *-es* for *he, she,* or *it* subjects if the verb ends with *-s, -sh, -ch, -x,* or *-z,* such as *miss* (*misses*), *wish,* (*wishes*), *reach* (*reaches*), *fix* (*fixes*), and *buzz* (*buzzes*).

Problem Verbs

There are two verbs that have irregular forms in the present tense. These verbs are *be* (am, are, is) and *have* (have, has). Another problem verb is *do* (do, does, don't, doesn't), which is sometimes used incorrectly.

The Verb to be

The verb *to be* is the only English verb that has three forms in the simple present: *am, are,* and *is.*

Simple Present	
I	*am*
he, she, it	*is*
we, you, they	*are*

EXAMPLES ➤   I   *am*   tired of working at the computer today.

              Bertha   *is*   probably tired of working at her computer, too.

              We   *are*   both tired of working at our computers.

With a few expressions using the verb *to be*—*there is, there are, here is,* and *here are*—the subject always follows the verb. Be sure to make the verb agree with the subject that follows it in sentences beginning with these expressions.

                    V   *S*

EXAMPLE 1 ➤   There are *fireworks* every Fourth of July.

The subject is *fireworks,* so *are* is the correct verb.

                    V   *S*

EXAMPLE 2 ➤   Here is the rent check.

The subject of the sentence is *check* (or *rent check*), so the verb is *is*.

                    V   *S*

EXAMPLE 3 ➤   There's no type AB blood available right now.

The subject of the sentence is *blood* (or *type AB blood*), so the verb must be the singular form *is*. In this sentence, the *'s* after *There* represents *is*. Unless you are writing something formal, it is generally acceptable to use the contractions *there's* for *there is* and *here's* for *here is*. However, there are no acceptable written contractions for *there are* or *here are*.

The Verb to have

The verb *to have* has an irregular form for *he, she,* and *it: has*.

EXAMPLES ➤   Huong   *has*   three daughters.

              Huong and Duc   *have*   three daughters.

The Verb to do

Many of us have heard or used expressions like the following at one time or another: "Verne don't need more work" or "Why don't he just stay for dinner?" These are examples of very casual speech, and while they may be acceptable for some users of the language, they are not considered correct standard English.

Standard English uses two forms for the present tense of the verb *to do: do* and *does*. The negative forms are *doesn't* (or *does not*) for *he, she,* and *it* subjects, and *don't* (or *do not*) for other subjects. Be especially careful to use the correct form *doesn't* (or *does not*) for *he, she,* and *it* subjects.

Here are some examples of *don't* and *doesn't* used with different subjects:

he, she, *and* **it** *Subjects*

Verne *doesn't* need more work.

Giselle *doesn't* speak Spanish.

It *doesn't* look like rain.

Other Subjects

We *don't* have any time to waste.

Don't you know the assignment?

Ray and Lisa *don't* know how to swim.

By understanding the basic rules of subject–verb agreement and applying them to your own sentences, you can be sure that your verbs agree with their subjects. (In Chapter 6, we will look at some additional subject–verb agreement situations with problem subjects.)

■ **CLASS PRACTICE** **5**

Proofreading for Subject–Verb Agreement

Directions: Carefully read the informal paragraph below, checking for correct subject–verb agreement. Draw a line through any verbs that are incorrect and write in the correct forms. It may be helpful to mark each subject with an *S* and each verb with a *V*.

Meet the Authors

As the authors of this textbook, Dan Moody and I (Anna Ingalls) wants to introduce ourselves to you. Dan teach basic English and ESL (English as a Second Language) at Southwestern College. In his free time, he enjoys riding his mountain bike. Sometimes in the summer he even ride his bike to school. Dan and his family live in a semi-rural area east of San Diego. On weekends, Dan spend quality time with his wife Kathleen and their three daughters. He also do various remodeling projects around the house. Dan's students often comes to him for help and advice. He don't turn anyone away. Like Dan, I also teaches at Southwestern College. My favorite courses is basic writing and creative writing. Students' success with writing is very important to me. Travel and photography are two of my personal interests. For exercise, I walk a three-mile course three times a week with my friend Marisol. As for my family, my son and daughter both attends college. There's also three cats and one dog in my family. The experience of writing this textbook has been enjoyable and rewarding for both Dan and me.

Learning about Prepositional Phrases

As you learned earlier in this chapter, a *prepositional phrase* is a group of words that begins with a preposition, such as *about, across, after, at, by, during, for, from, in, of, on, onto, to,* or *with,* and ends with a noun (or sometimes a pronoun). We often use prepositional phrases to help make sentences more complete and interesting. They can provide important information related to the subject, the verb, or another word in the sentence. Many of the example sentences that we have already looked at include prepositional phrases. Here are a few examples with the prepositional phrases in italics:

$$\overset{\textit{S}}{} \qquad \overset{\textit{V}}{}$$

EXAMPLE 1 ➤ A hot dog *at the ball park* tastes better than one *at home.*

In this sentence, the prepositional phrase *at the ball park* adds an important qualification to the meaning of the subject *hot dog,* and the prepositional phrase *at home* identifies another place where a hot dog could be eaten.

EXAMPLE 2 ➤ Javier's ancestors came *from Bolivia.*

The sentence in Example 2 wouldn't make sense without the prepositional phrase *from Bolivia* following the verb.

EXAMPLE 3 ➤ The Red Cross helps people *in other countries* as well as *in the United States.*

The prepositional phrases in Example 3 tell us the locations of the people—*in other countries* and *in the United States.*

Many prepositional phrases, like the ones in Examples 1, 2, and 3, identify locations or places related to the subject, the verb, or other words in the sentence. Prepositional phrases can also add various other kinds of information to our sentences, such as the time of the events or the way something occurs.

Can you find the prepositional phrases in the following sentences? Remember that they may be at the beginning, in the middle, or at the end, and there may be more than one prepositional phrase in a sentence.

1. After the earthquake, Deanna's family was homeless.
2. Joy has worked with handicapped adults for two years.
3. Randy and his crew sailed from San Diego to Hawaii.

Did you find the prepositional phrases *after the earthquake, with handi-capped adults, for two years, from San Diego,* and *to Hawaii?* Each one adds important information that makes the sentence clearer and more interesting.

Here is a list of commonly used prepositions:

Prepositions			
about	below	in	throughout
above	beneath	into	to
across	beside	near	toward
after	between	of	under
against	by	on	until
among	during	onto	up
at	except	out	upon
before	for	over	with
behind	from	through	without

Certain phrases that consist of two or three words are also used as prepositions. A few of the most common two- or three-word prepositions are *according to, because of, in front of,* and *in spite of.*

■ **CLASS PRACTICE** **6**

Recognizing Prepositional Phrases

Directions: Underline each prepositional phrase. Some sentences have more than one. Also mark each subject with an *S* and each verb with a *V*.

>   *S*   *V*
> **EXAMPLE ➤** Several <u>of Jane's poems</u> appeared <u>in *Rolling Stone* magazine</u>.

1. Alice wrote everything in her journal.

2. Steve and Rain followed the trail to Sacred Falls.

3. With trembling hands, Beth cut the rope and freed her friend.

4. There are two large bulletin boards near the Student Union.

5. Elephants greet each other by touching trunks.

6. After the concert, we asked the drummer for his autograph.

7. Jaden played beautiful music on the ancient flute.

8. Bill replaced the broken outlet with a new one.

9. The lions in the enclosure usually sleep during the day.

10. Digitalis, a well-known heart medicine, is made from the foxglove plant.

■ **CLASS PRACTICE 7**

Writing Prepositional Phrases

Directions: Write an appropriate prepositional phrase in each blank. Remember to begin the phrase with a preposition and end it with a noun.

EXAMPLE ➤   Do you spend a lot of time _____ ?
                                              prepositional phrase

Possible answers: *at the bowling alley* or *with Suzanne*

1. You should put all of the equipment _____ .
                                                          prepositional phrase

2. The huge white wolf leaped _____ .
                                                    prepositional phrase

3. _____ , everyone applauded.
              prepositional phrase

4. That man _____ looks familiar.
                              prepositional phrase

5. Several stolen vehicles were found _____ .
                                                        prepositional phrase

Now write a sentence of your own that has a prepositional phrase. Be sure that it is a complete sentence with at least one SV.

6. _____

_____

_____

Learning about Sentence Combining

An important part of developing the ability to write well is learning how to use a variety of sentence structures. Being able to write different types of sentences will help you express your ideas more clearly and make your writing more interesting. One way to build your sentence skills is through *sentence combining,* which means combining groups of short sentences into one longer, more effective sentence, without losing any of the original meaning. Sentence combining activities will give you an opportunity to practice some of the grammar and sentence elements presented in each chapter. In addition, sentence combining will help you develop a strong intuitive sense of what sounds right and what doesn't.

In each sentence combining activity, you will be given groups of two or more short sentences to combine, like this group of three simple sentences:

1.1   Marilyn enrolled in a class.
1.2   It was an English class.
1.3   It was at the community college.

Although these sentences are correct, they are not very effective. They are very short, and they sound repetitive because words such as "class" are used more than once.

Think about how you could combine the ideas in these three short sentences to make one good sentence. Start with the basic structure of the first sentence, and then add information from the other sentences. Leave out words that are unnecessary, and avoid repeating words. Write your sentence combination here:

SENTENCE COMBINATION:

_____

_____

If you used *and* in your first combination, see if you can find another way to combine the ideas. A long, wordy sentence like "Marilyn enrolled in an English class, and the class was at the community college" is not very effective. A clear, direct statement like this is much better:

SENTENCE COMBINATION:
Marilyn enrolled in an English class at the community college.

Instead of relying on *and* all the time, try to experiment with other ways to write sentences whenever possible. Usually the shortest sentence that conveys all of what you want to say is the best choice.

Now let's try another group of sentences. This time you may use *and* once, but don't use it twice. Find another connecting word instead by thinking about how the ideas in the first two sentences are related to the idea expressed in sentence 2.3.

2.1   She was nervous.
2.2   She was afraid.
2.3   Writing had always been difficult for her.

SENTENCE COMBINATION:

_____

_____

Although it would be possible to join all of the sentences by using *and* twice, other words such as *because* or *so* connect the ideas more effectively. Here are two possible combinations:

COMBINATION #1:

She was nervous and afraid because writing had always been difficult for her.

COMBINATION #2:

Writing had always been difficult for her, so she was nervous and afraid.

Is your sentence like one of these combinations? If not, ask your teacher to check your sentence. There is often more than one effective way to combine a group of sentences, so your answers may sometimes be different from anyone else's yet still be correct.

The sentence combining activity that follows uses sentences similar to these. Remember to make each group of short sentences into one good sentence. If you have trouble getting started with a combination, try beginning with the first sentence and then find ways to incorporate significant details from the other sentences.

Sentence Combining Paragraph

Directions: On your own paper, combine each group of sentences into one good sentence. You may use any sentences that sound natural and effective. Many of your combinations will be simple sentences.

Success Story

1.1   Marilyn enrolled in a class.
1.2   It was an English class.
1.3   It was at the community college.

2.1   She was nervous.
2.2   She was afraid.
2.3   Writing had always been difficult for her.

3.1   On the first day she sat alone.
3.2   She sat in the back of the room.

4.1 She didn't want to say anything.
4.2 She didn't want to write anything.

5.1 However, Marilyn wanted to learn something.
5.2 She wanted to learn how to write better.

6.1 The teacher encouraged her.
6.2 The teacher helped her.

7.1 Marilyn discovered that the textbook was helpful.
7.2 The textbook was interesting.

8.1 It explained everything clearly.
8.2 It had good examples.

9.1 Some of the assignments were challenging.
9.2 Some of the assignments were fun.

10.1 Marilyn began to like sentence combining.
10.2 Marilyn began to like writing in her journal.

11.1 Gradually she developed more confidence.
11.2 The confidence was in herself.
11.3 Gradually she learned how to write well.

12.1 This class will also help you.
12.2 It will help you become a better writer.

After you have finished combining the sentences in *Success Story*, you may want to compare your sentences with those written by other students. If some of your answers are not the same, check your sentences to make sure that they convey the meaning clearly and accurately, without repeating words or phrases unnecessarily. Remember that there is often more than one effective way to combine sentences.

ENRICHMENT SECTION:
Keeping a Journal

Goals

In the enrichment section of this chapter, you will learn how to do the following:

- Use a journal to improve your writing skills
- Express your thoughts and opinions in a personal journal
- Comment on class activities in a class response journal

One of the best ways to become a better writer is simply to write as much as you can, whenever you can. Practice is important in developing all kinds of skills, and writing is no exception. Can you imagine learning how to play a guitar just by reading about the right techniques and listening to guitar music? Although a few people are "natural" musicians who can just pick up an instrument and play it, most of us would need to practice and develop our skills gradually. The same is true for writing. A few people may be "natural" writers, but for most of us, practice is an essential part of building our writing skills.

Journal writing is more informal and less structured than regular writing assignments. For this reason, many people find that journal entries are easier to write. A journal gives you a chance to express your ideas and opinions in any way that you wish, without worrying about criticism. Also, you don't have to be as concerned about grammar and sentence structure when you are writing a journal, so you can let yourself relax and just write naturally. Even if you make some mistakes while you are writing, the great thing about keeping a journal is that your writing will start to improve all by itself.

There are two main types of journals—personal journals and class response journals. In a personal journal you can write your thoughts, feelings, and observations about almost anything. Topics could include things that are happening in your life, your goals and ambitions, problems that you are dealing with, your dreams, observations about other people, comments on current events, and so on. The choice of topics is up to you. Some people like to write things in a personal journal that they might write in a personal diary. However, a diary is not intended for anyone else to read, so it is usually more private and confidential than a journal.

A class response journal also gives you an opportunity to express your ideas, but everything should be related to your class assignments and activities. Class response journal entries can include your reactions to assignments, responses to readings in the textbook, comments on your progress in the class, questions that you may have, and your feelings about writing experiences. In a class response journal you can say whatever you want about these kinds of things without worrying about what others might think. This kind of journal can help you with other aspects of the class as well as improving your writing skills.

Your teacher may ask you to write a personal journal, a class response journal, or a combination journal that includes entries of both types. Even if a journal is not assigned, you may want to write one in order to build up your writing skills. Although journal entries can be any length, you will get the most benefit from your journal if you write as much as you can each time. Set a goal for yourself, such as one or two pages per week. If you want to, you can write at two or three different times during the week instead of doing your journal entries all at one time.

A special journal page is provided at the end of this section for your first journal entries. To help you get started, questions are already provided on the journal page, one for a personal entry and one for a class response entry. All of your other journal entries should be written in a special notebook or kept in a folder. Remember that your personal journal entries can be about anything that you want to write about, but your class response entries must be about something related to your class.

Here are some suggestions for class response journal entries:

Class Response Journal Topics

- **An Assignment:** Was this assignment easy or difficult? Helpful or not helpful? Interesting or boring? Clear or confusing?

- **A Class Session:** What are the most useful things that you learned during this class session? Is there anything that is still unclear? Do you have some questions that you would like to ask?

- **The Writing Process:** Write down all of the steps that you followed in the process of writing one of your papers, from prewriting activities to the final draft. How much time did you spend on each step? Which things were helpful or not helpful?

- **Learning:** Write about something that has helped you learn or something that made learning interesting for you in this class.

- **Feelings:** How did you feel about a specific activity or assignment? How do you feel about your writing? Do you feel better about your writing than you used to?

- **Problems:** Are you in a writing slump? Are you experiencing writer's block (a temporary feeling that you are unable to write)? What do you think is causing this problem? What do you think would help you pull out of it?

- **Assigned Topics:** Anything that your instructor asks you to write about in your journal.

- **Other Topics:** Anything else related to the class that you want to write about.

JOURNAL ENTRIES

Week #1

Personal Topic: What are your personal goals for this semester (or term)?

_____

_____

_____

_____

_____

_____

_____

_____

_____

Class Response Topic: What was the most useful or interesting thing that you learned in Chapter 1? Are there any questions that you would like to ask?

_____

_____

_____

_____

_____

_____

_____

_____

_____

∎∎∎ 2

Writing That Tells a Story

SECTION ONE:
The Writing Process for Narration

Goals

In this section of the chapter, you will learn how to do the following:

- Discover details by freewriting
- Organize a story using chronological order
- Use feedback from others to improve your writing
- Write an effective topic sentence and concluding sentence for narration
- Make your writing interesting by using vivid details
- Use dialogue effectively in a story
- Connect ideas with transitions that are appropriate for narration

Learning about Narration

What Is Narration?

Writing that tells a story is called *narration*. All of us use narration in our daily lives. Whenever you tell a friend about something that happened, such as a weekend trip or your first skydiving jump, you are using narration. You are telling a true story of events that actually occurred. Sometimes we also enjoy stories about imaginary events. For example, if you read a good novel or watch an interesting movie, part of what you are enjoying is the series of imaginary events—in other words, the story.

Both types of narration—true and imaginary—involve putting together a series of events that form a story. Enough details must be included so that readers or listeners can form a clear picture of the events and share the writer's experience. Usually the best way to present a story is to tell everything in order from beginning to end, although sometimes writers choose to withhold certain information from the reader in order to create suspense and make the story more interesting.

Writing Objective: Telling a Story

Your objective for this chapter is to write a true story about something that actually happened to you. To make your story interesting, you will need to include details about the events as well as your feelings and reactions. The events should be portrayed accurately and vividly so that readers will be able to picture everything that happened and share your experience.

Your story can be developed in one full paragraph, or if you prefer, you may write a longer story, a page or more in length. Although most of the student writing examples in this chapter are single paragraphs, the steps in the writing process are the same whether you are writing a paragraph or a longer paper that contains more than one paragraph. (You may want to discuss the length of your paper with your instructor before deciding.)

We all have many stories that we could tell about things that happened to us. However, before you choose one as your writing topic, consider which experiences would be most interesting for other people to read about. Think of situations that made you feel intense emotions such as excitement, fear, or pride. An experience from which you learned something or gained a special insight is also a good choice. Sometimes it's even possible to turn ordinary events into a good story—and most people love a good story!

Prewriting Activities

The first step in the writing process is to think of possible topics—in this case, stories that you would like to tell about your own experiences. Use the *Exploring Topics Worksheet* to help you think of some life experiences that could be used as writing topics. For each category on the worksheet, try to identify a significant or interesting experience in your life. Your teacher may ask you to do this in class or as a homework assignment.

After you have completed the *Exploring Topics Worksheet,* the next prewriting activities will help you decide which story to choose as your writing topic. By telling some of your stories orally, you will find out if other people enjoy them. You will also find out if you can think of enough details about a particular story to make it interesting.

■ **WORSHEET I** | # Exploring Topics for Narration

Directions: Recall some of your most interesting experiences and write a few words to identify each one. It is not necessary to write complete sentences.

1. The funniest thing that ever happened to me

2. My most unusual or strangest experience

3. An experience that was dangerous, adventurous, or exciting

4. An experience that made me feel proud or happy

5. A scary experience

6. An inspirational experience

7. An embarrassing experience

8. A sad or disappointing experience

9. A special "first time" experience (*such as your first date, your first job interview, the first time you achieved something, etc.*)

10. Any other significant experience

Discovering Details 1:
Telling Your Story Orally

Telling someone else one of your stories will help you decide if you want to use it for your writing topic. Look over the experiences that you listed on the *Exploring Topics Worksheet* and choose the one that you would like to tell first. Picture the events in your mind, remembering everything that happened. Now find two partners in the class to share your story with. Each of you should tell your story orally in about three minutes. Be sure to keep track of the time so that each person will have an equal opportunity to tell a good story. Try to make your story as interesting as you can, and remember to include feelings and reactions. If you finish before the three minutes are up, you should go back and add more details to the most important parts of the story. After each story is told, the listeners should respond by answering the following questions:

Listener's Response Guide

1. What do you like best about the story?

2. Which details are the most interesting?

3. Are there any parts of the story that you would like to hear more about?

4. Are the writer's feelings expressed?

5. Is the entire sequence of events clear and easy to understand?

You may want to practice telling your story again to other class members or to people outside of class. Later on, if you decide to change topics, it would be a good idea to try oral storytelling again with your new topic to help you think of interesting details.

Discovering Details 2: Freewriting

Another way to discover details about your topic is to *freewrite* for 15 to 20 minutes. *Freewriting* means writing whatever comes to your mind about the topic. Just write down all of the events and feelings that are part of your story without worrying about whether everything is written correctly. Try to write as fast as ideas come to you. Don't stop to correct or edit anything. Even if what you write seems disorganized, don't worry about it. The purpose of freewriting is simply to start getting ideas down on paper and to help you discover details that can make your story interesting.

If you wish, you may freewrite about the same experience that you chose for oral storytelling. You will probably think of new details while you are freewriting that did not occur to you before. However, if you would like to try another topic, go back to the *Exploring Topics Worksheet* and choose one of your other experiences.

Your teacher may ask you to do the freewriting in class. However, if you are freewriting at home, it is important to find a comfortable place to write where you will not be disturbed. Then simply write whatever comes to your mind about your topic for 15 to 20 minutes.

■ **WORKSHEET II** | # Freewriting

Directions: Write about the events and feelings that are part of your story, putting down whatever comes to mind.

Topic: _____

_____

_____

_____

_____

_____

_____

_____

_____

_____

_____

_____

_____

_____

_____

_____

_____

_____

_____

_____

If you were able to freewrite more than half a page, then this story will probably make a good topic for a narration paragraph or short paper. However, if you had difficulty thinking of things to say while doing the freewriting, you might want to try freewriting on a different topic.

If neither your oral storytelling topic nor your freewriting topic developed into an interesting story that you want to continue working with, go back to the *Exploring Topics Worksheet* and select another. Be sure to try telling your new story orally and freewriting again before making a decision about which topic to use. Whichever topic you can talk or freewrite about most fluently is probably the best choice.

Putting the Events in Chronological Order

In order to turn your freewriting into a good narration paragraph or short paper, you will need to make sure that the order of the events is clear and easy to follow. Usually the best way to organize a narration is simply to tell what happened, in the order that it happened. We call this *chronological order*. It means using the natural time order of the events, telling the story from start to finish.

As you read through your freewriting, think about the order in which everything actually happened. Are some things out of their natural time order? While you were in the middle of freewriting, perhaps you remembered things that you had forgotten earlier and thus wrote them out of sequence. If you find anything in your freewriting that is not in chronological order, underline or circle it. Then determine where each event belongs so that you can put the entire story in chronological order when you write your first draft.

Writing a Rough Draft

From Freewriting to First Draft

The next step is to write the first draft of your narration paragraph or short paper. The purpose of this first draft is to get you started. It gives you something to work with and to improve. Before you turn in the final copy, you will revise and rewrite it, so you will probably have a second draft and maybe a third draft. Occasionally writers use even more drafts if they want to make a lot of revisions. All of these drafts are "rough," meaning that they are not as "polished" as the writer wants to make them. That's why writers use the term *rough draft* to refer to all of the preliminary versions that they write before they are satisfied with the finished paper. Starting with a first draft and then revising it at least once or twice is an important part of the writing process.

Begin your first draft by simply writing the story that you want to tell, keeping everything in chronological order. Use your *Freewriting Worksheet* to help you remember things that you want to include in the story. You may even want to use some of the best sentences and phrases that you wrote on the Worksheet. However, you will probably want to change quite a few things to make the story better. For example, if you notice anything in your freewriting that doesn't seem relevant or interesting, don't include it in your first draft. Also pay special attention to parts of the story that were not in chronological order in your freewriting and be sure that they are correctly placed in your first draft. While you are writing, remember to include significant details about the events so that readers will be able to picture exactly what happened. Also include your feelings at significant points in the story. Intense feelings and vivid details help your audience to experience the events right along with you.

As you read the first draft that follows, *The Stalker*, notice the feelings and details that the writer includes in order to make the story effective. Also look for any events that are not in clear chronological order and try to figure out where they belong in the story.

First Draft

The Stalker

Last summer when I was taking a Spanish course in Mexico City, I had a frightening experience. There was a man following me, and I didn't know what to do. I changed directions several times and turned down different streets, but he still kept following me. I saw the man earlier at a coffee shop where I stopped to ask directions. He was sitting at the counter eating lunch. Shortly after I left the restaurant, I noticed that he was walking behind me on the other side of the street. At last I saw a taxi, so I quickly ran to it and jumped in. Then the man began to run along the street, trying to keep up with the taxi. Every time I looked at him, he smiled and waved at me. Before I got in the taxi, I went into a lot of different shops, but every time I looked behind me, he was still there. I felt very frightened and didn't know what to do. Finally I arrived safely at my hotel. When I had left the hotel that morning, I thought I could find my way to an area called the Zona Rosa where there were some clothing stores, but I got lost. That's why I decided to stop at the coffee shop to ask for directions, which turned out to be a big mistake. Later, when I told some of my Mexican friends about the man, they laughed and said that he probably just wanted to meet me and ask me to go out with him, but he was too bashful to say anything. I didn't know if they were right or not. Maybe it was just a cultural misunderstanding, or maybe I was being stalked by a dangerous person.

Response to *The Stalker*

1. Underline the parts of the story that are not in chronological order. Then try to figure out the order in which the events actually happened.

List the main things that happened in chronological order, as the writer should tell them:

1. _____

2. _____

3. _____

4. _____

5. _____

6. _____

7. _____

8. _____

2. Which parts of the story, if any, would you like to know more about? Where would you suggest that the writer add more details?

_____

_____

Make sure that the rough draft of your own story is in clear chronological order. Then continue working on your rough draft as you read the rest of this chapter. Try to follow all of the suggestions in the text for revising and improving it so that your finished paper will be as interesting and as effective as possible.

Learning about Topic Sentences for Narration

A good narration paragraph or short paper needs to have a *topic sentence*— a statement that expresses the main idea or the point of the story. For a paper that contains more than one paragraph, the topic sentence is often called a *main idea statement* or *thesis statement*. However, we will use the term *topic sentence* to mean the sentence that expresses the most important point of your paper, whether it is one paragraph or several paragraphs long. Although the topic sentence is usually just one sentence, occasionally two sentences may work together to state the main idea, especially in a longer story.

Is there a sentence (or two) at the beginning of your story that lets the reader know right away what the story is about? Does your first sentence introduce the story and capture the reader's attention? If so, you may already have a topic sentence in your first draft. If not, you will learn how to add a topic sentence that will emphasize the main point of your story.

Usually the topic sentence appears at the beginning of a paragraph or short paper. Putting the topic sentence first helps both you and the reader focus clearly on the most important thing about your story. However, sometimes the topic sentence may be more effective at the end, especially if a writer wants to create suspense or keep readers guessing for a while.

In order to write a good topic sentence, you need to decide what the most important thing about your story is. For example, the most important thing might be how you felt during the experience or how you feel about it now. Here are some examples of topic sentences that emphasize the writer's feelings. Circle the specific words that identify feelings in each statement.

TOPIC SENTENCES THAT EMPHASIZE FEELINGS:

1A. My first date was one of the most embarrassing experiences of my life.

2A. The most frightening experience I ever had was the time when I almost drowned.

3A. I felt very proud and happy when I became an American citizen.

Notice that all of these topic sentences tell what the story is about and also express the storyteller's feeling or attitude about it.

Sometimes a writer can make the topic sentence more interesting just by including a few more details. Topic sentences 1B, 2B, and 3B refer to the same experiences as the first group of topic sentences. However, they reveal more about the stories. As you read these topic sentences, what do you learn about each story that you didn't know before? Do any of these topic sentences grab your attention better than the previous ones? Underline the additional details that were not in the first group of topic sentences.

TOPIC SENTENCES THAT REVEAL MORE DETAILS:

1B. I was so nervous about my first date that everything went wrong, from losing my wallet to falling on my face.

2B. As I sank below the surface of the water for the third time, I knew this was the worst (and maybe the last) experience of my life.

3B. My entire family watched as I took the citizenship oath, and I felt very proud and happy to become an American.

Because these topic sentences include more specific details, the reader can already begin to anticipate and picture the events of the stories. Revealing more details in the topic sentence is one way of getting the reader interested in your story.

If you learned some kind of a lesson or gained some insight from your experience, another way to write a topic sentence is to emphasize what you learned. Here are more topic sentences for the same stories. Underline the part of each topic sentence that tells what the writer learned or realized as a result of the experience.

TOPIC SENTENCES THAT EMPHASIZE A LESSON:

1C. On my first date, I learned that if you're afraid everything will go wrong, it will.

2C. Although almost drowning was a frightening experience, it helped me understand the meaning of the saying, "Live for the day."

3C. Becoming an American citizen took a lot of hard work and determination, but it was worth the effort.

Notice that the lessons in topic sentences 1C and 2C relate to the writer's outlook on life. In fact, both statements use expressions that you may have heard before to explain the lesson, "If you're afraid everything will go wrong, it will" and "Live for the day." Topic sentence 3C implies the lesson that good things are worth the effort, although the writer refers only to the specific experience in the story rather than stating the lesson in general terms.

Now read all three groups of topic sentences again and think about which ones are the most interesting. Do some of them grab your attention better than others? Which ones make you want to read the story? On the lines below, write the numbers of the topic sentences that you like best (at least two) and briefly explain why you think they are effective.

_____

_____

_____

As you do the following exercise, *Evaluating Topic Sentences for Narration,* you will learn more about what makes an effective topic sentence.

Evaluating Topic Sentences for Narration

Directions: Decide which of the following would make good topic sentences for a narration paragraph or short paper. Write OK in the blank by each good topic sentence, and write NO by the others. Be ready to explain your answers.

EXAMPLE 1 ➤   _*NO*_   I went camping in the mountains last spring.

Example 1 is not *a good topic sentence because the main idea is not clear. The writer hasn't included enough details or feelings about the camping trip to make it interesting.*

EXAMPLE 2 ➤ _____*OK*_____ My camping trip to the Laguna Mountains last spring made me feel relaxed, refreshed, and glad to be alive.

Example 2 is a good topic sentence. It has a main idea, and it's more interesting because the writer included details and feelings.

_____ **1.** Our dog Topper died last year.

_____ **2.** Sailing from Boston to Prince Edward Island was an exciting and challenging adventure.

_____ **3.** There was nothing humorous about my date with "Cheap Charlie" at the time, but now I laugh whenever I think about it.

_____ **4.** Sometimes I like to live dangerously.

_____ **5.** I went to Mazatlán last summer, but my luggage stayed in Dallas.

_____ **6.** After weeks of aerobics classes, I could finally wear my bathing suit.

_____ **7.** Most people think getting stuck in an elevator happens only in the movies, but it happened to me on my wedding day.

_____ **8.** Teaching people to read in the adult literacy program.

_____ **9.** Strange events that happened one night made me wonder if ghosts might really exist.

_____ **10.** The story of my life is like a roller coaster ride because it has a lot of ups and downs.

Writing Your Own Topic Sentence

Directions: To write a good topic sentence for your paragraph or short paper, you need to figure out the most significant thing about the story that you are telling. Read through your first draft and ask yourself what the story is really about. To help you determine the main idea of your story, answer the following questions:

1. What was the high point of the action or the most significant event that occurred? It might be the most exciting part, the most frightening part, the moment when you (or someone else) learned the truth, or any part that was more intense or more memorable than the rest.

_____

_____

_____

2. How did you feel at the time when the events occurred? Are your feelings about the experience the same or different now?

_____

_____

_____

3. Did you learn something or gain some insight as a result of this experience? What was it?

_____

_____

_____

Now using one or more of your answers to questions 1 to 3, try to express the main idea of your story in one complete sentence:

TOPIC SENTENCE (DRAFT 1):

_____

_____

_____ .

What else could you include in this sentence that would make people want to read your story? Try to add something that will capture the reader's attention, such as more details about the events or your feelings. Then write your revised topic sentence here:

TOPIC SENTENCE (DRAFT 2):

_____

_____

_____ .

Next form a workshop group with three or four other classmates and read everyone's topic sentences aloud. Try to give helpful comments and suggestions to other group members about how to make their topic sentences effective. When you and your workshop group are satisfied with your topic sentence, write it here:

TOPIC SENTENCE (DRAFT 3):

_____

_____

_____ .

Now look over your rough draft and think about where your topic sentence would work best. Try putting it at the beginning to see how it sounds. By starting with the topic sentence, you can tell readers the most important thing that happened right away and get them interested in reading your story. After you add the topic sentence, you may also need to revise your previous opening sentence (now the second sentence) so that your topic sentence will lead smoothly and naturally into the story. For many narration paragraphs and short papers, the beginning is the most effective place to put the topic sentence.

For some stories, however, the topic sentence may work better at the end, especially if you want to create suspense. By placing the topic sentence at the end, you will be able to keep readers guessing. If they don't know what will happen next or how things will turn out, they may be more interested in reading your story. If you think that your story would be more interesting with the topic sentence at the end, try moving it. You may also want to make some other changes earlier in the story in order to make it more suspenseful.

As you read the following story by Mark Albarran about a frightening sky diving experience, notice that it has the topic sentence at the beginning. Remember that everything in the paragraph should relate to or lead up to the main point of the story, which is expressed in the topic sentence. Also notice that Mark tells everything in clear chronological order. After giving background information about weather conditions on the day of the jump, he starts the story with packing his parachute and ends it with the parachute opening. Underline the parts of the story that you think are the most interesting.

Sky Diving
by Mark Albarran

One of the scariest experiences in my life happened while I was jumping out of a plane at 12,000 feet, and my parachute almost didn't open. The day was great for sky diving. The sun was out, the sky was clear, and there was almost no wind. I wanted to jump so badly that I didn't watch how I packed my main parachute. I finished packing and I was in the plane ready to go. When the plane was in the air, everyone asked me how I had packed my chute so quickly, and I told them I had a reserve chute if my main didn't open. I really believed that the parachute was going to open, so I wasn't expecting to use my reserve. I always believed that there would be a time in my life when I would have to use it, so I was ready to pull my reserve anyway. The jump went as planned, but when it was time for the main to do its job, it just refused to open. I was so scared that I almost forgot I had a reserve. I jerked, pulled, and prayed to God for my life until the main opened. I wouldn't have had time to pull the reserve. That was a very scary experience, and it made me realize that not being careful was a stupid thing to do.

Response to *Sky Diving*

1. Which parts of the story are the most interesting? Why?

_____

_____

_____

2. Find several words and phrases in the story that show how scared the writer was during the experience (his topic sentence idea). Write these words and phrases here:

_____

_____

3. What lesson did the writer learn?

_____

Why do you think he stated this lesson at the end instead of at the beginning as his topic sentence?

_____

_____

4. Would this story also work with the topic sentence at the end? Why or why not?

_____

_____

Making Your Story Interesting

According to writer Jane Tassi, who is the author of several short stories and narrative poems,* good storytelling is "storying unboringly." The question is, how do you make sure that the way you tell your story is not boring?

*A narrative poem is a story written in the form of a poem.

Part of writing an interesting story, of course, is choosing a topic that will appeal to readers. However, even the best topic does not just automatically turn into a good story. It's up to the writer to hold the reader's attention by telling the events in an interesting way.

One way to make your story interesting is to include significant details that create a clear picture of the events and enable the reader to share your experience. Leave out unimportant things that don't really add to the story and that could be boring for the reader. Notice that in the previous example paragraph, *Sky Diving,* Mark Albarran didn't waste time with unimportant details like what he did before he got to the airport, the clothes he was wearing, or the names of everyone in the plane. Instead, he focused mainly on details about the parachute and the jump, which were very important to the story. Adding details about his thoughts and feelings also helped to make the story vivid and exciting. Of course, the kinds of details that make interesting reading will vary, depending on the particular story. To help you decide what to include and what to leave out, try asking yourself which things a reader would really like to know about the scene, the events, and the other people involved.

Using vivid, accurate words to describe people and things in your story is also important. Avoid words that are too general or vague. For example, if you're writing about climbing a hill and coming to some big rocks, try to create a more accurate picture with your words. Are the rocks actually huge boulders blocking your path? Are they large, smooth rocks that you can sit on? Or are they rough, jagged stones that are hard to walk on? Describing things accurately with precise words will enable the reader to picture the scene and make your story much more interesting.

In the story that follows, *The Howl* by Mark Field, notice how Mark uses vivid descriptive words that enable the reader to share his eerie experience. Although very few things actually happen, Mark builds an interesting, suspenseful story by adding thoughts, feelings, and speculations. He shows us what happened and how he and his companions reacted, detail by detail, and he describes the sounds so vividly that we can almost hear them ourselves.

The Howl
by Mark Field

While undergoing army basic training, I had one of the eeriest experiences of my life. It was the night I heard that chilling "Howl." My platoon was bivouacked out in the back country of Louisiana, miles from nowhere. The dark January night was cold and still. The only sounds were the croaking of bullfrogs and the occasional rustling of small animals in the bush. About 11:00 p.m. two of my buddies and I were trying to stay warm and awake while on guard duty. We were talking about all the things important to a young soldier. You know— girls, cars, home, and girls. Then we heard it, a sound I will never forget. From across the bayous came an unearthly growling noise, a kind of howling and snarling all combined. Instantly the night became deathly quiet, and we froze like rabbits. Our blood ran cold, and we stood paralyzed. Hearts racing, we spoke in whispers. "What was that?" And no one knew, for it was quite unlike anything we had ever heard before. For the remainder of the night, we discussed the possibilities among ourselves. Could it have been a dog? No, not way out here. A wildcat? No, it didn't sound like any type of cat I've ever heard. Okay then, how about a 'gator? Maybe, but I really didn't think so. Whatever made that sound, it was enough to keep three young men from resting peacefully that night. Many years have passed since that evening. Except in Hollywood movies, I have never heard anything like that howl again. So what was it that we heard that night? I'll probably never know. But I like to think that one cold, dark night in a Louisiana swamp, I heard Bigfoot's bayou cousin shouting out his existence to the world.

Response to *The Howl*

1. What do you think are some of the most vivid words and phrases used by the writer to describe the strange sound?

   _____

   _____

   _____

   _____

2. Which other words and phrases are especially effective in describing the place and setting the mood?

   _____

   _____

3. Notice that the first two sentences together act as the topic sentence. Even though the topic sentence is at the beginning, the story is still suspenseful. How does the writer create suspense?

   _____

   _____

4. Try to make sentences A, B, and C below more vivid and interesting by adding descriptive details about the truck, the men, the beach, and/or the events. Use your imagination to create a vivid picture of each scene with your words.
   A. The truck stopped.

   _____

   _____

B. Three men walked toward us.

_____

_____

C. I saw people on the beach.

_____

_____

   Now look at the rough draft of your own story again. Pretend that you are reading it for the first time and that you don't already know how the story turns out. Underline at least three words or phrases that you would like to change to make it more interesting. Look for vague words like _nice, good, big, small,_ or _pretty_ that could be replaced with more specific words. Look for descriptions that don't really create a clear picture, or action words such as _stopped_ or _saw_ that don't sound very interesting. Also see if there are places where you can add details to make the story more appealing to readers. Try to use vivid language throughout your story as Mark Field did in _The Howl._ If you make a lot of changes, you may want to recopy your rough draft so that it will be easier to read.

Rough Draft Workshop

After you have revised several words or phrases to make your sentences more vivid and interesting, it is time to let other people hear your story. Form a workshop group with three or four other class members and read your story to them, or read it to one of your previous storytelling partners. Ask your partner or group members which parts of your story they like best and where they think you should add more details, emotions, or vivid language. Use the following rough draft workshop questions as guidelines for your discussion.

> ### Rough Draft Workshop
>
> 1. What parts of the story are the most interesting?
> 2. Has the writer used vivid words to create a clear picture of the events?
> 3. Are there any places where more details or feelings should be added?
> 4. Does the topic sentence express the main idea of the story, and is it placed effectively at the beginning or at the end?
> 5. Is everything in chronological order? If not, which parts of the story need to be rearranged?
> 6. Can you think of anything else that could be added or changed to make the story better?

Bringing Your Story to Life with Dialogue

To make their stories seem realistic, some writers like to include words that were spoken by people involved in the action. For example, the young men in *The Howl* asked each other, "What was that?" Words that a person in a story says are called *dialogue*.

When you are writing dialogue, you should place quotation marks before and after the exact words that someone said, like this:

"It takes about forty-five minutes to get to the jungle," Rain told me.

Quotation marks are important because they signal to the reader that the words within the quotation marks were spoken by someone. If a phrase is added to identify the speaker, like *Rain told me* in the example above, notice that a comma is used inside the quotation marks instead of a period. (For additional information about how to use quotation marks, see Chapter 8, pages 431–432.)

Of course, it is important to choose dialogue that plays a significant part in the story and that will make the story more interesting. In most cases, readers will not want to hear ordinary conversations about routine things. For instance, if the writer of *The Howl* had included dialogue about things like the weather and the responsibilities of guard duty, it probably would have been boring, and these topics of conversation would not have contributed anything to the story.

Using dialogue gives the reader a sense of really being there, watching and listening as the story takes place. Hearing people speak brings them to life, which makes the story more enjoyable for the reader. Good dialogue should sound as real and life-like as possible, so the style should generally be casual. Grammar, sentence structure, and vocabulary can all be much less formal for dialogue than for regular writing.

Sometimes, instead of talking, we just think the words like a conversation inside our heads. We can use this technique in a story too. Thoughts are generally written in the same informal style as dialogue, usually without quotation marks. The writer of *The Howl,* for example, used thoughts that were going through his mind to build suspense: *Could it have been a dog? No, not way out here. A wildcat? No, it didn't sound like any type of cat I've ever heard.* Although the men talked about these possibilities, the writer is giving us his thoughts rather than their exact conversation.

In the next writing example, *The Sacred Falls,* Steve Wiggs begins his story with dialogue. The words spoken by his friend Rain get the story going as well as revealing a little about Rain's personality. In order to make the dialogue sound life-like, Steve uses very casual words, such as "gonna" instead of "going to." Since this is a fairly long story, Steve decided not to put everything into one paragraph. Instead, he divided the story into separate paragraphs, grouping events together that were closely related and that happened more or less at the same time. As you read *The Sacred Falls,* pay special attention to the dialogue and the paragraph divisions.

The Sacred Falls
by Steven E. Wiggs

"Do you want to go for a hike?" Rain asked. He was always full of natural energy. Every morning he would wake me up at eight o'clock and have our entire day planned. "First we're gonna go surf, then we're gonna eat breakfast, then we're gonna go hike to Sacred Falls," he announced confidently.

We surfed Velzyland, a reef break south of Sunset Beach, and ate some fruit for breakfast. Then we jumped on a bus and headed for Sacred Falls. On the way there, Rain told me, "This place is insane. We're gonna get to see what nature is all about. It's full of . . . well, . . . I can't explain it. You'll just have to see and feel it for yourself."

As we started the three-mile hike, I was a little disappointed. "It takes about forty-five minutes to get to the jungle," Rain told me. The jungle, I thought to myself, that's a pretty heavy word to use. It looked like we were going to be hiking through a park.

At last we made it around the final bend of the main trail, and there it was, the landscape I was expecting to see. We walked to the entrance where there were three trails. Rain had been on each of them in the past, and he wanted me to go on the most challenging one. I will never forget my first few steps. We entered into a pipe made of twining tree branches covered with neon-green moss. The sunlight from behind the clouds was almost completely blocked out by the dense tropical landscape. The air was musty yet very fresh and clean. The trees were full of noises of tropical birds and the rushing roar of the water in the stream next to us. I was actually experiencing nature in the works. I had become one with the Earth. We hiked through towering cliffs with palm trees growing from cracks in the walls. "Stop!" Rain shouted. "Can you hear it? We're almost there!" We started running through the trees toward the sound of the crashing water. I couldn't breathe as the waterfall of all my dreams appeared. "Let's jump in! Hey, Steve, let's jump in!" Rain shouted. My mind was frozen, blocking everything out except the waterfall. Rain finally got my attention, and we dove into the mineral pool lying beneath the fall. As I floated on my back looking up at the sky, the cliffs, and the water, I thought to myself, this is God, or God is in my presence, because I have never felt this way before in my life.

Our journey back to reality was filled with smiles and conversation about life. It felt as if I had opened a new door to thought. Since my experience at Sacred Falls, I give more respect to my personal spiritual life and to everything that is part of nature.

Response to *The Sacred Falls*

1. What would the story be like without dialogue? Would it seem less realistic? Explain.

_____

_____

2. Instead of using "he said" all the time to identify the speaker, the writer used a variety of different verbs. List some of the other words that he used:

_____

3. Find the topic sentence in *The Sacred Falls*. Why do you think the writer decided to put his topic sentence at the end instead of at the beginning?

_____

If you are thinking about adding some dialogue to your own story, remember that it must be interesting and relevant to the story. Think about the main events or the high point of the action, and try to recall the words that you or someone else actually spoke. Things that were said at intense or significant moments in real life are usually the easiest to remember and can contribute something special to your story. It may help to close your eyes, visualize the details of what happened, and try to hear words that were spoken. You may want to add a few lines of dialogue to your story to show your reactions, to intensify a conflict, or to reveal someone's personality. Be sure to use casual, natural words that sound like real speech.

After you have written the dialogue that you want to add to your story, read it to members of your workshop group and get their reactions. If they don't think it adds to the story, don't use it. You may want to try some other dialogue, or you may decide that having people talk in your story is not necessary. Although dialogue makes some stories more interesting, not all good stories need it.

Transitions for Narration

To make sure that the sequence of events in your story is always clear, you may need to use some special signal words to indicate time relationships and other connections between ideas. Words and groups of words that show relationships between events or ideas are called *transitions*. Some of the most commonly used transitions are time-order words like *then, next, soon, now,* and *at last.* You will probably need to use a few transition words like these in order to tell your story in clear chronological order.

You may also want to use some longer transitional expressions to connect specific events, like the italicized portions of these sentences from stories we have read:

> *Shortly after I left the restaurant,* I noticed that he was walking behind me on the other side of the street. (from *The Stalker*)

> The jump went as planned, but *when it was time for the main to do its job,* it just refused to open. (from *Sky Diving*)

For the remainder of the night, we discussed the possibilities among ourselves. (from *The Howl*)

As we started the three-mile hike, I was a little disappointed. (from *The Sacred Falls*)

These longer transitions show time relationships between closely related events. For example, by starting the sentence with, "As we started the three-mile hike," the writer lets us know that whatever follows (feeling disappointed) happened at the same time they started hiking. In addition to helping establish the right sequence for the events, transitional expressions can make your writing sound smoother and more polished. (To learn more about sentences like some of these examples, read about Basic Complex Sentences in Chapter 3.)

As you read the paragraph that follows, *Earthquake,* notice how Deanna Hernandez keeps the events in clear chronological order. Underline all of the transitional words and expressions that you find. Remember to look for single time-order words as well as longer transitional expressions beginning with words like *when* or *as.*

Earthquake

by Deanna Hernandez

I remember it all so well, just as if it were yesterday. It was January 17, 1994, and the time was 4:31 a.m. It seemed that at the very moment I had closed my eyes, they were forced open again by a frightening sound. It was a horrible rumbling sound. At first I thought to myself, "Oh my God! Someone's in the house; we're being robbed!" I heard things falling and shattering on the ground. All of a sudden, it felt as if something just picked up the house and dropped it back down and continued to do so repeatedly. My first reaction was to scream. No matter how hard I tried to get up, the enormous tremor kept on forcing me back down, like someone was actually pushing me. Then I remembered my little sister Marissa, and I covered her completely, like a shell on a turtle. When my mom reached my room, the earthquake had calmed down a little, but it had not stopped completely. My mom grabbed my little sister and ran out with her, but I still couldn't balance myself well enough to walk on my own. Suddenly the earthquake's strength increased. As I turned, I fell and couldn't get up. I thought, "God, we're going to die." Then I heard my name being called. It was my brother trying to find out where I was. With a sigh of relief, I called to him. I heard him say, "Let me go get Mom. I can't open the door." The door had apparently shut, and everything in the hallway closets had fallen in front of it. In the background, I could still hear objects falling and breaking. After many attempts, I finally managed to get out of there on my own. Just then I felt my brother's strong hand grab my arm and pull me as if I were a rag doll. Once outside, I felt safe, but still in a state of shock. Later that morning the city was still being ravaged by aftershocks, but we went back inside to check on everything. Our house, which we had lived in for all our lives, was ruined. We left the house with tears in our eyes. I realized all the things that I had taken for granted—my home, for example, a home I never appreciated until it was gone.

Response to *Earthquake*

1. After you have underlined all of the transitional words and expressions, choose the three that you think are the most effective and write them on the lines below:

   _____

   _____

2. Which details about the earthquake are the most vivid and interesting to read?

   _____

   _____

   _____

3. Where is the topic sentence? Do you think it is effective here? Why or why not?

   _____

   _____

Now check your own paragraph or short paper to make sure that the time order is clear and that events are smoothly connected. You may want to add a few transitional words or expressions, but be careful not to use too many. It isn't necessary to have a transitional word or expression in every sentence. To make your writing effective, try to use a variety of different transitions. If you discover that you have used the same transitional word, such as "then" or "next," more than two or three times, try to find some other words to use instead.

Ending Effectively

To end your story effectively, try to think of some "clincher" or final comment to use as a conclusion. If there is a message or lesson related to your story, the conclusion would probably be a good place for it. Another option is to use something similar to your topic sentence, as long as the wording isn't the same. If your topic sentence is at the end, it will probably work as the conclusion too, unless you want to add something more. Whatever you use as a conclusion, it should tie everything together and make the story seem finished.

Let's look at the concluding sentences of the example papers in this chapter. As you read each one, think about what makes it an effective ending for the story.

1. *The Stalker:* Maybe it was just a cultural misunderstanding, or maybe I was being stalked by a dangerous person.

2. *Sky Diving:* That was a very scary experience, and it made me realize that not being careful was a stupid thing to do.

3. *The Howl:* But I like to think that one cold, dark night in a Louisiana swamp, I heard Bigfoot's bayou cousin shouting out his existence to the world.

4. *The Sacred Falls:* Since my experience at Sacred Falls, I give more respect to my personal spiritual life and to everything that is part of nature.

5. *Earthquake:* I realized all the things I had taken for granted—my home, for example, a home I never appreciated until it was gone.

Three of these conclusions focus on the lessons that the writers learned from their experiences. Read the conclusions through again, and then write the numbers of the ones that tell what the writers learned or realized as a result of their experiences:

_____   _____   _____

Did you identify conclusions 2, 4, and 5? In all of these stories, the events had a major impact on the writer's life. Therefore, the insight that the writer gained because of the experience, or the lesson that he or she learned, makes an effective ending. In both *The Sacred Falls* and *Earthquake,* the concluding sentence also served as the topic sentence. Although the writer of *Sky Diving* used a separate topic sentence at the beginning of his paragraph, his conclusion includes the same idea—the scary experience.

In the other conclusions, 1 and 3, the writers analyze the events rather than emphasizing a lesson. At the end of both *The Stalker* and *The Howl,* there is still some mystery about the nature of the events, so the writers speculate in the conclusion about what might really have happened. In many stories, the writer's thoughts or reactions make the events seem more significant and are an appropriate conclusion.

These five conclusions show you some of the possible ways to end a story effectively. The main techniques are (1) restating the main idea in different words, (2) explaining a lesson that you learned, or (3) analyzing the events. What you choose as an ending, of course, will depend on what works best for your story. You may want to use a combination of these techniques rather than choosing just one, or you may come up with something else that makes the story seem complete.

Before you write your conclusion, read the example paragraph *Poolside* written by Jason Cross. Notice the topic sentence at the beginning and the conclusion at the end, which gives the paragraph a feeling of completeness.

Poolside
by Jason Cross

In high school I was a good water polo player with a cocky attitude until I had a very humbling experience. My girl friend was a cheerleader, so I finally convinced her to get the squad to cheer at one of our games—not just any game, but a play-off game. This was a home game, and at our pool the crowd sat up twenty feet above the deck looking down into the pool. In the first row was my girl friend along with seven other cheerleaders. Behind them sat my parents, my brother, and my grandmother. At poolside was a *Star News* photographer. This was my big chance to show off. I loved to show off, and besides, I was quite good at it. Everything went well for the first half of the game. I had a goal, and we were two goals ahead. Then it happened, the most embarrassing incident of my life so far. While I was swimming away from one of my opponents, my Speedo swimsuit was ripped from my body. There I was, butt-naked in the middle of the pool. The worst part was that the entire crowd, including my family and girl friend, was looking right down on me, and I mean all of me. All I could do was call time out and wait for a swimsuit. After that experience, I never showed off in the pool again.

Response to *Poolside*

1. Which sentence do you think is the writer's topic sentence?

_____

_____

2. The conclusion seems related to the topic sentence, but instead of repeating the same idea, it explains more about how the experience affected the writer. Although Jason didn't use the word "lesson," do you think the conclusion is based on a lesson that he learned? Why or why not?

_____

_____

3. Is the conclusion for *Poolside* effective, in your opinion? Why or why not?

_____

_____

Look at your own rough draft now to see if you have written an effective ending. Does your conclusion tie everything together and make the story seem complete? If your topic sentence is at the end, does it make an effective conclusion too, or would you like to add something else? If your story lacks a conclusion, or if you think that your conclusion needs to be revised, remember that there are three main techniques to choose from:

- Restate the main idea of the story in different words.
- Explain a lesson that you learned.
- Analyze the events.

If you have another idea for an effective ending that does not fit into one of these three categories, go ahead and try it. You may want to write more than one possible conclusion and have your workshop group help you decide which is most effective.

At this point, you have completed a good rough draft for your narration paragraph or short paper. The next step is to make sure that you have used correct sentence structure and grammar. In Section 2 of this chapter, you will learn some sentence and grammar skills that will help you edit and improve your rough draft. Then you will be ready to put the finishing touches on your paper and turn in the final draft.

SECTION TWO:
Sentence and Grammar Skills

Goals

In this section of the chapter, you will learn how to do the following:

- Recognize basic compound sentences
- Write basic compound sentences using Group A connecting words (coordinating conjunctions)
- Recognize and correct run-ons and comma splices
- Use past tense verbs correctly

Learning about Basic Compound Sentences

Using compound sentences is the simplest way of joining two clauses to make one sentence. These sentences are very common and useful in almost every kind of writing.

Chapter 1 presented a variety of *simple* sentences. Remember that a simple sentence has only one clause, that is, only one SV (subject and verb).

In this chapter you will learn an easy way of joining two clauses together in one sentence. Look at these sentences. How many clauses do they each have?

$$S \quad V \qquad\qquad\qquad\qquad\qquad S \quad V$$

EXAMPLE 1 ➤ Our whole family went horseback riding, and our guide got lost.

$$S \quad V \qquad\qquad S \quad V$$

EXAMPLE 2 ➤ Antonio loves soccer, but Marissa prefers scuba diving.

How many clauses are in the first sentence? _____

How many clauses are in the second sentence? _____

You can see that there are two clauses (two *SVs*) in each of the sentences above. These two sentences are examples of *basic compound sentences*.

Look at the two clauses in the first sentence: How are these clauses joined together?

Clause 1:		*Clause 2:*
Our whole family went horseback riding	, *and*	our guide got lost.
S V	, *and*	S V .

This sentence has *two* clauses that are joined by a comma and the word *and*.

Now look at the two clauses in the second sentence: How are these clauses joined together?

Clause 1:		*Clause 2:*
Antonio loves soccer	, *but*	Marissa prefers scuba diving.

These clauses are joined by a comma and the word *but*.

And and *but* are two examples of a group of connecting words that can be used to make a *basic compound sentence*.

What are the connecting words in the following sentences?

$$S \quad V \qquad\qquad\qquad S \quad V$$

EXAMPLE 3 ➤ Jaime has to complete his project, or he will not be ready for his presentation.

$$S \quad V \qquad\qquad\qquad S \quad V$$

EXAMPLE 4 ➤ Tricia was thirsty after the long hike, so she drank a whole quart of lemonade.

You can see that the word *or* and the word *so* are also in this group of connecting words. There are seven of these connecting words that can be used to connect two clauses together to make a basic compound sentence. The official name for these seven words is "coordinating conjunctions." This book will also refer to this group of connecting words as *Group A* connectors.

Here is the complete list of *Group A* connectors, or coordinating conjunctions:

Group A *Connector*	*Basic Meaning**
for	because
and	in addition, also
nor	neither, not one and not the other
but	in contrast, on the other hand
or	alternatively
yet	but (*yet* is a little bit more formal)
so	as a result, for that reason

One easy way to remember these Group A connectors is to memorize the first letter of each word. These letters form the words *fan boys*.

f	**a**	**n**	**b**	**o**	**y**	**s**	**=**	**fan boys**
o	n	o	u	r	e	o		
r	d	r	t		t			

The basic compound sentence pattern is the same for all of these *Group A* connectors:

S   V   , Group A   S   V .

Every basic compound sentence consists of the first clause (SV), a comma, the *Group A* connector, then the second clause (SV).

NOTE There are two exceptions to this basic rule:

> **Exception 1:** If the sentence is really short, the comma is not necessary.

EXAMPLE ➤ I looked at her and she recognized me.

> **Exception 2:** The *Group A* connector *nor* follows a slightly different pattern. (See number 7 in the following example sentences.)

---

*Some of these words have other meanings in other situations.

EXAMPLES ➤ Here are examples of each of the seven *Group A* connectors (coordinating conjunctions).

> *S*   *V*   *, and*   *S*   *V.*
> 1. And: Patricia walked up the beach, and Gary lazed in the sun.

> *S*   *V*   *S*   *V.*
> 2. But: Laurie visited Minnesota's lake country, but she didn't go fishing.

> 3. Or: We need to buy our tickets now, or we will miss the start of the movie.

> 4. So: Sharon was an experienced hiker, so she led the way.

> 5. Yet: I love my oceanography class, yet the homework is difficult.

> 6. For: The airport was crowded, for we arrived on a holiday weekend.

> *For* means the same as *because*, but sometimes *for* is more formal, and it is seldom used in conversation. By learning several ways to express an idea, you will have greater variety in your writing.

> 7. Nor: Scottsdale isn't a small town, nor is it a big city.

> The word order in sentences with *nor* is inverted: *SV, nor VS.* The subject and verb of the second clause switch places after the word *nor.* Other negative words such as *not* are not necessary in the second clause because *nor* makes the meaning negative.

■ **CLASS PRACTICE** **1**

Recognizing Basic Compound Sentences

Directions: Mark each subject and verb with *S* and *V.* If there is a Group A connector (coordinating conjunction) joining two clauses, circle the word and write *compound* in the blank to the left. If the sentence has only one *SV,* write *simple.*

>   *S*   *V*
> **EXAMPLE 1** ➤ _____ Louis is working as a teacher's aide.
>
> There is only *one SV,* so the sentence is simple. Write *simple* on the line.

EXAMPLE 2 ➤ _____
$\overset{S\quad\quad\quad V}{\text{Karen doesn't play basketball very often,}}$ $\overset{,\ but\ \ S\ \ V}{\text{but she is very good at it.}}$

There are two *SVs* connected by a *Group A* connector. Write *compound* on the line.

_____ **1.** Renate went home and put her feet up after work.

_____ **2.** Gabriel hasn't finished your portrait yet.

_____ **3.** Helga and Sharon packed for their trip to Europe.

_____ **4.** The defendant's story was believable, yet several of the jury members had doubts about it.

_____ **5.** Ahmad slipped in the dirt, so he didn't make it to first base.

_____ **6.** Colleen scored a goal, and the fans went wild.

_____ **7.** Fatima taught her daughter's class the words to a traditional Arabic song.

_____ **8.** The suspect tried to hide his face, but someone recognized him.

_____ **9.** You should practice your writing skills, for practice makes perfect.

_____ **10.** We learned to use a word processor in the computer lab.

■ **CLASS PRACTICE** **2**

Building Basic Compound Sentences

Directions: Combine the two simple sentences with a suitable *Group A* connector (coordinating conjunction) to make one compound sentence. If more than one *Group A* connector will work, choose the one that you like best.

EXAMPLE ➤ Pedro recently arrived from Ecuador. He wants to make new friends in this country.

Pedro recently arrived from Ecuador, and he wants to make new friends in this country.

Or:

Pedro recently arrived from Ecuador, so he wants to make new friends in this country.

1. Leticia works in a restaurant. She studies English after work.

   _____

2. Rita loves riding horses. She rides almost every day.

   _____

3. Patris may teach in China again. She might teach in India this time.

   _____

4. Many people believed the rumor. It wasn't true at all.

   _____

5. Dan forgot to save his file. It was erased from memory.

   _____

6. Carlos studies at Valparaiso University. He plays racquetball there after classes.

   _____

7. Larry works and plays hard. He believes in living life to the fullest.

   _____

8. Jody turned on the TV. She wanted to watch the World Cup soccer game.

   _____

9. Lisa just started snowboarding last December. She is already an expert.

   _____

10. The rhinoceros didn't come any closer to us. We didn't get any closer to him.

   _____

■ **CLASS PRACTICE** **3**

Writing Basic Compound Sentences

Directions: Now write your own compound sentences. Use several *Group A* connectors (coordinating conjunctions), and remember this pattern:

S　　V　　　, Group A　　　S　　V.

1. _____

2. _____

3. _____

4. _____

5. _____

6. _____

7. _____

8. _____

9. _____

10. _____

When you finish writing these sentences, check to make sure they follow the pattern.

Learning to Avoid Run-ons and Comma Splices

Up to now you have practiced two types of sentences—simple sentences, with only one *SV*, and basic compound sentences, which have two *SV*s joined by a *Group A* connector and (usually) a comma.

Here are the two patterns you have learned:

Simple Sentences	***Compound Sentence***
SV. SV.	*SV, Group A SV.*

One reason for learning the various types of sentences is so that you can check your sentences for errors and correct them. By the time you finish this book, you will have learned many correct ways to connect *SV*s. Of the nine most common ways of signaling where one clause ends and another begins, the first two are shown above—using a *period* to end a sentence, and using a *comma and a Group A connector* to make a basic compound sentence. The complete list of basic sentence patterns is in Appendix II on pages 449–451.

Certain ways of connecting *SV*s are not permitted in English writing. Here are some examples:

$$\overset{S \qquad V}{\text{INCORRECT EXAMPLE 1} \; ➤ \;} \overset{S \qquad V}{\text{The ferry operator spoke only French}} \; \overset{S \qquad V}{\text{we couldn't understand}}$$

INCORRECT EXAMPLE 1 ➤ The ferry operator spoke only French we couldn't understand him.

When you have two SVs with nothing connecting them, it is an error. This kind of sentence error is called a *run-on* because it "runs on" instead of stopping or pausing where it should.

INCORRECT EXAMPLE 2 ➤ Lisa wants to graduate in May, she wants to find a job this summer.

When there are two SVs connected only by a comma, it is an error. This kind of error is called a *comma splice* because it attempts to splice together two *SV*s using only a comma. This is acceptable in some languages, but not in academic written English.

Correcting Run-ons and Comma Splices

Here are the two correct patterns you have learned, as well as these two common errors to avoid:

Correct Sentence Patterns		*Incorrect Patterns*	
SV. SV.	*(simple)*	SV SV.	*(run-on)*
SV, Group A SV.	*(compound)*	SV, SV.	*(comma splice)*

Learning these sentence patterns will make it easy to check your writing for run-ons and comma splices. Look at the first incorrect example again:

INCORRECT EXAMPLE 1 ➤ The ferry operator spoke only French we couldn't understand him.

This is a run-on sentence because it consists of two SVs with nothing to connect them. Look at the correct sentence patterns in the chart above and see if you can find a way to correct this pattern: SV SV.

One correct pattern is SV. SV. Just add a period:

S $V.$ S $V.$

CORRECTED EXAMPLE 1A ➤ The ferry operator spoke only French. We couldn't understand him.

Now there are two correct simple sentences.
Another way of correcting this sentence is to make a basic compound sentence by adding a comma and a *Group A* connector:

S V , *Group A* S $V.$

CORRECTED EXAMPLE 1B ➤ The ferry operator spoke only French , so we couldn't understand him.

Let's practice with **Incorrect Example 2:**

S V , S $V.$
Lisa wants to graduate this year, she needs to take a full load of classes.

This is a comma-splice error because it has two clauses connected only by a comma. Again, there are two ways of correcting this type of error. One is to change the incorrect sentence into two correct simple sentences. Try this below:

_____

_____

The other way of correcting a comma splice error is to change it into a basic compound sentence using a *Group A* connector and a comma. Try this method too:

_____

_____

Now check your answers:

Simple: Lisa wants to graduate this year. She needs to take a full load of classes.

Compound: Lisa wants to graduate this year, so she needs to take a full load of classes.

Both of these answers are correct. By learning different ways to correct sentence errors, you will be able to choose the way that looks or sounds best to you in each case.

■ **CLASS PRACTICE** **4**

Identifying and Correcting Run-ons and Comma Splices

Directions: Mark the subjects, verbs, and Group A connectors, if you think it will help you. Then write *OK, run-on,* or *comma splice* in each blank, and correct the run-ons and comma splices by adding a *period* or a *comma* and a *Group A* connector.

_____ 1. Samantha loves all kinds of flowers roses are her favorite kind.

_____

_____ 2. The fog cleared, the mountain peak was straight ahead.

_____

_____ 3. Eduardo didn't cheat on his taxes. He is an honest man.

_____

_____ 4. Some glass products are fragile others are as strong as steel.

_____

_____ 5. I saw three alligators in the lagoon, I got out of there.

_____

_____ 6. It was almost time for Joan's appointment, and the car still wouldn't start.

_____

_____ 7. Humberto had never met the queen, he knew her from television.

_____

_____ 8. The tropical sun was hot and bright there was a cool breeze.

_____

_____ 9. A glider pilot must understand air currents, the glider may crash.

_____

_____ 10. I had almost fainted from the heat, so I appreciated the water.

_____

■ **CLASS PRACTICE** 5   # Proofreading to Correct Run-ons and Comma Splices

Directions: There are *several run-on sentences* and *comma splices* in the following paragraph. Find and correct all of them. Use a Group A connector and a comma, or add a period.

EXAMPLE ➤   *We thought a dangerous animal was running around in our tent,* ***but*** *it turned out to be only a little ground squirrel.*

A Moving Story

Moving from Michigan to California was an unforgettable and stressful adventure. My husband and I packed everything up and moved, it wasn't easy. We had too many things, so we decided to have a yard sale. For three weeks we sold extra clothes, dishes, and furniture lots of people came to look for bargains. After that, we built a huge trailer to hold everything else, including the dog. We were finally ready to leave our home in Michigan. We felt a little bit sad, we were also excited about going to California. It was a long trip we couldn't go very fast because of the heavy trailer. The dog was carsick for the first five hundred miles then she adjusted to traveling. We drove for ten or twelve hours each day, and at night we slept on a mattress in our trailer. At sunset on the fourth day, we arrived in Albuquerque, New Mexico. The city was surrounded by snow-capped mountains, it looked beautiful, we wanted to stay there. However, we had jobs waiting for us in California, we had to go on. Our trip ended in San Diego, and we still live there today.

■ **CLASS PRACTICE** 6   # Writing with Compound Sentences

PART A: Looking at Writing from an Example Paragraph

Directions: It is important to use a variety of sentence types when you write. In the following section taken from *Poolside* on page 58, look for clauses (SVs) joined by Group A connectors (coordinating conjunctions) and highlight or underline them. Notice that the author, Jason Cross, uses several sentences of this type, as well as other types of sentences that you will study in later chapters.

From *Poolside*

In high school I was a good water polo player with a cocky attitude until I had a very humbling experience. My girlfriend was a cheerleader, so I finally convinced her to get the squad to cheer at one of our games—not just any game, but a play-off game. This was a home game, and at our pool the crowd sat up twenty feet above the deck looking down into the pool. In the first row was my girlfriend along with seven other cheerleaders. Behind them sat my parents, my brother, and my grandmother. At poolside was a *Star News* photographer. This was my big chance to show off. I loved to show off, and besides, I was quite good at it.

PART B: Looking at Your Own Writing:

Directions: Find three compound sentences from your own *narration* rough draft and write them in the blanks below. Hint: Look for *Group A* connectors. If you don't have any compound sentences, you will probably want to replace some of your sentences with compound sentences for greater variety.

1. _____

_____

_____

2. _____

_____

_____

3. _____

_____

_____

Now check your compound sentences to be sure they each have two SVs connected by a comma and a Group A connector.

Narration Sentence Combining Paragraph

Directions: Combine each group of sentences into one good sentence. Most of the groups can be combined as compound sentences by using one of the Group A connectors: *for, and, nor, but, or, yet,* or *so.* Write your sentences on your own paper.

Tornado

1.1 Suddenly everything was quiet.
1.2 The sky began to turn a strange color.
1.3 The color was yellowish.

2.1 At first, the air was absolutely still.
2.2 Then the wind started to blow.

3.1 The sky got very dark.
3.2 I expected a thunderstorm.
3.3 The thunderstorm would be severe.

4.1 To my surprise, there was no thunder.
4.2 There wasn't any rain.

5.1 I heard loud cracking sounds.
5.2 Large branches were breaking.
5.3 They were falling into the yard.

6.1 Suddenly the wind roared.
6.2 I heard trees crashing to the ground.

7.1 When the electricity went off, I was frightened.
7.2 I hid under the kitchen table.

8.1 After awhile, I knew something.
8.2 I knew that the worst part of the storm was over.
8.3 The wind finally calmed down.

9.1 Later I found out about the tornado.
9.2 The tornado had touched down nearby.

10.1 It lifted roofs off houses.
10.2 It tore walls into pieces.
10.3 It wrapped cars around trees.

11.1 Some buildings were left standing.
11.2 The buildings were in its path.
11.3 Many were completely destroyed.

12.1 I saw how a tornado can be.
12.2 It can be frightening.
12.3 It can be destructive.

Learning about Past Tense Verbs

In this chapter the writing focus is *narration,* that is, telling a story. Most of these stories come from the past; we tell about something that we experienced, or imagined, or heard about. Look at these sentences taken from the example narration paper, *The Sacred Falls.*

> We *surfed* Velzyland and *ate* some fruit for breakfast.
>
> As we *started* the three-mile hike, I *was* a little disappointed.
>
> The trees *were* full of noises . . . .
>
> Rain finally *got* my attention, and we *dove* into the mineral pool . . . .
>
> I *floated* on my back looking up . . . .

These verbs, *surfed, ate, started, was, were, got, dove,* and *floated,* are in the *simple past tense.* The simple past tense is one of the most useful verb tenses in English. It is the most common tense that is used to talk about something that happened in the past—one hour ago, yesterday, last year, 500 years ago, or anytime in the past. Look at the verbs from *The Sacred Falls* again:

Simple Form	Simple Past Form	-ed Ending?
surf	*surfed*	*yes*
start	*started*	*yes*
be	*was, were*	*no*
get	*got*	*no*
dive	*dove**	*no*
float	*floated*	*yes*

Notice that three of these verbs, *surfed, started,* and *floated,* end with the letters *-ed.* These are called *regular verbs* because they all form the simple past tense the same way, that is, they all end with *-ed.* In English, most verbs are regular verbs.

The other verbs, *was, were, got,* and *dove,* do not end with *-ed.* These are examples of *irregular verbs,* verbs that form the simple past tense in a variety of different ways. Although there are fewer irregular verbs than regular verbs, many of the most common English verbs are irregular. This section will start with a very special irregular verb, the verb *to be.* After that you will look at other irregular verbs, and finally you will learn some spelling rules for regular *-ed* endings.

The *Verb* to Be (Was *and* Were)

As you know, the verb *to be* is the only English verb that has three forms in the simple present: *am, are,* and *is.* The verb *to be* is also the only verb in English that has *two forms* in the simple past tense: *was* and *were.*

---

*Although this writer used *dove, dived* is also accepted as correct by most authorities.

Simple Present		*Simple Past*	
I	*am*		
he, she, it	*is*	I, he, she, it	*was*
we, you, they	*are*	we, you, they	*were*

As you learned in Chapter 1, verbs must agree with their subjects. When you are using the past tense of the verb *to be,* you must choose *was* or *were,* depending on the subject of the sentence.

EXAMPLES ➤   1. Mark <u>was</u> on a soccer team, and he practiced several times a week.

Mark (he) is the subject of the sentence, so *was* is the correct form.

2. Many of the students <u>were</u> excited about learning to write better.

The subject of the sentence is *Many of the students* (they), so *were* is the correct form.

■ **CLASS PRACTICE** **7**

Using *Was* and *Were*

Directions: Identify the subject of the sentence first. Then write the correct verb, *was* or *were* for affirmative statements or questions, and *wasn't* or *weren't* for negatives, in each blank space below.

1. At dusk we still _____ ready to leave the Sacred Falls.

2. I tried to call and share the good news, but the telephone _____ working.

3. Kathleen _____ about to attempt a shot on goal.

4. _____ your friend with you in Jalisco, Mexico, last summer?

5. The hikers _____ hot, tired, and thirsty.

6. There _____ a big black car blocking the driveway.

7. _____ there first-aid supplies in the house?

8. There _____ many students trying to get into the aerobics class.

9. _____ they prepared for the earthquake?

10. _____ there any articles about space travel in last month's magazine?

Irregular Verbs

All verbs that do not end in *-ed* in the simple past tense are *irregular* verbs. Only the verb *to be* has two simple forms in the past tense. All other verbs use only one form no matter what the subject of the sentence is. For example, the simple past tense form of *think* is *thought* for all subjects: *I, we, you, he, she, it,* and *they*. Here is a list of the simple past forms of irregular verbs (besides *was* and *were*) that have been used in the sample papers in Chapters 1 and 2:

Simple Form	*Past Form*
become	became
begin	began
bring	brought
buy	bought
come	came
dive	dove (or *dived*)
do	did
drink	drank
eat	ate
fall	fell
feel	felt
find	found
forget	forgot
freeze	froze
get	got
give	gave
go	went
have	had
hear	heard
hurt	hurt
keep	kept
know	knew
leave	left
lose	lost
make	made
meet	met
run	ran
say	said
see	saw
sit	sat
speak	spoke
stand	stood
take	took
tell	told
think	thought
understand	understood

A more complete list of common irregular verbs is in Appendix III on pages 452–455.

■ **CLASS PRACTICE** **8**

Irregular Past Tense Verbs

PART A

Directions: Write the correct past form of the verb in parentheses.

1. Quietly, the old story-teller (begin) _____ to speak, and we all listened carefully.

2. Some of the nurses in the maternity ward finally (take) _____ a short break.

3. My dogs, Jake and Tanzy, (run) _____ to meet me.

4. Last Friday we (speak) _____ with the locker room attendant about the cold showers.

5. Rain and I (think) _____ about our wonderful experience.

6. Xavier (hear) _____ the voice of the ancient waterfall as he walked.

7. Jay (buy) _____ his watch in Japan last year.

8. The students (do) _____ a lot of work in that teacher's class.

9. The earthquake (make) _____ us realize the importance of being prepared.

10. My relatives (come) _____ to see me graduate from college.

PART B

Directions: Now choose three verbs from the list on the previous page and write past tense sentences of your own:

1. _____

   _____

2. _____

   _____

3. _____

   _____

Regular Verbs

Regular verbs end in *-ed* in the simple past tense, but there are several spelling rules to keep in mind. Here are a few more examples of regular verbs from the sample paragraphs and exercises in this chapter:

Simple Form	Past Tense Form
arrive	arrived
jump	jumped
stop	stopped
turn	turned
try	tried
wave	waved
pray	prayed

In the list above, only *jumped, turned,* and *prayed* add *-ed* without applying one of the spelling rules. Let's look at the spelling rules for the rest of these verbs:

1. *The silent -e rule:* If the verb already ends in a silent *-e,* you just need to add the *-d. Arrive, arrived* is an example of this rule.

2. *The consonant + -y rule:* If the verb ends with a consonant plus the letter *-y,* change the *-y* to *-i* and add *-ed.* In the list above, the past tense of *try* is *tried.* If the word ends in a vowel plus *-y,* however, don't change the *-y* to an *-i:* pray, prayed.

3. *The double consonant rule:* In certain cases, when the last three letters of a verb are a consonant, a vowel, and a consonant, the final consonant needs to be doubled before adding *-ed.*

    This is true with all one-syllable verbs except for those that end with the letters *w, x,* or *y.* Here are a few examples of this rule:

	Simple Form	Past Form
	hug	hugged
	grin	grinned
	rub	rubbed
but:	row	rowed

    If the verb has more than one syllable and ends with a consonant, a vowel, and a consonant, double the last consonant only if the stress is on the last syllable. Double the *-r* in *prefer,* for example, but not the *-l* in *travel.* Again, don't double the final consonants *w, x,* or *y.* Here are some more examples of this rule:

	Simple Form	Past Form
	commit	committed
	prefer	preferred
	regret	regretted
but:	deliver	delivered

This rule may seem strange, but there is a reason for it. The past tense of *tape* is *taped*—just add *-d*. But what is the past tense of the verb *tap?* If you added *-ed,* it would also be *"taped"*—and not the correct meaning at all. You can see that the last three (in this case the only three) letters of *tap* consist of a consonant (*t*), a vowel (*a*), and a consonant (*p*), so you have to double the final consonant (*p*) and write *tapped*. Now it still has the short *a* sound of *tap*.

■ CLASS
PRACTICE 9

Regular Past Tense Verbs

PART A

Directions: Write the correctly spelled past form of the verb in parentheses.

1. Dale (remember) _____ catching fish from his father's canoe.

2. The fishing boat accidentally (ram) _____ our tiny sailboat.

3. The allies (liberate) _____ France after many hard-fought battles.

4. Mrs. Conger (try) _____ to get someone to help her cook the giant pumpkin.

5. Daron (study) _____ electronics in school.

6. Martha (wait) _____ impatiently for the light to change.

7. Lori (hope) _____ for a gold medal in speed skating

8. The pirates (hum) _____ a sinister tune.

9. The Navajo children (listen) _____ intently until the story was over.

10. Our last night on the mountain, the wind (howl) _____ for hours.

PART B

Directions: Look at your own rough draft and see if you have used any past tense verbs that follow the *silent -e rule,* the *consonant + -y rule,* or the *double consonant rule.* If so, write them below. If not, choose two of the verbs above and write original past tense sentences with them.

1. _____

   _____

2. _____

   _____

Avoiding Past Tense Errors

It is important to check your own writing carefully to be sure that you avoid the most common past tense errors: using the wrong form of irregular verbs, not following the spelling rules, or writing an incorrect negative form.

Remember that the negative forms of regular and irregular verbs use *did not* (or *didn't*) and the simple form of the verb, with no *-ed* ending, like this example from *The Howl* by Mark Field, on pages 49–50.

A wildcat? No, it *didn't sound* like any type of cat I've ever heard.

By checking your past tense verbs to be sure that you have used the correct form and spelling, you can make your writing more accurate.

■ **CLASS PRACTICE 10**

Correcting Past Tense Errors

Directions: The following paragraph contains twelve past tense errors. Cross out each error and write the correction above the mistake.

Emergency

One night when I was in my junior year of high school, I had a really scary experience in an empty house. I arrived home at about 9:30, and I had forgotten my key to get in the house. No one answered when I knocking on the door. I taught I heard a noise inside, but I wasn't sure. I tryed to get in through the back door, but it was locked, so I get into the house through an attic window. Next, I stand at the kitchen counter and start to read the newspaper when I hear a heavy footstep in the hall. I ran to my room, closed the door, and grabed something heavy to hit the intruder with if he came into my room. Then I called the operator, and she asks me, "Is this an emergency?" In about five minutes I seen the red and blue lights from the police car in my driveway, and I ran to the front door to let the officers in. They was looking around the house but didn't found anyone, so I guess I heard the sound of the house settling. It was a scary and embarrassing experience!

Narration Sentence Combining Paragraph

Directions: Combine each group of sentences into one good sentence. Some of the groups can be combined as compound sentences by using one of the Group A connectors. Notice the past tense verbs, especially the irregular ones. Write your sentences on your own paper.

Coyote Sunset

1.1 It was late afternoon.
1.2 We arrived at our destination.
1.3 Our destination was far from the city.

2.1 We wanted to enjoy the view.
2.2 The view was from the top of the hill.
2.3 The hill was the highest one.
2.4 We started to climb.

3.1 Climbing was easy.
3.2 This was at first.
3.3 It began to get more difficult.
3.4 This was as we got higher.

4.1 We reached the top.
4.2 The sun was getting lower in the sky.

5.1 We stood there for a while.
5.2 We were enjoying the sunset.
5.3 The sunset was gold.
5.4 The sunset was crimson.

6.1 Then we heard the sounds.
6.2 The sounds were faint.
6.3 The sounds were of coyotes.
6.4 The coyotes were in the distance.

7.1   We began to get scared.
7.2   It was starting to get dark.
7.3   The sounds were getting closer.

8.1   We started down the hill.
8.2   We could hardly see where we were going.

9.1   We had been in a hurry.
9.2   We had forgotten to take along a flashlight.
9.3   We had forgotten to take along a compass.

10.1   Suddenly the direction of the sounds changed.
10.2   We were afraid of something.
10.3   The fear was that the coyotes were near our car.

11.1   We circled around the other side of the hill.
11.2   We circled cautiously.
11.3   We headed toward our car.

12.1   At last we reached the car.
12.2   We reached it safely.

13.1   We never saw the coyotes.
13.2   We didn't see their tracks.

14.1   Our experience taught us something.
14.2   Our experience was frightening.
14.3   It taught us to always take a flashlight and a compass.
14.4   It taught us not to climb so late in the day.

Putting the Finishing Touches on Your Writing

Before you turn in your completed narration paragraph or short paper, you should proofread it to make sure that you have used correct grammar and sentence structure. If you wish, you may also ask members of your workshop group or other classmates to help you with proofreading. Pay particular attention to things that you have studied in this chapter. For example, make sure that you have used the correct past tense forms for irregular verbs and that you have used the right spelling for regular verbs. Also make sure that when you have more than one clause in a sentence, you have connected the clauses correctly. If you find any run-ons or comma splices, correct them by adding a connecting word or a period.

After you have proofread your paper and completed your revisions, use the narration writing checklist that follows to make sure that you didn't forget anything. If you can answer *yes* to all of the questions on the checklist, you have done a good job of writing your story. However, if there are some questions that you cannot answer with a *yes* or that you are unsure about, you may need to do a little more revising before turning in your completed assignment. Ask your instructor if you have questions about anything on the checklist.

Narration Writing Checklist

Content and Organization

_____ 1. Is my story interesting to read?

_____ 2. Does my paper have a topic sentence?

_____ 3. Does the topic sentence express the main point of the story?

_____ 4. Is the order of events clear?

_____ 5. Have I included significant details ?

_____ 6. Have I expressed my feelings about the experience?

_____ 7. Are transitions used smoothly and effectively?

_____ 8. Does my concluding sentence make the story seem complete?

Sentence Structure and Grammar

_____ 1. In sentences with more than one clause, did I use connecting words correctly?

_____ 2. Have I avoided run-ons and comma splices?

_____ 3. Are past tense verbs used correctly?

_____ 4. Have I checked spelling and grammar?

ENRICHMENT SECTION:
Telling Someone Else's Story

Goals

In the enrichment section of this chapter, you will learn how to do the following:

- Write an interesting story about someone else
- Include your own observations and interpretations
- Plan and organize a story that is two or more paragraphs long

If you are ready for a slightly more challenging narration assignment, try writing the story of an experience that happened to someone else. Experiences that happened to friends or relatives can sometimes turn into even more intense or interesting stories than your own experiences. Even though you were an observer rather than a participant, you may know almost as much about the events as if you had experienced them yourself, and you may have very strong feelings about what happened. Your own observations and comments can add a lot to the story. Your topic can be something significant that happened in a brief period of a few hours or less, or it can be a series of events that took place over a longer period of time.

When you are writing the story of an experience that happened to someone else, almost all of the writing techniques are the same as for a story about yourself. You may want to begin by looking at the *Exploring Topics for Narration Worksheet* in this chapter (page 37) to get some good ideas for topics. Then practice telling the story orally and use freewriting to discover details, as you did with your own story earlier in this chapter. You will probably want to tell the events in chronological order, and you will need to use a few transitional words or phrases to help keep the time order clear. Think about whether your topic sentence should be at the beginning to make the point of the story clear right away or near the end to create suspense. If you decide to put the topic sentence at the end, remember that you may need to withhold other information at first in order to keep readers wondering about how things will turn out. The topic sentence may focus on your friend's feelings about the experience, a lesson that one or both of you learned, or your own observations about the experience.

Because you are telling the story as an observer, you will need to use *he* or *she* (third person) most of the time instead of *I* (first person). Of course, if you played a part in the events too, you should use *I* for those parts of the story. You may also use *I* to make observations about some of the things that happened. Your comments will give readers a clearer understanding of the person that your story is about, as well as his actions. (See this technique used in the story *A Lost Friend* that follows.)

Most of the example papers in this chapter have told about events that happened in one day or in only a few hours. If you write the story of events that happened over a longer period of time, you may want to divide the story into two or more paragraphs, as the writer of *The Sacred Falls* did earlier in this chapter (page 53). In this case, each paragraph should tell about one major part of the story or one group of related events. With a longer story, you may place the topic sentence in the first paragraph or in the last paragraph, whichever is most effective. You might even want to use more than one sentence to express the main idea.

Read the story that follows, *A Lost Friend* by Todd Louis. It is about what happened to a close friend of the writer over a period of a few weeks. There are several different events involving his friend that all lead up to the ending of the story. Notice that each paragraph contains events that happened during one time period or develops one part of the story. Most of the story is written in the third person (*he*), but the writer sometimes uses the first person (*I* or *we*) to express his own feelings or observations. Look for the topic sentence in the last paragraph of the story.

A Lost Friend
by Todd Louis

1   Carlos was under a lot of pressure. His parents had just kicked him out of the household, and he was on his own. His parents decided that it was time for him to start supporting himself. It wasn't a surprise thing for Carlos. His

parents had given him a six-month warning, and the day finally came. He had no job and no place to stay.

2   At first he seemed concerned, but later he seemed to not even care about what happened to him. The only money he had was the five hundred dollars that his dad gave him to help out with the first month's rent. He became irresponsible and was spending his money stupidly. One of the dumbest things he did was go out and buy a new wetsuit. He already had a perfectly good wetsuit that he had bought a few months ago.

3   One day I saw Carlos at the beach. "What's up, Carlos?" I said to him. "I'm not on drugs, man, I'm just being myself, I don't need money to live. You gotta be yourself, Todd. Open up to me, man. It's okay to cry, dude," he said to me in an emotional and scrambled manner.* That day, after surfing, Carlos ran into a telephone pole with his car. The passengers were not hurt seriously. There were only some cuts and bruises. The strange thing was that Carlos didn't even try to turn away from the pole. The passengers said he just ran straight into it. I began to wonder if he was trying to kill himself. My friends and I decided something had to be done before he got hurt.

4   Carlos became a hassle to hang out with. He wasn't the same friend I used to have. He would make a scene just about everywhere we went. For a while he would be fine and then some weird feelings of his would all of a sudden come up. For example, Carlos and some friends went to see the movie *The Doors*. Carlos began to dance and jump around while the movie was playing. Jim Morrison, the lead singer of The Doors, who is dead now, seemed to have some sort of psychotic effect on Carlos. After the movie, he began quoting Jim Morrison and wanted to drink the same kind of whiskey he drank. It was obvious that something was screwing him up. About a week of his madness passed, and he wasn't getting any better.

5   One morning Carlos got somebody to take him down to the bank to get some money out. He had forgotten his I.D. and was denied. He began to yell at the lady behind the counter, and eventually he was yelling at everybody in the bank. He didn't understand that he couldn't get his money out and went out of control. One of the ladies called Carlos's house and told his dad that he must be picked up immediately. After he was brought safely home, his dad came into Carlos's room and said, "Let's go to the hospital, Carlos." Carlos replied, "I knew it! Jim Morrison is alive, isn't he, Dad?"

6   At first, the doctors thought it was some form of acid that lasts about five or six days, but after a few days of tests and observations, they said it was some type of mental illness. There wasn't a trace of acid, crystal, or anything powerful enough to have that effect found in his system. After a few more days in the mental hospital, he was released. He was still weird, but really mellow.

7   Now he takes drugs to help calm the sickness, but they don't cure him. It seems like he's not really happy anymore. He is always worrying about something. Sometimes we go surfing together, but it's not the same. Taking his medicine makes it hard for him to have any social life. I've seen programs about mental illness on T.V., and I've heard about it from people, but I never

*Although all of this dialogue is in one paragraph, writers often put each person's words in separate, short paragraphs. Using this method, Todd's question would be in one paragraph, Carlos's response would be in another paragraph, and the incident that follows would also be in a separate paragraph.

thought it would happen to one of my friends. When I look at him I remember all the good times we had, because only on the outside is he still the same friend I used to have. I miss the old Carlos.

Response to *A Lost Friend*

1. Go back and underline all of the sentences in which the writer used the first person (*I* or *we*). Why did he use *I* and *we* in these sentences?

   _____

   _____

2. What is each paragraph about? On the lines below, briefly identify the main events and ideas that are included in each of the seven paragraphs.

   PARAGRAPH 1:

   _____

   _____

   PARAGRAPH 2:

   _____

   _____

   PARAGRAPH 3:

   _____

   _____

   PARAGRAPH 4:

   _____

   _____

   PARAGRAPH 5:

   _____

   _____

   PARAGRAPH 6:

   _____

   _____

PARAGRAPH 7:

_____

_____

3. Why is the final paragraph of the story written in the present tense instead of the past tense like the rest of the story?

_____

_____

4. Which sentence do you think is the topic sentence? (Look in the last paragraph of the story.)

_____

_____

   Now look back at _Worksheet I, Exploring Topics for Narration,_ earlier in this chapter to help you think of some good stories about people that you know. When you have decided on the story that you want to tell, answer the following questions:

1. Who and what will your story be about?

_____

_____

2. Are you going to write about one event or a series of related events?

_____

_____

3. What is the main point of the story going to be? (Suggestions: the other person's feelings about the events, your interpretation of the events, or something that one or both of you learned.) Remember that your topic sentence should focus on this main idea.

_____

_____

_____

Now use the freewriting technique that you learned earlier in this chapter to get the basic story down on paper. Then look over what you have written and decide if you want to break the story into paragraphs, as the writer of *A Lost Friend* did. If you decide to use two or more paragraphs, briefly explain on the lines below what part of the story you will include in each paragraph. There are places to plan four paragraphs. However, you may need more than four or less than four, depending on the length and complexity of the story. Use your own paper if you need more space.

PARAGRAPH 1:

_____

_____

_____

PARAGRAPH 2:

_____

_____

_____

PARAGRAPH 3:

_____

_____

_____

PARAGRAPH 4:

_____

_____

_____

Now you are ready to write an interesting and well-organized story. Remember to use vivid words, and try to include some dialogue at key points in the story.

■ ■ ■ 3

Writing That Explains How to Do Something

SECTION ONE:
The Writing Process
for Instructions

Goals

In this section of the chapter, you will learn how to do the following:

- Use listing to discover details
- Plan and organize step-by-step instructions
- Write an effective introduction and topic sentence for instructions
- Write at an appropriate level for your intended audience
- Include precautions to warn the reader about potential problems
- Write an effective conclusion for instructions

Learning about Instructions

What Are Instructions?

Writing that explains how to do something is called *instructions*. For most of us, instructions are a very important form of communication that we use almost every day. Either we need to follow instructions in order to do something ourselves, or we need to tell someone else how to do something. If those instructions are not clear, our daily lives might be disrupted. For example, without good instructions, the spark plugs in our car might not be adjusted right, we might not be able to set our VCR to record television programs when we're not home, we might not be able to fill out our income tax forms correctly, or our hot-air balloon might get caught in a treetop.

Sometimes we need to give instructions orally, and at other times we need to write the instructions, depending on the situation. For example, if you invite a friend to your house for the first time, you will probably just

87

tell the person how to get there. However, if you are inviting twenty people to a party, you might write out the instructions and make copies rather than saying everything twenty times. If the directions are complicated, you might also draw a map in addition to giving oral or written instructions. A map or diagram is simply a more visual way to give instructions. Whichever method (or methods) you use, the most important thing is to make the instructions clear and easy to understand.

Writing Objective: Explaining How to Do Something

Your objective for this chapter is to write instructions that explain how to do or make something. You will need to think of something that you know how to do or make really well so that you can explain it clearly. For this assignment, you will be the expert on your topic, and you will be telling other people how they too can learn your special skills and techniques. If your instructions are detailed and specific enough, whoever reads them will be able to do each step successfully as you have explained it. Your instructions may be written in one paragraph or in a longer paper that consists of two or more paragraphs, depending on your topic.

When you are writing instructions, it is very important to consider your *intended audience*—that is, who you are writing the instructions for. If your audience knows little or nothing about the topic, it will be essential to explain everything in very basic terms. For example, if you are explaining how to set up a spreadsheet on the computer to an audience that doesn't know anything about using a computer, you will need to include fundamentals such as how to turn it on, how to select the right application, etc., as well as how to actually set up the spreadsheet. On the other hand, if your audience is already knowledgeable about using a computer, your explanations should be at a more advanced level. For most topics, other class members will probably be your intended audience, so you can simply ask people in your workshop group if your instructions are at an appropriate level—not too basic and not too complicated.

Prewriting Activities

Exploring Topics

The best way to begin your writing assignment is to explore some possible topics. As you learned in Chapter 2, finding a good topic is always the first step in the writing process. Use the *Exploring Topics Worksheet* on the next page to help you think of a variety of things that you know how to do well. Even if you think at this point that you are not an expert on anything, you can find a good topic by doing the worksheet. Think seriously about each question and list as many possible topics as you can so that you will have a wide range of choices.

■ **WORKSHEET I** | # Exploring Topics for Instructions

Directions: Answer at least seven of the following questions. If you have more than one idea in response to some questions, write down all of your answers.

1. What is difficult for many people to do but easy for you?

2. What are some of your hobbies or favorite activities?

   Is there a special technique or procedure involved in one of these that you could teach others?

3. What are some of the interesting jobs or procedures that you do or supervise at work?

4. Are you good at remodeling or fixing things? Is there a special remodeling, repair, or maintenance job that you could explain how to do?

5. What can you make for yourself that most people have to buy?

6. Are you familiar with specific safety precautions or disaster procedures that you could explain to others? If so, what type of precautions or procedures?

7. What important procedure could you explain to a new student at your school—how to crash classes, how to apply for financial aid, how to locate a magazine article at the library, or something else?

8. What skill or technique have you learned in one of your classes that you could explain to others? (Suggestions: a biology or chemistry experiment; first aid or lifesaving techniques; communication techniques for specific situations.)

9. Could you suggest certain steps to follow in dealing with a personal problem such as low self-esteem, lack of assertiveness, or a difficult relationship? Identify a problem that you could give advice about.

10. What other procedure or technique could you teach someone else to do?

Discovering Details 1: Giving Oral Instructions

The best way to find out if instructions are really clear is to see if someone can follow them. This prewriting activity will help you develop your ability to give good instructions that are easy to understand. First, the class should be divided into groups of about five students. Each group will choose a topic and plan step-by-step instructions for something that can be done in the classroom. Then representatives from each group will present the instructions orally, and other class members will attempt to follow them.

STEP 1: FINDING A TOPIC:

Each group should select an instructions topic. It must be something that can be done in your classroom. Don't choose a topic that is too simple or that everyone already knows how to do (such as how to sharpen a pencil). Also avoid topics that are too broad or general, such as how to teach a class. Begin by looking over the topics that you listed on your *Exploring Topics Worksheet*. Think about which things you could teach someone to do in the classroom. Look for topics that require no equipment or only a few things that you could easily bring to class. Share and discuss your worksheet ideas with your group. Then write some of your group's best topic ideas here:

1. _____

2. _____

3. _____

4. _____

If you are having trouble thinking of topics, consider some of these suggestions:

1. How to do an exercise such as jumping jacks, sit-ups, or push-ups
2. How to do a simple line dance or square dance
3. A first-aid skill, such as how to bandage an injured ankle
4. How to make a boat, an airplane, or something else out of paper
5. How to write a good resumé or a short business letter
6. A relaxation technique, a self-defense technique, a Tai Chi movement, or some other useful technique
7. A communication technique such as how to be assertive in a specific situation or how to resolve a conflict
8. What to do in case of an earthquake or a disaster drill

Now discuss all of your topic ideas and decide which one you like best. If possible, choose a topic that at least two or three people in your group already know how to do well. They can teach other group members so that everyone will be able to assist with presenting the instructions.

STEP 2: LISTING STEPS:

Now decide on the steps that a person needs to follow in order to do the process or activity that you have selected. Someone in the group should make a list of the steps. You will have a chance to add more details orally, but your written list should include the most important things. Try to make everything as clear as possible so that your audience, the other class members, will be able to follow your instructions. Write your topic below and then list the steps, or you may use your own paper if you prefer. You may have fewer than eight steps or more than eight, depending on your topic.

Topic: _____

Steps:

1. _____

2. _____

3. _____

4. _____

5. _____

6. _____

7. _____

8. _____

STEP 3: TRYING OUT YOUR INSTRUCTIONS:

Select one or two people from your group to be the primary instructors. They will teach the rest of the class how to do the process by explaining it orally, one step at a time. If possible, one or more group members should also demonstrate the technique while it is being explained. If something isn't clear enough, class members who are trying to follow your instructions may ask questions. Everyone in your group should be ready to assist people who need help.

STEP 4: FOLLOW-UP QUESTIONS:

When all of the groups have finished presenting their instructions, answer the following questions about what happened during the activity. Discuss each question with your group before writing your answers here.

1. What parts of your group's instructions were easy for other people to follow?

2. What parts of your group's instructions, if any, were not clear enough?

3. What information, if any, did your group have to add so that people could follow your instructions?

4. What problems, if any, did you experience with instructions given by other groups?

5. What have you learned about giving instructions?

Discovering Details 2: Listing

Look again at the topics that you listed on the *Exploring Topics Worksheet* and pick the one that you are most interested in writing about. Use this topic for the following prewriting activity. If the topic that your group chose for oral instructions is the one you like best, it's all right to use it for this activity too. However, you may find another interesting topic on your worksheet that you like better and know more about. Be sure that the topic is not too complicated to explain in a paragraph or short paper. For example, if your topic is how to swim, your paper will be much too long if you try to explain all about floating, kicking, breathing, treading water, and various swimming strokes. A smaller topic such as how to tread water or how to do the backstroke would be a better choice.

After you have decided on a tentative topic, *listing* can help you think of steps and details to use in your paragraph or short paper. This prewriting activity is very similar to freewriting, which you did in Chapter 2. Both freewriting and listing involve putting everything that you think of down on paper, in whatever order the ideas occur to you, without editing. The main difference is that for listing, you simply make a list rather than writing sentences. Listing can be used to discover details about any kind of writing topic. However, listing is particularly good for instructions because it is an easy and natural way to write down a series of steps.

Begin by trying to list the steps in the process or technique that you have chosen as your topic. Also list anything else that might help the reader follow your instructions, such as the right equipment or safety precautions. Look at the listing example that follows, and then write your own list on Worksheet II.

LISTING EXAMPLE ➤ **Topic:** How to Paint a Room

need both roller and brush

buy the right kind of paint

apply paint evenly

protect furniture and carpet

wear old clothes

do ceiling first

paint edges and corners with a brush

brushing back and forth eliminates brush marks

put masking tape around edges and baseboard

paint one section at a time

wash brush and roller afterward—soap and water

importance of good ventilation

stir paint thoroughly before you begin

use even brush strokes

use long roller strokes

latex paint is easier to use

Now do the same thing with your topic on the worksheet that follows. Just make a list of everything you can think of that a person following your instructions will need to do or know.

■ **WORSHEET II** | # Listing

Directions: List as many steps as you can think of and any other important information about your topic. It is not necessary to write complete sentences, and don't worry if some things are not in the right order.

Topic: _How to_ _____

_____

_____

_____

_____

_____

_____

_____

_____

_____

_____

_____

_____

_____

_____

_____

_____

_____

_____

If your list is more than half a page long, you probably have found a good topic that you can develop into a paragraph or short paper. However, if you had trouble listing steps for your topic, you may want to try freewriting instead. (See Chapter 2, page 38, to review freewriting.) Telling someone the instructions orally might also help you think of more steps to write on your list. Then if you still can't find enough things to say about the topic, look over your *Exploring Topics Worksheet* again and change to a different topic. Use either listing or freewriting or both with your new topic. (See Appendix I for additional freewriting and listing worksheets.) These and other prewriting activities are essential steps in the writing process because they can help you discover what you want to say about your topic.

Putting Your List in Step-by-Step Order

The natural order for giving instructions is one step at a time, from start to finish—in other words, step-by-step order. For most kinds of instructions, step-by-step order is essential because certain things must be done before others. For example, if you are going to change an electrical outlet, you have to turn off the electricity and remove the old outlet before you can install the new one. In other words, step-by-step order is simply the logical and natural arrangement for most kinds of instructions. Since step-by-step order is based on time, it is very much like chronological order, which you used for narration writing in Chapter 2.

A lot of things on your *Listing Worksheet* are probably in step-by-step order already. However, before you begin your rough draft, it is important to make sure that all of the steps are in the right order. You should read through the entire list and think about the best sequence for the steps. Although most things will need to be done in a certain order, you may find a few things that can be done more or less at the same time. For example, if you are painting a room, preparations like buying the right kind of paint and getting a paint roller and brush can all be done anytime before you start painting. It doesn't matter which one you do first.

Before you start rearranging the list for your own topic, let's practice with the prewriting list for how to paint a room. As you read through the list, which is reprinted on the next page, try to imagine yourself actually painting a room by following these instructions. You don't have to be an expert on painting to see that some items are not in step-by-step order. For example, if you apply the paint (item #3) before you cover the furniture and carpet (item #4), your room may be a mess.

Circle all items that seem to be out of order. Then draw an arrow to show where you think each of these items should be placed.

Listing: How to Paint a Room

need both roller and brush

buy the right kind of paint

apply paint evenly

protect furniture and carpet

wear old clothes

do ceiling first

paint edges and corners with a brush

brushing back and forth eliminates brush marks

put masking tape around edges and baseboard

paint one section at a time

wash brush and roller afterward—soap and water

importance of good ventilation

stir paint thoroughly before you begin

use even brush strokes

use long roller strokes

latex paint is easier to use

What things did you find that are not in step-by-step order? Write them here:

_____

_____

_____

_____

_____

_____

_____

Compare your answers with those of other class members, and try to agree on the most logical step-by-step order for the painting instructions.

Now use this same method to organize your own list on your *Listing Worksheet*. Follow these steps:

STEP 1: Read through your complete list and circle all items that are not in step-by-step order.

STEP 2: Draw an arrow to show where each item that is out of place should be moved to create the most logical step-by-step order.

STEP 3: Look over your revised list to make sure that everything is in order. If you think of any additional steps that are missing, add them to your list. If you have moved or added several items, you may want to rewrite the list so it is easier to read.

STEP 4: Read your completed list to other classmates in your workshop group. Ask them to help you make sure that everything is in the best step-by-step order and that you have not left out any necessary steps.

Writing a Rough Draft

From Listing to First Draft

The well-organized list of steps that you have just completed will help you write your first draft in step-by-step order. Be sure to add details and explanations about how to do each step correctly. If you think of other important things that are not on the list, include them in your writing. If anything on your list seems irrelevant or not important to the instructions, you should, of course, leave it out.

Here is a first draft of *You Too Can Paint,* which was developed from the listing for how to paint a room. The writer did a good job of adding details about some of the steps but failed to explain others. As you read this first draft, think about whether the writer has told you everything that you would need to know if you were really painting a room. Underline any parts of the instructions that need more details and explanations.

First Draft

You Too Can Paint

Be sure that you have the right kind of paint. You will also need a paint brush, a paint roller, and old clothes to wear. Cover the furniture and carpet. Also protect the baseboard and door frames. Before you start to paint, open doors and windows for good ventilation. Stir the paint thoroughly, and then begin with the ceiling. After you have painted the edges and corners with the brush, use the roller to do the main part of the ceiling. The paint should be applied evenly with long, smooth, back-and-forth strokes. Do the walls the same way. Wash the paint brush and roller when you are finished. In a few hours, you will be able to sit back and enjoy your newly painted room.

Response to *You Too Can Paint*

Would you be able to paint a room by following these instructions? If you could talk to this writer, what additions or changes would you suggest to improve this first draft?

_____

_____

_____

As you write your own first draft, be sure to include details and explanations about every step. When you are finished, have two or three other classmates read what you have written and respond to the workshop questions below. If your instructions are intended for an audience that already has some background knowledge, remember that you may need to give classmates a little extra information about the topic so that they will be able to understand everything. Keep revising your rough draft until members of your workshop group agree that everything is clearly explained with adequate details.

Rough Draft Workshop Questions

1. Who is the writer's intended audience? Are the explanations at the right level for this audience? Is anything too technical or too basic?

2. What parts of the instructions are clearly explained and easy to follow?

3. What parts (if any) are confusing or inadequately explained? Can you offer any suggestions for improving these parts?

4. Can you think of anything else that could be added or changed to improve the instructions?

Learning about Introductions and Topic Sentences for Instructions

Introductions

Did reading the rough draft of *You Too Can Paint* make you want to go right home and paint your bedroom? Unless you just happen to want to paint a room, you probably didn't develop much enthusiasm because the writer didn't include anything to get readers interested in the topic.

Whenever you buy something that comes with written instructions, such as a new calculator or cordless phone, the manufacturer doesn't need to get you interested in the instructions. He can safely assume that a purchaser of the product will have some interest in the instructions.

However, for most academic writing, not all of your readers will automatically have an interest in your topic, so it is part of your job as a writer to *create interest*. In order to make your instructions more appealing to your audience (especially members of your class), you should begin with a brief introduction that captures readers' attention. Sometimes one sentence can act as both an introduction and a topic sentence. In other cases, you may want to use another introductory sentence or two in addition to the topic sentence so that you can include more information.

As you read the following introductions, notice that each one begins with something intended to get readers interested in the topic. Which introductions make you want to read more?

INTRODUCTION A:

When a great job opportunity comes along, it's important to be ready for it. If you prepare your resumé now and update it frequently, you'll have a head start.

INTRODUCTION B:

Are you bored, unhappy, or depressed? Try changing the color of your walls. Color has a tremendous effect on a person's well-being. Painting a room is an easy and inexpensive way to feel better.

INTRODUCTION C:

You probably have extra money hidden in your closets and cupboards, although you may not know it. Selling your unwanted items at a garage sale can put that cash in your pocket.

INTRODUCTION D:

AIDS is a sexually transmitted disease that has no cure at this time. Therefore, it is important to understand it and protect yourself.

INTRODUCTION E:

Do you like crisp green salads, fresh corn on the cob, sweet juicy watermelon, and strawberry shortcake? These are just a few of the homegrown treats that you can enjoy if you plant a small garden and take care of it properly.

Which introductions do you think are the most effective? What makes some of them capture your interest better than others?

_____

_____

_____

Did you notice that all of the introductions give readers a *reason* to want to learn how to do something? For example, you may never have considered having a garage sale, but if the idea of having extra money appeals to you, Introduction C may make you want to read the instructions. You may have been uninterested in the rough draft of *You Too Can Paint*, but perhaps you changed your mind when you read Introduction B and thought about having a light blue bedroom instead of a dull gray one. Giving readers a reason to read about your topic is one of the best ways to get them interested.

Topic Sentences

An important part of the introduction is the topic sentence, which should identify your instructions topic and include a main idea about it, such as why these instructions are important. For example, how will your instructions be helpful or useful to the reader? Why would someone want to learn this process or technique? Is there something unique or special about your method?

If the introduction is only one sentence long, that sentence will also be the topic sentence. However, if you use two or three sentences, like Introductions A through E above, the last sentence in the introduction is usually the topic sentence, and the other sentences should lead up to it.

Let's look again at Introduction C:

> *You probably have extra money hidden in your closets and cupboards, although you may not know it. Selling your unwanted items at a garage sale can put that cash in your pocket.*

Which sentence in Introduction C do you think is the topic sentence? Why?

_____

_____

Does the other sentence make the introduction more effective? Why?

_____

_____

Although the first sentence in Introduction C is the most interesting one for most readers, the second sentence focuses on the main idea that the writer plans to develop with instructions—having a garage sale to get cash from unwanted items. That's why the second sentence is the topic sentence.

Here are some possible topic sentences that one writer came up with for the topic of how to analyze dreams. As you read them, try to decide which one is the most effective. Circle the number of the topic sentence that you think is the best.

1. It's a good idea to analyze your dreams.

2. A knowledge of psychology will help you analyze your dreams.

3. Analyzing your dreams can give you a better understanding of yourself.

Did you select number 3 as the best topic sentence? It is the only one that tells us why analyzing dreams is important. Number 1 says, "It's a good idea," but it doesn't say *why* it's a good idea. Number 2 suggests that "a knowledge of psychology" is helpful, but it's not specific about a reason or a method for analyzing dreams.

Let's look at another set of three possible topic sentences on the topic of how to get more exercise by walking. Again, circle the number of the topic sentence that is most effective.

1. We should all walk wherever we go instead of driving a car.

2. Walking regularly will make you feel better, look better, and live longer.

3. Walking is good for you.

Number 1 may sound tempting, but it's not very practical. The writer can't seriously expect us to walk to work, school, and everywhere else, no matter what the distance. Number 3, "Walking is good for you," probably expresses the writer's main idea, but it would be a weak topic sentence because it's too general. The best topic sentence in this group is number 2 because it's very specific about how walking can be beneficial. This sentence would also do a better job of getting readers interested in the topic.

The topic sentence exercise that follows will give you an opportunity to look at and evaluate more topic sentences for instructions.

Evaluating Topic Sentences for Instructions

Directions: Decide which of the following are effective topic sentences for instructions. Write OK in the blank by each good topic sentence, and write NO by the others.

EXAMPLE 1 ➤ ___*NO*___ Always bring pencil and paper to class so you can take notes.

Example 1 is not a very good topic sentence. It does not include any method or reason for taking notes.

EXAMPLE 2 ➤ ___*OK*___ Using this easy method to take notes in your classes will help you improve your grades.

Example 2 is an effective topic sentence. It identifies a specific topic (a method for taking notes) and tells readers how they will benefit from the instructions.

_____ 1. Changing the oil in your car is not difficult and can save you money.

_____ 2. Illiteracy is a problem in our society.

_____ 3. Surprise your guests with a beautiful ice sculpture centerpiece.

_____ 4. The tango is a dramatic, fast-moving ballroom dance that you will enjoy learning.

_____ 5. Don't spend more money than you earn.

_____ 6. This is a method that world leaders can follow to bring about world peace immediately.

_____ 7. How to make a paper airplane.

_____ 8. Asking someone out on a date is not easy if you're shy.

_____ 9. Improve your bowling score by learning how to turn splits into spares every time.

_____ 10. Would you like to learn how to train tigers?

Writing Your Own Introduction and Topic Sentence

Now use what you have learned to write an interesting introduction that includes a topic sentence. If you wish, you can use one sentence that introduces the topic as well as stating your main idea about it. This kind of combined introduction/topic sentence can be effective if it does a good job of capturing readers' attention. However, you will probably want to try writing a slightly longer introduction with two or three sentences like some of the examples under _Learning about Introductions and Topic Sentences for Instructions_ on page 99.

First, think about how readers could benefit from your instructions. Why do people need to know about your topic? Why would someone want to read your instructions? What could you say that might make readers interested? List some of your ideas here:

IDEAS FOR INTRODUCTION AND TOPIC SENTENCE:

_____

_____

_____

_____

Using one or more of the ideas that you listed, write one or two opening sentences for your instructions. Try to make your topic sound as interesting as possible.

INTRODUCTION (FIRST DRAFT):

_____

_____

_____

_____

_____

Now make sure that your introduction includes a topic sentence. Would one of your sentences also be a good topic sentence? Does it state the purpose or importance of your instructions, as well as getting the reader interested? If not, you can either revise one of your introductory sentences so that it includes a main idea, or you can add a topic sentence as the last sentence of your introduction. If you already have a topic sentence, you may want to revise and improve it. Then write your revised introduction here:

INTRODUCTION AND TOPIC SENTENCE:

_____

_____

_____

_____

_____

Now read your introduction and topic sentence to other members of your workshop group. Ask them if the introduction captures their attention and makes them more interested in your topic. If they have suggestions about ways to make your introduction or topic sentence more effective, you may want to make some revisions before you add the introduction to your rough draft.

As you read the following example paragraph about how to make carnation leis by student writer Liza Torres, notice which sentences form the introduction, and identify the topic sentence.

Carnation Leis
by Liza D. Torres

Surprising someone with a home-made lei is far more imaginative than giving an ordinary bouquet of flowers. Making a lei is easy when you follow these instructions. Start by collecting the following items: a 3-inch long needle, fishing line, and 50–60 fresh carnations. Next cut the fishing line, taking into consideration that it will get smaller as you add the carnations. Test the length of the line around your own neck by making sure it at least reaches your navel. Now thread three inches of the line through the needle, so it will not slip out while you are sewing. Next cut the stems off the carnations, leaving the sepal (the fat green part that wrapped around the carnation when it was a bud). Continue by carefully peeling back the sepal so that the carnation fully opens. At this point, the carnations are very fragile, so handle them delicately so that you won't lose any petals. Arrange the carnations into a pattern that you like, laying them down to form a 'V.' It will be easier to work this way so you won't get lost and mess up your pattern while you are sewing the lei together. Simply thread your needle and line through each carnation, starting sewing at the bottom center through to the top center. Continue sewing until all the carnations are sewn and stacked together closely. Lastly, tie the lei together so that the first and last carnations meet. Secure the lei with 4–5 knots and cut off the extra line. Now congratulate yourself and surprise someone special with a lei uniquely created by you. With the gratitude and compliments you receive, you'll feel special too.

Response to *Carnation Leis*

1. Which sentences form the introduction? Which one is the topic sentence?

_____

_____

_____

2. How many steps did Lisa include for making a carnation lei? Number the steps in the paragraph, and list them on the lines below. Write only a few words to identify each step.

_____

_____

_____

_____

_____

_____

_____

_____

_____

_____

Including Precautions

When you are writing instructions, it is important to warn the reader about potential problems or anything that is likely to go wrong. A person following your instructions might make serious mistakes if you don't include precautions. For example, if you are explaining how to dive, you need to caution the reader that the water must be deep enough. Otherwise, someone might hit the bottom of the lake or pool and be seriously hurt. As an expert on your topic, you should be able to anticipate what could go wrong.

Of course, not all topics have potentially life-threatening dangers, but precautions may still be important. For instance, if someone using a word processor forgets to save a file, the work will be lost, so you might caution the reader: "Remember to save the file on your disk." If you are writing about how to make money with a garage sale, you might want to include a precaution about watching the cash box: "Don't leave the cash box unattended or you may lose all of your profits."

Look back at Liza Torres' paragraph about how to make carnation leis, and notice that she includes precautions with some of the steps. For example, she cautions us to be careful about handling the carnations, which are very fragile after their sepals are pulled back. In addition to this precaution, what other parts of the instructions caution the reader or emphasize the right way to do something in order to avoid problems? Underline all of Liza's precautions in the paragraph and then list them here:

_____

_____

_____

_____

The next instructions paragraph, *Protecting Yourself from AIDS,* is based on taking precautions. The author emphasizes being cautious about sexual relationships in order to decrease the risk of getting AIDS. As you read the paragraph, think about whether or not the steps would be effective.

Protecting Yourself from AIDS

AIDS is a sexually transmitted disease that has no cure at this time. Therefore, it is important to learn about it and protect yourself. If you are single, the most effective way to prevent AIDS is abstinence, which means saying no to sex. However, if you are thinking about having a sexual relationship with someone, there are steps you should take to protect yourself. First, get to know your partner well and find out about his or her background. Someone who has had many partners or who may have shared drug needles is a bad risk. Then ask your partner to have an AIDS test, and it's a good idea for you to be tested too. Another extremely important precaution is to use a condom every time that you have sex. A monogamous relationship is also important because having more than one partner increases the risk of getting AIDS. If you have questions about AIDS, don't be afraid to call a local clinic or your doctor for more information.

Response to *Protecting Yourself from AIDS*

1. Based on your own knowledge of the topic, has the writer included the most important points? Are there any other precautions that should be included? Explain your answer.

_____

_____

_____

_____

_____

_____

2. This paragraph actually presents *two* methods for protecting yourself from AIDS. The first method is explained in one sentence. What is it?

_____

The second method has four main steps. What are they?

Step 1: _____

Step 2: _____

Step 3: _____

Step 4: _____

Could the order of any of these steps be changed? Why or why not?

_____

_____

_____

Writing for a Specific Audience

Instructions for some topics, such as how to protect yourself from AIDS, are intended for almost anyone to read. Even the topics of how to paint a room or how to make a carnation lei might be of interest to a fairly wide range of people—anyone who wants to paint walls or who wants to be creative with flowers. No particular expertise is required to understand any of these instructions.

However, some instructions are written for a very specific audience that already has a lot of background knowledge. Auto repair manuals, for instance, are intended for people who already know what's under the hood of their car and understand mechanical terms. If your instructions are for an audience that already has a certain level of expertise, it's all right to use some technical words, and you should explain things at a more advanced level than you would for beginners.

The instructions that follow, *Saving a Diver's Life,* were written by a certified diving instructor, Denver Greiner, based on procedures set up by the Divers Alert Network. They are intended for a very specific audience— someone enrolled in a basic open-water scuba diving course. By the time Denver's diving students study this topic, they already have some technical knowledge and skills.

As you read these instructions, think about how the intended audience influenced the writer's word choices and explanations. Underline everything that seems technical or difficult to understand for readers who aren't knowledgeable about diving. Also notice that the writer includes a lot of introductory information in the first paragraph. Where do the actual instructions begin?

Saving a Diver's Life
by Denver Greiner

Arterial gas embolism, or simply air embolism, is a very dangerous condition where small air bubbles are released into the bloodstream by a rupture in the alveoli of the lungs. These bubbles travel through the bloodstream until they reach a passage that is too small for them to pass through, blocking that passage and depriving the tissues beyond it of oxygen. The symptoms of an embolism include chest pain, difficulty breathing, disorientation, visual impairment, unequal pupils, paralysis of both sides of the body, breathlessness, muscular weakness, bloody froth from the mouth, unconsciousness, and/or convulsions.

To give first aid for an embolism, lay the victim on his left side and elevate his feet to a thirty-five degree angle, which helps by drawing the bubbles away from the heart and brain. Administer 100% oxygen as this allows a higher level of oxygen to be carried into the area by the other passages. Treat the victim for shock by keeping him warm but not hot, and get him transportation to the nearest hyperbaric chamber. In the chamber, the victim will be pressurized to an equivalent depth of 165 feet (73.4 PSI). This compresses the bubbles to a much smaller size so that they can pass through the smaller blood vessels, and the bubbles will be absorbed by the victim's body in a fairly short time. By knowing and following these emergency procedures, you can save a diver's life.

Response to *Saving a Diver's Life*

1. Where do the actual instructions begin?

   _____

   _____

   _____

2. What is the purpose of the first paragraph?

   _____

   _____

   _____

3. Why did the writer divide his paper into two paragraphs?

   _____

   _____

   _____

4. Look back at the technical parts of the instructions that you underlined. Do you think that a scuba diver or diving student would be able to understand these parts of the instructions easily? Explain your answer.

_____

_____

_____

5. Look for a topic sentence that expresses the importance of the topic. It is not in the usual place at or near the beginning. Where is it?

_____

_____

_____

Transitions for Instructions

It is important to make the order of the steps in your instructions very clear. Using appropriate transitional words and phrases will help you keep the steps in order. Step-by-step order is very similar to chronological order, so you will probably want to use some time-order transitions such as *first, then, next,* and *now,* like the ones that you used for narration. (Refer back to *Transitions for Narration* on page 54 to review time-order transitions.) For example, here are some sentences from *Protecting Yourself from AIDS* (p. 106) that use time-order transitions:

> *First,* get to know your partner well and find out about his or her background.

> *Then* ask your partner to have an AIDS test . . . .

You can also create effective transitions by using other types of phrases or sentences that clarify the order of the steps. Words such as *before, after, when,* and *while* can help the reader follow your instructions by connecting the steps smoothly. The following transitional sentences from the first draft of *You Too Can Paint* (p. 97) use *before, after,* and *when* to indicate the order of the steps:

> *Before you start to paint,* open the doors and windows for good ventilation.

> *After you have painted the edges and corners with the brush,* use the roller to do the main part of the ceiling.

> Wash the paint brush and roller *when you are finished.*

In Section 2 of this chapter, you will learn more about writing these kinds of sentences.

As you read the next instructions, *How to Write a Limerick,* underline the transitional words and expressions that help to create step-by-step order.

How to Write a Limerick

A limerick is a short, humorous poem that anyone can write with a little practice and imagination. The most popular kind of limerick tells an entertaining story about a person in five lines. Begin by writing a first line that names a real or imaginary person, like this:

There once was a teacher named Ingalls

The words should have a natural rhythm, almost like music. Now think of something entertaining about the person that you can write about in the second line. The last word of the second line must rhyme with the last word of the first line.

There once was a teacher named Ingalls
Whose students would only write jingles.*

The next step is to continue the story with lines 3 and 4, using a different rhyme. These lines may be a little shorter than lines 1 and 2.

They said regular writing
Just wasn't exciting

The last step is the hardest for most limerick writers because line 5 has to end the story cleverly. It must also rhyme (or almost rhyme) with lines 1 and 2. Here is the entire limerick, including the last line:

There once was a teacher named Ingalls
Whose students would only write jingles.
They said regular writing
Just wasn't exciting,
But rhymes were such fun they felt tingles!

If you follow these steps, you too can have fun writing limericks.

Response to *How to Write a Limerick*

1. What steps did the writer give for writing a limerick?

    Step 1: _____

    Step 2: _____

*Jingles are simple verses that rhyme.

Step 3: _____

Step 4: _____

2. To make the order of the steps easy to follow, the writer began each one with a transitional word or phrase of some kind. List the transitional words that lead into each step.

Transition 1: _____

Transition 2: _____

Transition 3: _____

Transition 4: _____

3. See if you can write a limerick by following these instructions. First complete the limerick below for practice, and then try writing your own. You may want to work with a partner or small group to write the limerick.

There once was a pilot named Bill
Who'd do anything just for a thrill.

_____

_____

_____

YOUR OWN LIMERICK:

_____

_____

_____

_____

Ending Effectively

Instructions that come with products or appear in reference manuals generally end with the last step. However, since you are writing a college paper, it needs to have a conclusion to tie everything together. One of the best ways to write a conclusion is to say something about how the reader will benefit from the instructions or will enjoy the finished product.

Look at these concluding sentences from example papers in this chapter and think about what makes each one effective:

1. *You Too Can Paint:* In a few hours, you can sit back and enjoy your newly painted room.

2. *Carnation Leis:* Now congratulate yourself and surprise someone special with a lei uniquely created by you. With the gratitude and compliments you receive, you'll feel special too.

3. *Protecting Yourself from AIDS:* If you have questions about AIDS, don't be afraid to call a local clinic or your doctor for more information.

4. *How to Write a Limerick:* If you follow these steps, you too can have fun writing limericks.

5. *Saving a Diver's Life:* By knowing and following these emergency procedures, you can save a diver's life.

1. Which conclusions do you think are the most effective? Why?

   _____

   _____

   _____

2. Which conclusions focus on enjoying the finished product?

   _____

   _____

3. Which conclusions emphasize the importance or significance of the topic?

   _____

   _____

Occasionally a conclusion may provide related information that was not stated in the body of the paper as a part of the process. For example, the writer of *Protecting Yourself from AIDS* suggested that readers could consult a local clinic or a doctor for more information (Conclusion 3).

As you read the following instructions by Richard D. Munholand about how to get the most enjoyment out of a baseball game, pay special attention to the way Richard gets readers interested with his introduction and then uses the same ideas in his conclusion. People might think they already know how to enjoy a baseball game, so it is especially important for him to convince readers that his advice will be useful. Since the instructions are fairly long and detailed, Richard decided to use several paragraphs instead of just one. In order to divide the instructions into paragraphs, he grouped things together that would be done more or less at the same time: one paragraph for preparations, one for pre-game batting practice, one for what to do after you take your seat, and one for after the game. The introduction and conclusion are also separate paragraphs.

A Day at the Murph
by Richard D. Munholand

Are you working too much? Do you need to just get away? Well, a day at the ballpark may just be the answer. Therc are over fifty home games a year at Jack Murphy Stadium, and one day at the stadium may be all you need to help yourself relax.

The first thing you'll need to do is buy a field level ticket on the first base side. This allows you to sit close to the field on the same side as the home team and at the same time be close enough to have a great view of the game. Next pack a backpack with what I consider the essentials for watching a baseball game: a Walkman radio, a pair of binoculars, paper, a pen, a pencil, a baseball glove, a baseball, some bottled water, some sort of snack, and at least $25.00.

You should arrive at the ballpark a couple of hours early to avoid traffic and, the most important, to watch batting practice. Before doing anything else, purchase a program for a couple of bucks. The program is very useful for the first timer and also makes a good autograph book. Shortly after that, you'll want to head over to the outfield wall and position yourself in a good spot to catch batting practice home run balls. Everyone going to a baseball game dreams of catching a major league baseball, and this is a good opportunity to do so.

After batting practice is finished, it is time to find your assigned seat. This is the time the players start fielding warm-ups and a great chance to get autographs signed on your new baseball. Sitting on field level gives you an advantage over others who are not seated on field level. When fielding practice is over, situate yourself in your seat and get ready for the game to start. In the meantime, pull out your binoculars, program, and pencil, and start filling out the game lineup. I find it exciting to keep score during the game, and it allows you to keep up on all the events. In addition, get the vendors' attention and get yourself a Coke, a hot dog, and some peanuts. There is nothing like watching a live ball game and having a hot dog. Now that you have done all that, get your Walkman out and find the station the ball game is on. This is always beneficial because it allows you to get play-by-play results so you know what is going on. Now that you're set, sit back and enjoy the game.

After the game, I always find it enjoyable to sit and let everyone else leave first. After almost everyone has cleared out, start walking over to the players' parking lot. There you can try to get a few more autographs from your favorite players. But remember not to be pushy in your quest as the players are tired and sometimes don't want to be bothered after a game.

All in all, you should feel so overwhelmed by the day's events that any problems or stress you had before the game should be quite forgotten. So the next time you need to just get away, plan a day at the ballpark and let the kid in you come out and play.

Response to *A Day at the Murph*

1. According to the introduction and conclusion, how would readers benefit from attending a baseball game?

_____

_____

2. What special tips does the writer give to help readers get the most enjoyment out of a ball game?

_____

_____

_____

Now try writing a conclusion for your own instructions. To help you come up with some ideas, answer the following questions about your instructions.

1. How will the reader enjoy the finished product or the completed process?

_____

_____

2. How will your instructions be useful or important to the reader?

_____

_____

3. What ideas did you use in the introduction to get readers interested?

_____

_____

4. Is there anything else related to your topic that you would like to tell readers, such as where to get additional information?

_____

_____

After you have listed a few ideas, look them over and circle the ones that you like best. Then, using one or more of the ideas that you have circled, write an effective conclusion for your instructions. If you use some of the same ideas that were in your introduction, be sure that the wording is different in the conclusion.

CONCLUSION:

_____

_____

_____

Now read your conclusion to members of your workshop group. They may have some more ideas about how readers can benefit from your instructions. After listening to their comments and suggestions, revise your conclusion if you want to, and then add it to your rough draft.

Now your instructions paragraph or short paper is almost finished except for proofreading and editing, which are the final steps in the writing process. In Section 2 of this chapter, you will learn additional sentence and grammar skills that will help you proofread and edit your writing.

SECTION TWO:
Sentence and Grammar Skills

Goals

In this section of the chapter, you will learn how to do the following:

- Recognize basic complex sentences
- Write basic complex sentences using Group B connectors
- Recognize and correct sentence fragments
- Correctly use adjectives and adverbs to add interest to your writing

Learning about Basic Complex Sentences

Complex sentences are valuable in all kinds of writing and have many functions. They may show time relationships such as *before, after,* or *while,* which are especially useful in giving instructions, or how some things cause others (*so that, because*). They can also be used for conditional situations (*if, unless*), conceding a point (*although, even though*), and other important relationships between ideas.

In Chapter 1 you looked at *simple* sentences, and in Chapter 2 you learned about basic *compound* sentences, which have two clauses, or *SVs*, joined by a *Group A* connector and a comma. Here is an example:

S	*V*	*, Group A*	*S V.*

EXAMPLE ➤ Jeannelle agreed to sing in the choir,   but   she was nervous about it.

In this chapter you will learn how to use another group of connectors to join two *SVs* together. This will give you a greater variety of different sentence structures to choose from to help make your writing more interesting.

Look at these sentences:

EXAMPLE 1 ➤ Helen felt proud because she had done well on her chemistry lab project.

EXAMPLE 2 ➤ Nathan finished his homework even though his roommate had the TV on.

In Example 1, what word is used to join the two SVs together? _____

Clause 1: Helen felt proud

Clause 2: she had done well on the chemistry lab project.

Helen felt proud *because* she had done well on the chemistry lab project.

These clauses are joined by the word *because*. Notice that no comma is used before the word *because* in the middle of the sentence.

Now look at Example 2: How are the two clauses joined together?

Clause 1: Nathan finished his homework

Clause 2: his roommate had the TV on.

S   V   even though
Nathan finished his homework *even though* his
S   V.
roommate had the TV on.

This sentence has two clauses that are joined by the words *even though*. *Because* and *even though* are two examples of a group of connectors that can be used to connect the two clauses that make a *basic complex sentence*. One official name for these connectors is *subordinators*. In this book we will refer to this group of words as *Group B connectors*. What are the connecting words in the following sentences?

     S   *V*   *S*

Ali started playing the piano when the orchestra conductor

     V

signaled.

     S   *V*   *S* *V*

Martha worked out in the gym as soon as she got off work.

You can see that the word *when* and the words *as soon as* are also in this second group of connectors.

Here is a list of some of the most useful *Group B* connectors (subordinators):

after	although	as	as if	as soon as
because	before	even though	how	if
since	so (that)*	than	that†	though
unless	until	what	whatever	when
whenever	where	whereas	wherever	whether
while	why			

A few Group B connectors include two or three words used together, like *even though*, *such as*, *as if*, *as soon as*, and *so that*. Using Group B connectors correctly will help you to link ideas smoothly and clearly. Keep this list where you can refer to it when you are proofreading and preparing the final drafts of your papers.

Most Group B connectors can be used in the following *two* different patterns.

Pattern 1

      S   **V**   **Group B connector**   **S**   **V.**

All four of the example sentences above follow this pattern. Here are some more examples:

EXAMPLE 1A ➤ Georgia took inventory of the stock while Ruben handled a customer complaint.

EXAMPLE 2A ➤ Everyone stood up as the bride came down the aisle.

*The Group B connector *so* (or *so that*) means *in order to* or *for the purpose of*. Be sure not to confuse this word *so* with the Group A connector *so*, which means *as a result* or *therefore*.

†*That* can be used both as a subordinator in a noun clause and as a relative pronoun (see Chapter 4).

EXAMPLE 3A ➤ You should do warm-up exercises so that you don't injure your muscles running.

EXAMPLE 4A ➤ Transactional analysis is a useful method of examining interpersonal relationships although it is not the only valid model.

These sentences can also be written in a different order, with the Group B connector at the beginning of the sentence:

EXAMPLE 1B ➤ While Ruben handled a customer complaint, Georgia took inventory of the stock.

EXAMPLE 2B ➤ As the bride came down the aisle, everyone stood up.

EXAMPLE 3B ➤ So that you don't injure your muscles running, you should do warm-up exercises.

EXAMPLE 4B ➤ Although transactional analysis is not the only valid model, it is a useful method of examining interpersonal relationships.*

These sentences with the Group B connector at the beginning are examples of the second pattern:

Pattern 2

     Group B connector   **S**   **V**   **,**   **S**   **V.**

Both patterns of complex sentences consist of two clauses, the *main clause* and the *subordinate clause*. The subordinate clause begins with a Group B connector, which connects it to the main clause. The main clause, also called an *independent clause*, could be a complete sentence by itself. Here are some more examples of sentences that can use Group B connectors both ways:

          S   *V*   *Group B*   *S*   *V*

EXAMPLE 5 ➤ Tidepools are a good place to learn about sea life   if   you visit them at low tide.

Or:

  Group B   *S*   *V*   *,*   *S*   *V*

         If you visit them at low tide, tidepools are a good place to learn about sea life.

---

*In this example, *transactional analysis* needs to be mentioned in the first clause so that the reader will know what the word *it* refers to.

EXAMPLE 6 ➤

            (S)V   *Group B* *S*   *V*

Be sure to bow deeply to the hosts when you visit a Japanese house.*

Or:

    Group B *S*   *V*   *, (S)V*

When you visit a Japanese house,   be sure to bow deeply to the hosts.

In some situations Group B connectors only work with the first pattern.

Here is an example with *than.*

EXAMPLE 7 ➤

                  S   *V*   *Group B* *S* *V*

Hua was a better student   than   she was willing to admit.

Sometimes one pattern feels more natural than the other. Use the one that you like best in each situation. If you are in doubt about which pattern to use in a certain sentence, check with some of your classmates to get their opinion.

A few of the Group B connectors, including *that* and *wh- words* such as *what, where,* and *why,* can be used both in Pattern 1 and in a third pattern.

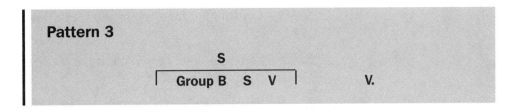

Pattern 3

                          S

                ⌐ **Group B** **S** **V** ⌐   **V.**

This third pattern is more complicated than the others because one entire clause, called a *noun clause*, is the subject of the main clause. Here is one example that will help you recognize this kind of pattern in case you use it in your own writing.

EXAMPLE 8 ➤

                         S

        ⌐*Group B* *S*   *V*   ⌐ *V*

What we decided at the meeting solved the problem.

In this sentence, the subject of the main clause is the entire noun clause, "What we decided at the meeting," and the verb of the main clause is *solved.* In this book we will focus mainly on patterns 1 and 2 because they are used more often than pattern 3, both in writing and in speaking.

---

*The subject of the first clause is understood to be *You.* With imperative verbs (commands), like *be* in this clause, the subject *you* doesn't need to be stated.

Group B words are very important and useful in your writing. In later chapters you will learn how to use these and other connectors to write sentences with three or more SVs.

■ **CLASS PRACTICE** **1**

Recognizing Complex Sentences

Directions: Mark each subject and verb with *S* and *V* and circle the connector in each sentence if there is one. Then write *simple, Group A,* or *Group B* in the blank. Remember: Most *Group B* connectors may be used either at the beginning or in the middle of the sentence.

_____ 1. Dan wanted to correspond with people in other countries, so he subscribed to an online computer service.

_____ 2. Debbie went back to school because she wanted a better job.

_____ 3. Before you drive away from the pump, put the gas cap back.

_____ 4. Rachel wrote a thesis. Most students in her program took the comprehensive test instead.

_____ 5. Chuck remodeled the interior of our house last summer.

_____ 6. The desert smelled like rain, and the wind played sweet melodies through the narrow ravine.

_____ 7. Cynthia let Joe use her mountain bike since she wasn't using it.

_____ 8. Separate your recyclable items from the trash when you take it out to the curb.

_____ 9. You can achieve whatever you set your mind to.

_____ 10. While Matt was in college, he enlisted in the Navy reserves.

■ **CLASS PRACTICE** **2**

Building Basic Complex Sentences

Directions: Combine the two simple sentences with a *Group B* connector from the list on page 117 to make one complex sentence. Choose a suitable *Group B* connector for each sentence. Practice both patterns.

1. Tom will be a counseling intern this summer. He needs the experience.

   Because he needs the experience, Tom will be a counseling intern

   this summer.

Or:

Tom will be a counseling intern this summer because he needs the experience.

2. Dedicate quality time to your children. Children need caring interaction with adults.

3. You can deal with your emotions better. You analyze the underlying reasons for them.

4. People try to do too much all at once. They can end up under a lot of stress.

5. Tell your kids that you love them. They grow up and move out.

6. Choose a therapist or counselor wisely. You have time and money to waste. (try: *unless*)

7. Self-discovery can be a painful process. It is certainly worth the effort.

8. It's important to have quiet, reflective moments. You can get to know yourself.

_____

_____

9. You can break the spiral of negative self-talk. You stop thinking negative thoughts about yourself.

_____

_____

10. Mid-life crisis often occurs in the late thirties. People become aware of their own mortality.

_____

_____

■ **CLASS PRACTICE** **3**

Writing Basic Complex Sentences

Directions: Now write your own basic complex sentences. Use a different *Group B* connector (subordinator) in each sentence, and write each sentence twice, once for each pattern (if possible):

> ***Pattern 1:*** S V   *Group B connector*   S V.

and

> ***Pattern 2:*** *Group B connector*   S V ,   S V.

1. _____

_____

2. _____

_____

3. _____

_____

4. _____

_____

5. _____

_____

When you are finished, ask another student to help you check your sentences. Be sure that each sentence has two SVs linked by a Group B connector.

Learning to Avoid Fragments with Group B Connectors

When a sentence includes a Group B connector, it needs to have two SVs. One common error is using a Group B connector with only one SV:

S   *V*   . *Group B* *S*   *V*   .

INCORRECT EXAMPLE 1 ➤ You should start writing your report tonight. If you have time.

When a Group B connector is used in a group of words with only one SV, it is an error. This kind of sentence error is a *fragment* because it is only part of a complete sentence. It is important to be able to recognize and correct fragments if they occur in your own writing.

Because one correct pattern is **SV   Group B connector   SV,** you can connect the fragment to a neighboring SV, like this:

S   *V*   *Group B* *S*   *V*   .

You should start writing your report tonight   if   you have time.

Now it is a correct sentence. Another way to correct this fragment is to put the Group B connector first. You can correct the fragment above using the Group B connector first, like this:

Group B   *S*   *V*   ,   *S*   *V*   .

If   you have time, you should start writing your report tonight.

Now let's practice with another example. Which one of the word groups in the following incorrect example is a fragment?

INCORRECT EXAMPLE 2 ➤ Please represent us at the awards ceremony. Because we can't attend this year.

The second group is a fragment because it has a Group B connector, *because*, with only one SV. It's easy to correct this error. Just combine the two clauses into one good complex sentence:

> *Correct:* Please represent us at the awards ceremony because we can't attend this year.

You may also want to try using pattern 2:

> *Because we can't attend this year, please represent us at the awards ceremony.*

It's important to use the correct form that seems best to you. The following exercise will give you more practice correcting this type of fragment.

Correcting Fragments

Directions: If there is no fragment, write CORRECT. If one of the word groups is a fragment, underline it, and then correct it by joining it to the appropriate sentence.

EXAMPLE ➤ Don't be afraid of conflict. Because conflict can help to resolve problems. Many people try to avoid conflict.
(*Because conflict can help to resolve problems* is a fragment because it begins with a Group B connector and contains only one SV. It should be corrected by joining it to the sentence where it makes the most sense—the first sentence.)

Answer: Don't be afraid of conflict because conflict can help to resolve problems.

1. If you want to get good grades. You need to begin studying early. You shouldn't wait until the night before the test.

_____

_____

2. You should read each chapter. When it is assigned. Don't wait until you are three or four chapters behind.

_____

_____

3. It's a good idea to underline or highlight the most important ideas. As you read.

_____

_____

4. Take careful notes in class. If you are absent. You can ask for a copy of someone else's notes.

_____

_____

5. After each class, it's important to review your notes. It is a good idea to underline or highlight the most important parts of your notes too.

_____

_____

6. Whenever you don't understand something. Ask questions. Your teacher will probably be glad to help you.

_____

_____

7. You may want to form a study group with other students from your class. Try to study together at least once a week.

_____

_____

8. With your study group, you should review the lessons each week. Because then you won't have to cram during finals.

_____

_____

■ CLASS
PRACTICE 5

Proofreading for Fragments

Directions: Underline each fragment that you find in the following paragraph. Then correct the fragments by joining each one to a neighboring sentence where it makes sense.

Don't Forget to Vote

Voting is both a responsibility and a privilege. Although marking a ballot is easy. Voting intelligently requires some thought and effort. When you are eighteen. You should register to vote. Then you will receive information in the mail about every election. Study the voting information carefully. Because it is important to understand the issues. Decide how you will vote. Before you go to the polling place. If you mark your sample ballot. You can take it with you. Each person's vote is confidential. This means that no one can watch you or talk to you. While you are voting. Afterward, you don't have to tell anyone else how you voted. Although you may think that your one vote is not very important. Sometimes just a few votes can make a big difference.

■ CLASS
PRACTICE 6

Writing with Complex Sentences

PART A: Looking at Writing from an Example Paragraph

Directions: Look at the following sentences from the first draft of *You Too Can Paint* on page 97 and highlight or underline the complex sentences. Notice that the author used several sentences of this type as well as other types of sentences. Hint: Look for *Group B* connectors.

You Too Can Paint

Be sure that you have the right kind of paint. You will also need a paint brush, a roller, and old clothes to wear. Cover the furniture and carpet. Also protect the baseboard and door frames. Before you start to paint, open doors and windows for good ventilation. Stir the paint thoroughly, and then begin with the ceiling. After you have painted the edges and corners with the brush, use the roller to do the main part of the ceiling. The paint should be applied evenly with long, smooth, back and forth strokes. Do the walls the same way. Wash the paint brush and roller when you are finished. In a few hours, you will be able to sit back and enjoy your newly painted room.

PART B: Looking at Your Own Writing

Directions: Find three complex sentences from your own *Instructions* rough draft and write them in the blanks below. If you don't have any complex sentences, you will probably want to replace some of your sentences with complex sentences for greater variety. Write your new complex sentences in the blanks below.

1. _____

   _____

   _____

2. _____

   _____

   _____

3. _____

   _____

   _____

Now check your sentences by marking the subject and verb in each sentence and circling the Group B connector.

Instructions Sentence Combining Paragraph

Using Group B connectors to link ideas can help you add variety to your sentences. Several of the sentence groups in *Listen to This* can be joined effectively with Group B connectors (subordinators) such as *before, because, when, although, if, after,* and *while*. Use both patterns if you can. Other sentence groups may be joined in any way that creates clear, effective sentences.

Listen to This

1.1 Learning to listen effectively is important. *(because)*
1.2 It can improve communication.
1.3 The communication is between you and other people.

2.1 We may think that we hear the words. *(although)*
2.2 We may think that we understand.
2.3 Sometimes we don't hear accurately.

3.1   For example, someone is talking angrily. *(if* or *when)*
3.2   It may be especially difficult to listen to the meaning.
3.3   The meaning is of the words.

4.1   The other person is speaking. *(while)*
4.2   Try to remain calm.
4.3   Try to remain objective.

5.1   The person has finished speaking. *(after)*
5.2   Repeat what you heard.
5.3   Repeat exactly.

6.1   You may be surprised.
6.2   The surprise will be that you didn't hear.
6.3   You didn't hear clearly.
6.4   You didn't hear correctly.

7.1   If this happens, try repeating.
7.2   Try again.
7.3   Try until you get it right.

8.1   You are sure that you have understood the words. *(after* or *when)*
8.2   Listen for feelings.
8.3   The feelings may be unspoken.

9.1   A person may feel frightened. *(although* or *even though)*
9.2   A person may feel insecure.
9.3   A person may feel lonely.
9.4   He may not want to say how he feels.

10.1   You should ask about the person's feelings.
10.2   Listen to the answers.
10.3   Listen compassionately.

11.1   People's feelings are accepted and understood. *(if* or *when)*
11.2   They feel better about themselves.
11.3   They feel better about others.

12.1   You can improve your relationships.
12.2   You can do it just by listening better.

Learning About Adjectives and Adverbs

In order to make your papers more interesting to the reader, it is important to have interesting details. One way to do this is by using *adjectives* and *adverbs* to describe or modify nouns and verbs.

Adjectives

An *adjective* is a word that describes or modifies a *noun.* In Chapter One you learned that a noun names a person, place, thing, or idea, and can be either singular or plural. In the following sentence, which words describe the noun *convertible?*

EXAMPLE 1 ➤ John bought a classic red convertible.

Red and *classic* are words used to describe the noun *convertible,* so they are adjectives.

Here are two more example sentences using adjectives. Look for two adjectives in each sentence and underline them:

EXAMPLE 2 ➤ High voltage is dangerous.

EXAMPLE 3 ➤ This new software looks fantastic!

High and *dangerous* are the adjectives in Example 2. *New* and *fantastic* are the adjectives in Example 3. In English, adjectives are often used in the following two ways:

1. Before a noun, like *high* in Example 2 and *new* in Example 3 above.
2. After a linking verb, like *dangerous* after the verb *is* in Example 2 and *fantastic* after the verb *looks* in Example 3. (Remember from Chapter 1 that linking verbs show a condition or state instead of an action. They include *be, look, sound, smell, feel, taste, appear, seem, become,* and a few others.)

Adverbs

An *adverb* is a word that usually describes or modifies a *verb.* Some adverbs also modify adjectives or other adverbs, but we will concentrate on modifying verbs in this chapter. Remember that a verb is a word that shows an action or condition. In the following sentence, which word is the verb?

EXAMPLE 1 ➤ John carefully washed his new car.

The verb is *washed.*

Which word describes how John washed his car? _____

The word *carefully* describes the manner in which John washed the car. In other words, the word *carefully* modifies the verb *washed.* Therefore, the word *carefully* is an example of an *adverb.*

Here are two more example sentences using adverbs. Underline the adverb in each sentence:

EXAMPLE 2 ➤   Tony easily lifted the 200-pound patient.

EXAMPLE 3 ➤   Carol balanced her checkbook accurately.

You can see that adverbs sometimes come before the verb and sometimes come at the end of the clause or sentence. Sometimes they work at the beginning of the sentence too:

EXAMPLE 4 ➤   Swiftly and silently, the pirate ship glided into the unprotected harbor.

What are the adverbs in this sentence?   _____ and _____

What is the verb that they modify?   _____

Most adverbs are formed by adding the ending *-ly* to an adjective, as in the examples above (*swift—swiftly, silent—silently*), but there are some exceptions. Some common adverbs that don't end in *-ly* are *well, fast, hard, very,* and *quite.*

Well is the adverb that corresponds with the adjective *good.* For example:

> **Adjective:** She is a *good* dancer. (The adjective *good* describes the noun, dancer.)

> **Adverb:** She dances *well*. (The adverb *well* modifies the verb by telling how she dances.)

Fast and *hard* don't change forms. They are both adverbs and adjectives. For example:

> **Adjective:** Writing a textbook is a *hard* job.

> **Adverb:** We worked *hard* to write this textbook.

Very and *quite* are adverbs that are used to modify adjectives and other adverbs. For example:

> It's *very* important to clean the wound before you bandage it.

There are also a couple of spelling rules for adverbs that end in *-ly*. First, for adjectives like *realistic* and *stylistic* that end in *-ic*, don't add *-ly* to form the adverb. Instead, add *-ally: realistically, stylistically.* Finally, for adjectives that end with a consonant plus *-y*, like *sturdy*, change the *-y* to *-i* before adding *-ly: sturdily.*

The following exercise will give you more practice with adjectives and adverbs.

■ CLASS
PRACTICE   **7**

Creating Adverbs from Adjectives

Directions: Change each adjective in italics to an adverb, and write the adverb in the second sentence. Follow the spelling rules, and use the correct form for irregular adverbs.

1. *Adjective:* Be *careful* when you chop the wood.

   Adverb: Chop the wood _____ .

2. *Adjective:* The blending of the base paint and pigment must be *thorough*.

   Adverb: Blend the base paint and pigment _____ .

3. *Adjective:* *Regular* exercise is important.

   Adverb: It is important to exercise _____ .

4. *Adjective:* Setting *realistic* goals is the first step.

   Adverb: We need to set goals _____ .

5. *Adjective:* We revved the engine to make the car sound *fast*.

   Adverb: The tuneup helped the car run _____ .

6. *Adjective:* Ridesharing may be the *perfect* solution to the parking problem.

   Adverb: Ridesharing may solve the parking problem _____ .

7. *Adjective:* The architect's cabin design is *appropriate* for the wilderness setting.

   Adverb: The architect designed the cabin _____ for the wilderness setting.

8. *Adjective:* A test will seem *hard* for someone who hasn't studied.

   Adverb: If you study _____ , you will be more prepared for the test.

9. *Adjective:* Try to do a *good* job on your assignments.

   Adverb: Try to do _____ on the test.

10. *Adjective:* The *playful* baby hippo came up to the edge of the enclosure.

    Adverb: The baby hippo romped _____ .

■ **CLASS PRACTICE** **8**   **Using Adjectives and Adverbs to Add Interest**

Directions: Add an appropriate adjective or adverb in each space below.

EXAMPLE ➤   Jesse watched the _____ basketball player make a rim shot.

Here are some possibilities: *tall, young, athletic, famous,* or *talented*. What other possibilities can you think of?

_____

1. You should be _____ when you speak in front of a group.

2. In a debate, _____ analyze your opponent's argument.

3. Don't hesitate to contradict any _____ information or propaganda.

4. It's _____ to be assertive in that type of situation.

5. You should make your points _____ .

Now write two original sentences that use adjectives to add interest:

6. _____

7. _____

Write two original sentences that use adverbs:

8. _____

9. _____

Now find one sentence that uses an adjective or an adverb from your own instructions rough draft and copy it below. If you prefer, *add* an adjective or adverb to one of your sentences, and copy your revised sentence below.

10. _____

■ **CLASS**
PRACTICE **9**

Proofreading for Adjective and Adverb Errors

Directions: Some of the adjectives and adverbs in the following passage are correct and some are incorrect. Draw a line through the incorrect forms and write in the corrections.

Starting an Exercise Program

Most of us have sedentary lifestyles, and finding time to exercise is not easily. If you are not accustomed to exercising, it may be difficult to develop a newly habit, but you will feel better and probably live longer if you do. Experts say that you should begin with a moderate amount of non-impact exercise at least 4 days per week. It's more importantly to exercise frequent and regular than to exercise for a long time. Walking, swimming and bicycling are real good exercises for heart and lungs because they exercise major muscle groups without dangerous, high-impact movements that could possible lead to a serious injury. By gradual starting one of these exercises today or tomorrow, you will soon enjoy excellent results. Within a few weeks, you will be able to exercise for an hour easy. If you continue your exercise routine, you can get in great shape, have well health, and enjoy life more.

Instructions Sentence Combining Paragraph

Directions: Be sure to use adjectives and adverbs correctly in your sentence combinations. A few of the sentence groups can be joined effectively with Group B connectors (subordinators) such as *if, because,* or *when.*

Money Matters
1.1 You sometimes spend more money than you earn.
1.2 It's time to start managing your money.
1.3 Manage it effectively.
1.4 Manage it with a budget.

2.1 First make a list of your expenses.
2.2 The expenses should be monthly.
2.3 The list should be complete.

3.1   Begin with your rent or house payment.
3.2   Begin with utilities.
3.3   Begin with groceries.
3.4   These expenses are essential.

4.1   Don't forget transportation expenses.
4.2   Don't forget school expenses.
4.3   Don't forget entertainment expenses.

5.1   Estimate the amounts that you spend.
5.2   The amounts are approximate.
5.3   Do this as accurately as you can.

6.1   Then add all of your expenses.
6.2   Add them together.
6.3   Figure out your total income.
6.4   The income is monthly.

7.1   The expenses are higher than the income.
7.2   Try to cut out some expenses.
7.3   Some expenses are unnecessary.

8.1   Make your total expenses less.
8.2   They must be less than your income.

9.1   Next is the part.
9.2   This part is the most difficult.
9.3   This part is following your budget.

10.1   You must take control of your spending.
10.2   Spending is in all categories of your budget.

11.1   Keep track of all the money.
11.2   Do it carefully.
11.3   This includes money that you spend.
11.4   This includes money that you earn.

12.1   You spend over the limit in one category.
12.2   You will have to spend less in another category.

13.1   Follow your budget.
13.2   Do this faithfully.
13.3   You will enjoy having money left.
13.4   This is at the end of the month.

Putting the Finishing Touches on Your Writing

Before you turn in your completed instructions paper, you should read your rough draft at least once more to make sure that you have applied everything you have learned in this chapter. Read through it slowly, with a pen or pencil in hand to mark anything that you want to change. Think about both content and mechanics. Does any part need more details and explanations? If so, add a few words or even a few sentences. Is there anything that might be confusing for a reader who is trying to follow your instructions? If there is, change the wording to make it clear. Also pay special attention to the proofreading skills that you have studied in this chapter, and apply them to your paper. Be especially careful to check for fragments and correct any that you find.

To help you proofread for content, organization, sentence structure, and grammar, use the instructions writing checklist below. You should be able to answer *yes* to all of the questions. If you are not sure about your answers to some of the questions, ask your workshop group or your teacher to look at your rough draft again and help you decide whether you need to make any revisions.

Instructions Writing Checklist

Content and Organization

_____ 1. Are the instructions clear and easy to understand?

_____ 2. Does my paper have an interesting introduction and topic sentence?

_____ 3. Have I used step-by-step order?

_____ 4. Have I included details and explanations about each step?

_____ 5. Are precautions included where they are necessary?

_____ 6. Is the level appropriate for the intended audience?

_____ 7. Are transitions used smoothly and effectively?

_____ 8. Is there an effective concluding sentence after the last step?

Sentence Structure and Grammar

_____ 1. Did I use Group A and Group B connectors correctly?

_____ 2. Have I avoided using fragments?

_____ 3. Have I avoided run-ons and comma splices?

_____ 4. Have I used verbs correctly, especially imperative verbs?

_____ 5. Have I used adjectives and adverbs effectively?

_____ 6. Have I checked the spelling of any unfamiliar words?

ENRICHMENT SECTION:
Making a Class Booklet

Goals

In the enrichment section of this chapter, you will learn how to do the following:

- Plan and organize a booklet of instructions written by class members
- Work cooperatively with others to edit and revise instructions

If several class members write about related topics, you may want to create a useful and interesting booklet of instructions. There are many possibilities for topics, depending on your interests. If several people are interested in dancing, for example, you could make a booklet with instructions for different kinds of dances. People who have experience working on cars could make a useful auto repair booklet. A recipe booklet may be a good idea if a lot of people have favorite original recipes or family recipes to share. Here are some other possible ideas for instruction booklets:

> Health and Fitness Topics
> First Aid Techniques
> Related Job Skills (drafting skills, clerical skills, nursing skills, etc.)
> Home Repairs and/or Remodeling Projects
> Sports Skills and Strategies
> Skills for Academic Success
> Arts and Crafts Projects

List some of your own ideas for an instructions booklet here:

_____   _____

_____   _____

_____   _____

Now discuss your booklet ideas with other classmates. Perhaps the entire class will want to work together on one booklet, or you may want to form two, three, or four separate groups. Your group should consist of at least six or eight people so that there will be enough instructions papers to make an interesting booklet. It is important to discover an interest that group members share so that everyone can participate.

As soon as you have formed a group and agreed on the kind of booklet you are going to make, select an editor-in-chief and an assistant editor who will take charge of organizing and supervising the project. Other members of your group should also have specific job assignments. In the blanks that follow, put the names of the people in your group who will be responsible for each of the jobs listed. If you have a large group, you may want to assign two people for some of the jobs. There are extra blanks so that you can add additional jobs to the list if you want to.

EDITOR-IN-CHIEF   _____

ASSISTANT EDITOR   _____

PROOFREADING EDITORS   _____

                                _____

FORMAT EDITORS   _____

                                _____

ILLUSTRATOR (OPTIONAL)   _____

OTHER JOBS (LIST):   _____

                                _____

                                _____

In addition to the jobs listed above, each person in the group should be responsible for writing one instructions paragraph or short paper to be included in the booklet. Spend some time with your group discussing possible topics. Then make a list of all of your group members and the topics that they are writing about. This list may be the responsibility of the editor-in-chief, or another group member may be assigned to keep track of it. It's all right to use the paragraph or short paper that you wrote earlier in this chapter if the topic is appropriate, or you may decide to write a new one.

After you have written a rough draft, have at least three group members read your instructions. Ask for their comments and suggestions. Even if you are using the instructions that you wrote earlier in the chapter, you may still want to revise and edit some things. Each person in the group should help others with proofreading and editing their writing. Then have your group's proofreading editors check everything to make sure that there are no errors in grammar or sentence structure. You may want to have your instructor look over your writing also.

Before making copies of your booklet, be sure that the pages are arranged neatly and attractively. Use your imagination to create an interesting design for the pages of your booklet. The format editors should be in charge of this part of the project, but other people can help. The following pages illustrate how a recipe booklet can be set up. When you have all pages ready, your instructor can probably help you arrange to have photocopies made. If your booklet looks attractive and contains useful information, you will feel good about sharing it with others. In fact, you may even want to make extra copies for friends and relatives!

CHICKEN KILAWI

Recipe by Karmina Charfauros

✳ ✳ ✳

2 pounds chicken legs
1 dozen limes
1/4 pound spinach
2–3 green peppers
salt and soy sauce for seasoning

The best way to keep your loved ones happy is to delight them with a special meal. If you don't want to spend too much time or money, then follow this delicious but easy recipe for Chicken Kilawi. First wash the chicken legs thoroughly and then remove the skin. Put the chicken in a big pan with some water so it can be boiled. While the chicken is cooking, wash the green peppers and the spinach so you can start cutting them in small pieces. Next, cut the limes in half and squeeze the juice from them, pouring the juice into a small container with some salt. After the chicken is cooked, cut it in small pieces too, and put it in a large bowl. Add the spinach, the lime juice, and the green peppers to the chicken and mix them very well. Finally add some salt and soy sauce, spreading it over the chicken. Now you can decorate the dish with some limes on top, and you will be ready to serve and enjoy Chicken Kilawi.

STUFFED CHILES

Recipe by Pilar Guerrero

✳ ✳ ✳

8 chiles
2 tomatoes
1 can tomato sauce
1 small onion
1 cup oil
1 cup flour
2 eggs
Monterey jack cheese
1 glove garlic

First put the chiles in a flat pan on high heat, and when the skin is almost toasted, peel the skin off the chiles. Then make a slice in each chile and remove all the seeds that are inside. Stuff the chiles with slices of cheese and set aside while you beat the whites of the eggs. Dip the chiles into the flour first and then into the egg whites. Cook in a frying pan with hot oil until they are golden brown. Then quickly remove them. (It takes about five minutes.)

Now prepare the sauce. Put one whole clove of garlic into the frying oil until it is golden brown, almost toasted, and then remove it. Add finely chopped tomato and onion, and then add one can of tomato sauce and a little water. Cook the sauce until it is thoroughly heated, and then pour it over the chiles.

Now try them and you will know why stuffed chiles are so delicious!

PANCIT

Recipe by Maria Teresa B. Barron

✳ ✳ ✳

INGREDIENTS AND EQUIPMENT
1 package rice noodles (pilipino noodles)
1 lb. pork (meat for stew) or 1 lb. chicken meat
1 lb. medium size shrimp
1/2 cabbage
1 medium onion
2 cloves garlic
1/4 lb. peapods
1 stalk celery (optional)
1 small carrot
2 T. cooking oil
soy sauce (to taste)
salt and pepper (to taste)
MSG food seasoning (to taste)
wok
medium size casserole

This delicious recipe is easy to make, and for sure everybody will love it once they taste it. First, wash the pork or chicken with warm water, put the meat in a medium size casserole, and add just enough water for boiling. Boil the meat on medium high heat until tender. While the meat is boiling, peel off the shells of the shrimp, rinse with warm water, and set aside. Rinse all the vegetables. Slice the cabbage, peapods, celery, and carrots lengthwise, and set them aside. Slice the onion, chop the garlic, and set them aside also. When the meat is tender, slice it lengthwise, and save the broth for later use. Heat the wok on medium high. (Do not overheat. Otherwise, you will burn the oil and other ingredients and affect the taste.) Add the cooking oil, and sauté the garlic, onion, and vegetables. Add the meat and shrimp, and cook the mixture for about five minutes. Then add a cup of broth that you saved. Season the mixture with soy sauce, salt, pepper, and food seasoning, and let it boil for five minutes. Turn the heat down to medium to prevent it from burning. Next cut the noodles in half, wet them to prevent their sticking together, and add them to the mixture. Stir the noodles and the mixture together until well blended. You might need to add more broth (or water if you don't have more broth) because noodles absorb a lot of water. Cook the noodles to the desired softness, but do not overcook. Serve the pancit as a main dish alone or with eggroll as a side dish. Enjoy the meal!

LEMON MERINGUE PIE

Recipe by William S. White

✳ ✳ ✳

To make a really good pie, you need the following ingredients:

3 eggs, separated
1 can (14 oz.) of Eagle brand
    sweetened condensed milk
1/2 cup lemon juice (fresh or
    reconstituted)
1 tsp. grated lemon rind
1 graham cracker pie crust
1/4 tsp. cream of tartar
1/3 cup of sugar

While combining ingredients, preheat the oven to 350 degrees. In a medium bowl, mix using an electric mixer until the following ingredients are blended together smoothly: egg yolks, lemon juice, Eagle brand condensed milk, and don't forget the lemon rind. Now pour the mixture into a graham cracker pie crust that you purchased or made. To make the meringue, beat the egg whites in a small bowl with the cream of tartar until foamy, and add the sugar gradually. Beat the egg whites for the meringue until they are stiff but not dry. A good way to check the egg whites is to remove the beaters and see if the meringue forms peaks. Spread the meringue on top of the pie, making sure you seal the edges of the crust with the meringue. Bake the pie for about fifteen minutes or until the meringue is golden brown. Cool the pie and chill it before serving. Make sure that you refrigerate any leftovers so that the pie doesn't spoil.

CHOCOLATE ELEPHANT

Recipe by Sadie Sullivan-Greiner

✳ ✳ ✳

12 eggs
1 tsp. vanilla
1/2 lb. sweet butter
3 T. almond liqueur
1 lb. German sweet chocolate
4 T. sugar
whipped cream (optional)

Anyone who likes rich chocolate desserts will want the recipe for Chocolate Elephant. To make Chocolate Elephant for twelve people, you will need the quantities of the ingredients listed above. Begin by separating the eggs, and then beat the yolks with the vanilla and butter. When these are thoroughly blended, add the almond liqueur. Next melt the chocolate in a double boiler. While the chocolate is cooling a bit, beat the egg whites and sugar until stiff. Then blend the chocolate with the butter/yolk mixture, adding the chocolate a little at a time. The final step is to gently fold the chocolate into the egg whites. Be careful to just barely turn the spoon so that the egg whites don't go flat. Put the mixture in small glasses or serving dishes and chill before serving. Because Chocolate Elephant is extraordinarily rich, it should be served in tiny portions. With or without whipped cream on top, Chocolate Elephant is sure to please real chocolate lovers.

Writing That Describes Something

SECTION ONE:
The Writing Process for Description

Goals

In this section of the chapter, you will learn how to do the following:

- Use visualizing to discover details about your topic
- Write a topic sentence by selecting the most important details
- Choose descriptive words that are clear, accurate, and interesting
- Use the senses of sight, sound, smell, touch, and taste in your writing
- Organize a description using spatial order, group order, or time order

Learning about Description

What Is Description?

Writing that tells how something looks, sounds, smells, feels, or tastes is called *description*. Description is a very natural form of speaking and writing that we use all the time. For example, whenever we tell someone about a new mountain bike or surfboard, a new class ring or engagement ring, a new apartment or condo, we almost always describe what it looks like. In addition to visual details, we may also use the senses of sound, smell, touch, and occasionally even taste to make the description more complete. For instance, you might use the sense of touch to describe the texture of something, such as the *rough, uneven* surface of a stone fireplace or the *soft leather* seats in your new car. You might also want to mention distinctive sounds or smells like the *powerful sound* of your car's engine or the *sweet, perfume-like scent* of the night-blooming jasmine by the entrance to your new apartment.

Since descriptive details are often included in other kinds of writing, you may already have used some description in your narration or instructions (Chapters 2 and 3). For example, the narration paragraph *The Howl* (page 49) used vivid details like "an unearthly growling noise," "one cold, dark night," and "the croaking of bullfrogs." *The Sacred Falls* (page 53) included "twining tree branches covered with neon-green moss," "towering cliffs," and "crashing water." In the instructions paragraph *Carnation Leis* (page 104), the writer used description to explain the part of the flower called the sepal—"the fat green part that wrapped around the carnation when it was a bud." Descriptive details like these often make writing more interesting because they enable the reader to picture what you are talking about and to share the experience.

Writing Objective: Describing a Place

Your objective for this chapter is to write a description of a specific place. Your description may be one paragraph long (like most of the example descriptions in this chapter), or, if you prefer, you may write a longer description that consists of more than one paragraph. In addition to creating a visual picture of the place, you should also include things that can be perceived with some of the other senses—sound, smell, touch, and taste. Your reading audience should be able to see what the place looks like, hear the sounds of the place, and experience any distinctive smells, tastes, or touch sensations associated with the place. Your topic should be a place that you know well so that you will be able to describe it accurately with plenty of details, and a place that others would be interested in reading about.

It is important to choose a place that is neither too large nor too small to describe well in a paragraph or short paper. A place as large as a country or a state or even a city would be difficult to write about because there would be too many details to include. For example, you probably wouldn't be able to describe the city of San Francisco effectively in a paragraph or two because there wouldn't be enough room to include all the interesting details about the steep hills, the trolley cars, the downtown area, Golden Gate Bridge, Alcatraz Island, nearby University of California at Berkeley, Chinatown, Fisherman's Wharf, evening entertainment, and so on. On the other hand, a place that is very small will give you little to write about. A bird house, for instance, would probably be too small to write about—unless, of course, it's a very special birdhouse, such as one built in a Victorian style.

Prewriting Activities

Exploring Topics

In order to find a good topic, you need to think of some places that you could describe well. Begin by looking at the preliminary topic ideas listed below. In the blanks provided, identify a specific room, a building, and an outdoor area that you might like to write about. You may use ideas that are already listed or think of others.

PRELIMINARY TOPIC IDEAS:

ONE ROOM: cafeteria, science lab, theater lobby, waiting room, business office, courtroom, living room, or . . . .

Is there a room that you might like to describe? _____

ONE BUILDING: house, restaurant, hotel, cabin, sports stadium, health spa, bowling alley, library, place where you work, or . . . .

Is there a building that you might like to describe? _____

AN OUTDOOR AREA: a park, camping area, boat dock, playground, outdoor theater, area where you go horseback riding, or . . . .

Is there an outdoor area that you might like to describe? _____

Now use the worksheet that follows to explore possible topics. When you fill out the worksheet, it is all right to use some of the preliminary topic ideas that you just wrote in the blanks above, or you may think of entirely different topics.

■ WORKSHEET I | Exploring Topics for Description

Directions: List specific places in at least seven of the categories below. Choose places that you know well and can picture easily in your mind.

1. A room that has special significance for you

   _____

2. An outdoor place where you like to spend time

   _____

3. A special place that most people don't know about

   _____

4. A place where you spend many hours every week

   _____

5. A store where you like to shop or a restaurant where you like to eat

   _____

6. Someone's house or another building that you admire or dislike

   _____

7. A place that is sometimes stressful or uncomfortable for you

   _____

8. Someplace that you would like to be right now

   _____

9. Anyplace where you will be sometime today or tomorrow

   _____

10. Any other interesting place that you could describe in detail

   _____

Discovering Details 1: Observing with All of Your Senses

In order to write a good description, you will need to carefully observe sights and sounds, as well as smells, touch sensations, and perhaps even tastes. One way to develop your ability to observe these kinds of details is to practice by going to different places and noticing everything that you can see, hear, smell, touch, or taste.

Choose someplace on campus to observe such as the Student Union, the library, the admissions office, an outdoor patio area, a swimming pool, the tennis courts, or any other location. This activity may be done with groups of five or six people working together, or it may be done individually. The whole class may observe the same place, or groups may go to different parts of the campus to make observations. While you are actually in the place that you have selected, carefully observe everything listed in the Observation Guide below. You may want to write down some notes to help you remember details.

Observation Guide

1. General impression of the place

2. Location, size, and shape (or shapes)

3. Colors, textures, special features

4. Furniture, equipment, or other objects

5. People (if any)

6. Actions or activities taking place (if any)

7. Sounds that you hear

8. Smells or tastes associated with the area (if any)

9. Anything else that you observe

When you meet back at the classroom, share your observations with other students. If some of you observed the same place, did you notice the same things? If not, discuss the different things that you noticed. As you tell others about everything that you saw, heard, smelled, touched, or tasted, you should include as many details as possible. Remember that you want your audience to be able to experience the place too, so try to describe everything as vividly and accurately as you can. In addition to sharing your observations orally, you may also want to write an informal paragraph about your observations.

Another way to practice observing and describing places is to use pictures. Look through magazines for some interesting pictures of places, or perhaps you have some photographs of special places that you would like to bring to class. After you have selected a picture, notice the same kinds of things that are on the Observation Guide above. Since you will be able to use only one sense, *sight,* as you look at the picture, try to imagine what you would observe with your other senses if you were actually in the place. Share your observations with your classmates.

You can continue to practice observation techniques by noticing details about sights, sounds, smells, touch sensations, and tastes wherever you go. Becoming a keen observer will help you write a good description that will make your reading audience feel almost as if they have been there themselves.

Discovering Details 2: Visualizing

Look over the topics that you listed as preliminary ideas on page 143 and on the *Exploring Topics Worksheet,* and select one that you think you would like to write about. If possible, go to the place that you have chosen and write down detailed observations about the sights, sounds, smells, touch sensations, and tastes (if any), as you did in the previous activity. However, if going to the place is not practical, a good way to remember details is to *visualize* the place in your mind. *Visualizing* allows the conscious mind to relax so that details from the subconscious mind can be recalled. Sometimes it's even possible to visualize and remember things that you think you have completely forgotten. Visualizing can be a helpful prewriting technique for any writing assignment, but it's particularly useful for describing a place because it's the next best thing to actually being there.

In order to do this activity, you need to be relaxed. Sit down and make yourself as comfortable as possible. Then take a few deep breaths. Close your eyes and imagine that you are in this place right now. Look all around you and start noticing details, especially the sights, sounds, smells, and touch sensations. Spend a few minutes visualizing everything about the place that you can recall. Imagine walking all around, noticing what you see and how you feel. After you have visualized the place clearly, open your eyes and write your observations on the *Visualizing Worksheet* that follows. You may want to close your eyes and come back to the place again in your mind in order to answer some of the questions.

■ **WORKSHEET II** | # Visualizing

Directions: Answer the following questions about the place that you visualized. If you do not remember something, close your eyes and visualize it again.

The Place: _____

1. As you look all around you, what do you see? What is in front of you? To your right? To your left? Behind you? In the distance?

   _____

   _____

   _____

2. What specific objects do you see? Furniture? Personal items? Equipment? If the place is outdoors, are there any trees or other plants? How about animals?

   _____

   _____

   _____

3. What other people are in this place? What are they doing?

_____

_____

_____

4. What colors and textures do you see? Be specific.

_____

_____

_____

5. What sounds do you hear? Who or what is making these sounds?

_____

_____

_____

6. Imagine taking a deep breath, inhaling slowly. What smells do you notice?

_____

_____

_____

7. How do you feel while you are in this place? What makes you feel this way?

_____

_____

8. What time of day or night is it? If you visited the same place at a different time, would anything be different?

_____

_____

If you were able to visualize the place easily and to recall a lot of interesting details, this place will probably make a good writing topic. However, if you would like to try another topic before deciding which one to use, you can choose another place from your *Exploring Topics Worksheet* and use the same visualization technique to discover details. If freewriting or listing worked well for you in the previous chapters, you may want to use one of these prewriting techniques as well in order to come up with more details about the place you are going to describe.

Selecting the Most Significant Details

The next step is to decide which details on your *Visualizing Worksheet* are the most significant. Look over your answers to each question and think about the things that you visualized. Which words and phrases give the clearest, most accurate picture of the place? Which information is most interesting? Which details show the unique qualities of the place that you are going to describe? Put a check mark (✓) by everything on the worksheet that you think is especially important. If you find some things that don't seem very interesting or relevant, draw a line through them.

The following example worksheet shows details that one writer selected about her favorite vacation spot in the Florida Keys. The details that she thought were the most significant are marked with a ✓. Things that she decided to eliminate have a line drawn through them. As you read her worksheet, see if you agree with her choices.

Example Visualizing Worksheet

The Place: *Summerland Key — view from the porch*

1. As you look all around you, what do you see? What do you see in front of you? To your right? To your left? Behind you? In the distance?

   ✓ *the ocean — a small peaceful bay*

   other houses to the left and right but not close

   Behind us — quiet street...the rest of Summerland Key

2. What specific objects do you see? Furniture? Personal items? Equipment? If the place is outdoors, are there any trees or other plants? How about animals?

   ✓ *comfortable chairs and tables on screened porch*

   glasses with drinks, books, newspapers

3. What other people are in this place? What are they doing?

Jim, Dot, David, Bill, Joan

✓ *boating, fishing,*   ✓ *relaxing on porch*

4. What colors and textures do you see? Be specific.

✓ *shades of blue & turquoise in the water*

✓ *clear blue sky;*   ✓ *boats and sails, mostly white*

5. What sounds do you hear? Who or what is making these sounds?

✓ *birds — pelicans following fishing boats*

sounds of motorboats

6. Imagine yourself taking a deep breath, inhaling slowly. What smells do you notice?

✓ *fresh sea smell, clean air*

7. How do you feel while you are in this place? What makes you feel this way?

✓ *peaceful, relaxed, contented*

8. What time of day or night is it? If you visited the same place at a different time, would anything be different?

~~*more or less the same all day*~~

✓ *evening — sunset*

early morning, more boats going out

As you are marking your worksheet, you should place check marks by all of the details that seem significant—at least five or six. When you write your rough draft, you will probably want to use most of the details that you have checked and leave out things that you have drawn a line through. If there are some things that you didn't mark at all, you can decide later whether you want to use them or not.

Writing a Rough Draft

Learning about Topic Sentences for Description

With some types of writing, it works well to go directly from prewriting activities to your first draft. Then, after you have your ideas down on paper, you can write a good topic sentence. This was the writing process we used for narration and instructions in Chapters 2 and 3. With both of these writing assignments, the first draft could be developed directly from your freewriting or listing worksheet by putting everything in the right order. However, when you are writing a description, it is usually a good idea to decide on a topic sentence first. Then you can develop your rough draft more easily with details that relate to the topic sentence.

One thing that your topic sentence must do is identify the place that you are going to describe. In addition, it must state something important about the place, such as its most significant features, your impressions of the place, or your feelings about being there. You should review the key words or phrases that you identified on your *Visualizing Worksheet* to help you come up with a main idea. As you read over everything that you checked, try to decide which features, impressions, or feelings are the most important. For example, when the writer of the example worksheet looked over the items that she had marked with a ✓, these were the things that she thought were the most significant:

✓ the ocean—a small peaceful bay

✓ relaxing on porch

✓ peaceful, relaxed, contented

These phrases seemed to express her strongest impressions of the place. She also noticed that a lot of the other details, such as the fresh sea air, the blue and turquoise water in the bay, and the sunset, seemed related to her feelings of peacefulness and relaxation. Therefore, she decided to include some of these feelings in her topic sentence. Here is the first topic sentence that she tried:

> *Draft 1:* I enjoyed a relaxing vacation on Summerland Key.

Although this topic sentence emphasized her feeling of relaxation, she didn't think it sounded very interesting. Therefore, she decided to add something about peacefulness as well. This is the second version of her topic sentence:

> *Draft 2:* Summerland Key was a peaceful and relaxing place for a vacation.

She liked this second topic sentence better, but her workshop group suggested that she should add more details about the place to make it sound more appealing to readers. This is the revised topic sentence that she decided to use for her description:

> *Draft 3:* The best part of my vacation on Summerland Key was relaxing in a beautiful, peaceful setting, with a magnificent ocean view.

This topic sentence included everything that the writer wanted to focus on: her feeling of relaxation, the peaceful setting, and the ocean view.

Now do the following activity to practice evaluating topic sentences for description before writing your own.

Evaluating Topic Sentences for Description

Directions: Write OK in the blank by each good topic sentence, and write NO in the blank by the others. Be sure that the place is identified, and look for something important about the place, such as the significant features or the writer's impressions. Be ready to explain your answers.

EXAMPLE 1 ➤ ___*NO*___ From the helicopter, we had a good view of the glacier.

Example 1 is not a good topic sentence because it does not identify the specific place and does not mention significant features or impressions.

EXAMPLE 2 ➤ ___*OK*___ As we flew over Mendenhall Glacier, our view of the vast river of ice was breathtaking.

Example 2 is an effective topic sentence because it identifies the place and includes something important about the main features.

_____ **1.** Mount Pleasant has a city park.

_____ **2.** There are many wineries in Napa Valley, California.

_____ **3.** Although many buildings along the canals in Venice, Italy, have deteriorated, the former splendor of the city is apparent.

_____ **4.** Tree-lined Palmer Lake near Lakebay, Washington, is small but picturesque.

_____ **5.** Hong Kong is a huge city.

_____ **6.** The waiting room at my dentist's office is beautifully color-coordinated and comfortably furnished.

_____ **7.** One of the warmest and most loving places in my house is my baby's room.

_____ **8.** That house on Evergreen Street is painted pink with coral trim.

_____ **9.** There are five apricot trees and two plum trees in Dan's small orchard.

_____ **10.** The spacious tiger enclosure at Lincoln Zoo is designed to resemble the tigers' natural habitat.

Writing Your Own Topic Sentence and Introduction

Writing Your Topic Sentence

Now read over everything that you checked on your *Visualizing Worksheet* and think about which features or impressions of the place are the most important. What makes this place unique and special? If you could use only a few of your descriptive details to tell someone about the place, which ones would you choose? In the blanks below, write the words or phrases from your *Visualizing Worksheet* that describe the most significant features or your strongest impressions of the place:

_____

_____

_____

_____

Now try writing a topic sentence that uses one or more of the ideas that you listed above. Be sure that your topic sentence also identifies the place you are going to describe.

TOPIC SENTENCE (DRAFT #1):

_____

_____

Ask your workshop group or other classmates to read your topic sentence. If they have any suggestions, or if you want to change the wording to make your description sound more interesting, write your revised topic sentence here:

TOPIC SENTENCE (DRAFT #2):

_____

_____

Now answer the following questions to make sure that your topic sentence does everything it is supposed to:

1. Does your topic sentence identify the place? _____
2. Does your topic sentence say something significant about the place? _____

3. Does your topic sentence make this place sound interesting? _____

4. Will you be able to think of other details to include in your description that relate to your topic sentence? _____

5. Is your topic sentence a complete sentence? _____

Were you able to answer "Yes" to all of the questions? If so, you have a good topic sentence that will help you get started with your first draft. If you're not sure about some of the answers, ask members of your workshop group to help you decide, or you may want to show your topic sentence to your instructor. Keep working on the wording of your topic sentence until you are satisfied with it.

Adding an Introduction

Although the topic sentence alone can often introduce a paragraph or short paper effectively, you may be able to make your description sound more interesting to your reading audience by adding another introductory sentence or two. Having a two- or three-sentence introduction is especially important if your description is going to be a page or more in length or if it will contain more than one paragraph. Some writers make the place sound appealing in the introduction by including background information or a brief story about how they happened to go there. However, anything that captures readers' attention and gets them interested in your topic will be an effective introduction. (It may be helpful to review introductions in Chapter 3, pages 98–100.)

Here is the introduction for a description called *Horsethief Canyon*, by Shawn McPherren, which appears later in this chapter on page 158:

> Horsethief Canyon, in the Cleveland National Forest, is a close and concealed retreat from the city. Although it's only a 20–30 minute drive from the city, it's one of those places that few people even know about, so its use is limited to the lucky few. Within the walls of Horsethief Canyon is a realm of total isolation and serenity.

By using three sentences as an introduction instead of just the topic sentence (the third sentence), Shawn was able to get readers interested in going to Horsethief Canyon themselves. In fact, some people in his workshop group even asked him for directions!

Now try to write an introduction for your own description. What would make the place that you are describing sound appealing to readers? Or, if it's not an appealing place, what would give readers a strong sense of how terrible or unpleasant it is? Could you say something that would arouse readers' curiosity about the place? Using some of these ideas or other ideas of your own, try adding another sentence or two before the topic sentence to capture the reader's attention. Write your introduction below, including the topic sentence. (If you prefer to use only the topic sentence as an introduction, write a third draft of your topic sentence here, making it as interesting as possible.)

INTRODUCTION WITH TOPIC SENTENCE:

_____

_____

_____

_____

From Topic Sentence to First Draft

As soon as you are satisfied with your introduction and topic sentence, you can start planning and working on your first draft. The topic sentence will help you decide which details to include in the body of your paper. Everything that you write must be related in some way to your topic sentence. For example, if your topic sentence says that the place makes you feel uncomfortable or uneasy, the body of your paper must give details that show why you feel that way. If your topic sentence says that the view from a mountaintop is spectacular, the body must emphasize the details that make it spectacular.

It is important to include enough details so that the reader has a clear and accurate impression of the place that you are writing about. Try to show what sets this place apart from other similar places—its special qualities and characteristics. For example, if you are describing a park, think about what makes it different from other parks. What special features does it have? Is there a tile-roofed gazebo? Is there a small petting zoo for children? Is there a three-mile walking trail around the perimeter of the park? Are the barbecue grills exceptionally well-located and convenient? You may want to look over your *Visualizing Worksheet* on pages 146–147 and perhaps even visualize the place again in order to recall special features and characteristics.

Here is the first draft of *Summerland*, which uses details from the example visualizing worksheet earlier in this chapter. In some sentences, the writer uses words like "relaxed" or "comfortable" to tell us how she felt and to reinforce her main idea. In other places, she describes the view, the smells, the sounds, and other things that contributed to her impressions of the place. As you read *Summerland*, think about whether it includes enough details to make the place sound special and interesting. Try to find several sentences where the writer could improve this first draft by adding more details.

First Draft

Summerland

The best part of my Florida vacation was relaxing in a beautiful, peaceful setting, with a magnificent ocean view. Our house on the west side of Summerland Key overlooked a small, turquoise blue bay, and I spent many happy hours in my favorite lounge chair, enjoying the view. Early each morning, we heard the sounds of boat motors and watched Big Jake's lobster boats. During the day, other boats moved back and forth across the bay. Sometimes we heard the cries of pelicans. In the evenings, there were magnificent sunsets of purple, crimson, and gold. Every day I relaxed on the porch for hours, enjoying the ever-changing view and the fresh, invigorating smell of the salt water. With cool drinks in our hands, fresh fish on the dinner menu, and views that looked like postcards, life seemed perfect for one wonderful week.

Response to *Summerland*

1. Are there enough details in this first draft to give readers a clear picture of the place and its special features? What kinds of details would you like to see added to this first draft?

_____

_____

_____

2. Which details in *Summerland* do you think are the most interesting and effective? List three of your favorite details on the lines below.

_____

_____

_____

Organizing the Details

As you are writing your first draft, you will need to decide how to organize it. Where should you start? What order should you put things in? It is important to present the details in a way that is clear, logical, and easy for readers to follow. Three methods of organization that are often used for descriptive writing are *spatial order, group order,* and *time order.*

Spatial Order

One way to organize a description is *spatial order.* This means arranging the points in your paper according to the physical arrangement of the place that you are describing. In other words, consider where everything is located in the "space" of the room, building, or other area. For example, if you are describing your favorite restaurant using *spatial order,* you would think about how the restaurant is arranged in order to figure out a logical organization. You might start with the entrance, then describe what you see as you go into the dining room. You could describe everything in the dining room from left to right, right to left, floor to ceiling, or according to any other spatial order that makes sense for the particular restaurant. When you organize a description according to spatial order, you can start anywhere that you want and then move to other areas in any order that makes sense.

As you read *Waiting Room* by Todd Tenbrook, notice how he uses the technique of spatial order to give us a clear, well-organized picture of his dentist's waiting room.

Waiting Room

by Todd Tenbrook

I sat viewing the dentist's neat, orderly lobby while anxiously waiting for the nurse to call my name. The room is square-shaped with three gray padded chairs against each of the three walls. Against the west wall in addition to the chairs there are two dark wood end tables with lamps, one in each corner of the room. Within arm's reach of the chairs, there is a three-foot long coffee table with glass in the middle. On the coffee table is a variety of magazines, from *National Geographic* to *Newsweek*. On the east side of the lobby are the entrance and the receptionist's desk. To the left of the receptionist's desk is the door leading to the doctor's office. In the center of the north and south walls there are paintings of dolphins. The lobby is consumed by the smell of fluoride, and if you listen really hard, you can hear the sound of drilling. After twenty minutes of waiting nervously in that room, the nurse beckoned me to enter the doctor's office, and I knew I was doomed.

Response to *Waiting Room*

1. Try to draw a picture of everything in the waiting room, putting the chairs, tables, lamps, doors, receptionist's desk, and paintings in their places according to the spatial order that Todd described.

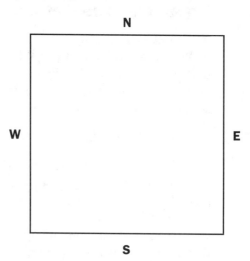

2. Are there any features of the waiting room that you would like to hear more about?

_____

_____

3. Some descriptions are written in the present tense to give readers a feeling of being there, while others may be written in the past tense if the writer visited the place in the past. Why do you think this writer used the past tense for the topic sentence and the conclusion but used the present tense for the rest of the paragraph?

_____

_____

Group Order

With some description topics, it may be possible to use *group order,* which means grouping together things that are related. Similar items can be placed in the same group and described together even if they are not located near each other. Using this method, a park or picnic area might be described using groups of items such as these:

GROUP 1—grass, trees, other plants

GROUP 2—picnic tables, barbecue grills, trash cans

GROUP 3—walking trails or hiking trails

GROUP 4—playground areas

GROUP 5—animals or people observed in the park

Group order works better than spatial order for this topic because the same kinds of things are likely to be found throughout the park. For example, there may be trees near some of the picnic tables, trees along the trails, trees near the park entrance, and so on. Organizing a description according to groups allows you to describe similar things together, even if they are located far apart.

Time Order

It is also possible to organize a description according to the *time order* in which an observer might see each part of the place. This works particularly well if you observed the place during an extended time period of several hours or more. The writer of *Summerland,* for example, organized her description according to what she saw at different times of day, from morning to evening.

Combining Different Methods of Organization

Sometimes two or more methods of organization—spatial order, group order, and/or time order—can be combined effectively. For example, if you are describing a fairly large area that you observe over a period of time, you might want to combine time order and spatial order. In this case, you could write as an observer moving through the area and describing things in different locations as you see them. This is the way Shawn McPherren decided to organize his description, called *Horsethief Canyon.* Because Shawn's description was more than a page long, he decided to divide it into separate paragraphs. After the introduction, each paragraph describes things that Shawn observed at a certain time of day or in a certain part of the canyon area. As you read *Horsethief Canyon,* think about whether or not the organization is effective.

Horsethief Canyon
by Shawn McPherren

Horsethief Canyon, in the Cleveland National Forest, is a close and concealed retreat from the city. Although it's only a 20–30 minute drive from the city, it's one of those places that few people even know about, so its use is limited to the lucky few. Within the walls of Horsethief Canyon is a realm of total isolation and serenity.

The dry, dusty parking lot is on the top of a hill, and from this vantage point, you can see other tan and green hills and the dense canopy of trees snaking on the valley floor. The trees that shade the hiking trails along the stream bed are ancient oaks. Some of these trees are over two hundred years old. The splendor of this beauty is nearly invisible from anywhere other than the valley floor.

Within the canopy of trees can be heard the faint babbling of the stream over stones, the loud buzzing of a dragonfly darting by, the sweet songs of the birds high in tree tops, and the rustling of rabbits fleeing from us. As the hot summer sun lays down upon us its warming sunlight, the scent of the vegetation gets thick. Strong are the smells of sagebrush, daisies, and other wildflowers. Walking down the trail, we smell the dust as it's kicked up by our boots. As breezes cool our necks, we catch the stray scent of distant pines on the wind.

As we move on, so does time, and sunset approaches. The air feels much cooler on our trip out of the canyon. Facing west, we can see the golden light that sunset produces and the vivid clouds in their shades of pink and gold. All these colors in such bright shades on the deep blue sky make it easy to get caught up in the ethereal beauty of nature.

To avoid getting caught in the dark, we hurry back up the hill we came down (the Espinoza Trail). Back up on the dirt parking lot, we can see the hills and the canopy of ancient oaks. Now they have a dark shadow cast upon them as the sun has slipped down past the horizon. As sunlight fades, the fiery sky calms down and is replaced with a deep azure that twinkles with the freckles of the night's face. As the air is much cleaner out in the country, many more stars are visible at night, and the heavens seem much closer to us.

Heading down the hills and along the winding country roads, we listen to the stereo and enjoy the glow of a long day of physical exercise coming to an end. Next stop: Carl's Junior and then a nice, hot shower.

Response to *Horsethief Canyon*

1. Does Shawn's description make you want to visit Horsethief Canyon? Why or why not?

   _____

   _____

2. Which visual details are most appealing and interesting?

   _____

   _____

3. Which sounds or smells do you think the writer has described especially well?

   _____

   _____

4. Do you think that the combination of time order and spatial order is an effective way to organize this description? Why or why not?

   _____

   _____

Now think about which method of organization would work best for your own description topic. Whether you use spatial order, group order, time order, or some combination of these techniques, an effective pattern of organization is an important part of writing an accurate description.

When you have completed your rough draft, using an appropriate pattern of organization and interesting details, it is time to have your workshop group take a look at your description and give you some feedback. Here are some rough draft workshop questions to help you give constructive suggestions to your classmates.

Rough Draft Workshop Questions

1. Is there a clear topic sentence?
2. Has the writer included enough interesting details?
3. Are the details organized logically and effectively?
4. Are other senses used in addition to sight?
5. Can you suggest anything that could be added or revised to make the description better or more interesting?

Writing with All of Your Senses

Most descriptions emphasize visual details because readers want to be able to picture the place that is being described. You will need to tell them about the main features or characteristics of the place, giving details about what everything looks like—colors, sizes, shapes, and so on. For example, if a bird cage is hanging in one corner of the room, is it a small gold cage or a large black one? How many birds are in it, and what kind of birds are they— twelve canaries or one parrot? What is the parrot doing—standing, eating, looking at you? Visual details like these make your writing interesting and give your audience a sense of actually being in the place that you are describing.

In addition to creating a visual picture, a good description usually includes some other senses as well—sound, smell, touch, and sometimes taste. Most places have distinctive sounds, such as frogs croaking at night near the shore of the lake, the whining of lathes and screeching of table saws in a woodshop, the reverberating metallic tones of a steel drum band at the Wild Animal Park, the shrill whistle of trains on a nearby railroad track. Telling readers about the kinds of sounds made by people, machines, animals, or something else will make your description more complete and more interesting.

How things feel when you touch them or how they smell or taste may also add interest to your description. If you're writing about a beach, is the water cool or warm? As you wade into the water, what does the bottom feel like on your feet—sandy? uneven? rocky? mushy? Are there any plants or fish close enough to touch? Do you smell fresh, clean air or rotting seaweed and dead fish on the shore? How about Lou's Gym? Does it smell musty and sweaty? Do the locker rooms smell disinfectant clean? Are the tile floors in the shower room slippery, or do they have a nonslip surface? When you are in the pool or jacuzzi at the gym, can you taste the chlorine in the water? Of course, some places may not have any noticeable smells or tastes that you can write about, but with other places it may be possible to use all of your senses effectively. A place will seem very real to the reader if you describe how things smell and taste, as well as how they feel, how they sound, and what they look like. It is not necessary to use all five senses in order to write a good description, but you should try to include some details that use at least one or two other senses besides sight.

When Yanina Swiderski described the island beach of Cozumél, she included a talking parrot (*sound*), colorful fish that she could *touch,* and the *smell* of the ocean breeze, as well as a lot of other interesting details. As you read *One Perfect Place*, try to picture Cozumél in your mind, and think about which details are the most effective.

One Perfect Place
by Yanina Swiderski

My favorite part of my Cancún vacation was relaxing and swimming at a beautiful little island beach named Cozumél. It was the most peaceful and gorgeous place I've ever been. Cozumél beach didn't have waves, and it seemed as if I was getting into a swimming pool. The water was lukewarm, turquoise in color, and clear enough to see and touch some of the colorful fish swimming around me. Deep in the water was a sunken ship that everybody could swim near and touch. There was an exciting section in the ocean where people could really swim with a young shark named "Pancho." Relaxing in the white sand, I could smell the ocean breeze, feel the hot sun, and see a paradise all around me. Near the beach was a little restaurant made of red bricks, and its ceiling was made of leaves from palm trees. Its wooden tables and chairs looked almost like picnic tables from a park. The white walls were covered with fishing nets, several jawbones of sharks, and different paintings of the ocean. Near the cash register was a cute green parrot with a yellow mark on his head. He was standing on top of his big, black cage. He could say "Hola, ¿cómo estas?", sing "La Cucaracha," and imitate a child crying or laughing and the waiter saying "¿Listos para ordenar?", which means "Ready to order?" I could scratch the back of his head and feed him sunflower seeds, pieces of tortilla, or hard bread. I will never forget the wonderful day I spent at that paradise named Cozumél.

Response to *One Perfect Place*

1. What sounds has the writer included in her description? List them below. Mark the ones that you like best with a ✓.

   _____

   _____

   _____

2. Which details involve the sense of smell? List them below. Mark the ones that you like best with a ✓.

   _____

   _____

   _____

3. Which details involve the sense of touch? List them below. In some cases the writer may not tell us exactly how something feels, but we can imagine it from her description.

   _____

   _____

   _____

   _____

4. Which visual details do you think are most interesting?

_____

_____

_____

_____

    Now look at the kinds of details that you included in your own rough draft and answer the following questions:

Have you included any sounds? If so, what are they?

_____

_____

Is there anything that uses the sense of smell or taste? Which details use one of these senses?

_____

_____

Are there any details that involve the sense of touch, such as textures, temperatures, or how the surface of something feels? Which details are they?

_____

_____

Which visual details in your rough draft do you think are the most effective?

_____

_____

    If your rough draft has only visual details, you should try to add something that uses sound, smell, taste, or touch. These kinds of details, as well as visual details, can help the reader share your experience more completely.

Checking for Unity

As you are writing and revising your rough draft, it is important to make sure that all of the details relate to your topic sentence. Everything that you include should somehow support, explain, or give more information about your topic sentence. If something seems irrelevant or creates a contradictory impression, your writing will not have *unity*—that is, it will not be clearly focused on a main idea. In most types of academic writing, the details in the body of the paragraph or paper should work together, or *unite,* to develop the writer's main idea.

For example, if your topic sentence about a new shopping mall says that the unusual architectural style is ugly and grotesque and the shops are too expensive, you must stick to those ideas throughout your description. If you start writing about how much fun you had with your friends the last time you were at the mall, that story is not related at all to the topic sentence, so your paper will lack unity. Don't digress with anything that is irrelevant or is inconsistent with your topic sentence. Omit things like the great foot massager that you bought for your dad in one of the shops, directions for taking the bus or trolley to get there, and the spicy chicken burritos you ate at the Mexican restaurant in the mall.

As you read the following rough draft, *The Apartment,* look for problems with unity. At several points, the writer gets off the topic and starts telling about things that are irrelevant to her topic sentence. Draw a line through all of the sentences that do not belong in the paragraph.

Rough Draft

The Apartment

I remember my first apartment with a mixture of pride and embarrassment. It was a tiny studio apartment on the second floor of an old, run-down building, with mismatched furniture, but I was thrilled because it was all mine. It was all I could afford. I had only a part-time job, reading for a blind person who was working on his doctoral thesis, and I also had a scholarship that paid for my tuition and books. Unlike most studios, my apartment did have the luxury of a separate kitchen, which was about the size of a small closet. The bathroom was the same size—barely big enough to turn around in—but at least it had indoor plumbing! I remember staying at my aunt's farmhouse when I was about seven or eight years old, before she had indoor plumbing put in. Going outside to the outhouse at night with a flashlight was scary! Anyhow, my apartment had running water, but in the winter the pipes would freeze, so sometimes there was no water for a day or two. The landlord was nice, but he wasn't very prompt about fixing things. When I moved into the apartment, the windows were bare, so I bought some inexpensive material with an aqua floral print and made curtains. Aqua was a popular color for kitchens then. The kitchen had only a few rough shelves instead of cupboards, so I hung panels of the same material in front of the shelves. The effect was really not bad at all. At least my kitchen was color-coordinated. The chartreuse green couch with black arms and the sagging brown recliner didn't match anything, but they were comfortable enough. In fact, I've had more expensive furniture since then that wasn't nearly as comfortable! There was no other furniture except for a cheap coffee table with lots of ring marks where people had set glasses on it over the years. I hate it when people do inconsiderate things like that! To anyone else, my little apartment probably looked dreary and depressing, but it felt good to come home to my own place after classes and curl up on my own couch/bed in the evenings. I hardly noticed the inconveniences.

Response to The *Apartment*

1. What main idea about the apartment does the writer express in her topic sentence? (Remember that everything in the paragraph should somehow relate to this main idea.)

_____

2. After you have drawn lines through everything that you think does not belong in the paragraph, discuss the things that you marked with your workshop group or other classmates. Try to agree on which details should be eliminated so that the description of *The Apartment* will have unity.

Now read through your own rough draft to check for unity. If you find things that seem irrelevant or inconsistent, the best solution is probably to cross them out. However, if it turns out that a lot of your most interesting details don't relate to the main idea in your topic sentence, you may want to consider changing the topic sentence. Having a topic sentence that expresses what you really want to say about your topic is an important part of writing a unified paragraph or paper.

Transitions for Description

To make everything in your description clear to the reader, you will probably need to use transitions to connect some of your ideas. One function of transitional words and phrases for description is showing the physical arrangement of things, especially where objects are located in relation to each other. If you don't explain where things are, it may be difficult for readers to picture the scene accurately. For example, in the following brief description of the grounds of a museum, the writer has not used transitions to show where the pond, rocks, footbridge, benches, and hanging plants are located, so it's difficult to figure out where things are in relation to each other:

> Outside of the museum is a small pond with several gold-colored fish swimming back and forth and sometimes hiding. A lot of large rocks can be seen, and there is a wooden footbridge with high railings. Two old-fashioned park benches provide places for people to sit. Several hanging baskets of pink and purple fuchsias add color to the scene.

Which things are not clearly located? Are the rocks near the pond, in the pond, or somewhere else? Where are the benches? What are the baskets of fuchsias hanging from? Although we can picture each item individually, it is not possible to put the entire scene together accurately because we don't know where things are in relation to each other.

In the revised description below, the writer has added phrases to show the locations of things more clearly, making it easier for the reader to get a clear mental picture of the scene:

> Outside of the museum *to the left of the main entrance* is a small pond. Several gold-colored fish are swimming back and forth, sometimes hiding among the large rocks that are half-submerged *around the edges of the pond*. *Arching across the pond* is a wooden footbridge with high railings. *Hanging from the railings* are several baskets of pink and purple fuchsias that add color to the scene. *On a small hill overlooking the pond*, two old-fashioned park benches provide places for people to sit.

How do the phrases in italics help to explain the physical arrangement of things?

_____

_____

_____

Words and phrases like these that show the location of things in relation to each other are examples of transitions.

Many transitions that show location consist of prepositional phrases, like *to the left of the main entrance, around the edges of the pond,* and *on a small hill,* or include prepositional phrases along with other constructions, like *hanging from the railings.* (You may want to review prepositional phrases in Chapter 1, pages 26–28.) Some of the transitions in the above description also use -ing words and phrases, which we will learn about later in this chapter. (See pages 189–196.) Other types of words, phrases, and clauses can be used as transitions too. Remember that transitional expressions can also be used to show time relationships (as we saw in Chapters 2 and 3), as well as other kinds of connections between ideas.

Activities with Transitions

Each numbered group of words contains five or more items that are located in the same general area. Picture these things in your mind and imagine how they are arranged. Then write a short description that explains where all of the items in each group are located in relation to each other, similar to the previous example with the pond, rocks, footbridge, hanging baskets, and benches. You may also add interesting details about size, shape, color, texture, or other characteristics if you want to.

1. Computer, file cabinet, telephone, desk, three chairs, lamp

   _____

   _____

   _____

   _____

2. Lilac bush, birdbath, two blue spruce trees, tulips, lawn

   _____

   _____

   _____

   _____

3. Merry-go-round, ferris wheel, bumper cars, arcade, cotton candy

   _____

   _____

   _____

   _____

Compare your descriptions with those of other classmates. Did you arrange the items similarly, or are your descriptions quite different?

Now read *Christmas Eve in Saudi Arabia,* and notice how Danny Banda used transitions effectively to give us a clear picture of the room at the Oasis where he spent one memorable Christmas Eve.

Christmas Eve in Saudi Arabia
by Danny Banda

My favorite Christmas was at the Oasis in December of 1990 during the Gulf War in the city of Jaibal, Saudi Arabia. I remember seeing British women and United States Navy nurses dancing with male Marines. The perfume the women were wearing smelled so good that I had to take a deep breath. Behind me there were British and U. S. personnel mingling and chatting with each other. The front of the room had a bunker built out of sandbags. As I looked deep inside the bunker, I saw a D.J. playing music, with a red light in the background. To the rear of the room there was a 20-foot bar made out of sandbags and camouflage blankets. Behind the bar there were metal trash cans full of ice with cold non-alcoholic beer and sodas. In the center of the room there was a huge Christmas tree decorated with various types of lights that were blinking. Wrapped nicely underneath the tree were various size gifts with pretty bows on them. I could hear people talking here and there and the music drowning out some of their conversations. Although the party was for the young troops, some high-ranking officers crashed the party and started dancing with some of the pretty British women. I felt good just watching everybody enjoying themselves, but the best thing was knowing that the young troops had a merry Christmas instead of spending it in a foxhole. If I had returned the following day to the Oasis, it would have been different because all the allied troops would be on their way to Kuwait City.

Response to *Christmas Eve in Saudi Arabia*

1. Where are each of the following located? Find the transitional phrase that tells us the location of each item and write it in the blank.

   A. bunker built out of sandbags _____

   B. D.J. playing music _____

   C. red light _____

   D. bar made of sandbags and camouflage blankets _____

   E. metal trash can full of ice and drinks _____

   F. Christmas tree _____

   G. gifts _____

2. Which details in this description do you think are the most interesting?

   _____

   _____

   _____

Ending Effectively

Like the other types of writing that we have studied, your description needs to have a conclusion—one or two sentences at the end that tie everything together and make your paper seem complete. Many writers end their descriptions by saying something that refers back to their topic sentence. Other options include a final comment about the significance of the topic or what happens after the time of the description. Let's look at the concluding sentences of the example descriptions in this chapter to see how different writers ended their papers effectively.

1. *Summerland:* With cool drinks in our hands, fresh fish on the dinner menu, and views that looked like postcards, life seemed perfect for one wonderful week.

2. *Waiting Room:* After twenty minutes of waiting nervously in that room, the nurse beckoned me to enter the doctor's office, and I knew I was doomed.

3. *Horsethief Canyon:* Heading down the hills and along the winding country roads, we listen to the stereo and enjoy the glow of a long day of physical exercise coming to an end. Next stop: Carl's Junior and then a nice, hot shower.

4. *One Perfect Place:* I will never forget the wonderful day I spent at that paradise named Cozumél.

5. *The Apartment:* To anyone else, my little apartment probably looked dreary and depressing, but it felt good to come home to my own place after classes and curl up on my own couch/bed in the evenings. I hardly noticed the inconveniences.

6. *Christmas Eve in Saudi Arabia:* If I had returned the following day to the Oasis, it would have been different because all the allied troops would be on their way to Kuwait City.

Three of these conclusions say something that refers back to the topic sentence used at the beginning of the description. The ending sentences for *Summerland* and *One Perfect Place* both reinforce the writer's main idea about how enjoyable it was to be there on Summerland Key or in Cozumél. The writer of *The Apartment* emphasized mixed feelings of pride and embarrassment in the topic sentence, and the conclusion is related to those feelings too.

The other conclusions, 2, 3, and 6, all mention something that happened immediately after the time of the description. Todd left the waiting room to see the dentist (Conclusion 2), Shawn drove home from Horsethief Canyon, stopping to get a hamburger on the way (Conclusion 3), and the allied troops left the Oasis to head for Kuwait (Conclusion 6). If an area is described at a specific time or over a period of time, what happens at the end of the time period can be an effective final comment for the conclusion.

In the description that follows, *The Nepa Hut*, Estel Manito-Stokholm gives us a clear picture of the hut that her family lived in when she was a child. Her topic sentence and her conclusion both emphasize how she felt about living there.

The Nepa Hut
by Estel Manito-Stokholm

I vividly remember the nepa hut that my two brothers, grandfather, and I lived in with a mixture of contentment and despair in a small village in the Philippines. It was a very small one-room hut built in the corner of one acre of land with a roof made of cross-linked nepa leaves. (A nepa leaf is wider than a coconut leaf.) The wall and floor consisted of bamboo stems cut in halves and polished with a knife. Inside the nepa hut were a few things necessary for survival. In the corner on the west side lay neatly folded mats and blankets. In the east corner were a few iron plates and drinking glasses made of bamboo. On the north side of the room was the stove, which consisted of three medium size stones stuck in the dirt in a triangle-like arrangement. Next to it was a stack of firewood used for cooking. Pots, pans, and a lantern fueled with petroleum were also located around this area. In the backyard was a garden planted with different kinds of filipino vegetables varying in color—green, yellow, purple, etc. As I looked around outside the nepa hut, I could see acres and acres of rice fields with rice plants sprouting. I could also smell the clear, fresh air unpolluted with automobile fumes and other city pollutants. As I look back now at that meager existence, I can still feel the contentment and despair: contentment because it was a very simple way of living, despair because it was deprived of luxuries that other people could afford.

Response to *The Nepa Hut*

1. What feelings about the hut does Estel express in her topic sentence at the beginning?

_____

_____

2. How does the conclusion reinforce the main idea in her topic sentence? What related information is included in order to give the reader a better understanding of the writer's feelings about living in the nepa hut?

_____

_____

_____

3. Do you think this conclusion is effective? Why or why not?

_____

_____

    Now write your own conclusion. You may emphasize the same features or feelings about the place that you focused on in your topic sentence, write about something that will happen after the time of the description, or use anything else that will make your description seem complete and finished. After you have added the conclusion to your rough draft, ask your workshop group to read it and comment on its effectiveness. If they have some good suggestions, you may want to revise it.
    In the next section of the chapter, you will learn more about using different sentence patterns and phrases that can help to make your writing

more interesting. You may continue to revise and improve your description while you are doing the Sentence and Grammar Skills activities. At the end of Section Two, you will have an opportunity to put the finishing touches on your description before you turn it in.

SECTION TWO:
Sentence and Grammar Skills

Goals
In this section of the chapter, you will learn how to do the following:

- Recognize relative pronouns, relative adverbs, and relative clauses
- Write sentences using relative clauses
- Avoid common sentence errors with relative clauses
- Use -ing words and phrases to add variety to your writing

Learning about Relative Clauses

In Chapter 3 you learned about basic complex sentences, which have two clauses joined by a Group B connector. In this chapter you will study another kind of complex sentence. These sentences also have two clauses, but one of them is a *relative clause* that begins with a *relative pronoun,* such as *who, whom, that, which,* or *whose;* or a *relative adverb: where* or *when.* These words can also be called *relative connectors.*

Relative clauses provide more information about the subject or another important noun in your sentence. The following examples will show you what relative clauses look like and give you a general idea about how they work. In each sentence, the relative clause is in italics, and the noun that it gives information about is underlined.

EXAMPLE 1 ➤ Cristina got the promotion *that she wanted.*

EXAMPLE 2 ➤ The city council will present an award to the firefighter *who saved three children from the fire.*

EXAMPLE 3 ➤ The stage *where the president spoke* was shielded from the public.

In Example 1, the relative clause *that she wanted* gives more information about the promotion. The relative clause in Example 2, *who saved three children from the fire,* tells us which firefighter received the award. Example 3 uses the relative clause *where the president spoke* to identify which stage the writer means. In this chapter you will learn how to use relative clauses like these in order to make your writing more interesting and descriptive. Learning the correct patterns will also help you avoid run-ons, comma splices, and fragments in your writing.

There are two main sentence patterns that are used with relative clauses, as well as a couple of variations.

Pattern 1:

This pattern is the same as the first pattern used for Group B connectors, but the two clauses are joined by a relative connector instead of a Group B connector.

SV	Group B	SV.
SV	Rel	SV.

The words *who, whom, that, which, whose, where,* and *when* can all be used with this pattern. The following rules tell you when to use which relative connector.

   I. For animals and things, use *which* and *that*.

   Look at the following example sentence:

	S	*V*		*Rel*	*S*	*V*

EXAMPLE 4 ➤ Matilda works at the electronics factory that her uncle owns.
which

In this example, either word, *that* or *which,* can be used to join the two SVs (or clauses) together. We normally use the relative pronouns *that* and *which* when we are referring to animals and things, but *which* is sometimes considered to be more formal. In the following example also, either relative pronoun may be used. Notice that the relative clause gives more information about the noun it follows, *prewriting technique.*

EXAMPLE 5 ➤ You should use the prewriting technique which you like best.
that

Which and *that* are not always interchangeable—in some sentences you will have to choose either one or the other. One general rule of thumb is to use *which* whenever the information in the relative clause isn't absolutely essential to identify the noun it relates to, as in the following example:

EXAMPLE 6 ➤ Tickets are sold out for the new play *Bandido!*, which
Luis Valdez wrote.

The relative clause in Example 6 is not essential to identify which play we are talking about, so *which* is the correct connector. Essential and nonessential relative clauses, as well as punctuation rules, are explained more fully in *Punctuation of Relative Clauses*, beginning on page 176.

II. Use *who* or *whom* only for people.

In the following example, *who* or *whom* begins the relative clause that gives more information about a person or people.

		Rel	*S*	*V*

	S	*V*		*Rel*	*S V*

EXAMPLE 7 ➤   Kris interviewed Bill Clinton,   who   she met at the rally.
                                                             whom

In traditional grammar, *who* is used only for the *subject* of a clause and *whom* is used for grammatical *objects*, such as *direct objects* and *objects of prepositions*. However, today many teachers and professional writers accept *who* in both cases. You will need to choose *who* or *whom* depending on what your teacher requires and on how formal you want your paper to be, but even in formal writing *whom* can never be used as a subject.

III. You may use *that* for an unnamed person or people.

In certain cases the relative pronoun *that* can start a clause that gives more information about people, but only if the person isn't named. The following example sentence uses *who*, *whom*, or *that* in a relative clause to give more information about the noun *applicant*.

EXAMPLE 8 ➤   The committee hired the applicant   who   they liked best.
                                                                whom
                                                                that

Here is another example:

EXAMPLE 9 ➤   The manager approves of the new cashier   who   you hired.
                                                                   whom
                                                                   that

In Examples 8 and 9, the applicant and the new cashier aren't named, so *that* can be used as the relative connector. *That* and *who* are considered to be less formal than *whom*.

IV. Use *whose* to show that the noun you are referring to possesses a quality, person, or thing.

EXAMPLE 10 ➤   The curator complimented the artist whose sculptures he admired most.

We usually use another noun with *whose,* like *whose sculptures* in Example 10, to make the meaning clear.

> **V. Use *where* to give more information about a place, and *when* to give more information about a time.**

S   V   *Rel*   S   V

EXAMPLE 11 ➤   I saw the place where the treaty was signed.

Where and *when* can be either Group B words or relative connectors, depending on how they are used. When either *where* or *when* follows a noun and gives more information that relates to that noun, it is a relative connector.

S   V   *Rel* S   V

EXAMPLE 12 ➤   I will never forget the day when I first met my sweetheart.

The words *who, whom, that, which, whose, where,* and *when* can all be used with this pattern: *SV   Rel   SV.*

Variation of Pattern 1

The relative pronouns *who, which, whose,* and *that* can be used in a variation of Pattern 1. These words can function as the subject of the relative clause as well as being the connector. Here are some examples:

S   V   *Rel = S*   V

EXAMPLE 1 ➤   I try to wear the colors   that   look good on me.

S   V   *Rel = S*   V

EXAMPLE 2 ➤   Boris Yeltsin led the government   that   replaced Gorbachev.

S   V   *Rel = S*   V

EXAMPLE 3 ➤   The contest judges chose the student *whose photograph* was the best.

Whose is not usually used alone; instead, it is often used with a noun or noun phrase, like *whose photograph* in Example 3. As in all of the sentence structure sections, the important thing is to identify the two clauses and the connector to see if they form a complete and accurate sentence.

Pattern 2:

Relative connectors can also be used in another very different pattern. Look at the following example:

S   *Rel*   S   V   V

EXAMPLE 1 ➤   The class *that you recommended* taught me a lot.

The main clause is: *The class taught me a lot*. The relative clause is: *that you recommended*. It gives more information about the word *class* by answering the question, "Which class?" Remember that relative clauses must follow the word they refer to. When that word is the subject of the first clause, the relative clause is placed in the middle of the first clause, between the subject and the verb. The pattern looks like this:

<u>S</u>   Rel   S   V   <u>V.</u>

Here are some more examples of this pattern:

EXAMPLE 2 ➤
                 S   *Rel*   *S* *V*
The University of Arizona, where Frank plans to attend
              V
graduate school, is a well-known research center.

EXAMPLE 3 ➤
         S   *Rel* *S* *V*   *V*
Mexico City, which I visited in 1992, is the largest city in the world.

Variation of Pattern 2

With Pattern 2, just like with Pattern 1, the relative pronouns *who*, *which*, *that*, and rarely *whose* may also function as the subject of the relative clause. Here are some examples:

EXAMPLE 1 ➤
          S   *Rel = S* *V*
The Bedouin Arabs, who united against the Turkish Empire,
       V
invaded Damascus.

The main clause is *The Bedouin Arabs invaded Damascus*. The relative clause is *who united against the Turkish Empire,* which gives additional information about the Bedouin Arabs. In this pattern, the relative pronoun *who* is the subject of the relative clause as well as being the word that connects the two clauses. Only the words *who, which, whose,* and *that* can be used with this pattern.

EXAMPLE 2 ➤
        S *Rel = S* *V*   *V*
The tree   that   had been burned by lightning was a
          which
well-known landmark.

EXAMPLE 3 ➤
        S *Rel = S*   *V*   *V*
The frame   which   best suited the painting was worth the extra money.

Sometimes the subject of the relative clause is a noun used with *whose*. The following example shows this construction.

$$\underline{S} \quad\quad Rel = S \quad\quad V \quad\quad\quad\quad\quad\quad\quad\quad \underline{V}$$

EXAMPLE 4 ➤ Marco, *whose family* owned a jet-ski rental shop, could swim extremely well.

The following class practice will help you learn more about relative clauses and how they are used.

■ **CLASS PRACTICE** **1**

Recognizing Relative Clauses

Directions: Some of the following sentences contain a relative clause, some have a Group A or Group B connector, and some are simple sentences. Mark each subject and verb with *S* and *V* and circle the connector if there is one. Write RELATIVE, GROUP A, GROUP B, or SIMPLE in the blank.

_____ 1. Lydia picked some homegrown tomatoes for the man who sells vegetables at the Swap Meet.

_____ 2. I will always remember the rocky outcropping where you proposed to me.

_____ 3. The high dive looked safe, yet I couldn't make myself jump.

_____ 4. The king whose laws are just will be remembered for many centuries.

_____ 5. Tony tried to avoid the burly construction worker whom he had insulted.

_____ 6. Larry worked in real estate for three years before he switched careers.

_____ 7. Giraffes, which seem slow and graceful, can actually run 30 miles per hour.

_____ 8. The business department is offering a popular new International Business Certificate.

_____ 9. We stayed with some Hopi Indians who still live in an ancient adobe pueblo.

_____ 10. Someone crashed into my newly painted Toyota pickup, which I had just picked up from the automobile dealer.

Another Variation of Patterns 1 and 2

In certain cases we can omit the relative connector entirely if the meaning of the sentence is clear without it. Here is one of the first examples that we looked at, which can be written without the relative connector as well as with it:

EXAMPLE 1 ➤ Matilda works at the electronics factory *that* her uncle owns.

Or:

Matilda works at the electronics factory her uncle owns.

Even though we don't see the connector, we understand it to be the relative connector, *that,* which has been omitted from the sentence. This works only if the meaning of the sentence is clear without the relative connector. Here are some more examples where the relative connector can be omitted:

EXAMPLE 2 ➤ The manager approves of the new cashier   who   you hired.
                                             whom
                                             that

Or:

The manager approves of the new cashier you hired.

EXAMPLE 3 ➤ You should use the prewriting technique   which   you like best.
                                             that

Or:

You should use the prewriting technique you like best.

EXAMPLE 4 ➤ I will never forget the day when I first met my sweetheart.

Or:

I will never forget the day I first met my sweetheart.

Omitting a relative connector, especially the relative pronoun *that,* is often done in conversation and casual writing. For most formal academic writing, however, it is usually a good idea to include the relative connector. Otherwise, your sentence may seem unfinished or unclear.

Punctuation of Relative Clauses

Sometimes relative clauses have commas around them, and sometimes they don't. Here are some example sentences from earlier in this chapter. In the first one no commas are used, but in the second example there are commas around the relative clause.

EXAMPLE 1 ➤   The waves *that crash on the beach* are called breakers.

EXAMPLE 2 ➤   Juan, *who plays football at Southwestern College,* works out every day.

When are commas necessary? Sometimes the information contained in a relative clause is absolutely essential in order to identify the word it refers to, but sometimes it's not necessary. If it's necessary to identify the word it refers to, use commas. When it's not necessary for identification, don't use commas.

Some books refer to a necessary relative clause as a *restrictive* or *essential* relative clause. In Example 1, the relative clause *that crash on the beach* is essential because without it the sentence would be unclear. *The waves are called breakers* doesn't make sense because not all waves are called breakers, and the reader doesn't know which waves the writer means.

A relative clause that contains interesting or useful information but isn't necessary to identify the word it refers to is known as a *nonrestrictive* or *nonessential* relative clause. In Example 2 above, the relative clause isn't necessary to identify *Juan* because he is already identified by name. This sentence still makes sense without the relative clause: *Juan works out every day*. The information in the relative clause, *who plays football at Southwestern College,* is interesting, but it is not essential to identify who Juan is. Commas are used to show that the information is *nonessential*.

It is especially important not to use the relative pronoun *that* in nonessential clauses. *That* is used only in essential clauses and never with commas.

Here are some more examples of essential and nonessential relative clauses:

EXAMPLE 3 ➤   Sallie, who had worked as the program coordinator for many years, was looking forward to her retirement.

In this example commas are used with the relative clause because Sallie is already identified. The information about Sallie in the relative clause is important, but it is *not essential* to identify Sallie because she is already identified by name.

EXAMPLE 4 ➤   The woman who had worked as the program coordinator for many years was looking forward to her retirement.

In Example 4, commas are not used around the relative clause because the information it contains is absolutely *essential* to identify which woman the writer is talking about.

EXAMPLE 5 ➤   The Americas Cup races were held off the peninsula which separates San Diego Bay from the Ocean.

In this case the relative clause is necessary to explain which peninsula is meant, so no comma is used. It is an *essential* relative clause.

EXAMPLE 6 ➤ The Americas Cup races were held off Point Loma, which separates San Diego Bay from the Pacific Ocean.

In Example 6, the reader already knows which peninsula it is (Point Loma), so the information in the relative clause is not necessary to identify it. This is a *nonessential* relative clause, so you need to use a comma.

Keeping the following points in mind will help you know whether or not to use commas to set off the relative clause. First of all, ask yourself if the relative clause is needed in order to identify which person, place, thing, or idea it refers to. For example, if what it refers to is already identified by name, then the relative clause is *not essential* for identification, so use commas. But if the relative clause is *essential* to identify the noun it follows, don't use commas.

■ **CLASS PRACTICE** **2** ## Punctuation and Meaning of Relative Clauses

Directions: Mark the relative connectors and underline the relative clauses. If the relative clause is *essential* to identify the word it refers to, write *correct*. If it is *not essential* to identify the word it refers to, add a comma before and after the relative clause.

EXAMPLE ➤ Mr. Ybarra and Mrs. Fenton who were both small business owners competed for the same customers.

In this sentence Mr. Ybarra and Mrs. Fenton are identified by name, so the relative clause isn't necessary to identify who they are. Therefore, commas are necessary. Write them in before and after the relative clause.

Rel
CORRECTED EXAMPLE ➤ Mr. Ybarra and Mrs. Fenton, *who were both small business owners,* competed for the same customers.

1. Houses that were built before 1950 often do not meet modern earthquake safety standards.

2. Los Cabos which is a beautiful Baja California vacation area offers everything from fancy resorts and nightclubs to shoestring-budget camping on the beach.

3. We celebrated Thanksgiving with some friends whom we have known for years.

4. Our primary care physician is Dr. Krenz whom I first saw 20 years ago.

5. The meeting had been scheduled for late December when everybody would be gone for the holidays.

6. Allyn and Bacon which publishes a full line of English textbooks is also starting to look at the ESL market.

7. As an adult, I revisited the small town where I had grown up.

8. Subliminal advertising is a means of persuasion that tries to communicate directly with the subconscious mind.

9. Malibu where many famous Hollywood personalities live is subject to mudslides and road closures every time it rains.

10. The neighbor whose pig keeps getting into our trash refuses to take responsibility.

Building Sentences with Relative Clauses

By using relative clauses, you can combine some of your shorter sentences to give your writing more variety. When you use relative clauses, it is important to place them correctly so that the meaning will be clear. Remember that a relative clause has to follow the noun that it relates to.

Here are two simple sentences that can be combined by changing the second one to a relative clause:

EXAMPLE 1 A ➤ *(simple sentences):* In the 1940's families used to gather around the radio. The radio was often their main source of entertainment.

These two sentences can easily be combined by using the relative pronoun *which* in place of subject of the second sentence, *the radio*.

EXAMPLE 1 B ➤ *(relative clause):* In the 1940's, families used to gather around the radio, *which* was often their main source of entertainment.

How could you combine the following two simple sentences?

EXAMPLE 2 A ➤ *(simple sentences):* A brush fire threatened homes on the rim of the canyon. It was started by sparks from a motorcycle.

There is more than one way to combine these two sentences with a relative clause. One way is to replace the pronoun *it* in the second sentence with a relative pronoun. Then make sure the relative clause follows the noun it refers to. Since the relative clause gives information about the brushfire, it should come immediately after brush fire.

EXAMPLE 2B ➤ A <u>brush fire</u> *that was started by sparks from a motorcycle* threatened homes on the rim of the canyon.

Another option is to make part of the first sentence into a relative clause, like this:

EXAMPLE 2C ➤ A brush fire *that threatened homes on the rim of the canyon* was started by sparks from a motorcycle.

In the exercise that follows, you will practice combining two simple sentences by adding an appropriate relative connector after one of the nouns in each sentence and creating a relative clause.

■ **CLASS**
PRACTICE **3**

Building Sentences with Relative Clauses

Directions: Combine the two simple sentences with a relative connector to make one complete sentence that includes a relative clause. Use *who, that, which, whom, where, when,* or *whose,* whichever is correct.

1. The viola player received a standing ovation. She is visiting from Taiwan.

   _____

   _____

2. I bought a new bicycle at Performance Bicycles of Baltimore. It is part of a national chain of stores.

   _____

   _____

3. Spanish ranchers used to water their cattle in Spring Valley. It was called "El Aguaje de San Jorge" (St. George's Spring).

   _____

   _____

4. We want to buy a house in a peaceful neighborhood. The people are friendly and outgoing.

   _____

   _____

5. I have a friend named Carlos. His uncle owns a rancho near Tecate, Mexico.

_____

_____

6. Some comic books are now selling for thousands of dollars. They cost 12¢ in 1965.

_____

_____

7. Mariana and Sylvia finished the work. Someone else had started the work.

_____

_____

■ **CLASS PRACTICE** **4** ## Using Relative Clauses to Give Additional Information

Directions: Add an appropriate relative clause to give additional information about one of the nouns in the main clause. Try to use each of the patterns more than once.

EXAMPLE ➤ We visited an ancient temple.

We visited an ancient temple which had been buried for centuries.

1. The divers encountered a long-forgotten underwater cave.

_____

_____

2. My sister likes the mixed bouquet of pink roses and white carnations.

_____

_____

3. Several angry parents came to the school board meeting.

_____

_____

4. Tim is trying to choose a university.

_____

_____

5. Sarah went rock-climbing in Joshua Tree National Monument.

_____

_____

6. The weekend racquetball group decided to buy new racquets.

_____

_____

■ **CLASS PRACTICE** **5** | ## Writing Original Sentences with Relative Clauses

Directions: Now write your own relative clause sentences. Use a different *relative connector* in each sentence. Use each pattern at least once:

SV Rel SV   and   <u>**S**</u> Rel SV <u>**V**</u> .

Remember that sometimes a relative pronoun can be the subject of the relative clause.

1. (use *who*) _____

_____

2. (use *whom*) _____

_____

3. (use *whose*) _____

_____

4. (use *which*) _____

_____

5. (use *that*) _____

_____

6. (use *where**)_____

_____

7. (use *when†*) _____

_____

Check your sentences yourself or with your workshop group to make sure that each sentence has two SVs joined by a relative connector. Also check to see that the relative clause is correctly placed after the noun that it relates to.

Learning to Avoid Common Errors with Relative Clauses

One common error with relative clauses is writing a relative clause as a sentence by itself. When you use a relative clause, you must always have at least two SVs in the sentence. Look at the following example where a relative clause has been incorrectly written as a complete sentence:

INCORRECT EXAMPLE 1 ➤   Randy picked the beets. *That the previous owners of his new house had planted.*

When you have a relative connector in a group of words with only one SV, it is an error. This sentence error is a *fragment* because it contains only part of a complete sentence. The corrected sentence is below:

CORRECTED EXAMPLE 1 ➤   Randy picked the beets that the previous owners of his new house had planted.

---

*After the *place* it refers to.

†After the *time* it refers to.

                                    Rel = S   V
INCORRECT EXAMPLE 2 ➤   The train *that   was called the Orient Express.*

This is another fragment error. There is a relative connector with only one subject and verb, and to fix it you need to add another SV. You can use *train* as the subject of the main clause and add a verb after the relative clause. Now you will have a correct Pattern 2 sentence:

CORRECTED EXAMPLE 2 ➤   The train that was called the Orient Express carried passengers through the Swiss Alps.

Another common error is using the wrong relative connector. It is especially easy to confuse *who* with *whom*, and *that* with *which*.

INCORRECT EXAMPLE 3 ➤   Pastor Brindisi, whom has twelve children, has a big house.

In this sentence *whom* is incorrect because *whom* cannot be used as the subject of a relative clause.

CORRECTED EXAMPLE 3 ➤   Pastor Brindisi, who has twelve children, has a big house.

INCORRECT EXAMPLE 4 ➤   Bicycling that I enjoy very much has increased my cardiovascular fitness.

In this sentence the relative clause isn't essential to identify the sport, bicycling, because it is already named, so you must use *which* instead of *that*, and commas.

CORRECTED EXAMPLE 4 ➤   Bicycling, which I enjoy very much, has increased my cardiovascular fitness.

The third common error with relative connectors is putting them in the wrong place in the sentence. Remember that the relative clause should follow the noun that it describes or refers to. Look at the following sentence:

INCORRECT EXAMPLE 5 ➤   A student has a better chance of finding a job who learns to use computers.

Who will learn to use computers—the student or the job? The sentence should be written like this:

CORRECTED EXAMPLE 5 ➤   A student who learns to use computers has a better chance of finding a job.

The relative clause *who learns to use computers* clarifies the meaning of the subject *student*, so it should be placed immediately after *student*.

The following exercise will give you practice recognizing and correcting all of these types of errors.

■ **CLASS**
PRACTICE **6**

Correcting Common Errors
with Relative Clauses

Directions: If the sentence is correct, write CORRECT on the line. If there is a fragment, an incorrect relative connector, or a comma error, rewrite the sentence to make it complete and correct.

EXAMPLE ➤   Pirates of the Caribbean, which is one of the most popular attractions at Disneyland.

Pirates of the Caribbean, which is one of the most popular

attractions at Disneyland, had a long line.

1. The soldiers cut the ropes that they had used to climb up into the cave.

   _____

2. Henry didn't tell me whose car.

   _____

3. I watched Sarah, whom was playing outside in the snow.

   _____

4. Matar whose name means "rain" lived in the dry desert country of Saudi Arabia.

   _____

5. Many people were stopped at the traffic light, who was stuck on red.

   _____

6. New Orleans, that is a popular tourist destination, has a wonderful mix of cultures.

   _____

7. Quentin interviewed the politician whom we had met at the airport.

   _____

8. The 6:00 ferry, which was the last ferry off the island.

_____

9. I read an article that dealt with spies and technology secrets, and then I went to the park.

_____

10. The gemologist appraised the stones. Which were really very beautiful.

_____

■ **CLASS PRACTICE** **7**

Proofreading for Common Errors with Relative Clauses

Directions: Correct all of the fragments and relative connector errors in the following paragraph. Most of the fragments involve relative clauses, although a few other types of fragments that you have studied previously are also included for review. (You may want to review fragments in Chapter 3.)

Waiting for the Future

I waited for my appointment in a small room that smelled of incense. The soft, harmonious music that was playing. Made me start to relax. I was nervous because I had never been to a tarot card reader before. However, I wanted to know. What the future would be. The straight chair who I was sitting on. Felt hard and uncomfortable. The minutes went by slowly. Finally a woman called my name who appeared in the doorway . She led me to another room. Which was about the size of a closet. To my surprise, she looked like an ordinary person which you might meet anywhere. There was nothing in the room. Except a tiny square table, two folding chairs, and a floor lamp. Which was as old as my grandmother. As I sat down, she began to shuffle the cards who would foretell my future. I am still waiting to find out if what she saw in the cards will really happen.

■ **CLASS**
PRACTICE

Writing with Sentences that Have Relative Clauses

PART A: Looking at Writing from an Example Paper

Directions: Look at the sentences in Estel Manito-Stokholm's paper, *The Nepa Hut* (from pages 168–169). Highlight or underline the sentences that use relative connectors. Notice that the author used several sentences of this type as well as other types of sentences.

The Nepa Hut

I vividly remember the nepa hut that my two brothers, grandfather, and I lived in with a mixture of contentment and despair in a small village in the Philippines. It was a very small one-room hut built in the corner of one acre of land with a roof made of cross-linked nepa leaves. (A nepa leaf is wider than a coconut leaf.) The wall and floor consisted of bamboo stems which had been cut in half and polished with a knife. Inside the nepa hut were a few things necessary for survival. In the corner on the west side lay neatly folded mats and blankets. In the east corner were a few iron plates and drinking glasses made of bamboo. On the north side of the room was the stove, which consisted of three medium size stones stuck in the dirt in a triangle-like arrangement. Next to it was a stack of firewood used for cooking. Pots, pans, and a lantern fueled with petroleum were also located around this area. In the backyard was a garden planted with different kinds of filipino vegetables varying in color—green, yellow, purple, etc. As I looked around outside the nepa hut, I could see acres and acres of rice fields with rice plants sprouting. I could also smell the clear, fresh air that was unpolluted with automobile fumes and other city pollutants. As I look back now at that meager existence, I can still feel the contentment and despair: contentment because it was a very simple way of living, despair because it was deprived of luxuries that people who had more money could afford.

PART B: Looking at Your Own Writing

Directions Find one or two sentences with relative clauses from your own *Description* rough draft and write them in the blanks below. If you don't have any relative clauses, you will probably want to add one or more for greater variety. Write your new sentences that have relative clauses in the blanks below.

1. _____

   _____

   _____

2. _____

   _____

   _____

3. _____

   _____

   _____

Now check your sentences by marking the subjects and verbs in each sentence and circling the relative connectors.

Description Sentence Combining Paragraph

Directions: Some of the sentences can be combined effectively by using a relative connector. Other combinations use sentence patterns that you have studied in previous chapters.

The Wrong Hotel

1.1   We made a mistake.
1.2   We went to a low-priced hotel.
1.3   The hotel had been recommended by a friend.

2.1   The desk clerk greeted us.
2.2   He looked as if he had slept in his clothes.
2.3   He took us to our room.

3.1 The room was dimly lighted.
3.2 It was lighted by one bulb.
3.3 The bulb was bare.

4.1 The carpet was old.
4.2 The carpet was worn.
4.3 It had been walked on by many feet.

5.1 The walls were gray.
5.2 The walls had streaks.
5.3 The streaks had been made by unknown substances.

6.1 There was an odor.
6.2 The odor was musty.
6.3 The odor was throughout the room.

7.1 My roommate tried to open the windows.
7.2 She wanted to get some fresh air.
7.3 The windows were stuck shut.

8.1 The bed had a mattress.
8.2 The mattress was lumpy.
8.3 The mattress sagged in the middle.

9.1 Cockroaches lived in the bathroom.
9.2 The cockroaches were a family.
9.3 The cockroaches were huge.

10.1 I started to brush my teeth.
10.2 Cockroaches crawled out of the drain.
10.3 The cockroaches had been waiting for me.

11.1 We tried to sleep.
11.2 We heard sounds all night.
11.3 The sounds were strange.

12.1 Early in the morning we left.
12.2 We left quickly.
12.3 We left before breakfast.

13.1 We found a hotel room.
13.2 The room was clean.
13.3 The room was comfortable.
13.4 The room had no insect inhabitants.

Learning about -ing Words and Phrases

Interesting descriptive details can help make your writing more effective. One way to add descriptive details is by using -*ing* words as adjectives. They can be used alone or as part of a phrase to give additional information about people, places, things, or ideas. Several of the example paragraphs in this chapter used *-ing* words as adjectives to add interesting details. Here are some of the *-ing* words that the writers used in their descriptions:

fishing boats	*exciting* section in the ocean
invigorating smell	*sagging* brown recliner
ever-*changing* view	*running* water
hiking trails	*depressing* apartment
warming sunlight	*hanging* baskets
winding country roads	high-*ranking* officers

The *-ing* words in these examples add important information about the nouns they describe. They help to give us a clearer picture of what the writer is talking about. For example, the word *boats* could mean any kind of boat, from rowboats to submarines, but *fishing* boats tells us more specifically what the writer means. *Trails* could be trails for 4-wheel drive vehicles, joggers, or horses if the writer hadn't said *hiking* trails. As you can see, *-ing* words are often used the same way that regular adjectives are used—to describe nouns.

You can create an *-ing* adjective from almost any verb just by adding *-ing* to the simple form of the verb, like these examples:

fish + *-ing* = *fishing*
hang + *-ing* = *hanging*
depress + *-ing* = *depressing*

The official name for *-ing* forms created in this way is *present participles*.

There are two important spelling variations for present participles, which are similar to the spelling rules that you learned in Chapter 2 for adding -ed endings to verbs.

1. **The silent -e rule:** If the simple form of the verb ends with the letter -e, omit the -e before adding *-ing*:

   hike (-e) + *-ing* = *hiking*

   change (-e) + *-ing* = *changing*

   excite (-e) + *-ing* = *exciting*

2. **The double-consonant rule:** If a one-syllable verb ends with a single consonant preceded by a single vowel, like *run*, or *sag*, the final consonant must be doubled before adding *-ing*:

   run + n + *-ing* = *running*

   sag + g + *-ing* = *sagging*

   drip + p + *-ing* = *dripping*

If a two- or more syllable verb ends with a single consonant preceded by a single vowel, double the final consonant only if the stress is on the last syllable:

refer + r + *-ing* = *referring*

but   travel + -ing = traveling

Verbs ending in -w, -x, or -y are an exception to this rule. For these verbs, just add *-ing*: *relax* + ing = relaxing, *play* + ing = playing, *snow* + ing = snowing, and so on. (For more complete spelling guidelines, see Appendix IV on page 456.)

Generally, *-ing* adjectives are used the same way as other adjectives. They can add information about any noun (person, place, thing, or idea) in a sentence. In most cases, the *-ing* word comes before the noun that it describes. Which word (or words) in each of the following sentences does the *-ing* word describe?

EXAMPLE 1 ➤ We jumped off the dock into the cool, *refreshing* water.

EXAMPLE 2 ➤ The *smiling* Cheshire cat is a favorite character in *Alice in Wonderland*.

In the first sentence, *refreshing* adds an interesting detail about the *water*. In the second sentence, *smiling* describes the *Cheshire cat*. Sometimes an *-ing* word describes the subject, as it does in the second example, and sometimes an *-ing* word is used to describe another noun in the sentence.

Now try to think of some appropriate *-ing* words to use as adjectives in these sentences:

EXAMPLE 3 ➤ In the middle of class, the _____ sound of an alarm startled us.

EXAMPLE 4 ➤ The wild animal show at the zoo features a _____ elephant.

How did you describe the sound of the alarm in Example 3? Some possibilities are *buzzing, screeching*, or *deafening*. The elephant in Example 4 might be described with the words *dancing, performing, trumpeting* or any other *-ing* adjective that could apply to an elephant. You may want to compare your answers with those of other classmates.

Although *-ing* words used as adjectives are usually placed before the noun that they describe, as in the previous examples, occasionally they are also used in other places. For example, *-ing* adjectives sometimes appear after linking verbs, just as regular adjectives do:

S   *V*

EXAMPLE 5 ➤ For people who are visual learners, lectures sometimes seem *boring*.

In this sentence, the *-ing* adjective *boring* comes after the linking verb *seem* and describes *lectures*.

Using -ing Words as Adjectives

Directions: Fill in each blank with an appropriate *-ing* word that will make the sentence more interesting.

EXAMPLE ➤ The crowd screamed as the charging bull headed straight toward the matador.

1. The accident was caused by a _____ motorcycle.

2. If you see a _____ star, remember to make a wish.

3. The _____ lights of the police car illuminated the park.

4. Millions of viewers watched the _____ murder trial on television.

5. Janine and Jeff thought that the music festival was _____.

6. _____ snow made it difficult to see the road ahead of us.

7. When we drove through the area right after the fire, we could see _____ trees not far from the road.

8. Now check the rough draft of your description to see if you have used any *-ing* words as adjectives. If you have, copy one of your sentences that uses an *-ing* adjective below. If you don't have any, find a sentence where you may want to add one.

_____

_____

Using -ing Adjective Phrases

Sometimes an *-ing* adjective does not act alone to describe something. Instead, it may be the first word of a descriptive phrase. The entire phrase is used to add details about someone or something, so it is called an *-ing* adjective phrase.

Adjective phrases that begin with *-ing* words are often used at the beginning of a sentence, followed by a comma. In this position, the *-ing* phrase describes or gives information about the first person or thing that is named after the *-ing* phrase, which is almost always the subject of the sentence. Here are some examples from *Horsethief Canyon:*

*   S   V*

EXAMPLE 1 ➤ *Walking down the trail*, we smell the dust as it's kicked up by our boots.

*   S   V*

EXAMPLE 2 ➤ *Facing west*, we can see the golden light that sunset produces and the vivid clouds in shades of pink and gold.

In both of these sentences, the *-ing* adjective phrase applies to the subject *we*. Although the *-ing* words *walking* and *facing* refer to something that the subject is doing, they are considered adjectives rather than verbs. They actually describe a situation or condition that applies to the subject at the time the main clause takes place. *Walking down the trail* is the situation that we must be in if we want to smell the dust, and *facing west* is a necessary condition in order to see the sunset. Here are two more examples:

*   S V*

EXAMPLE 3 ➤ *Seeing her friend fall out of the boat*, Eva threw him a life preserver.

*   S V*

EXAMPLE 4 ➤ *Pretending to be interested*, Mindy smiled.

Notice that the main clause of each sentence expresses the main action: Eva threw a life preserver and Mindy smiled. The *-ing* adjective phrases at the beginning describe a situation or condition that is related to the main action. Seeing her friend fall was a necessary condition for Eva to throw the life preserver, and pretending to be interested was the condition that caused Mindy to smile.

Now use your imagination to complete the *-ing* phrase at the beginning of this sentence:

Hoping _____ , Leo bought a lottery ticket.

What was Leo hoping? What condition can you think of that would relate to buying a lottery ticket? You might use *hoping to win a million dollars, hoping to get lucky, hoping to get rich quick*, or something similar.

Let's try another sentence. This time you will need to think of your own *-ing* word to use at the beginning of the adjective phrase.

_____ , Roy started to drive faster.

What made Roy start to drive faster? What situation or condition affected his driving? Was it *noticing the time, wanting to get there before dark, hearing a police siren*, or something else? You may want to share your answers with your classmates or have your teacher check your *-ing* phrase to make sure that it is correctly written.

Another position where -*ing* adjective phrases can be placed is after a noun. They may follow the subject, or they may be used to describe another noun in the middle or at the end of a sentence. In this type of construction, the -*ing* phrase usually comes immediately after the noun that it describes. Which noun does the -*ing* phrase describe in each of these sentences?

EXAMPLE 5 ➤   The Marines *spending Christmas Eve at the Oasis* probably missed their families. (from Danny Banda's *Christmas Eve in Saudi Arabia*, page 166)

EXAMPLE 6 ➤   To our surprise, we saw a duck *swimming in the pool*.

The phrase *spending Christmas Eve at the Oasis* identifies which Marines the writer was talking about, so it describes *Marines,* and of course *swimming in the pool* describes the duck.

Now try adding an -*ing* phrase to identify or describe the man in the following sentence:

Everyone was watching the man _____ .

How did you imagine him—*standing on the roof, swimming toward the submarine, wearing gold tights?* Any of these conditions could make people watch him. You may enjoy comparing your answer with phrases written by some of your classmates.

Occasionally an -*ing* phrase that describes the subject may also be used at the end of a sentence, like this example:

EXAMPLE 7 ➤   The big cat circled slowly, *waiting for the right moment to pounce.*

Even though the -*ing* phrase in Example 7 does not come immediately before or after "the big cat," it is clear that it describes the cat because there are no other nouns that it could describe.

Although these are not the only ways to use -*ing* adjective phrases, they will give you a basic understanding of how adjective phrases work. Knowing how to use an -*ing* adjective phrase following a noun, at the beginning of a sentence, or at the end of a sentence can help you add variety to your writing.

■ **CLASS PRACTICE** **10**

Using -ing Adjective Phrases

Directions: Fill in each blank with an appropriate -*ing* adjective phrase that will make the sentence more interesting.

EXAMPLE ➤   If you stand very still, you may see a golden eagle

__*landing on its nest*__ .
-ing phrase

1. _____ , Fred enrolled in a computer class at
    -ing phrase

   the community college.

2. We all listened to Irene and Roger _____ .
                                       -ing phrase

3. _____ , we took shelter from the storm in
    -ing phrase

   an old barn.

4. Passengers on the Alaskan cruise ship stood at the rail and watched the

   iceberg _____ .
            -ing phrase

5. _____ , you can see the fireworks over the water.
    -ing phrase

6. The forest fire was started by someone _____ .
                                            -ing phrase

7. Now check the rough draft of your description to see if you have used any *-ing* adjective phrases. If you have, copy one of your sentences that uses an *-ing* adjective phrase below. If you don't have any, find a sentence where you may want to add one.

   _____

   _____

Placing -ing Phrases Correctly

When you are using *-ing* phrases to describe someone or something, it is extremely important to place them correctly in your sentence. If they are not in the right place, they may seem to describe the wrong word, which can result in a confusing or even humorous sentence like this one:

> ***Incorrect:*** Chuck saw a big snake riding his bicycle the other day.

Who is riding the bicycle, Chuck or the snake? In order to correct this sentence, we need to move the *-ing* phrase so that it clearly applies to Chuck.

> ***Correct:*** Riding his bicycle the other day, Chuck saw a big snake.

In this case, the *-ing* phrase works well at the beginning of the sentence because it applies to the person who is named immediately afterward, Chuck.

If an *-ing* phrase at the beginning of a sentence does not apply to the following noun, however, it is an error. Here is an example:

> ***Incorrect:*** Echoing across the canyon, we heard our voices.

Are *we* echoing? Or are our *voices* echoing? In this example, the *-ing* phrase is not correctly placed at the beginning because it should be describing the word *voices*. To correct the problem, move the *-ing* phrase so that it comes after the word *voices*, like this:

> ***Correct:*** We heard our voices echoing across the canyon.

Now check the sentences below, and write OK by the one that has the *-ing* phrase in the correct place.

_____ **1.** Joy tried on the water skis wearing her new bikini.

_____ **2.** Wearing her new bikini, Joy tried on the water skis.

Did you choose the second sentence, which has the *-ing* phrase placed correctly to describe Joy? If you chose the first sentence, think about it again. Someone reading Sentence 1 might picture the water skis wearing the bikini.

Now try the next two sentences. Again, mark OK by the one that is correct.

_____ **3.** Spinning a web on the deck, I noticed a large spider.

_____ **4.** I noticed a large spider spinning a web on the deck.

Did you choose the sentence where the *spider,* not the person, is spinning a web? Sentence 4 is the correct choice.

In order to place these kinds of *-ing* adjective phrases correctly, you need to figure out which noun the phrase should describe, and then place the *-ing* phrase immediately after the appropriate noun or immediately before it at the beginning of the sentence.

■ **CLASS PRACTICE** **11**

Proofreading for Misplaced -ing Phrases

Directions: Some of the *-ing* phrases are misplaced and need to be moved to an appropriate location. Draw a circle around the misplaced phrases and use an arrow to show where they should be moved.

Camp Woodland

Before the campers arrived, Camp Woodland was quiet and peaceful. I

was anxious to see the campground area, so I started to explore. I saw ground

squirrels and lizards hiking along the trails. A large crow scolded me loudly sitting in a tree. Jumping out of the water, I saw several fish and a few wild ducks swimming lazily on the surface. There were several canoes along the shore. I thought about the young campers that would soon be paddling the canoes wearing orange life vests. Blowing across the lake, I noticed that there were small ripples made by the wind. Approaching one of the cabins, I decided to go inside and look around. The beds, sleeping soundly after a day of fun and exercise, would soon hold children. These children, coming from disadvantaged homes in nearby cities, would discover unexpected pleasures that summer. For me, the experience as a camp counselor would be unforgettable.

Description Sentence Combining Paragraph

Directions: Use *-ing* phrases in some of the sentence combinations. You may also want to use a few Group B connectors (such as *when*) and relative connectors (such as *that* or *where*) to create complex sentences.

Memories

1.1 Every room in the house brought back something.
1.2 It brought back memories.
1.3 The memories were of my childhood.

2.1 In the kitchen I could smell something.
2.2 The smell was cookies.
2.3 The cookies were freshly baked.
2.4 They were chocolate chip cookies.
2.5 Another smell was chicken.
2.6 The chicken was roasting in the oven.
2.7 The chicken was for Sunday dinner.

3.1 I could picture myself as a little girl.
3.2 I was setting the table.
3.3 I did it carefully.
3.4 I set it with the best china.

4.1 In the living room I remembered my dad.
4.2 He was sitting.
4.3 He was in his favorite chair.
4.4 He was reading the newspaper.

5.1 I was little.
5.2 He let me climb onto his lap.
5.3 He read to me.
5.4 He read the comics.

6.1 I looked around the living room.
6.2 I saw the piano.
6.3 I used to play the piano.
6.4 I saw the record player.
6.5 The record player was old-fashioned.

7.1 I could hear familiar melodies.
7.2 The melodies were on records.
7.3 I listened to the records long ago.
7.4 The records were by Elvis Presley.
7.5 The records were by Pat Boone.

8.1 I entered my bedroom.
8.2 I lay down on the bed.
8.3 This bed was where I used to sleep.

9.1 I liked to stay awake at night.
9.2 I listened to the sounds of crickets.
9.3 I listened to the wind.
9.4 The wind blew through the cottonwood trees.

10.1 My mother would come into my room.
10.2 She would tuck me into my bed.
10.3 She made me feel safe.

11.1 Going back to the house makes me remember.
11.2 The memory is my childhood.
11.3 The memory is like a movie.
11.4 It is a wonderful old movie.

Putting the Finishing Touches on Your Writing

Now it's time to take another look at your rough draft and make any final revisions before you turn it in. Use the checklist on the next page to make sure that you have not forgotten anything.

Checking your sentences for completeness is an important part of editing and revising your paper. The sentence patterns that you have learned can help you make sure that the structure of your sentences is correct. Here is a list of the five main sentence patterns that you have studied and practiced in this book so far:

Simple Sentences:	SV. SV.
Compound Sentences:	SV, Group A SV.
Complex Sentences:	SV Group B SV. (or SV Rel SV.)
	Group B SV, SV.
	<u>S</u> Rel SV <u>V.</u>

Use this list to help you check your sentences and eliminate errors such as fragments, run-ons, and comma splices. These types of errors can interfere with the reader's understanding of what you are trying to say. (A more complete list of basic sentence patterns is in Appendix II on page 449.)

Also pay special attention to the sentence and grammar skills that you have studied in this chapter: using relative clauses correctly and using *-ing* words and phrases as adjectives. Both relative clauses and *-ing* adjectives can be especially useful for adding details to a description. If you have questions about whether some of your sentences are correctly written, ask your instructor for assistance.

Description Writing Checklist

Content and Organization

_____ 1. Have I created a clear and accurate picture of the place?

_____ 2. Does my paper have a clearly focused topic sentence?

_____ 3. Does everything in my paper relate to the topic sentence?

_____ 4. Is my paper clearly organized according to spatial order, group order, time order, or some other logical pattern?

_____ 5. Have I included sounds, smells, touch sensations, or tastes?

_____ 6. Do transitions smoothly and effectively connect ideas?

_____ 7. Have I ended with an effective concluding sentence?

Sentence Structure and Grammar

_____ 1. Did I use relative clauses correctly?

_____ 2. Did I use Group A and Group B connectors correctly?

_____ 3. Have I avoided run-ons, comma splices, and fragments?

_____ 4. Have I used appropriate adjectives and adverbs to add details?

_____ 5. Have I used *-ing* words or phrases effectively?

_____ 6. Did I check for spelling and grammar errors?

_____ 7. Does my writing use a variety of different sentence patterns?

ENRICHMENT SECTION:
Describing a Person

Goals

In the enrichment section of this chapter, you will learn how to do the following:

- Write a description that focuses on a person's special characteristics
- Select significant details and examples that show personality traits
- Use brief stories about a person to illustrate characteristics

Another interesting kind of description that you may want to try is a description of a person. Most of the techniques for describing a person are very similar to the techniques that you learned in this chapter for describing a place. When you are describing someone, your objective should be to explain what makes that person unique or special. Although you may include a few details of physical appearance if you want to, it is more important to emphasize personality, values, and distinctive characteristics. In order to do this, you should write about someone that you know well. It could be someone that you like, admire, and respect, or it could be someone that you dislike or resent. Your strong feelings about the person, whether they are positive or negative, will help you develop your description with vivid details and examples.

An effective description should focus on characteristics that set this person apart from others. For example, how is one special friend different from other friends that you've had? What do you admire about your aunt or your grandfather? What makes a certain teacher or supervisor memorable? Why is your cousin always in trouble with the family? Why do you think that your brother's friend will never get ahead in life? What is it about your neighbor that you find annoying?

As you develop your description, try to *show* readers what the person is like instead of just telling them. For example, if you tell us that your grandfather was always nice to you when you were a child, the word "nice" won't give us a very clear picture. Instead, you should try to *show* him being nice to you with details and examples, like this:

> When I went to visit my grandfather, he would always have my favorite cookies waiting for me—chocolate-covered graham crackers—and I was allowed to eat as many as I wanted. Sometimes we'd go for a walk along the river near his house, and he'd tell me interesting names for every wildflower that we saw, like Queen Anne's lace and Jack-in-the-pulpit. On one of our walks, he carved a whistle from a willow branch and taught me how to play a melody on it. I've wished many times that I still had that whistle to remember my grandfather by.

These details and examples *show* us a grandfather doing caring, thoughtful things that made a big impression on the child, such as giving her chocolate-covered graham crackers and carving a willow whistle. Now her grandfather begins to seem like a real individual with his own special characteristics.

It is important to create a realistic picture of the person that you are describing. Consider including flaws or weaknesses as well as the good points. After all, nobody is perfect, so a description of someone who seems too perfect will not be believable. One way to make your description seem realistic is to include an interesting story about something that the person did. Although we often think of storytelling or narration as a separate type of writing, stories can also be used effectively in description and other types of writing to illustrate a point. For example, if you want to show readers that someone is very forgetful, you could make your point by telling a few stories that illustrate the person's forgetfulness. This is how Armando Barcelon described his mother in the following paragraph. As you read *My Forgetful Mother,* think about which stories illustrate the point most effectively.

My Forgetful Mother
by Armando Barcelon

My mother is so forgetful. I still remember some of her funny and embarrassing situations. In one incident she unintentionally locked her car while the engine was still running, and our neighbor had to unlock the door. Another time she baked chicken for dinner, but she forgot to turn on the oven, so we ended up having hot dogs that night. One day she came home crying and said that her car had been stolen from Plaza Bonita. After we informed the police, my brother and I searched all over the parking lot and found that her car was parked on the other side of the mall, not where she claimed. Last month a concerned neighbor called the police and reported that he saw a burglar trying to open our window from the backyard. The police responded right away, and they found my mother still in the backyard because she had forgotten her house key. When the police called me at work, I rushed home to let my mother in and apologize to the policemen for their inconvenience. These were some of my mother's embarrassing experiences because of her forgetfulness.

Response to *My Forgetful Mother*

1. Which stories about Armando's mother do you think best illustrate her forgetfulness?

_____

_____

2. Which of these stories do you like best? Why?

_____

_____

Stories like the ones that Armando told about his mother can help to illustrate some of a person's special characteristics. They enable the reader to see the person doing something or experiencing something, which makes the description more interesting. Whenever possible, you should try to *show* readers examples rather than just telling them that the person has certain qualities.

The next description, called *Spoiled Rotten*, by Trent Parker, also includes interesting stories about the person that he is describing, his cousin Mickey. As you can guess from the title, Mickey is "spoiled rotten." After you have read some of the true stories about him, try to decide if Mickey is portrayed realistically—that is, if he seems like a real person. Because Trent's description is fairly long, he decided to divide it into five paragraphs: an introduction, three body paragraphs, and a conclusion.

Spoiled Rotten
by Trent Parker

Have you ever seen somebody who was given too much love? Sometimes people are given so much love that they take it for granted. Take my cousin Mickey, for example. He is probably one of the most spoiled kids in the United States. Mickey has had four motorcycles, including a NINJA, and he is only sixteen years old. He is a little daredevil and wrecks his bikes. Then he turns his baby blue eyes into the sad puppy dog look and wants a new bike.

Mickey knows how to con his father and his grandmother. He thanks them for his expensive toys, and then if he doesn't tear them up, he will trade them away for something else. Last year his dad bought him a Jeep, which was worth about four thousand dollars. He sold it, without even consulting his dad, for two thousand dollars and a used snowboard. His way of wheeling and dealing makes me mad because he is never going to amount to anything if he continues to get handed everything on a silver platter. He had a job once for about a month, washing dishes at a restaurant, but he said it was just too hard for him, so my uncle let him quit.

To top it off, he is also always in trouble. He's been busted for shoplifting, drugs, reckless driving, speeding, and being truant. He gets D's and F's and still gets whatever he wants. I don't have very much respect for Mickey because he never thinks of the consequences before he does something that will get him in trouble. Even if he does get caught, he knows that he can get out of it because my grandma and my uncle are usually pushovers. With that kind of attitude, I'm almost positive that he'll end up in jail by the time he's eighteen years old.

When Mickey had barely turned sixteen, he was promised a vehicle worth up to ten thousand dollars. He received a Toyota 4×4 and was happy until he found out that it cost only about eight thousand dollars. He had the nerve to ask his father for the other two thousand dollars. Surprisingly, his dad refused. So within a week, Mickey rolled his truck in the hills and totaled it. It is unbelievable that a kid could be so unappreciative.

Mickey is spoiled with love and material goods but is just a little troublemaker who doesn't deserve anything that he receives. Hopefully he'll graduate from high school sometime in the future and get a diploma. But the way that he has everyone trained right now, he has no ambition to try in school. If he excelled in something positive, then receiving the gifts he gets wouldn't make him such a little weasel. But he is a weasel because deep down inside I know that he knows that he doesn't deserve them. If I had three wishes, one of them would be to have my uncle become stern and demand respect and to have Mickey straighten up and learn to give that respect.

Response to *Spoiled Rotten*

1. Which stories about Mickey do you think are the best examples of his being spoiled rotten?

_____

_____

2. If you could choose only a few words or phrases to describe Mickey's main characteristics, what would you say about him? List at least three words or phrases, but no more than six.

_____   _____

_____   _____

_____   _____

3. Which sentence in the introduction do you think is the topic sentence for this description?

_____

_____

The first step in writing your own description of a person is selecting someone interesting to write about. Here are a few suggestions to consider:

1. A unique individual from your past
2. Someone that you admire or envy
3. Someone who has had a significant impact on your life
4. Someone you can't stand
5. Someone you know who did something unfair or unethical
6. Anyone who is special to you for some reason

After you have decided on a person to write about, figure out the main characteristics that you want to emphasize. What makes this person unique? What special characteristics does he or she have? Think about faults or weaknesses that you might want to include, as well as qualities that you like. List your ideas here:

_____   _____

_____   _____

_____   _____

Now choose the characteristics from this list that you think are the most significant and use them as the main idea in your topic sentence. Then, as you develop your description, be sure to add details and examples that illustrate these qualities and show what the person is really like.

Are there any interesting stories about this person that you would like to use as examples? Try to think of stories that illustrate one of the person's main characteristics, like the stories that showed Armando's mother being forgetful or Trent's cousin acting spoiled. Write some of your story ideas here:

1. _____

2. _____

3. _____

Try to include at least one of these stories in your description. Tell the story briefly, in just a few sentences, but make it sound interesting.

At the end of your description, remember to write a conclusion that ties everything together and makes it seem complete.

Writing That Explains Similarities and Differences

SECTION ONE:
The Writing Process for Comparison/Contrast

Goals

In this section of the chapter, you will learn how to do the following:

- Analyze similarities and differences
- Discover details by dividing and listing
- Organize a comparison/contrast using the Block Method
- Organize a comparison/contrast using the Point-by-Point Method
- Plan and write a comparison/contrast paragraph or short paper
- Write an effective introduction and conclusion for a comparison/contrast
- Use appropriate transitions to show similarities and differences

Learning about Comparison/Contrast

What Is Comparison/Contrast?

Sometimes people use the word *comparison* to include both similarities and differences, especially in conversation. However, in this book we will use the word *comparison* to mean explaining similarities and the word *contrast* to mean explaining differences. Writing that explains both similarities and differences is called *comparison/contrast*. Comparison and contrast are generally combined because considering one without the other can give an incomplete picture.

Looking for similarities and differences is a very natural way of thinking. We use this kind of thinking often, especially when we have to choose between two alternatives. For example, suppose you are trying to decide between two different part-time jobs. Before you decide which job to take, you would consider several factors: Which job pays more? Does one of the jobs have better hours or better working conditions? Which job would be more enjoyable? Does it take longer to get to one place of work than to the other? And so on. Although there may be some similarities between the two jobs, the differences are probably more important because they will help you decide which job to take. Analyzing similarities and differences in a situation like this often helps us make important decisions in our lives.

In some situations, we may also use comparison/contrast thinking to analyze more than two alternatives. You might have several job choices, for example, instead of just two. However, comparison/contrast writing usually focuses on two items. In a short paper, it would be difficult to analyze more than two items effectively.

Writing Objective: Comparing and Contrasting

Your writing objective for this chapter is to compare and contrast two people, places, things, or experiences. Most comparison/contrast papers analyze things that are somewhat similar but have significant differences, such as two friends, two movies, two musical groups, two political philosophies, two types of planes, two kinds of hiking boots, and so on. It is also possible to compare and contrast two things that appear to be very different yet have significant similarities. For example, sometimes people and their pets, although obviously very different, have been known to develop similar personalities, so a comparison/contrast of you and your golden retriever or of your sister and her Appaloosa might be very effective and interesting. However, if the two parts of your topic are not similar at all, a comparison/contrast will not work. For example, a topic like the Pacific Ocean and jazz music would be a poor choice because they are completely different, with no similarities, so there would be no point in trying to compare and contrast them.

The purpose of a comparison/contrast is to present clear, accurate information about both parts of a topic, calling attention to features that are the same or similar and features that are different. With many comparison/contrast topics, the differences are more significant than the similarities, especially if two choices or alternatives are involved. For instance, if you are comparing and contrasting a CD player and an audio tape player, differences in the quality of the sound and the price would help you decide which one you wanted to buy. With some topics, however, similarities can be just as important as differences, or perhaps even more important. For example, if you are transferring to a different college, it would be a good idea to look for one that has similar course requirements. If you do not find a college with similar requirements, you might not receive credit for some of the courses that you have already taken, and you might have to take additional courses to meet the new requirements. In order to present an accurate picture of different kinds of topics, comparison/contrast writing sometimes emphasizes similarities, sometimes differences, and sometimes both.

Although it is possible to write a comparison/contrast in one paragraph, you will probably find that you need more than one paragraph in order to include enough details about both parts of your topic. Later in the chapter, the section called "From Topic Sentence to First Draft" will show you how to develop a longer comparison/contrast paper that has four or more paragraphs. All of the example papers in this chapter are at least four paragraphs long, so you can also use them as models for organizing and developing your own paper.

Prewriting Activities

Exploring Topics for Comparison/Contrast

Your topic may be two places, people, or things that you know about through your own experience, such as two people that you know well, two places where you have lived, or two schools that you have attended. Another option is to choose two things that you would like to find out about, such as two possible careers that you are considering or two kinds of computers. If you select a topic that you want to learn more about, planning and writing your comparison/contrast will help you discover useful information. The *Exploring Topics Worksheet* that follows will help you think of some possible topics.

■ **WORKSHEET I** | ### Exploring Topics for Comparison/Contrast

Directions: Write down as many possible topics as you can think of. If you wish, you may also add a few words about their similarities or differences.

1. A choice that you made or need to make between two alternatives

2. Two significant people in your life, past or present

3. Two places where you have lived or that you have visited

4. Two schools, two restaurants, two recreational areas, or two other locations

5. Two sports, two athletes, or two teams

6. Two different cultures or languages, especially if you have experience with both

7. Two different ways of doing something, especially if one method is better

8. Two different goals or objectives for the future, such as two majors or two careers

9. Did some experience or decision change your life? If so, how were you different "before" and "after"?

10. Any other two people, places, things, or experiences that you could compare and contrast

Discovering Details 1: Analyzing Similarities and Differences Orally

When you are comparing and contrasting two things, you need to identify and explain their most important similarities and differences. This prewriting activity will help you get started by discovering details about your topic. First choose one of your most interesting topic ideas from your *Exploring Topics Worksheet* and find a partner to talk with. Your partner should ask you questions about your topic, starting with the questions listed below. Try to give detailed answers so that your partner will have a clear understanding of all the similarities and differences. If there is time, your partner may also ask additional questions to find out more about your topic. Then change roles and ask your partner questions about his or her topic.

- Why do you want to write about this topic?
- Which characteristics or features of the two parts of your topic are alike or similar?
- Are some of these similarities more important than the others? Why?
- Which characteristics or features are different?
- Are some of these differences more important than the others? Why?
- Are some of the similarities or differences unusual or surprising?
- Do any of the differences make one person, place, thing, or experience better than the other in some way?
- Any other appropriate questions to help your partner express more details about the topic.

If you can't find much to say about the first topic you choose, change to a different one. You may want to do this activity with two or three of your topics to see which one you like best. After you and your partner have answered all of each other's questions, go on to the next prewriting activity, *Dividing and Listing,* where you will make a written list of all the similarities and differences.

Discovering Details 2: Dividing and Listing

With any writing topic that deals with two separate things, such as a comparison/contrast, one useful way to begin discovering details is to make a list for each part. The *Dividing and Listing Worksheet* will help you come up with ideas about both parts of your topic so that you can look closely at the similarities and differences.

Before you begin, read the following example *Dividing and Listing Worksheet.* Notice that there are two columns, one for each part of the topic. The writer began by writing one part of her topic, *renting a movie,* at the top of the left column, and the other part of her topic, *going out to a movie theater,* at the top of the right column. Then she listed all the details she could think of in each column. When she thought of related points, she put them side by side. For example, the first item in both columns is the cost, and the second item is movie selections. If she didn't think of a related similarity or difference right away, she left a blank space in the other column and continued listing her ideas.

Example Worksheet: Dividing and Listing

Directions: Write one part of your comparison/contrast topic at the top of each column. Then write all the details that you can think of.

COMPARISON/CONTRAST TOPIC:

renting a movie	going out to a movie theater

DETAILS:

cheaper to rent—costs about $2	costs $6–$7 to go to a movie
older movies, good selection	new movies
invite several friends no annoying audience members	crowds, annoying people

snacks cheaper at home
    more variety
eat anything you want
	limited snacks—more expensive
	    popcorn & candy

can take a break any time	

can watch more than once for
    same price
	watch once—miss part of movie if
	    you take a break

no need to dress up	more of a "special occasion"
smaller screen	big screen experience
Cost of VCR—$200–$400? should be considered too	Evening for two costs $20 with snacks 10–20 movies for two = cost of VCR

Now try dividing and listing with one of your own topics that you think you would like to write about. You may use the same topic that you analyzed with your partner for the previous activity, or you may try another topic from your *Exploring Topics Worksheet* if you wish. Begin by writing one part of your topic in the left column and the other part of your topic in the right column of the *Dividing and Listing Worksheet.* Then list all the details that you can think of for each part of your topic. Write down everything that comes to mind without stopping to edit your list. Whenever possible, try to put related similarities or differences side by side, but it's not necessary to match up everything. Just leave a blank space if nothing comes to your mind quickly about the other part of the topic and go on with the list. You will have an opportunity later to organize your lists and decide which details you want to use in your comparison/contrast.

■ WORKSHEET II | Dividing and Listing
=====

Directions: Write one part of your comparison/contrast topic at the top of each column. Then list all the details that you can think of. Put related points side by side if possible.

COMPARISON/CONTRAST TOPIC:

_____   _____

DETAILS:

_____   _____

_____   _____

_____   _____

_____   _____

_____   _____

_____   _____

_____   _____

_____   _____

_____   _____

_____   _____

_____   _____

_____   _____

_____   _____

When you have finished dividing and listing, look over what you have written. Did you fill most of the page with details about the two parts of your topic? For most of the points that you listed, were you able to write something in the other column, either a similarity or a difference? If so, your topic can probably be developed into an interesting comparison/contrast paragraph or short paper.

As you are looking over your worksheet, if you notice some details that are related but are not listed side by side, you can draw arrows to indicate where they belong, or you can rewrite them in the right place. For instance, on the example worksheet, the writer didn't think of mentioning the cost of a VCR until the end, but this information actually belongs earlier with other information about costs, so the writer could draw an arrow to show where it belongs.

If you didn't come up with very many similarities or differences, try another topic from your *Exploring Topics Worksheet*. Be sure to divide and list again with your new topic. You may also want to try one or more of the other prewriting techniques that we have studied, such as freewriting or visualizing. (Extra worksheets can be found in Appendix I in the Reference Section in this text.) Even professional writers often use a variety of prewriting techniques like these to help them get ideas and discover details.

Writing a Rough Draft

Learning about Topic Sentences for Comparison/Contrast

In the previous chapters, we have used the term *topic sentence* to refer to the sentence (or two) that states the main idea of a paragraph or short paper. When a paper consists of three or more paragraphs, many writers prefer to call this sentence a *main idea statement* or a *thesis statement* instead of a topic sentence. A *main idea statement* or *thesis statement* serves the same purpose in a longer paper that a topic sentence serves in a paragraph: it focuses the paper on the most important point that the writer plans to make. If you are going to write a comparison/contrast that has three or more paragraphs, you or your instructor may prefer to use one of these terms, *main idea statement* or *thesis statement*. However, since the comparison/contrast writing process in this chapter applies to both one-paragraph papers and longer papers, in this book we will continue to use the term *topic sentence* most of the time.

A topic sentence (or main idea statement) for a comparison/contrast paper identifies the topic and usually states the kinds of similarities or differences that the paper will be about. Before you write your topic sentence, you should try to decide on the main similarities or differences that you want to include. Depending on your topic, you may want to focus on similarities, differences, or both.

Let's look at how one writer used some of the ideas on his *Dividing and Listing Worksheet* to develop a good topic sentence. Being bilingual, he had decided to compare and contrast his two languages—English and Spanish. When he read over his *Dividing and Listing Worksheet*, he found that he had identified several differences but only two similarities:

Differences

Spelling—Spanish words are spelled the way they sound; English words are not.

Spanish has masculine and feminine words; English does not.

Grammar rules—double negatives, where adjectives are placed, etc.

Word order.

Similarities

Both languages are spoken by large numbers of people around the world.

Some grammar and sentence structure rules are similar.

Since this writer had listed more differences than similarities, he decided to emphasize the differences in his comparison/contrast paper. He chose not to include the similarities because readers would already be aware that both languages are spoken around the world and that some characteristics of the languages would naturally be similar. Therefore, the differences would be more informative and interesting. In addition, an explanation of the differences might be helpful to readers learning one of the languages.

This is the first topic sentence that the writer came up with:

TOPIC SENTENCE (DRAFT #1):

English and Spanish have differences in grammar and pronunciation.

This topic sentence is a good start. It identifies the topic (English and Spanish), and it focuses on two differences—grammar and pronunciation. However, the writer wanted to include other differences in his paper as well, so he decided to add more to his topic sentence:

TOPIC SENTENCE (DRAFT #2):

English and Spanish have significant differences in pronunciation, word order, gender of nouns and adjectives, and certain grammar rules.

This topic sentence worked very well because it included all of the points that he wanted to write about in his paper: pronunciation, word order, masculine and feminine words, and grammar rules.

With some topics, your comparison/contrast may show that one part of the topic is superior to the other in some way. If so, you will probably want to include that idea in your topic sentence too. For example, the writer of the example *Dividing and Listing Worksheet* intended to show that renting a movie is a better option than going to a movie theater, so she tried this topic sentence:

TOPIC SENTENCE (DRAFT #1):

Renting a movie to watch at home is better than going to a movie theater.

This topic sentence tells us which alternative the writer thinks is better, but it doesn't tell us anything about the differences that explain why it's better.

Therefore, the writer's workshop group suggested that she add something about the differences between the two ways of watching a movie. This is the second draft of her topic sentence:

TOPIC SENTENCE (DRAFT #2):

Renting a movie to watch at home is better than going to a movie theater because it costs less.

Although this topic sentence tells us the main reason why the writer thinks that renting a movie is a better choice, the writer realized that it didn't include any of the other differences that she wanted to write about. By reviewing her notes on the *Dividing and Listing Worksheet*, she was able to make the topic sentence more complete. Here is her third version:

TOPIC SENTENCE (DRAFT #3):

Renting a movie costs less than going to a movie theater and offers a more convenient, comfortable viewing environment.

This topic sentence is very effective. Instead of simply stating that one alternative is better than the other, it identifies specific differences that back up the writer's opinion. In the body of the paper, the writer can give details about the costs, as well as about the comfort and convenience of watching movies at home.

If you decide to mention in your topic sentence that one part of your topic is better than the other, be sure that your opinion sounds reasonable and that you will be able to back it up. Notice that the person writing about English and Spanish did not try to establish that one language is superior to the other. He had thought about saying that Spanish is an easier language to learn or perhaps that Spanish is more poetic and romantic. However, he realized that it might be hard to come up with enough evidence to support either of these topic sentences. Therefore, he decided to state the differences objectively instead of favoring one language over the other.

Sometimes, if there are several similarities and differences that a writer wants to include, it may not be possible to put all of them into one good topic sentence. In this case, the topic sentence can give a general idea about the nature of the similarities or differences instead of identifying each one. For example, one writer who was comparing and contrasting the neighborhood where she lives now with her old neighborhood wanted to write about all of these similarities and differences:

New neighborhood is farther from friends and stores.

New neighborhood has fewer teens, more adults and children.

We always had to lock doors in old neighborhood, not in the new neighborhood.

Neighbors used to fight and argue in old neighborhood, new neighbors don't.

Street is quieter than old neighborhood, although nearby main road is noisy.

Both neighborhoods have police cars and sirens in the area often.

Surrounding areas are similar.

She realized that her topic sentence would have to be very long to include all of these similarities and differences. Therefore, she decided to write a topic sentence that would tell readers her overall opinion about the two neighborhoods instead of trying to say everything in one sentence. This is the statement that she wrote:

TOPIC SENTENCE:

Although the neighborhood where I live in Paradise Hills is better in some ways than where I used to live in National City, I would rather live in National City to be closer to my friends.

This statement expresses her overall opinion about living in the two neighborhoods: the new neighborhood is better in some ways, but she prefers her old neighborhood because of her friends. Although it does not tell us the specific things that make the new neighborhood better, it is an effective topic sentence. In the body of the paper, she can give more details that show why she feels the way she does about the two neighborhoods, including all of the similarities and differences that she listed above.

Before you write your own topic sentence (or main idea statement), do the following exercise, *Evaluating Topic Sentences for Comparison/Contrast*. Remember that a good topic sentence usually identifies the kinds of differences or similarities that the writer plans to emphasize, or it gives the writer's overall opinion about the topic. The topic sentence may show that one part of the topic is better than the other in some way, or it may state the differences objectively, without taking sides.

Evaluating Topic Sentences for Comparison/Contrast

Directions: Write OK in the blank by each good topic sentence (or main idea statement). Write NO in the blank by the others. Remember that the topic sentence should focus on significant similarities or differences or should express the writer's overall opinion. Be ready to explain your answers.

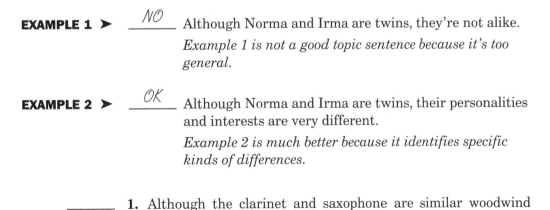

EXAMPLE 1 ➤ _____*NO*_____ Although Norma and Irma are twins, they're not alike.

Example 1 is not a good topic sentence because it's too general.

EXAMPLE 2 ➤ _____*OK*_____ Although Norma and Irma are twins, their personalities and interests are very different.

Example 2 is much better because it identifies specific kinds of differences.

_____ **1.** Although the clarinet and saxophone are similar woodwind instruments, their different shapes and sizes create different sounds.

_____ **2.** St. Bernards are a much larger breed of dogs than poodles.

_____ **3.** Cordless phones are more convenient than regular phones, but they generally cost more and often have poorer quality sound.

_____ **4.** Women's fashions of the 1990's have brought back several styles from the 1960's.

_____ **5.** My two favorite restaurants are Angelo's and Mister J's.

_____ **6.** Buy your child a hamster because hamsters are much more interesting than other pets.

_____ **7.** Although IBM computers are popular for business use, the Macintosh is easier and more fun for home users to learn.

_____ **8.** Type A personalities are generally aggressive and forceful, whereas Type B personalities are calmer and more relaxed.

_____ **9.** Many Japanese customs and American customs are different.

_____ **10.** The American bald eagle can be compared with many other endangered species whose environment is threatened.

Writing Your Own Topic Sentence

In order to write a good topic sentence (or main idea statement), first read over everything that you listed on your _Dividing and Listing Worksheet_. Think about which characteristics of the two parts of your topic are different and which ones are the same (or similar). If you notice individual items on the list that are closely related, you may want to group them together in order to organize the information more effectively.

As you look over your complete list for each part of your topic, try to decide which points are the most important. Are some of the similarities (or differences) especially interesting or surprising? Which things would the reader need to know about in order to really understand how the items are different? If your topic deals with a choice between two alternatives, what information would you or your audience need in order to make the choice?

Remember that your paper does not need to have an equal emphasis on similarities and differences. Some topics may have several important differences but hardly any similarities. In other cases, the similarities may already be well-known by your audience, so you don't need to explain them. Therefore, it would make sense to write mostly about the differences. On the other hand, if there are not many differences, or if the differences seem obvious, you should concentrate on explaining the similarities. Readers will be especially interested in any similarities that are unexpected or surprising.

When you have decided on the main points that you want to include in your comparison/contrast (the most important similarities and/or differences), write them on the following lines:

Main Points

_____

_____

_____

_____

Now try writing a topic sentence (or main idea statement) that identifies your topic and says something about the similarities or differences that you listed above:

TOPIC SENTENCE (DRAFT #1):

_____

_____

Does this topic sentence include all of your main points? Does it give an accurate picture of how the two parts of your topic are alike or similar or how they differ from each other? Have your workshop group read your topic sentence too and make suggestions. Then if you want to revise it, write a second draft of your topic sentence here:

TOPIC SENTENCE (DRAFT #2):

_____

_____

If your topic consists of two alternatives or options, do you think that one is better than the other in some way? By explaining the differences, will your comparison/contrast *show* that one is somehow better? If so, you may want to revise your topic sentence to include the idea that one is a better choice. Try writing a third draft of your topic sentence below:

TOPIC SENTENCE (DRAFT #3—OPTIONAL):

_____

_____

Be sure that this topic sentence sounds reasonable and states the situation fairly. If you have doubts about using it, have your workshop group read it and give you some feedback before making your decision.

If your topic includes a lot of similarities and differences, you may want to use a topic sentence that states your main idea or overall opinion without including everything that is similar or different. If you would like to try this kind of topic sentence, think about these questions: What is most important about the two things that you are comparing and contrasting? Could you tell readers the essential idea without including specific similarities and differences? Try your topic sentence here and see how it sounds:

TOPIC SENTENCE (DRAFT #4—OPTIONAL):

_____

_____

If you are having trouble deciding which one of your topic sentences will work best for your topic (Draft #2, Draft #3, or Draft #4), have your workshop group read them and help you choose the most effective one. You may also want to ask your instructor's opinion. Having a good topic sentence is important because it will help you get started with your first draft. However, at any time while you are in the process of writing your paper, if you find that your topic sentence does not adequately identify the main points that you want to compare or contrast, you may decide to revise it again.

Your first draft should begin with one of the topic sentences that you just wrote or with a short introduction that includes your topic sentence. Adding another introductory sentence or two is a good idea if you would like to give readers some additional background information about your topic or if your paper is going to be longer than one paragraph. (For examples of comparison/contrast introductions, see some of the example papers later in this chapter, such as *Judo Versus Wrestling* on pages 223–224.)

From Topic Sentence to First Draft

Before you begin writing the body of your paper, you will need to choose between two different patterns of organization: the Block Method and the Point-by-Point Method. You should read about both of these patterns of organization in the following pages and look at the examples of comparison/contrast writing in each pattern. Then you can decide which method will work best for your topic.

Using the Block Method

One way to organize a comparison/contrast is to divide it into *two blocks of information*, one block for each part of the topic. This is called the *Block Method*. After your topic sentence, or a short introduction that includes your topic sentence, you write about one part of your topic, including all of the characteristics that you intend to compare and contrast. In the middle of the comparison/contrast, there should be a transitional sentence to introduce the second part of the topic smoothly. Then write another block of information about the second part of the topic, explaining how it is similar to or different from the first part. You must be careful to include the same kinds of information about the second part of your topic that you included about the first part. At the end of the paper, of course, you should have a conclusion that ties everything together.

Here is a diagram representing the Block Method of organizing a comparison/contrast in one paragraph.

Block Method for a Comparison/Contrast Paragraph

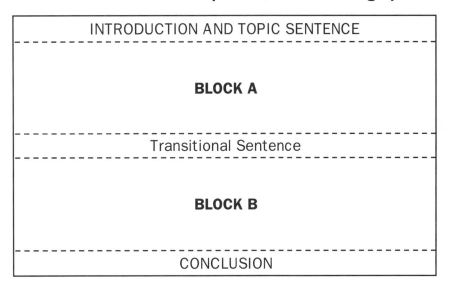

If you're using the Block Method to compare and contrast two TV programs, for example, you would write about one program in Block A and about the other program in Block B. If you are comparing the *Encyclopaedia Britannica* with the *World Book Encyclopedia,* you would write about one of the encyclopedias in Block A and about the other one in Block B. It is important to remember that both blocks of writing must cover the same kinds of information. This means that if you write about the reading level of one encyclopedia, you must also write about the reading level of the other encyclopedia. If you discuss how comprehensive one of the encyclopedias is, you have to consider how comprehensive the other one is too. In most cases, the clearest way to present the information is to arrange the points in the same order in both blocks. By following these guidelines, you can use the Block Method to organize almost any comparison/contrast.

The Block Method will also work for a longer comparison/contrast paper. Writing a longer paper will allow you to include more details about your topic so that the similarities and differences will be clearer to the reader. To write a longer comparison/contrast using the Block Method, start with an introduction of two or three sentences, including your topic sentence. The introduction should be a separate paragraph. Then write one paragraph about part A of your topic and one paragraph about part B, being sure to include the same types of information about each, in the same order if possible. When you write your conclusion, it should be a separate paragraph also. Here is a diagram representing the Block Method for a longer paper:

Block Method for a Longer Comparison/Contrast

INTRODUCTORY PARAGRAPH

PARAGRAPH A

Transitional Sentence

PARAGRAPH B

CONCLUDING PARAGRAPH

The following comparison/contrast, *Where I Live* by Carla Garcia, uses the Block Method of organization. Following the introduction, there is one paragraph about the neighborhood where Carla used to live in National City, followed by another paragraph about the neighborhood where she now lives in Paradise Hills. Then there is a brief conclusion where the writer makes a final comment on the two neighborhoods. As you read *Where I Live,* notice that the writer presents the same kinds of information about each part of the topic.

Where I Live
by Carla Garcia

My experience of moving a lot has given me the opportunity to see the differences in living in many communities, such as National City and Paradise Hills. Although the neighborhood where I live in Paradise Hills is better in some ways than where I used to live in National City, I would rather live in National City to be closer to my friends.

The neighborhood where I lived in National City was very close to the main part of the city, so we had the advantages of having all the stores, restaurants, and small plazas close by. The area where we lived had a combination of good and bad qualities. During the day, most of the time the neighborhood was quiet since everybody was either at school or work, but at night the neighborhood turned into a social place; we could hear people talking, loud music playing, and cars passing by every five to ten minutes. Many nights this would go on past the hour of midnight. Neighbors were fighting constantly, and men were always arguing. We could hear the sirens of police cars almost every night. At least once a week a helicopter with a spotlight on would fly so close above the houses that we would think it was for us or one of our neighbors. It was a type of area where we would not leave the car doors unlocked, and we would always double-check the windows and doors on the house. Even though my mom put a lock on the gate to our backyard, a man managed to jump the gate once and steal my sister's bike. The majority of our neighbors were Mexicans. They were friendly and occasionally would socialize with us. Since I had lived there almost six and a half years, I made very good friends with peers from junior high and high school.

The neighborhood where I live in Paradise Hills is different. It is a very isolated area, and in order to get to the stores, we have to travel to a nearby town, either Spring Valley or Lemon Grove. The neighborhood itself is safer than our neighborhood in National City, but the surrounding area is almost the same. Since a very busy main road is just one block away from my house, we can hear cars driving by day and night. Many police cars and fire trucks pass by with their loud sirens. I have also heard driveby shootings. There is a bus stop at the corner of our block, so we hear buses from very early in the morning until very late at night. The street on which we live is a dead-end, so there isn't any traffic there, and most of the time it is quiet. Most of our neighbors are Oriental people, and they usually keep to themselves. They are either adults in their late thirties or little grade school kids. There are no people my age to meet and be friends with, and it is very hard to visit my friends in National City without a car.

It may seem that the neighborhood where we live in Paradise Hills is nicer than the one in National City, and in some ways it probably is. But to me, it isn't, because I miss all of my friends.

Response to *Where I Live*

1. The topic sentence says that Carla's new neighborhood is better in some ways. By looking at details in both body paragraphs, find two ways in which it seems to be better.

_____

_____

2. Read both body paragraphs over again and find at least three other differences between the two neighborhoods.

_____

_____

_____

3. Which sentence acts as a transition between the first block of information and the second block of information?

_____

Using the Point-by-Point Method

Another way to organize a comparison/contrast is the Point-by-Point Method. To use this method, you need to decide on a few main points (probably three or four), and for each point you will write first about one part of your topic and then about the other. If there are a lot of details about the two parts of your topic that you want to compare and contrast, it will probably be necessary to group related details together in order to figure out what your main points really are. For example, one writer who was comparing and contrasting her two sisters, Miho and Emi, wanted to include all of the following kinds of details:

hair color and style
hobbies
attitude toward marriage
style of dress
sense of humor
goals
outgoing or shy personality
job
attractiveness
friendliness
home life

Looking over all the things she wanted to include, she realized that these details could be grouped into three main points: appearance, personality, and lifestyle:

Appearance	*Personality*	*Lifestyle*
hair color and style	sense of humor	hobbies
style of dress	outgoing or shy	home life
attractiveness	friendliness	attitude toward marriage
		goals

This chart shows how she organized her paper according to the Point-by-Point Method:

Introduction and Topic Sentence		
Point 1: Appearance	A. Miho	B. Emi
Point 2: Personality	A. Miho	B. Emi
Point 3: Lifestyle	A. Miho	B. Emi
Conclusion		

This type of point-by-point organization can be used for any comparison/contrast topic. All you need to do is decide on the main points or kinds of information that you want to compare and contrast, and then discuss how each point applies to both parts of your topic. In order to avoid confusion, it is generally a good idea to discuss the two parts of your topic in the same order: details about Point 1 A and B, then details about Point 2 A and B, and so on.

Like the Block Method, the Point-by Point-Method can also be used to write a longer comparison/contrast paper that consists of more than one paragraph. To do this, begin with an introductory paragraph, including a topic sentence (or main idea statement). Then develop each of your main points into a separate paragraph with details, explanations, and examples. These paragraphs will form the body of your paper. After that, write two or three sentences for a concluding paragraph.

The following comparison/contrast paper uses the Point-by-Point Method, with a separate paragraph to explain each point. Ray Jensen effectively contrasts judo and wrestling by explaining three points: the throws, the pinning techniques, and the scoring system. Since he is writing for an audience that already knows something about one or both of the sports, he does not give a complete explanation of all the rules. His purpose is to explain the differences, not to give instructions that would enable the reader to compete in either judo or wrestling. Notice that as Ray explains each point, he discusses wrestling first, then judo.

Judo Versus Wrestling
by Ray Jensen

Many people believe judo and wrestling are basically the same because they are both one-on-one contact sports that have pinning and points for the means of winning. However, judo is easier and less dangerous because of the differences in the throws, the pinning techniques, and the scoring system.

One of the main differences between judo and wrestling is the throws. In wrestling, there are very few throws that are legal, and most of them are very painful to the receiver. In fact, most of the throws are not intended, and they can result in broken bones. If a throw is done in wrestling, it rarely accomplishes much. However, in judo there are many throws, and the throws are taught as an art. A judo student learns the kata (the motions of the throw) before he learns the actual throw. The judo student is trained to throw his opponent in such a way as to give the least pain and danger. Also, the judo student is trained to fall correctly to avoid hurting himself.

Besides the throws, the pinning techniques make competition in judo easier. In wrestling, the wrestler has to have both shoulders of his opponent touching the mat in order to win. The count is for approximately five seconds, and sometimes the referee does not or cannot see whether or not both shoulders are actually touching. Many times, the wrestler gets his opponent's shoulders on the mat, and just before the count is over, his opponent moves, forcing him to lose all the effort he put into it. In contrast, the judo student only has to have his opponent in a "controlled hold," which does not require both shoulders touching. It is much easier to get the opponent in a controlled hold for 30 seconds than to try to get both of the opponent's shoulders to touch the mat.

In addition to the throws and pinning techniques, the scoring system in wrestling is more complicated than in judo. In wrestling, for example, the wrestler gets points for a reversal, which means that the wrestler was in a down position but then made a fast move to get out from under his opponent's control and then another move to gain control of his opponent. Other moves that gain points are a takedown, which is when the wrestler forces his opponent to the mat, and an escape, which is when the wrestler escapes from a hold that his opponent put on him. The scoring system for judo is simpler. The judo student can get a full point, which means a win, if he throws his opponent directly on his back. If the judo student only throws his opponent halfway, he gains half a point, which also allows him to be given five seconds off the time he has to have his opponent in a controlled hold.

With all the advantages of the throws, pinning techniques, and scoring system, it is no surprise that judo is easier and less dangerous. More people should try judo for exercise and for the competition.

Response to *Judo Versus Wrestling*

1. Do you think that the Point-by-Point Method of organization is effective for this topic? Why or why not?

_____

_____

2. Which sentence do you think is the topic sentence (main idea statement)?

_____

_____

3. What evidence has the writer used to back up his idea that judo is easier and less dangerous than wrestling?

_____

_____

Choosing the Block Method or the Point-by-Point Method

Choosing which method to use for your own comparison/contrast is largely a matter of personal preference. Some writers simply feel more comfortable with one method than with the other. Other writers who have practiced both methods may find that one works better for a particular topic than the other.

The Block Method may seem easier because it allows you to write about each part of the topic separately instead of going back and forth. However, if you are using the Block Method, you must be careful not to write two separate, unconnected blocks of information. When you write about the second part of your topic, you must be sure to include the same kinds of details that you wrote about the first part of your topic. Also, you must be sure to emphasize ways in which the second part is similar to the first part and ways in which it is different. Otherwise, readers may not remember whether the first part is similar or different, especially if your paper is very long.

A Point-by-Point comparison/contrast usually takes a little longer to plan and organize because you have to group the details into a few main points. However, presenting the information point-by-point may make it easier for readers to understand the similarities and differences. For this reason, many writers prefer using the Point-by-Point Method, especially if they are going to explain a lot of similarities or differences. When you are writing a Point-by-Point comparison/contrast, you must be careful to follow the organization that you have planned. For each point, you must present enough information about both parts of your topic so that readers can easily understand the similarities and differences.

With either method of organization, an essential part of writing a good comparison/contrast is including the same kinds of information about both parts of your topic. If your topic sentence identifies specific similarities or differences, use it as a guideline to make sure that you cover everything. As you develop the body of your paper, explain to readers exactly how the two things are similar and how they are different, being sure to include plenty of details.

If the first method of organization that you try doesn't seem to be working well for you, try changing to the other method. You may want to discuss the organization of your comparison/contrast with your workshop group or ask your instructor to help you decide which method to use.

As you read the following first draft, *Living Alone,* identify which method of organization the writer used. Then check to see if the writer has explained all of the similarities or differences identified in the topic sentence and if the same kinds of details are included about both parts of the topic.

First Draft

Living Alone

After living alone for two years, I have discovered that the advantages definitely outweigh the disadvantages. Even though you may occasionally get lonely, living alone gives you much more freedom and privacy than living with someone else.

When you live alone, you have the freedom to do whatever you want, whenever you want, without having to consult anyone. For example, if you're tired and want to go to bed at 7:00 P.M., you can. On the other hand, if you want to stay up until 3:00 A.M. and watch horror movies, there's no one to complain. If you want to have a huge chocolate milk shake and banana cream pie for dinner, no one will accuse you of being a pig. You are also free to choose whatever style of furnishings you want—beanbag chairs or leather couch, waterbed or futon, lamps or candlelight. At times you may feel a little lonely and wish you had someone around to talk to, but at least there will be no one to annoy you or to argue with you about what you want to do.

If you live with someone, however, your freedom and privacy will be much more limited. Your roommate will find out everything about you: how you look when you get up in the morning, how you brush your teeth, how messy you are, and all kinds of things that you might not want to share. You won't be able to have private phone conversations without someone else listening, unless your roommate is gone. It's true that a roommate will often keep you company, so you probably won't ever feel lonely, but it isn't always easy to get along smoothly with a roommate and still have the lifestyle that you want. Of course, one advantage of living with someone is that your roommate will pay half of the rent, so you will have more money to spend on other things.

If you live with someone else, you will have to sacrifice some of your privacy and maybe even some of your independence. Unless you find a roommate with whom you are very compatible, living alone may be much less stressful and more enjoyable than living with another person.

Response to *Living Alone*

1. Which method of organization does this comparison/contrast use, the Block Method or the Point-by-Point Method?

2. In the topic sentence, the writer identifies three differences that she plans to write about. What are they?

(Difference #1) _____

(Difference #2) _____

(Difference #3) _____

3. Has the writer mistakenly included any information that does not relate to the topic sentence? If so, what is it?

_____

What should the writer do to fix this problem?

_____

4. Has the writer included the same kinds of information about both parts of the topic? (Remember that all three of the differences should be discussed for each part of the topic.)

_____

If not, what do you think is missing from the paragraph about living alone?

_____

_____

What do you think is missing from the paragraph about living with a roommate?

_____

_____

As you write your own first draft, try to avoid the kinds of problems that you observed in *Living Alone*. Make sure that everything you include relates to the topic sentence. Anything that does not relate to the topic sentence, such as the comment about a roommate helping pay the rent, should not be included, unless you change your topic sentence. Double-check to be sure that your paper covers the same kinds of information about both parts of your topic. The writer of *Living Alone* forgot to do this. She wrote about freedom and loneliness in the first block of information but left out privacy; in the second block of information she discussed privacy but left out freedom. By following the pattern for the Block Method or the Point-by-Point Method carefully and using your topic sentence as a guideline, you can avoid these types of problems.

When you have finished your rough draft, meet with your workshop group and read each person's comparison/contrast paper. If you see any ways that other writers could improve their first drafts, make suggestions. Use the following rough draft workshop questions as guidelines for your discussion:

Rough Draft Workshop Questions

1. Has the writer used either the Block Method or the Point-by-Point method correctly?
2. Does the topic sentence (or main idea statement) identify the kinds of similarities and differences? If not, does it state an appropriate main idea about the topic?
3. Are the same kinds of details included about each part of the topic?
4. Are the similarities and differences clearly explained?
5. Can you think of anything else that should be added?

Transitions for Comparison/Contrast

Transitional words and phrases can be very useful in comparison/contrast writing to connect your ideas smoothly and clearly. They can help you emphasize characteristics that are similar or call attention to characteristics that are different.

Some transitional words that may be helpful when you are writing about similarities include the following:

> similar to
> similarly
> likewise
> like
> both
> the same as
> as _____ as
> also

Here is a sentence from *Where I Live* that uses *the same as* to make one of the similarities between the writer's old neighborhood and her new neighborhood clear:

> The neighborhood itself is all right, but the surrounding area is almost *the same as* in National City.

Although the writer goes on to give details about the surrounding area in her new neighborhood, she has made sure that readers understand the similarity by using the transitional phrase *the same as*.

Transitional words and phrases that can help you emphasize differences include the following:

Group B Connectors:	whereas although even though

Group C Connectors:	in contrast however on the other hand instead	*(See Section Two of this chapter to learn about using Group C connectors.)*

Other Words and Phrases:	differs from different unlike one of the differences another difference more _____ than less _____ than _____ -er than (comparative adjectives)

Here are some sentences from *Judo Versus Wrestling* that use transitions to help point out the differences between the two sports:

> *One of the main differences* between judo and wrestling is the throws. In wrestling, there are very few throws that are legal, and most of them are very painful to the receiver. In fact, most of the throws are not intended, and they can result in broken bones. If a throw is done in wrestling, it rarely accomplishes much. *However,* in judo there are many throws, and the throws are taught as an art. . . .

The phrase "one of the main differences" leads into a discussion of the writer's first main point, differences in the throws. Then, after giving some details about the throws in wrestling, he switches to judo by using *however* as a transition. Notice that the writer also uses phrases like "in judo" and "in wrestling" in some of his sentences to remind the reader about which sport his statement applies to. Since these phrases help to connect the ideas smoothly, they could also be considered transitions.

Here are some more examples of transitions from *Judo Versus Wrestling*:

> The scoring system in wrestling is *more complicated than* in judo.

> With all the advantages of the throws, pinning techniques, and scoring system, it is no surprise that judo is *easier* and *less dangerous.*

Words like *more* and *less* and adjectives that end with *-er,* such as *easier,* are sometimes very useful in comparison/contrast writing. They help to express specific differences that the writer wants to call our attention to.

(In Section Two of this chapter, you will learn more about using these types of words correctly.)

As you read the next comparison/contrast, *Japanese and American Customs* by Toshiko Williams, look for some transitional words and expressions that help to connect ideas smoothly. Although there are only a few transitions in each paragraph, they make it easy for the reader to understand when Toshiko is referring to customs in Japan and when she is referring to customs in the United States. Also, think about why this paper is organized according to the Point-by-Point Method rather than the Block Method.

Japanese and American Customs
by Toshiko Williams

After I decided to marry my American husband, I started to learn American culture in my way. I watched American movies, read American magazines, and even made a few American friends. I thought I knew most things about America, so I wasn't worried about living in the United States. But after I came to America from Japan, I found out that there are many differences between customs in Japan and America.

The first thing that surprised me was the difference in manners between Japanese and Americans. One day, my husband and I invited a couple to dinner. They were nice people, and we were talking for a while. Suddenly, the guy stood up, went to the kitchen, and opened the door of the refrigerator to get something to drink. In Japan, it is extremely impolite to open somebody's refrigerator, especially without asking. Another example is that American people sometimes put their feet on a table. Most of my husband's friends do this when they are sitting in the living room. To me, it seems very dirty. They walk with their shoes and then put their feet on the table which I put coffee or some snacks on. In Japan, it is a very rude thing to do. If somebody goes to somebody else's house in Japan and puts his or her feet on the table, Japanese people will be very disappointed with the person.

The way to express feelings is also very different for Japanese people than for American people. Japanese people don't express their feelings a lot. Sometimes, even when they get mad, they don't express their anger directly. Instead, they express their feelings in a roundabout way. In Japan, people can understand each other in a roundabout way, and people who don't show their anger are considered good because they don't hurt others. In the United States, it is a different story. The first time I had an American friend, I was very happy, but she asked me many private things about my husband and me. I don't talk about those kinds of things, but I couldn't say that, so she kept asking me. I tried to let her know indirectly that I didn't want to talk about it, but she never understood that. On the other hand, American people express their feelings straightforwardly. If they don't like somebody's opinion, they just say, "I don't think so," or "You are wrong." When my American friend told me, "You are wrong," I used to wonder why she couldn't have said that in a nicer way, but now I can understand that she didn't mean to hurt me.

The most interesting difference between Japan and America is how people greet each other. My mother-in-law was the first woman who kissed me, and I thought she was a lesbian because in Japan we don't kiss friends and family. Kissing is only for boyfriend and girlfriend in Japan. When my father-in-law tried to kiss me, I ran away from him because I felt that it was not right. My father-in-law seemed sad because of my reaction, so I hugged him, which Japanese people don't do either. I still don't feel comfortable when American people kiss or hug me. Also, when my father-in-law told me, "I love you," I was troubled because I misunderstood what he meant; I thought he loved me as a woman! One day, I dared to tell my husband about it. He started laughing at me, and he told me that it is the usual thing to say "I love you" to family and close friends in American society. I felt so stupid at that time. In Japan, we don't say "I love you" to family and friends. These words are only for lovers.

I have lived in America for three years, but I still have difficulty understanding American people sometimes. I tried so hard to learn about the United States before I came here from Japan, yet the knowledge didn't help me a lot. It will take a long time to understand the differences between Japan and America.

Response to *Japanese and American Customs*

1. Underline all of the transitional words and phrases that you can find in this comparison/contrast paper. Then compare your answers with other students' answers. Do you think that there are enough transitions? Why or why not?

    _____

    _____

2. Do you think that the Point-by-Point Method of organization is the most effective way to present this topic? Why or why not?

    _____

    _____

3. Toshiko has included stories about some of the things that have happened to her since she moved to the United States. How do these stories help readers understand the different customs?

    _____

    _____

    _____

Now look at the rough draft of your own comparison/contrast paper and circle all of the transitional words and phrases that you used. Make sure that there are enough transitions to connect your ideas smoothly. With the Point-by-Point Method of organization, the most important places to use transitions are usually where you begin each new point and where you change back and forth from one part of the topic to another. If you are using the Block Method, you will probably need a transitional phrase to begin the second block of information, and you will also need some transitional words to emphasize similarities and differences in the second block of information.

If you think that your rough draft should have a few more transitional words or phrases, add them in the appropriate places. Then have your workshop group read your paper again to be sure that your transitions are effective. Don't try to add transitional words to every sentence, or your writing style may sound very formal and artificial. Remember that your goal is to connect ideas smoothly, so make sure that the transitions you use sound natural.

Ending Effectively

An effective way to end a comparison/contrast is to weigh the similarities and differences that you have written about and analyze their significance. Have you shown that one part of your topic is better than the other in some way because of their differences? Does one thing have certain advantages over the other, or are they about equal? There may also be some benefit for the reader in knowing about the similarities and differences, or something important that the reader can learn from your paper. If so, you can use any of these ideas in your conclusion. Some writers also like to comment on what they have learned personally by analyzing the similarities and differences.

The sample papers in this chapter have all used one or more of these approaches for writing an effective conclusion. Notice that each conclusion analyzes the similarities and differences in some way and gives the writer's overall idea or opinion about the topic:

1. *Where I Live:* It may seem that the neighborhood where we live in Paradise Hills is nicer than the one in National City, and it probably is. But to me, it isn't, because I miss all of my friends.

2. *Judo Versus Wrestling:* With all the advantages of the throws, pinning techniques, and scoring system, it is no surprise that judo is easier and less dangerous. More people should try judo for exercise and for the competition.

3. *Living Alone:* If you live with someone else, you will have to sacrifice some of your privacy and maybe even some of your independence. Unless you find a roommate with whom you are very compatible, living alone may be much less stressful and more enjoyable than living with another person.

4. *Japanese and American Customs:* I have lived in America for three years, but I still have difficulty understanding American people sometimes. I tried so hard to learn about the United States before I came here from Japan, yet the knowledge didn't help me a lot. It will take a long time to understand the differences between Japan and America.

Which of these conclusions do you like best? Why?

_____

_____

Sometimes a comparison/contrast conclusion also reviews the main points that the writer made, especially in a longer paper. Which of the conclusions shown above do this?

_____

_____

The last example paper in this chapter, _Becoming an EMT or a Paramedic,_ compares and contrasts two similar careers. In the conclusion, instead of analyzing the similarities and differences or reviewing the main points, the writer tries to persuade readers to consider one of these exciting and rewarding careers. Although this conclusion is a little different from the others we have looked at, it is appropriate because it presents the writer's overall opinion about the topic. Notice that Damon has used a variation of the Point-by-Point Method. There are three paragraphs explaining the differences between the two careers, followed by one paragraph about the points that are similar.

Becoming an EMT or a Paramedic
by Damon Aikens

Becoming a Basic Emergency Medical Technician and becoming an Emergency Medical Technician Paramedic are two different processes. Although many of the job duties are somewhat the same, an Emergency Medical Technician Paramedic must undergo more extensive training and learn more advanced skills.

Becoming a Basic EMT includes going to school from one to six months. The class emphasizes anatomy and physiology of the body and the skills required to be an EMT. Some of the skills that you must learn are basic airway management, the application of oxygen inhalation equipment, the use of suction equipment, bandaging and splinting, control of bleeding, cervical spine immobilization, and cardiopulmonary resuscitation. In the state of California, you are tested on these skills twice, once at the end of your class and once at your county certification test. Once you have successfully demonstrated all of these skills to the county evaluators, you can be certified as an EMT 1-A. Then you must obtain an ambulance driver's license, which requires taking a physical exam and having a doctor complete the form given to you by the Department of Motor Vehicles.

After you have been a Basic EMT practicing or working for a minimum of one year, you can apply to paramedic school, which takes about nine months to complete. Other prerequisites for paramedic school are a four-unit anatomy and physiology class, a medical terminology class, and an entrance exam. A lot of the skills are the same as the skills that an EMT has to learn, with advanced components added, such as more sophisticated techniques of airway management. Some additional skills that a paramedic must learn include how to correctly administer 30–35 different medications, how to properly defibrillate a patient in cardiac arrest, how to read an EKG, and how to start IV's. You will also learn pre-hospital trauma life support and advanced cardiac life support, and believe me, these skills will be your best friend out there.

If you decide to go to paramedic school, you will probably be glad that you did because being an EMT 1-A usually does not have all the fame and glory of being a paramedic. EMT's aren't always looked on as having knowledge, and they generally don't get the exciting calls. In fact, in San Diego County, 90% of Basic EMT calls are inter-facility transports, unless you work with a fire department that uses ambulances as first responders to 911 calls, which are few and far between. However, some counties that don't have paramedics depend on EMT's for all emergency medical services. In these areas, EMT's have to handle major medical emergencies even though they have only a few advanced skills.

There are a lot of similarities between the two jobs, such as riding around in an ambulance, responding to emergency calls, and just being your own boss. In this line of work, it's just you and your partner, and maybe a fire engine that responds to calls with you for manpower support. You don't have anyone telling you what to do, so it makes your job a lot easier and more enjoyable. The hours are about the same for both jobs, with twelve and twenty-four hour shifts, and you make a decent income. You have little to do until you get a call, which is great for students.

If you are looking for an exciting career and can overcome a few obstacles, becoming an EMT or a paramedic may be for you. You will feel good about yourself, and the job will be rewarding. In addition, a career as an EMT or a paramedic may open up other doors in the medical field for you.

Response to *Becoming an EMT or a Paramedic*

1. Do you think that the conclusion gives an accurate impression of the two careers? Why or why not?

_____

_____

2. Damon's first point is differences in education and training for the two careers. Why did he use two paragraphs to present this information instead of just one?

_____

_____

3. What other differences does the writer mention?

_____

_____

4. Why do you think the similarities are all in one paragraph?

_____

_____

5. Do you think Damon himself is an EMT or a Paramedic? How can you tell?

_____

_____

To help you get some ideas for your own conclusion, answer the following questions:

- What can readers learn from your comparison/contrast, or how can they benefit?

  _____

  _____

- What do you want readers to remember the most about your topic?

  _____

  _____

- What insights have you personally gained or what have you learned by writing about this topic?

  _____

  _____

- Have you shown that one part of your topic is better than the other in some way because of their differences? If so, in what way is it better?

  _____

  _____

- Does one alternative have certain advantages over the other? If so, what are they?

  _____

  _____

• What else would you like to tell readers about your topic?

_____

_____

_____

_____

One of these ideas may be enough for a good conclusion, or you may combine a couple of them. Don't try to include all six of your answers because your conclusion would be way too long. For most comparison/contrast papers that are a page or two in length, a conclusion with two or three sentences is appropriate. If your paper is less than a page, one concluding sentence can end it effectively.

Write the first draft of your conclusion here:

CONCLUSION (DRAFT #1):

_____

_____

Is this the thought that you would like to leave readers with? Does this conclusion add a feeling of completeness to your paper? Read it to your workshop group and ask for their opinions. They may have some good suggestions about other ideas to include.

If you want to revise your conclusion to make it more effective, write another draft of it here:

CONCLUSION (DRAFT #2):

_____

_____

Now add your conclusion to your rough draft.

At this point, your instructor may ask you to turn in your rough draft, or you may continue to revise and improve it while you are doing Section Two of this chapter, Sentence and Grammar Skills. In Section Two you will learn about using another group of sentence connectors to help you write a greater variety of sentences. Then you will learn about comparative adjectives and adverbs so that you can be sure you have used these kinds of words correctly in your comparison/contrast. The paragraphs in Class Practices 5 and 9 and the two sentence combining paragraphs in Section Two will give you additional examples of comparison/contrast thinking and writing.

SECTION TWO:
Sentence and Grammar Skills

Goals

In this section of the chapter, you will learn how to do the following:

- Recognize advanced compound sentences
- Use semicolons and Group C connecting words to write advanced compound sentences
- Use comparative and superlative forms of adjectives and adverbs

Learning about Advanced Compound Sentences

In Chapter 2 you learned about basic compound sentences, that is, sentences that consist of two SVs joined by a Group A connector. In this chapter you will learn other ways of connecting SVs to make a compound sentence.

Look at the following sentences. How are they connected?

EXAMPLE 1 ➤ Pat wanted to apply for the new position; however, she didn't want to give up her old job.

$$S \qquad V$$
The first clause is *Pat wanted to apply for the new position*.

$$S \qquad V$$
The second clause is *she didn't want to give up her old job*.

They are connected by a *semicolon, however,* and a *comma*, like this:

SV   ; however,   SV.

Here is another example of this type of sentence:

Clause 1   *Clause 2*
Canada has a liberal immigration policy; therefore, many immigrants have come to British Columbia in recent years.

In this sentence, the two clauses are connected by a *semicolon, therefore,* and a *comma*, like this: **SV ; therefore, SV.** *However* and *therefore* are two examples of a group of connectors that follow the same patterns of sentence structure. The formal name for these connectors is *conjunctive adverbs* (or sometimes *adverbial conjunctions*), but in this textbook we will refer to them as *Group C* connectors.

Here is a list of common *Group C* connectors:

as a result	instead
consequently	moreover*
furthermore	nevertheless
however	on the other hand
in addition	otherwise
in contrast	then
in fact	therefore

The first pattern using *Group C* connectors can be written like this:

SV   **; Group C connector,**   **SV.**

In addition to the first pattern shown above, these connectors can be used with a period instead of a semicolon, as in the following examples:

EXAMPLE 1 ➤   Pat wanted to apply for the new position. *However,* she didn't want to give up her old job.

EXAMPLE 2 ➤   Canada has a liberal immigration policy. *Therefore,* many immigrants have come to British Columbia in recent years.

These examples follow the pattern:

SV   **. Group C connector,**   **SV.**

This pattern consists of two simple sentences instead of one compound sentence, but the basic meaning and style are essentially the same as in the first pattern. The Group C connector still joins the idea in the first clause with the idea in the second clause.

You have seen examples of two of the Group C connectors on our list. Here are examples of the rest of them. Some of the examples show the first pattern, and some show the second pattern.

1. **as a result:** Hurricanes often destroy or damage beachfront homes. As a result, homeowner's insurance is more expensive and limited in beach areas.

2. **consequently:** Tokyo is in a very active earthquake zone; consequently, the Japanese government has stored water and supplies in case of a major earthquake.

3. **furthermore:** An earthquake and fire nearly destroyed San Francisco in 1906; furthermore, another large quake is expected sometime in the next 50 years.

---

*Moreover has been included here because it is used in formal academic writing, although not as commonly as the other connecting words listed above. Other words less often used as Group C connectors (at least in recent years) include *also, hence, indeed, rather, similarly,* and *thus.*

4. **in addition:** To reduce the danger of a house fire, store gasoline away from the house and garage. In addition, keep brush cleared a good distance from the house.

5. **in contrast:** Some houses were totally destroyed in the Laguna Beach fire of 1993. In contrast, neighboring houses were sometimes untouched.

6. **in fact:** Many California homeowners have stored water in case of an earthquake; in fact, authorities recommend storing at least three days' worth of water.

7. **instead:** In an earthquake, don't try to run outside right away; instead, experts recommend staying inside and taking cover until the shaking stops.

8. **moreover:** In earthquake areas, storing water is important. Moreover, first aid and other necessary supplies should be included in your earthquake kit.

9. **nevertheless:** There may not be a major earthquake or other natural disaster in your lifetime; nevertheless, it is a good idea to be prepared for the worst.

10. **on the other hand:** Thinking about natural disasters can be scary; however, not thinking about them can be dangerous.

11. **otherwise:** Plan for earthquakes and other natural disasters in advance. Otherwise, things may get rather chaotic.

12. **then:** After the earthquake, get your family outside. Then turn off the gas to your house or apartment building.*

Still another type of compound sentence follows the pattern shown below.

	Clause 1	*Clause 2*
EXAMPLE 3 ➤	Mike was hot and sweaty; he had picked tomatoes for hours in the hot sun.

In this example the two closely related clauses are joined with just a semicolon. A semicolon alone can sometimes be used to join two clauses together if they are closely related in meaning.

These three ways of connecting clauses to make compound sentences can be written as follows:

SV	**; Group C connector,**	**SV.**
SV	**. Group C connector,**	**SV.**
SV	**;**	**SV.**

*The *Group C* connecting word *then* usually isn't followed by a comma.

These three types of compound sentences are fairly formal, and most people do not use them much in short papers. However, it is often useful to include one or two of them to give your writing more sentence variety.

■ CLASS
PRACTICE **1**

Recognizing How Clauses Are Joined

Directions: Mark each subject and verb with S and V if it helps you. Then circle the connector and write one of the following on the line: GROUP A, GROUP B, RELATIVE, GROUP C, or SEMICOLON. If there are two simple sentences, write SIMPLE.

EXAMPLE 1 ➤ _____ The hospital emergency room was very busy; however, the pharmacy was almost empty.

There are two SVs joined by a *Group C* connector. Write *Group C* on the line.

EXAMPLE 2 ➤ _____ Most pine trees don't lose their leaves in the fall, so they are called evergreen trees.

There are two SVs joined by a *Group A* connector. Write *Group A* on the line.

_____ **1.** The medical profession is demanding; however, it pays well.

_____ **2.** Tina chose classes that would help her transfer to the university.

_____ **3.** Jeremy likes the University of Washington, but he was accepted at Loyola.

_____ **4.** Be sure to give credit when you quote someone.

_____ **5.** Lena Gillespie and Renée Williams made a presentation at the Optimists Club meeting. The club members applauded them.

_____ **6.** There was a small explosion in the lab; one group of chemistry students had accidentally mixed the wrong chemicals.

_____ **7.** The museum director praised Tom's art framing ability. Tom thanked him for the compliment.

_____ **8.** I need to mail my application today or it may arrive late.

_____ **9.** A major earthquake is predicted for California in the next 30 years; people living there should take precautions.

_____ **10.** The literature class discussed a new book by Alice Walker, who wrote *The Color Purple*.

■ **CLASS PRACTICE** **2**

Building Sentences with Group C Connectors and Semicolons

Directions: Correctly combine the two simple sentences with an appropriate *Group C* connector or a *semicolon* alone to make one compound sentence. If you prefer, just add a *Group C* connector at the beginning of the second sentence.

EXAMPLE ➤ Sharon wanted to go out. She stayed home and studied for final exams.

Sharon wanted to go out; however, she stayed home and studied for final exams.

Or:

Sharon wanted to go out. Instead, she stayed home and studied for final exams.

1. Mrs. Montes de Oca studies in the library after her classes. She sees a tutor twice a week.

2. Winnie-the-Pooh is a famous character created by A. A. Milne. Most children have not heard of Milne.

3. Sigmund Freud is the father of modern psychology. Nearly all psychology students study his writings.

4. Doing well in college takes a lot of hard work. It can pay off in the long run.

5. Very few ranchers today use traditional methods of raising cattle. They use more profitable modern methods.

_____

_____

6. Plan time for yourself every day. Your health and mental attitude may suffer.

_____

_____

7. The U.S.–Mexico border is heavily traveled. The San Diego–Tijuana border crossing is the busiest in the world.

_____

_____

8. In the days of the early typewriters, keys would often become stuck. The standard typewriter keyboard arrangement was designed to slow the typist's speed and prevent keys from jamming.

_____

_____

■ CLASS
PRACTICE 3

Writing Sentences with Group C Connectors and Semicolons

Directions: Now write your own sentences using a *Group C* connector or a *semicolon* between the two clauses. Use a different *Group C* connector in each sentence, and write at least one sentence for each pattern:

Pattern 1:	S V	; Group C connector,	S V.
Pattern 2:	S V	. Group C connector,	S V.
Semicolon:	S V	;	S V.

1. _____

_____

2 _____

_____

3. _____

_____

4. _____

_____

5. _____

_____

When you are finished, ask another student to check that each sentence uses a *Group C* connector or a *semicolon* correctly.

Avoiding Common Sentence Errors

In previous chapters you learned about correct sentence structures as well as how to avoid common sentence structure errors. Here is a chart of the eight main ways of connecting two clauses (or separating them, in the case of the period) that you have seen so far:

Correct			*Connected by:*
SV	.	SV.	a period.
SV	, Group A connector	SV.	a comma and a Group A connector
SV	Group B connector	SV.	a Group B connector (or relative connector)
Group B connector SV,		SV.	a Group B connector at the beginning
S	Rel SV	V.	a relative connector
SV	. Group C connector,	SV.	a period, Group C connector, and a comma
SV	; Group C connector,	SV.	a semicolon, Group C connector, and a comma
SV	;	SV.	a semicolon alone

When your clauses are not connected in one of these eight ways, there is a strong possibility that they are incorrect. A sentence can be incorrect for many reasons. For example, it could be punctuated incorrectly. If you put a comma before a *Group B* connector, for instance, it is nearly always incorrect. It is also incorrect if you use a comma instead of a period or semi-colon in front of a *Group C* connector, or if you forget to put a comma before a *Group A* connector, unless the sentence is short. You should also check for run-on sentences, comma splices, and fragments. Refer back to previous chapters if you need to review these common errors.

■ **CLASS PRACTICE** **4**

Correcting Sentence Structure Errors

Directions: Correct all comma splices, run-ons, fragments, and punctuation errors with any of the correct sentence patterns you have studied.

1. Population growth is a worldwide concern; although, countries differ as to which course to take.

   _____

   _____

2. Education can be the key to a better job; therefore, learn all you can while you're in school.

   _____

   _____

3. Travel is enlightening it can expand your horizons.

   _____

   _____

4. The earth is a precious and irreplaceable resource therefore we must take good care of it.

   _____

   _____

5. Gambling and other addictions can be overcome; don't be afraid to ask for help.

_____

_____

6. The biology instructor required a 12-page paper, furthermore. It had to be typed.

_____

_____

7. City officials in Tucson, Arizona, don't wear a suit and tie in the summer, the official summer uniform is the Guayabera, or Mexican wedding shirt.

_____

_____

8. The windsurfers on San Diego's Mission Bay were thankful for the steady breeze, however. They watched the dark clouds with apprehension.

_____

_____

9. A new variety of insect was discovered in the Peruvian Andes; and it was named after its discoverer.

_____

_____

10. In a very wintry storm on the Bay of Biscayne.

_____

_____

Proofreading for Sentence Structure Errors

Directions: Check the sentences in the following paragraph. Correct run-ons, comma splices, fragments, and punctuation errors by using a period, a *Group A, B,* or *C* connector, a relative connector, or a semicolon between the clauses.

Julian and Borrego Springs

When most people think of San Diego County, palm trees and beaches come to mind. That picture is an incomplete one in fact the county of San Diego has a wide variety of climate zones ranging from desert to seashore to mountains. There are nine coastal cities in the county, there are also some communities with completely different settings and climates, two of these communities are Julian, in the mountains, and Borrego Springs, in the desert.

Julian, a historic mining town in the nearby Cuyamaca mountains, is a popular destination for native San Diegans. It is famous for its apple pies, bed-and-breakfast inns, and fresh mountain air it is just an hour's drive from downtown San Diego. It almost never snows in metropolitan areas of San Diego County, consequently; after a winter storm, locals often head for Julian to show their children what snow is and just enjoy the small-town atmosphere more adventurous types can tour the Eagle Gold Mine visitors can also spend the day hiking or cross-country skiing in the thickly-forested state parks nearby.

East of Julian, the highway takes a sudden drop out of the mountains, and within 30 minutes travelers find themselves driving through the high desert on the way to Borrego Springs, a town set in the Anza-Borrego Desert State park, every spring, tourists come from all over the United States and foreign countries in the hope of seeing the sometimes-spectacular desert wildflowers bloom. Some people come for the many excellent hiking trails, others explore the incredible geological formations on foot or in four-wheel-drive vehicles. For those who prefer less exercise, there are several good camping areas; and comfortable lodge-type accommodations can be reserved as well. Accommodations can be very crowded at certain times of the year therefore; be sure to make reservations.

On your next trip to San Diego, consider visiting one or both of these towns for a taste of a different side of San Diego County. You will enjoy some of the lesser-known attractions of the region and begin to see the San Diego that the locals know.

■ **CLASS PRACTICE** 6

Writing with Advanced Compound Sentences

PART A: Looking at Writing from an Example Paper

Directions: Look at the following sentences from *Judo Versus Wrestling*, by Ray Jensen, on page 224, and highlight or underline the advanced compound sentences. Notice that the author used a few sentences of this type as well as other types of sentences. Hint: look for *Group C* connectors.

One of the main differences between judo and wrestling is the throws. In wrestling, there are very few throws that are legal, and most of them are very painful to the receiver. In fact, most of the throws are not intended, and they can result in broken bones. If a throw is done in wrestling, it rarely accomplishes much. However, in judo there are many throws, and the throws are taught as an art. A judo student learns the kata (the motions of the throw) before he learns the actual throw. The judo student is trained to throw his opponent in such a way as to give the least pain and danger. Also, the judo student is trained to fall correctly to avoid hurting himself.

Besides the throws, the pinning techniques make competition in judo easier. In wrestling, the wrestler has to have both shoulders of his opponent touching the mat in order to win. The count is for approximately five seconds, and sometimes the referee does not or cannot see whether both shoulders are actually touching. Many times, the wrestler gets his opponent's shoulders on the mat, and just before the count is over, his opponent moves, forcing him to lose all the effort he put into it. In contrast, the judo student only has to have his opponent in a "controlled hold," which does not require both shoulders touching.

PART B: Looking at Your Own Writing

Directions: Find one or two sentences from your own *Comparison/Contrast* rough draft where you have used a Group C connector or a semicolon to join two clauses, and write them in the blanks below. If you don't have any of these sentences, you may want to replace one or two of your sentences in order to achieve greater variety. Write your new sentences in the blanks below.

1. _____

   _____

   _____

   _____

2. _____

   _____

   _____

Now check your sentences by marking the subjects and verbs in each sentence and circling the *Group C connector* or the *semicolon*. In addition, check to see if the sentences sound natural in your paper.

Comparison/Contrast Sentence Combining Paragraph

Directions: You may use Group A, Group B, and Group C connectors, semicolons, relative connectors, or any other effective way of joining the sentences.

Speaking and Writing

1.1   Spoken English is usually casual.
1.2   Written English is more formal.

2.1   Written English requires sentence structure.
2.2   Written English requires grammar.
2.3   Written English requires punctuation.
2.4   Written English requires spelling.
2.5   All of these must be correct.

3.1   In contrast, someone is speaking.
3.2   Sentence structure is less important.
3.3   Formal grammar is less important.
3.4   Spelling does not matter.
3.5   Punctuation does not matter.

4.1   People often use slang words.
4.2   People often use fragments.
4.3   People often use sentences that go on and on.
4.4   This happens when they are talking.

5.1   Most listeners don't pay any attention to errors.
5.2   The only important thing is the message.
5.3   This is the message that the speaker wants to communicate.

6.1   Unlike speaking, writing requires planning.
6.2   The planning is careful.
6.3   The planning is of what you are going to say.

7.1   For example, you are writing a composition.
7.2   Your paper must be clearly organized.
7.3   You must state the main idea clearly.
7.4   All of the details must relate to your topic sentence.

8.1   On the other hand, speaking is almost always informal.
8.2   We do not usually plan what we are going to say.

9.1   Most of us just say something.
9.2   It's whatever comes to mind.
9.3   This is done without any planning.
9.4   This happens unless we are making a speech or presentation.

10.1 However, when we write, we have to think more.
10.2 We think about what we are saying.
10.3 We say it with our pen.
10.4 We say it with our typewriter.
10.5 We say it with our computer.

11.1 Speaking and writing are different in many ways.
11.2 We need both of them to communicate effectively.
11.3 The communication is in different situations.

Learning about Comparatives and Superlatives

In Chapter 3 you learned about using adjectives and adverbs to add interest to your writing. In this chapter we will look at two special forms of adjectives and adverbs that are used to compare and contrast the people or things you are writing about or to point out that one person or thing stands out from the others in some way.

Comparative Forms of Adjectives and Adverbs

Comparative Form for One-Syllable Adjectives

Look at the sentences below and notice the comparative form of the one-syllable adjectives:

EXAMPLE 1 ➤   high

Dmitri received a *high* grade on his description paper.

Dmitri's description paper received a *higher* grade *than* his narration paper.

High is the adjective that describes what kind of grade Dmitri received. *Higher* is the comparative form of *high*; it compares the grades Dmitri received on his two papers. Notice that the word *than* is often used with the comparative form. Use *than* before the second person or thing that you are comparing.

EXAMPLE 2 ➤   new

Roy bought his car in 1995, and Cindy bought her *new* Toyota pickup truck in 1996.

Cindy's truck is *newer than* Roy's car.

Newer is the comparative form of the adjective *new*.
Did you notice the pattern?
For short adjectives, that is, adjectives that have only one syllable, add *-er* to the adjective.

Spelling Rules

There are a couple of rules that affect the spelling of *-er* comparative adjectives. Look at how the comparative form is spelled in the following examples:

The Silent -e Rule

EXAMPLE 3 ➤   large

The new authors hoped for a *large* advance on their royalties.

In fact, they received a *larger* advance than they had anticipated.

Notice that the comparative form *larger* just adds an *-r* to the adjective *large*. If the adjective ends with an *-e*, just add *-r*. Here is another example of this rule:

EXAMPLE 4 ➤   late

Sulema usually gets up *late*, around 9:00.

Louis gets up even *later than* Sulema, around 10:00 or 11:00.

The Double Consonant Rule

EXAMPLE 5 ➤   thin

Before his illness, Rob was *thin*.

After being sick, Rob was even *thinner*.

In this case, the final consonant is doubled when the last three letters of the adjective are a consonant, a vowel, and a consonant. See Appendix IV on page 456 if you want to review the complete spelling rule.

Some Two-Syllable Adjectives: -er Ending

Most two-syllable adjectives that end in *-y* or *-ow* also end in *-er* in the comparative form. For two-syllable adjectives that end in *-y*, change the *y* to *i* and add *-er*.

EXAMPLE 6 ➤ narrow

Debbie's feet are *narrow*.

Dee's feet are *narrower than* Debbie's feet.

EXAMPLE 7 ➤ happy

Teresa's supervisor is usually *happy*.

In fact, her supervisor seems *happier than* most of the other supervisors.

Comparative Form for Longer Adjectives: More

Two-syllable adjectives that don't end in *-y* or *-ow* form the comparative by adding *more*, and so do all adjectives of three or more syllables. Look at the examples below:

EXAMPLE 8 ➤ modest

Rachel was very *modest* about her swimming trophy.

She was even *more modest* about winning the spelling bee at school.

EXAMPLE 9 ➤ impressive

Yerma's diploma looked *impressive* on her dresser.

Her diploma looked *more impressive* on her wall *than* it did on her dresser.

Exceptions

Finally, there is a group of adjectives that don't follow these rules. Here are examples of a few of them:

The adjective *good* has an irregular comparative form: *better*.

EXAMPLE 10 ➤ good

Julie thinks that Ben's poetry is *good*.

Kate thinks that Raúl's poetry is *better than* Ben's.

Worse is the irregular comparative form of the adjective *bad*.

EXAMPLE 11 ➤   bad

Walter was having a *bad* day.

The day before had been even *worse*.

-ly Adverbs

To form the comparative of adverbs with *-ly* endings, just use *more*. (To review adverbs, see Chapter 3.) Here is an example of a comparative adverb:

EXAMPLE 12 ➤   quietly

The librarian *quietly* answered my question.

He reshelved the books even *more quietly*.

Irregular Adverbs

There are also a few other irregular comparative adverbs. *Well* is one of the most common:

EXAMPLE 13 ➤   fast

It's important to think *fast* in an emergency.

Some people react *faster* than others.

EXAMPLE 14 ➤   well

Jaime dances *well*.

He dances *better than* his partner does.

Some adverbs don't end in -ly. For example, *faster* is the comparative form of the adverb *fast*.

 ■ CLASS PRACTICE 7

Comparative Forms of Adjectives and Adverbs

Directions: For each sentence below, write another sentence using the comparative form of the adjective or adverb given. Use *than* where it is appropriate.

1. Tami has fine hair that doesn't take a perm well.

   Pat's hair is even finer than Tami's.

2. Ryusuke thought his old car was *ugly*.

   _____

3. Linda *carefully* checked her homework in her workshop group.

_____

4. Helena skated *well* in the competition.

_____

5. The warm sun on my back felt *wonderful*.

_____

6. Scott's cheeks were *red* from the intense sun.

_____

Superlative Forms of Adjectives and Adverbs

In your comparison/contrast paper, when you want to point out that one person or thing is exceptional, or "super," you can use the superlative form of adjectives and adverbs. The rules are very similar to the rules for the comparatives:

To make the superlative form of one-syllable adjectives or adverbs, or two-syllable adjectives that end in *-y* or *-ow*, add *-est*.

EXAMPLE 1 ➤ loud

The band played *loud* music.

It was *the loudest* music I had ever heard.

Don't forget to apply the silent *-e* and double consonant spelling rules. Also, notice that the word *the* is often used with the superlative form.

EXAMPLE 2 ➤ lazy

Your cat is so *lazy* it won't even move out of the way when someone tries to open the door.

That cat is *the laziest* cat I have ever seen!

For longer adjectives and adverbs, use *the most*.

EXAMPLE 3 ➤ difficult

Digging the ditch was very *difficult*.

It was *the most difficult* job I did this summer.

EXAMPLE 4 ➤   beautifully

This blanket is *beautifully* woven.

It's *the most beautifully* woven blanket I've ever seen.

Finally, there are also some irregular superlatives:

EXAMPLE 5 ➤   good

What a good idea!

That is *the best* idea I have heard in a long time.

EXAMPLE 6 ➤   bad

It was a *bad* day for catching trout.

It was *the worst* day for fishing that we had all season.

■ **CLASS PRACTICE** **8**   ## Superlative Form of Adjectives and Adverbs

Directions: For each sentence below, write another sentence using the superlative form of the adjective or adverb given.

1. Dagmar's sketches are *inspiring*.

   Dagmar's sketches are **the most inspiring** *in the exhibition.*

2. Tony is a very *fast* typist.

   _____

3. Socorro danced *gracefully*.

   _____

4. This paper is very *good*.

   _____

5. The music in the department store was very *mellow*.

   _____

6. The Sonora Desert gets very *hot* in the summer.

   _____

■ **CLASS**
PRACTICE 9

Proofreading for Comparatives
and Superlatives

Directions: The following paragraph contains several errors with comparative and superlative forms of adjectives and adverbs. Cross out the incorrect forms and write in the correct form above the error.

Ask for Help or Handle it Alone?

Most people have experienced serious problems at one time or another. Sometimes these problems are more big than others. There are two basic ways of dealing with a problem. You can either ask for help or handle the problem alone. If you decide to get help, you will probably feel more relaxed than if you go it alone, and you may solve your problem more fast and more better than if you face it alone. It may be the most difficult to tell someone about your problem, though. On the other hand, facing and overcoming a problem by yourself can make you feel more stronger than before, and the most confident you have ever been. However, some problems are more scary, and you should not be embarrassed to ask for help when you think it is necessary. It's OK to try to solve a problem by yourself as long as you are willing to ask for help when it is necessary. Asking for help may be the bestest thing you have ever done.

Comparison/Contrast Sentence
Combining Paragraph

Directions: Many of the following sentences use comparative adjectives and adverbs. You may combine the sentences any way that sounds natural and effective.

Crazy about Both

1.1 I'm crazy about Tom.
1.2 I'm crazy about Cecil.
1.3 They have different personalities.
1.4 They have different habits.

2.1   Cecil has a more laid-back personality than Tom.
2.2   He accepts things as they happen.
2.3   He is one of the most relaxed friends that I have.

3.1   Tom is more aggressive.
3.2   He is also more selfish.
3.3   He always wants to have his own way.

4.1   He is more likely to get into fights than Cecil is.
4.2   Sometimes he shows up with cuts on his face.
4.3   Sometimes he shows up with a bump on his head.

5.1   However, Tom also tends to be friendlier.
5.2   He tends to be more affectionate.
5.3   He is this way with me.

6.1   Sometimes he curls up with me on the couch for hours.
6.2   He seems to enjoy my company more than Cecil does.

7.1   Tom also talks to me more often than Cecil.
7.2   Cecil seems to be the silent type.
7.3   He keeps his opinions to himself.

8.1   As for appearance, they are both handsome.
8.2   Each one has his own distinctive look.

9.1   They are both about the same height.
9.2   Tom is built more sturdily.
9.3   Cecil has a more delicate bone structure.

10.1   Cecil's hair is much longer.
10.2   His hair is much lighter in color.
10.3   This is in contrast to Tom's short, dark hair.

11.1   Tom is usually more neatly groomed.
11.2   Cecil sometimes looks a little bit scruffy.
11.3   He doesn't bother with his appearance as much as Tom does.

12.1   One of Cecil's best qualities is that he never complains.
12.2   Tom often complains about things.
12.3   These are things that he doesn't like.

13.1   However, Cecil likes to go out by himself.
13.2   He does this more often than Tom does.
13.3   I think Tom is the happiest at home.
13.4   Tom is the most contented at home.

14.1   I have to admit something.
14.2   I love both of them.
14.3   This is in spite of their odd ways.
14.4   This is in spite of their faults.

15.1   Our family would be incomplete without these two cats.
15.2   They seem more like people than pets.

Putting the Finishing Touches on Your Writing

Before you turn in your completed comparison/contrast paper, read it again and see if you are happy with it. Pay attention to the organization, especially the topic sentence and comparison/contrast pattern that you have chosen, and make sure that the information in the body supports your topic sentence. Check your sentences as well. You should have a wide variety of sentence types, without run-ons, comma splices, or fragments. The sentences should also be correctly punctuated.

The following comparison/contrast writing checklist is useful for making a final check before you hand in your final draft. If you cannot answer *yes* to all of the questions, ask your teacher or workshop group to help you decide if you need to revise anything.

Comparison/Contrast Writing Checklist

Content and Organization

_____ 1. Does my paper give an accurate picture of the two parts of my topic?

_____ 2. Are the most important similarities and/or differences explained?

_____ 3. Does the topic sentence (or main idea statement) identify the similarities or differences or express an overall idea about them?

_____ 4. Is my comparison/contrast organized effectively using either the Block Method or the Point-by-Point Method?

_____ 5. Have I included enough details to make all of the points clear?

_____ 6. Are transitions used smoothly and effectively?

_____ 7. Does my conclusion tell the reader something important to remember about the topic?

Sentence Structure and Grammar

_____ 1. Did I use Group C connecting words correctly?

_____ 2. If I used a semicolon to connect two clauses, are the clauses closely related in meaning?

_____ 3. Have I avoided using fragments?

_____ 4. Have I avoided run-ons and comma splices?

_____ 5. If comparative or superlative adjectives and adverbs are used to describe some of the differences, are they correctly written?

ENRICHMENT SECTION:
Writing an Imaginative Comparison

Goals

In the enrichment section of this chapter, you will learn how to do the following:

- Use your imagination to create comparisons
- Write a paper based on an imaginative comparison
- Illustrate your main idea with interesting details

In addition to being an informative way to analyze two related topics, comparison/contrast thinking can add interesting and imaginative details to other kinds of writing. For instance, in some of the example papers that we have read in previous chapters, writers used these imaginative comparisons:

Then I remembered my little sister Marissa, and I covered her completely, *like a shell on a turtle.* (from *Earthquake*, by Deanna Hernandez)

Instantly the night became deathly quiet, and *we froze like rabbits.* (from *The Howl* by Mark Field)

As sunlight fades, the fiery sky calms down and is replaced with a deep azure that twinkles with *the freckles of the night's face.* (from *Horsethief Canyon* by Shawn McPherren)*

If an imaginative comparison is developed with more details, it can become the basis for writing an interesting comparison paragraph or short paper.

The enrichment activity for this chapter is to write an imaginative comparison that is one full paragraph or more in length. Your topic must be two things that are not normally considered to be similar, but by using your imagination you will show that they are actually alike in some ways. For example, a student once claimed that writing a paper was like having a tooth pulled: he was nervous beforehand, and the process was sometimes agonizing, but he felt relieved and happy when it was finished! Someone else might have said that writing is more like riding a camel, trying to catch a butterfly, climbing a mountain, planting a garden, or something else. As you can see, there is no right or wrong comparison to use. Whatever you choose, you simply need to discover enough unexpected similarities to make it work.

---

*Brief comparisons like the first two examples are also called *similes*. The third example, which compares things without using the word *like,* is a *metaphor*. Imaginative similes and metaphors often appear in poetry as well as in other types of writing.

Writing an imaginative comparison can actually be more fun than most kinds of writing—not at all like having a tooth pulled. You may want to write something humorous for this assignment, or you may choose a serious topic. Either way, the key to enjoying the process of writing is to find a topic that appeals to you. Feel free to try some unconventional, even outrageous topic ideas if you want to. For example, is your best friend like a kitten, a shark, a fairy godmother, or a brick wall? Of course, your friend does not *look* like one of these, but maybe he or she is playful like a kitten, can sometimes attack viciously like a shark, tries to fulfill everyone's wishes like a fairy godmother, or is solid and immovable like a brick wall.

The writer of *A Tree Like Me*, Aurora Alvarez, got her unusual topic idea one day while she was driving to school. She happened to notice a huge, beautiful tree and suddenly imagined herself like that tree. Before you read her paper, think about her topic for a moment. In what ways do you think she might be like a tree? Do you expect her to be tall and leafy? Are there any ways in which *you* could be compared with a tree? See if any of her points of comparison surprise you.

A Tree like Me
by Aurora Alvarez

Although I have climbed a tree, have eaten fruit from a tree, and have felt the breeze when I sat under a tree, I've taken this wondrous woody plant for granted. Even though a tree and a human being are very different, we have many things in common. Just like a tree has roots, a trunk, and branches, I also have them. A tree provides food and shelter to many creatures, reproduces, and eventually dies, and I'm also capable of doing these same things.

A tree's roots are essential for its development. Roots serve as the support system to draw and store food. The more roots expand, the taller a tree will grow. A tree without roots wouldn't be able to stand on its own; therefore, any wind would blow it away. My roots are my spiritual beliefs and the relationship I have with God, the values I get from my family, and the traditions I have gained from my culture. As I increase my knowledge of my roots, I have a better chance of understanding myself and of having confidence in who I am. Roots are a vital part of a tree and of me because with them we can know where we came from and where we're going.

The woody part of a tree is its trunk. The trunk holds the vessels that make it possible for water and food to reach the branches and leaves. It also serves as a torso which the roots and branches are connected to. My trunk is where my vital organs are as well as vessels so that blood and other liquids can travel through my body. Like a tree, I can't be a complete person without the torso that my limbs and head are attached to.

I see the branches of a tree like my arms. A tree's branches offer the comfort of shade and cool air. The way branches are spread and open is like when I open my arms to give someone a nurturing, affectionate, or caring hug. I can also give people comfort with my arms when they are sad or hurt. If the branches of a tree fall on someone, the person may be injured, just as hands can hit someone and cause an injury.

A tree can provide food and shelter for many insects, animals, and humans too. Just as a tree provides leaves, seeds, and fruit that can be eaten, my body also has the ability to provide food. I was capable of feeding the fetus when I was pregnant and producing milk after my baby was born. A tree can protect people from the strong rays of the sun, from strong winds, and from heavy rains. The way I provide shelter for myself and for my family is by having a home.

A tree may reproduce itself when a seed has fallen to the ground and gotten covered with soil; afterwards, nature provides the essentials for it to grow. I can also reproduce when I have a baby. The baby is a product of the union of my egg with the sperm of my partner. So even when a tree dies, or when I die, it is not a loss because we both have left something of ourselves on this earth.

Trees are something that we need to be thankful for because without them this planet wouldn't have enough natural oxygen for us to breathe. Maybe if people could start relating more to trees, they would respect them and give them the space that they rightly deserve.

Response to *A Tree Like Me*

1. List all the characteristics that the writer says she has in common with a tree.

   _____

   _____

   _____

   _____

   _____

2. Instead of using just one sentence for her topic sentence idea, this writer used two. Which two sentences are they?

   _____

   Why do you think she used two sentences?

   _____

   _____

You too may be able to write an interesting comparison about yourself if you are willing to stretch your imagination. What could you compare yourself with? Are you like a good book? Or are you more like a bag of popcorn? Do you sometimes act like a lion or maybe like a monkey or a wild mustang? Remember that your comparison must be something imaginative, not something that is literally true. Try answering these questions to explore some topic ideas about yourself:

1. If you were an animal, what animal would you be?

   _____

2. If you were a cartoon character, which one would you be?

   _____

3. If you were a food or a plant, what would you be?

   _____

4. If you were a country, city, state, or other geographical location, what would you be?

   _____

5. If you were a song, which song would you be?

   _____

6. If you were a car, plane, or some other vehicle, which model would you be?

   _____

7. If your life were a book, television show, or movie, which one would it be?

   _____

8. Other Ideas:

   Sometimes I feel like or act like a _____

   Sometimes my life seems like a _____

   I'd like to compare myself to a _____

If you don't want to write about yourself, try answering the same questions about some of your friends or relatives. You may also have some other creative ideas of your own for an imaginative comparison topic. If you have trouble choosing a topic idea to write about, you may want to check with your instructor before making your decision.

Once you have found a topic that you like, make a list of all the similarities that you can think of. If you want to use a *Dividing and Listing Worksheet* like the one that you used earlier in this chapter, there are extra worksheets in Appendix I. Remember that your topic sentence should identify the kinds of similarities that you are going to write about. It probably will not be necessary to mention differences because they will most likely be obvious. (Readers will know that you don't actually look like a red Corvette, for example.) If possible, organize the body of your paper using the Point-by-Point Method explained earlier in this chapter so that the points of comparison will be easy to follow. Then develop your paper with interesting details and examples showing how the two parts of your topic are alike or similar, and add a conclusion that leaves readers with a final thought or insight about your topic.

■ ■ ■ **6**

Writing That Classifies Things

SECTION ONE:
The Writing Process for Classification

Goals

In this section of the chapter, you will learn how to do the following:

- Use sorting to identify categories
- Use outlining to organize a classification
- Plan and develop a classification paragraph or short paper
- Write an effective classification topic sentence and conclusion
- Write clear, accurate definitions

Learning about Classification

What Is Classification?

Whenever we place things into categories, we are using *classification*. There are many useful classifications that are part of our daily lives. For example, if we are trying to decide which movie to see, we may want to consider the ratings of the movies: G, PG, PG-13, R, NC-17, or X. These ratings are one way of *classifying* movies. That is, they place the movies into categories, which are based on the appropriateness of the content for different audiences.

263

Another example of classification is the organization of our public school systems into categories that represent different levels. These categories are generally identified as elementary school, junior high school, high school, and college. In some parts of the country, different terms may be used, such as middle school instead of junior high, but the classification is basically the same. Students are placed at different levels (in different categories) according to their age and/or the difficulty of the classes at each level.

In any classification, items are placed into appropriate categories by using some specific guideline or criterion, which is the *organizing principle*. In the previous examples, the *organizing principle* for movie ratings is the content of the movies, and the *organizing principle* for the school system is students' age and/or the level of difficulty. An organizing principle always serves as the basis for identifying and naming the categories in a classification, as well as for placing items into the categories.

Many classifications, like movie ratings and the school system, are widely accepted and generally agreed upon by everyone. However, in other cases, we may create our own classifications. For example, what about the types of friends that you have? Could you place your friends in categories based on some organizing principle? Are you closer to some than to others? Do you spend more time with some than with others? Most of us would probably agree that our friends could be sorted into categories such as best friends, close friends, and casual friends. The organizing principle for this classification might be how close we feel to different friends or the activities we do with them. With this type of classification, we can name the categories ourselves.

There are also times when we use classification to examine things very objectively, such as in scientific experiments or investigations. For example, if you are trying to identify several rocks that you have found, you could do various tests on them and then classify the rocks according to the results. One test might be how they react with a weak acid solution such as vinegar. Rocks that have no reaction at all would be grouped together in one category. Rocks that bubble and dissolve when vinegar is dripped on them would be in another category. Classifications like this can help us understand our physical environment. Thus classification is a very useful scientific process, as well as a way of thinking that we use in our everyday lives.

Writing Objective: Identifying Categories and Explaining Them

Your writing objective for this chapter is to set up a classification with two or more categories and write an informative paper that explains the categories. Unless your instructor asks you to write a one-paragraph classification, you should consider writing at least four paragraphs: an introductory paragraph, one paragraph about each category in your classification, and a concluding paragraph. The basic writing process that you will learn in this chapter will work for any classification paper, no matter how short or how long.

One option is to write about a traditional classification that has well-known categories, such as types of college degrees or basic food groups. For this kind of classification, you should choose a topic that you are knowledgeable about so that you can write an informative paper. A classification that you have recently read about or studied in one of your other classes might be a good topic.

Another option is to create your own classification by identifying and naming the categories yourself, using one organizing principle. For example, if you decide to classify the various student clubs at your college, you might sort them into categories such as academic clubs, ethnic clubs, service clubs, and social clubs, based on the common interests that bring club members together. These common interests would be the organizing principle for the classification. In the body of the paper, you would define and explain each category that you have set up.

Whether you are writing about a traditional classification or one that you set up yourself, don't choose a topic that has too many categories to cover in a short paper. A classification of all the courses offered at a local community college, for example, might require pages and pages to explain because you would have to write about every kind of course that is offered: mathematics, science, art, economics, political science, history, business, sociology, drama, physical education, health sciences, psychology, auto repair, architecture, English, and so on. A better choice for a topic would be the types of courses offered in just one subject area or field, such as vocational courses.

As you begin your classification paper, you should explain the organizing principle that your categories are based on. Then the categories should be discussed, one at a time, with emphasis on the unique features that distinguish items in each category from items in the other categories. Explain to readers how each category differs from the other categories, as well as what the items in each group or category have in common. If possible, mention a few examples of typical items that will help readers understand each category. Many classifications also include specific comparisons or contrasts between different categories.

Prewriting Activities

Before exploring topics for your classification paper, it is important to understand how classification works. In the first prewriting activity, *Practice with Classifying,* you will learn how to set up a classification by finding an appropriate organizing principle and then sorting items into categories. Then you will be ready to think about possible topics for your own paper. After you have selected a topic, a special prewriting activity will help you figure out an effective organizing principle and identify categories. Finally, outlining will show you another way to make sure that your classification is planned and organized effectively.

Practice with Classifying

If possible, do this activity with a group of classmates so that you can share your ideas. Using an imaginary situation, you will work together to find an organizing principle and set up categories for a classification.

Classification Situation: Kinds of Pets

Joy decided to write about different kinds of pets that parents might choose for their children, including some of the special characteristics of each. Because she was working at a pet store, she thought this classification would be helpful to some of her customers. In order to plan her classification paper, she needed to figure out an organizing principle so that she could set up categories of animals to write about. She began by listing all of the kinds of pets she could think of. This is her list:

mice	puppies
snakes	finches
hamsters	tropical fish
canaries	cockatiels
kittens	tarantulas
rats	rabbits
turtles	guinea pigs
goldfish	iguanas
gerbils	parakeets
pot-bellied pigs	lizards

Next she had to decide what organizing principle to use. Can you suggest one? Think about the different characteristics of each pet on the list, and try to find an organizing principle that would allow you to sort the animals into groups. The animals in each group must be similar in some way. Write your idea for an organizing principle here:

ORGANIZING PRINCIPLE #1:

_____

Using the principle that you have identified, what groups, or categories, could the animals be placed in? Identify at least two categories but no more than six. To make sure that your classification works, write the names of the categories on the lines below, and then list all of the animals that belong in each category. Be sure that every animal on the list can be sorted into one of the categories. If some animals don't fit into any of your categories, try renaming some categories or using a different organizing principle.

Category 1	Category 2	Category 3
_____	_____	_____
_____	_____	_____
_____	_____	_____
_____	_____	_____
_____	_____	_____
_____	_____	_____

Category 4	Category 5	Category 6
_____	_____	_____
_____	_____	_____
_____	_____	_____
_____	_____	_____
_____	_____	_____

The first classification that Joy thought of was based on the different types of animals, such as birds, fish, rodents, and so on. However, she decided to consider some other organizing principles too before writing her paper. What other ways can you think of to sort all of the pets on the list into two or more categories? Try to come up with other organizing principles that would work and write them on the lines below. The list is started for you.

ORGANIZING PRINCIPLE #2:
whether animals make noise or don't make noise

ORGANIZING PRINCIPLE #3:

_____

ORGANIZING PRINCIPLE #4:

_____

Share your ideas for organizing principles with some of your classmates. You may also want to sort the animals again using categories based on principles 2, 3, or 4. After discussing the different organizing principles, do you like one better than the others? Why?

_____

_____

_____

_____

_____

_____

An effective classification paper could be written using any organizing principle that allows all of the pets to be placed in an appropriate category. However, for her paper, Joy decided to classify the pets according to the type of enclosure they needed. Using this organizing principle, she had three categories: pets that need no special enclosure (kittens, puppies, pot-bellied pigs), pets that can be kept in an aquarium (goldfish, tropical fish, snakes, lizards, tarantulas, turtles, mice), and pets that usually need a cage (canaries, finches, cockatiels, parakeets, hamsters, guinea pigs, gerbils, rats, rabbits, iguanas). Since customers at the pet store often needed to purchase a cage or an aquarium along with their new pet, this classification would be useful for her and her audience.

Exploring Topics for Classification

Your topic for your classification must consist of several items (things, people, or ideas) that can be sorted into categories, like the pets in the previous activity. For this reason, it will be helpful to begin by thinking of your topic as a group of similar items to place in categories, such as rocks, restaurants, drugs, clocks, boats, hairstyles, athletic shoes, picnics, jewelry, branches of government, planets, or just about any other group of things. With some topics, such as branches of government, well-known categories may come to mind immediately. However, with most topics, the next step will be finding an organizing principle to use in setting up categories.

On the _Exploring Topics Worksheet,_ write down some things that you are interested in and may want to consider as possible topics. Although any group of items can be classified, be careful not to choose a huge topic with hundreds of items or lots of categories, such as cities of the world or breeds of dogs. If your topic has more than four or five categories, it will probably be too much to explain in a paragraph or short paper.

■ **WORSHEET I**

Exploring Topics for Classification

Directions: Fill in the blanks with some possible topics. Try to think of things you are interested in that could be placed in categories. A few ideas are already listed to help you get started.

1. What things at your workplace could be sorted into different categories?

   Types of jobs _____   _____

   Types of computers _____   _____

   _____   _____

   _____   _____

2. Can you think of some objects, ideas, or other things to classify that are related to one of your classes? Try to recall classifications that have been presented in your classes or textbooks.

   Types of sentences *(English class)*   _____

   _____   _____

   _____   _____

3. People can be sorted into categories too. List some interesting kinds of people that you could classify.

   Types of students _____   _____

   Types of musicians _____   _____

   _____   _____

   _____   _____

4. List any other classification topics that you can think of.

   Types of sports _____   _____

   Types of jokes _____   _____

   _____   _____

   _____   _____

Discovering Details 1: Identifying Categories

In order to identify categories to use in your classification, you will need to decide on an organizing principle. For most topics, there is more than one organizing principle that could be used, so you may want to consider several possibilities. For example, it would be possible to classify sports on the basis of whether they're played by teams (team sports, individual sports), whether there is body contact (contact sports, noncontact sports), or even according to the type of footwear that participants use (regular athletic shoes, shoes with cleats, shoes with blades, non-shoe footwear, bare feet, etc.).

Can you think of any organizing principles that would work for the topic of *crimes?* Do some crimes have certain characteristics while others have different characteristics? The idea is to find an organizing principle that will allow you to put crimes with certain characteristics in one group and crimes with other characteristics in other groups. Here is a chart that shows one possible organizing principle and categories that are based on it:

Topic	*Organizing Principle*	*Categories*
Crimes	seriousness of the crimes	1. misdemeanors
		2. felonies

Using the organizing principle of *seriousness of the crime,* the two categories are misdemeanors and felonies. This is a well-known classification in the United States legal system.

Another way to classify crimes could be according to the type of injury to victims. Here is a chart showing categories that could be set up with this organizing principle:

Topic	*Organizing Principle*	*Categories*
Crimes	type of injury to victims	1. death
		2. physical injury
		3. financial injury
		4. emotional injury

The writer could choose either organizing principle, seriousness of the crimes or type of injury to victims, as the basis for an effective classification of crimes.

The next chart shows one way that the topic of recreational boats could be classified by using the organizing principle of how the boat is powered:

Topic	*Organizing Principle*	*Categories*
Recreational boats	how the boat is powered	1. sailboats
		2. motorboats
		3. oar-powered boats

Other organizing principles could be used for boats too: size, color, cost, or anything else that would separate boats into different groups. The writer can choose whichever organizing principle seems to work best for a particular topic.

It is important to choose only one organizing principle. If you mix two or more organizing principles, the categories will not be parallel and the classification will probably seem confusing. For instance, *sports* could not be effectively classified as team sports, individual sports, and professional sports because *team sports* and *individual sports* use one organizing principle, but the category of *professional sports* is based on a different organizing principle. Sports that are played by professionals, such as football, baseball, soccer, and tennis, would also belong in the category of team sports or individual sports. Because two different organizing principles are being used, the categories overlap.

Now choose two or more of the topics that you listed on your *Exploring Topics Worksheet.* Using *Worksheet II: Identifying Categories,* try to figure out at least one organizing principle for each topic. Then use the organizing principle to identify at least two or three categories.

■ WORKSHEET II | Identifying Categories

Directions: For each topic, think of an organizing principle, and then name at least two or three categories. If you wish, you may use the same topic more than once with a different organizing principle.

Topic #1	*Organizing Principle*	*Categories*
_____	_____	1. _____
		2. _____
		3. _____
		4. _____

Topic #2	*Organizing Principle*	*Categories*
_____	_____	1. _____
		2. _____
		3. _____
		4. _____

	Organizing Principle	*Categories*
Topic #3		
_____	_____	1. _____
		2. _____
		3. _____
		4. _____

	Organizing Principle	*Categories*
Topic #4		
_____	_____	1. _____
		2. _____
		3. _____
		4. _____

If you had trouble deciding on categories, you may want to try listing the items that you want to classify and then sorting them into categories as you did earlier in *Practice with Classifying*. First you will need to make a list of all the items that are part of your topic, like the list of pets in *Practice with Classifying*. Then you can experiment with different ways of setting up categories until you find an effective organizing principle and categories that work.

Discovering Details 2: Outlining

Another way to plan and organize a classification is *outlining*. Outlining is based on dividing a topic into subtopics or categories and using different headings for each division of the topic, so it is especially useful for classification. Some writers like to use outlining as a prewriting technique for other types of writing as well.

The basic process of outlining is to divide the topic into at least two parts, and then, if there are subdivisions for some parts of the topic, to divide those parts into at least two more parts, and so on. You can continue subdividing each part again and again if you want to have a very detailed outline. However, for most writing situations, dividing topics two or three times is enough to give you a helpful and accurate outline.

The major categories in an outline are always identified with Roman numerals: I, II, III, IV, V, VI, and so on. For example, types of college degrees could be classified and outlined like this:

I. Certificates
II. Two-year degrees
III. Four-year degrees
IV. Graduate degrees

This basic outline identifies the four categories and puts them in the order that the writer plans to use in his paper. The organizing principle for this well-known classification is the academic work that a person must complete in order to obtain each type of degree (number of units, kinds of courses, courses at a certain level, etc.).

With many topics, there may also be *subcategories,* or further divisions of some of the categories. If any of the categories can be divided into two or more subcategories, the subcategories should be identified by capital letters in the outline. For example, the fourth category in the outline above, graduate degrees, could be subdivided into master's degrees and doctoral degrees by adding an A and a B, like this:

IV. Graduate degrees
    A. Master's degrees
    B. Doctoral degrees

If you want to develop the outline further, subcategories on the next level should be identified by numbers. For instance, if the writer wants to identify the kinds of master's degrees and doctoral degrees offered at a specific university, section IV of the outline might look like this:

IV. Graduate degrees
    A. Master's degrees
        1. Master of Arts
        2. Master of Science
        3. Master of Fine Arts
        4. Master of Business Administration
        5. Master of Social Work
    B. Doctoral degrees
        1. Doctor of Philosophy
        2. Doctor of Jurisprudence
        3. Doctor of Medicine
        4. Doctor of Education

Of course, if the writer plans to identify subcategories for graduate degrees, it would be appropriate to show subcategories for certificates, two-year degrees, and four-year degrees also. When it is not possible to divide a category into subcategories, however, that part of the outline should not go any further. Do not write down an A to show one subcategory unless there is another subcategory that you can identify as B.

Now outline your own classification topic on the *Outlining Worksheet* if you think that outlining will help you plan and organize your paper. Roman numerals I, II, III, and IV are already on the worksheet, as well as subcategories A, B, and C under Roman numeral I. If you don't need all of the categories and subcategories, cross out the extra ones. If you need to, you may add more Roman numerals, letters for additional subcategories, or numbers for smaller subcategories. Refer back to the example outline of college degrees for the correct format.

■ **WORKSHEET III** | **Outlining**

Directions: Write your main categories after the Roman numerals. If any of the categories can be divided into two or more subcategories, list the subcategories as A, B, C, etc. There is extra space so that you can add more letters or numbers if necessary.

Topic: _____

      I. _____

          A. _____

          B. _____

          C. _____

     II. _____

     III. _____

     IV. _____

Writing a Rough Draft

Learning about Topic Sentences for Classification

After you have decided on an organizing principle and categories for your classification, the next step is writing a topic sentence. As with other types of writing, the topic sentence (or main idea statement) must express the main idea of your paragraph or paper. Since the main idea of a classification is how things are placed into categories, the topic sentence usually identifies the categories.

One writer who was classifying men's hairstyles wrote this first draft of her topic sentence:

TOPIC SENTENCE (DRAFT #1):

Some men have conservative hairstyles while others have long hair or styles that are extreme.

As she looked at this topic sentence, she realized that the names of the categories were based on different organizing principles. Both *conservative* and *extreme* identified attitudes that she thought were reflected by certain hairstyles, but *long* obviously referred only to length, not to a person's attitude. Another problem was that the categories seemed to overlap because certain long hair styles might also be considered extreme or conservative. Since she wanted to use the attitudes associated with different hairstyles as the organizing principle, she decided to eliminate the category of long hair. Instead, she included *stylish* as an additional category. Here is the second draft of her topic sentence:

TOPIC SENTENCE (DRAFT #2):

Men's hairstyles may be classified as conservative, stylish, or extreme.

Now three parallel categories based on the same organizing principle are clearly identified, so this topic sentence would work. However, the writer wanted to make her classification sound a little more interesting to readers, so she decided to revise the topic sentence again. This is her third version:

TOPIC SENTENCE (DRAFT #3):

Men generally choose one of three types of hairstyles to reflect something about their attitude or outlook on life: conservative, contemporary, or extreme.

Do you like this revised topic sentence better? The idea that hairstyles reflect a person's attitude or outlook on life probably makes the topic seem more appealing to readers. Since this idea is the organizing principle, it also helps us to understand the categories better. Including the organizing principle in the topic sentence is often a good idea, especially if it will be interesting to readers or will help them understand your classification.

Let's look at some more topic sentences about different kinds of underwater diving. As you read each version of the topic sentence, think about whether the categories are clearly identified. Circle the number of the topic sentence that you think is the best.

1. Underwater diving can be divided into different categories, depending on how the diver breathes.

2. Some people dive underwater by holding their breath while others use diving equipment.

3. Three types of underwater diving that people can enjoy are skin diving, scuba diving, and surface-supplied diving.

Which topic sentence did you pick as the best one? Sentence 1 states the organizing principle (how the divers breathe), but it doesn't identify the categories. Sentences 2 and 3 both identify categories. However, the categories in Sentence 3 are more specific than the categories in Sentence 2. "Diving equipment" in Sentence 2 could include anything used by a diver; it doesn't distinguish between scuba equipment and air hoses connected to an air supply on the surface. These two different methods of breathing underwater are clearly identified in Sentence 3. Therefore, Sentence 3 is the best topic sentence.

As you read the following classification of styles of dress at Southwestern College by Cynthia Uribe, notice that her topic sentence clearly identifies four categories. Then she explains each category with details and examples that show us what the main characteristics of each style are. Notice that she used one paragraph for the introduction, one paragraph about each category, and one paragraph for the conclusion.

Variations
by Cynthia Uribe

Students in college have already developed their idea of who they want to be, and they express this decision in the way that they dress. Four different styles of dress can be observed on the Southwestern College campus: Hip-hop, Casual, New Wave, and Gang-affiliated.

The Hip-hop name is given to the style of dress that reflects the type of music the dresser likes. The people who dress in this style generally like reggae, rap, and modern jazz. They usually wear baggy pants and bold-colored, oversized T-shirts with logos like "Phunk This." A lot of logos also have a marijuana plant painted next to them, or a marijuana plant medallion will be around the person's neck. Both men and women like wearing beanies or other types of hats that cover most of their forehead. Sometimes there may be a whole new trend that fits into the Hip-hop category because this style of dress is rapidly changing.

In the Casual style of dress there are lots of variations in attitudes. Comfortable shoes, like tennis shoes, sandals, or Ug boots, seem to be the most obvious in this style of dress. T-shirts, sweatshirts, jeans, sweats, and even boxer shorts are often worn. Casual dressers like to wear baseball caps or visors to protect their eyes and face from the sun, which they are forever in.

Most of the time their hair is worn away from their face, either in a ponytail for the women, or clean cut for the men.

The New Wave style allows many variations of clothes, from seventeenth century dresses to thigh-high black plastic go-go boots. Many women wear thigh-high nylons with red, black, green, or blue combat boots, or some other shocking style of footwear. Long, beautiful dresses made of velvet, silk, or rayon are also popular. Their hair may be dyed, usually black. The men wear combat boots with cut-off shorts and long trench coats. They like to wear their hair long, and they also may have it dyed. Black clothing and pale faces will often distinguish these dressers from the other categories.

The name Gang-affiliated is given to a certain style whether the people are or are not actually gang-affiliated. Men wear a white tank top T-shirt under a regular white T-shirt with sharp starched creases. They wear jeans or Dickies brand pants with shiny creases on the front and back. Their shoes are usually bright white tennis shoes or black Nike running shoes. The women wear crop tops or short blouses, sometimes with a flannel shirt over them. They also wear chokers and red lipstick. Sometimes they wear baggy pants so low at the waist that their belly buttons can be seen. Other times they wear tight pants with high heels or platforms.

Many students consistently dress in the same style every day to express their identity. However, others dress in one style one day and another style the next day, depending on their personality, their mood, and their feelings about the different styles of dress.

Response to *Variations*

1. Do you think that the names Cynthia used for the categories are appropriate? Why or why not?

_____

_____

2. What organizing principle are the categories based on?

_____

_____

3. If you were writing a classification about ways that people dress at your school, would the categories be the same as these or different?

_____

_____

_____

Before you write your topic sentence and begin the first draft of your own classification, do the following activity, *Evaluating Topic Sentences for Classification*. As you read each topic sentence, think about whether or not it clearly identifies categories that could be explained and discussed in a classification paper.

Evaluating Topic Sentences for Classification

Directions: Decide which of these topic sentences (or main idea statements) are effective. A well-written topic sentence should identify specific categories based on one organizing principle. Write OK in the blank by each good topic sentence, and write NO by the others.

EXAMPLE 1 ➤ ___*NO*___ Some rocks were formed by volcanic action, while others are huge boulders.

Example 1 is not effective because it mixes two organizing principles: geologic origin and size.

EXAMPLE 2 ➤ ___*OK*___ Rocks are classified as igneous, sedimentary, or metamorphic, according to how they were formed.

Example 2 correctly identifies three kinds of rocks based on their geologic origin.

_____ **1.** Four kinds of bears are native to the United States: grizzly bears, brown bears, polar bears, and black bears.

_____ **2.** White mice make better pets than other kinds of mice or rats.

_____ **3.** Members of Lifestyle Spa can choose from five kinds of aerobics classes: high impact, low impact, high/low combo, step aerobics, and aqua aerobics.

_____ **4.** Many species of animals are classified as endangered.

_____ **5.** Halloween costumes can be funny, attractive, realistic, or scary.

_____ **6.** Many different kinds of people make life interesting.

_____ **7.** Some trees have flowers or fruit, some lose their leaves, and others stay green all year.

_____ **8.** The only types of TV programs for children are cartoons, *Sesame Street*, and movies on the Disney channel.

_____ **9.** An orchestra is made up of string instruments, woodwind instruments, brass instruments, and percussion instruments.

_____ **10.** Clarity, cut, and size are three characteristics used to classify diamonds.

Writing Your Own Topic Sentence

In order to write a good topic sentence (or main idea statement) for your classification, you need to know what categories you are going to use. Look back at your *Identifying Categories Worksheet* and select the topic that you like best. Check to make sure that all of your categories are based on the same organizing principle and that they do not overlap. Then write your topic, organizing principle, and categories here so that you can look at them while you are writing your topic sentence:

Topic	*Organizing Principle*	*Categories*
_____	_____	1. _____
		2. _____
		3. _____
		4. _____

Your topic sentence should focus on the categories because they are what your classification paper is all about—in other words, the main idea of your paper. Be sure that your topic sentence also identifies the topic itself. If you wish, you may include the organizing principle as well, like Example 2 in the previous exercise:

> Rocks are classified as igneous, sedimentary, or metamorphic, *according to how they were formed.*

Write the first draft of your topic sentence here.

TOPIC SENTENCE (DRAFT #1):

_____

_____

Would this topic sentence appeal to readers? If you would like to add something to make your topic sentence more interesting or informative, answer these questions to help you come up with some ideas:

1. Why did you choose this classification to write about?

_____

2. What can someone learn from reading your classification?

_____

3. What is the most interesting thing about your topic?

_____

You may want to add one of these ideas in order to make your topic sentence more interesting. Try writing another draft of your topic sentence here:

TOPIC SENTENCE (DRAFT #2):

_____

_____

Now share your topic sentence with your workshop group and ask for their comments. Make sure that everyone's topic sentence clearly identifies specific categories based on one organizing principle. If it is difficult to figure out what someone's organizing principle is, you may want to suggest that the writer include the organizing principle in the topic sentence.

If your workshop group has some suggestions that you think would improve your topic sentence, try revising it again:

TOPIC SENTENCE (DRAFT #3):

_____

_____

If your classification is going to consist of more than one paragraph, you should also add another introductory sentence or two before the topic sentence in order to get readers interested, and the introduction (including the topic sentence) should be a separate paragraph. To help you write an introduction, look again at your answers to questions 1–3 above to get some ideas, such as the most interesting thing about your classification or what someone can learn from reading it. Some writers also like to include a little bit of background information about the topic in the introduction. The classification called _Variations_ that we read on pages 276–277 and a number of other example classifications later in the chapter, such as _The Lineup_ (page 283), have effective introductions that are two or three sentences long.

From Topic Sentence to First Draft

After you have written your topic sentence, you are ready to start working on the first draft of your paper. Classification is a type of writing that generally follows a certain pattern of organization, which means that each category has to be explained in order, one at a time. It is a good idea to use the same order that you used for naming the categories in your topic sentence. In order to give a balanced picture, you should include the same kinds of information and write approximately the same amount about each category.

Your paper should include details and examples that will show readers what the items in each category have in common. What characteristics do the items in each category share? What features identify members of that category? What distinguishes items in one category from items in another category?

Without details and examples, your classification may be unclear or confusing. For example, we can classify poems into three categories according to their form: free verse, traditional poetry, and experimental poetry. However, unless the special features of the categories are explained, most readers will not understand the classification. The writer must give us details about the characteristics of each category: free verse has no regular pattern of rhyme or rhythm; traditional poetry has regular patterns of rhyme and rhythm; experimental poetry takes unconventional forms, such as shapes representing an object. With these explanations of what the names of the categories mean, the classification starts to make more sense. Of course, the writer would still need to add more details and give a few examples of the different types of poems in order to have an effective classification paper.

One of the best ways to figure out what information you should include is to put yourself in the position of your audience. If you are writing for a general audience, such as your classmates, ask yourself what they would need to know in order to fully understand each category, as well as what details and examples would be interesting to them. If your audience does not know much about your topic, you may want to include more basic facts and perhaps even background information about the classification, the organizing principle, or the categories. On the other hand, if your intended audience is already knowledgeable about your topic, both your vocabulary and the information that you include can be at a higher level.

As you read the following first draft, which is a classification of different learning styles intended for an audience of college students, think about what additional details or examples the writer could include to explain each of the three learning styles.

First Draft

Learning Styles

Different people have different learning styles. Many people are visual learners, others are auditory learners, and some are kinesthetic learners. The first group, visual learners, learn best by seeing something. They often pay more attention to notes written on the board than to lectures. Handout sheets, overhead transparencies, and other visual methods of presenting information are also very helpful for visual learners. Auditory learners, on the other hand, prefer to listen to something in order to learn. Unlike visual and auditory learners, kinesthetic learners need to experience what they are learning. They learn best by *doing* something, so they tend to excel in laboratory classes that provide hands-on learning experiences. Understanding whether your learning style is visual, auditory, kinesthetic, or some combination of these styles can help you find ways to learn more effectively.

Response to *Learning Styles*

1. Although this first draft has a good topic sentence and conclusion, it needs more details and examples. Can you think of anything else that the writer could add about visual learners?

   _____

   _____

2. The category of auditory learners is the least well-developed, with only one sentence to explain how they learn. The writer needs help with this category, so try to come up with some examples of techniques that would be effective for auditory learners or things that could be problems.

   _____

   _____

3. Can you think of anything else to add about kinesthetic learners? What kinds of problems do you think kinesthetic learners sometimes experience in school?

   _____

   _____

Other students are likely to have a variety of different suggestions for improving the first draft of *Learning Styles*, so be sure to discuss your answers with some of your classmates.

By adding more details about helpful techniques and problem areas for each category of learners, the writer of *Learning Styles* can turn his first draft into a well-developed classification. He might also want to include examples from his own learning experiences or the learning experiences of other people that he knows.

Now read *The Lineup* by Richard Munholand, which classifies the three different types of players that a baseball lineup consists of. Notice that Richard introduces each category with an explanation of what the name of the category means, followed by more details about players who belong in that category.

The Lineup
by Richard D. Munholand

The baseball lineup is made up of the order in which players bat and the positions they will play for the game. A manager needs to go through a lot of planning to put the most effective players on the field in order to win. A lineup consists of three types of players: power hitters, contact hitters, and those players who excel in defense but are usually weak hitters.

Power hitters are those who are blessed with the art of hitting home runs. Not everyone can hit the longball like these monsters do. These hitters are put in the lineup for their mighty bats that enable a team to put runs on the board. Power hitters tend to have a low batting average, but they also lead the team in RBI's and home runs. Home run hitters tend to hit third or fourth in the lineup so they can hit in the runs. Without these hitters, runs are hard to come by.

Contact hitters are a precious commodity on any team. These hitters are likely to get on base more often than other hitters, which gives them higher batting averages. Contact hitters are likely to be found in the beginning of the lineup, so they can get on base for the power hitters. A long career is inevitable for these hitters because of their strong desire to play ball and their contribution to winning games.

Defensive players are put in the lineup for their defensive skills rather than their offensive ones. Although they are apt to have really low batting averages, they make up for it in their efforts on the field. Defensive players are usually found in the bottom of the lineup, along with the pitcher, who himself generally lacks the ability to hit the ball.

When a lineup is constructed in the proper way, a team can find itself winning many ball games and may even find itself enjoying the sights of the playoffs at the end of the season.

Response to *The Lineup*

1. Do you think that all of the categories are clearly explained with enough details? Why or why not?

\
\

2. The writer identified two categories of hitters—power hitters and contact hitters. What is the difference between these two categories?

\
\

3. Why is the pitcher mentioned along with defensive players in the third category?

\

As you develop your own rough draft, be sure to include enough details so that readers will have a clear understanding of your categories. Remember to emphasize the special characteristics shared by people or things that make up each category. It is usually not necessary to name everyone or everything that belongs in a category. A few examples will generally be enough to show readers what types of people or things are included.

When you are ready to show your rough draft to your workshop group, here are some questions to use as guidelines:

Rough Draft Workshop Questions

1. Does the topic sentence clearly identify the categories?
2. Are the categories based on one organizing principle?
3. Are the special characteristics of each category explained?
4. Has the writer used enough details and examples?
5. Is the classification well-organized?

Defining Terms

It is often helpful to begin the explanation of each category with a one-sentence definition, as the writer of *Learning Styles* did. Unless the names of the categories are very well-known or obvious, defining them will help the reader understand your classification. For example, if someone is writing a classification of people's different styles of walking, using the categories of power walkers, steady walkers, and leisurely walkers, it would be a good idea to define the names of these categories. If readers have to guess what the names mean, their guesses may not be accurate.

A good definition must be clear, accurate, and easily understandable. Avoid using the same word in the definition that you are trying to define. For example, this definition of "steady walkers" doesn't really tell us anything:

Poor Definition: Steady walkers are people who walk in a steady manner.

Instead, the writer should use different words to explain what he means by "steady."

Good Definition: Steady walkers have a consistent pace that is neither fast nor slow.

This is a much better definition because now we have a clearer understanding of what the writer means by "steady."

Also avoid using expressions like "is when" or "is where" in your definitions. Unless you are defining a time period or a place, "when" and "where" do not really apply. For example, this definition of "leisurely walking" is poor because walking is not a time period.

> ***Poor Definition:***   Leisurely walking is when people walk in a slow, relaxed manner.

This definition of "leisurely walkers" is much better:

> ***Good Definition:***   Leisurely walkers are people who walk in a slow, relaxed manner.

This definition will help readers understand the style of walking that the writer has in mind. Since readers already know the meaning of "walking" or "walker," this part of the category name does not need to be defined.

Which one of the following definitions do you think is effectively written? Write *Good* in one of the blanks and *Poor* in the others.

> _____ ***Definition:***   Power walking is where people walk quickly and forcefully.

> _____ ***Definition:***   Power walkers are people who walk quickly and forcefully.

> _____ ***Definition:***   Power walkers are people who have a powerful walking style.

Sometimes writers prefer to use what is called a *formal definition*. This kind of definition is very precise. A formal definition has three parts: the term to be defined, the class (or group) of things that it belongs to, and its distinguishing characteristics. For example, what is a *vegetarian*?

> ***Term:*** vegetarian
>
> ***Class:*** person
>
> ***Distinguishing Characteristics:*** doesn't eat meat
>
> ***Formal Definition:***   A vegetarian is a person who doesn't eat meat.

The formal definition begins with the term *(vegetarian)*, then identifies a vegetarian as a person *(class)*, and finally adds the characteristic that distinguishes a vegetarian from other people—not eating meat.

Let's use the same pattern to write a definition for a *high school diploma*.

> ***Term:*** high school diploma
>
> ***Class:*** document

After deciding that a high-school diploma is a document, we need to figure out what makes this particular document different from other documents—in other words, the distinguishing characteristics.

> ***Distinguishing Characteristics:***   given for completion of grade 12
>
>   presented to individuals at graduation

Then the distinguishing characteristics need to be combined into one good sentence, along with the term and the class:

> ***Formal Definition:***   A high school diploma is a document that verifies an individual's successful completion of grade 12.

Look at your rough draft again and check to see if the names of your categories are clear. If your audience might have trouble understanding what the names of all or some of the categories mean, you may want to add definitions. Also, if you have used any technical or special terms in your paper, you should make sure that they are clearly defined. You will probably find that formal definitions are very effective for some topics. However, in other cases, you may prefer to use more informal definitions or explanations without necessarily naming the class and all of the distinguishing characteristics. Remember to avoid expressions like "is when" or "is where," and don't use the same word that you are trying to define as part of the definition.

After you have written your definitions, have your workshop group read them to make sure that they are clear and accurate. If you and your workshop group think these definitions will help readers understand your classification, add them to your rough draft.

As you read the following classification of tools by Steven Tanciatco, notice that he defines each category, as well as the tools that he mentions as examples. In addition, he includes a formal definition of tools in the introduction. Although most people already have a general understanding of tools, he wanted to write this classification so that a beginner in a school shop class (perhaps in junior high) would understand it very clearly. With this audience in mind, he decided that accurate definitions were important.

Tools

by Steven Tanciatco

What are tools? Tools are devices which help us accomplish a certain task, such as building and fixing objects. There are two different kinds of tools, power and non-power.

Power tools must use energy (non-human power) to operate. One example, a chainsaw, is two to four feet in length and has a long blade with a jagged-edged chain which surrounds it. The motor located in the rear drives the chain around the blade and cuts into wood. Unlike a conventional hand saw that can cut a 2″ × 4″ block of wood in about a minute, a chainsaw can cut it in a few seconds. Another power tool is a drill, which is about one foot in length, shaped like a hand gun, and uses pointed, cylindrical spiral blades called bits, which are usually at least two inches long and vary in diameter. The drill has a motor which spins the bit at a high speed and is used to drill through wood and steel. Next, unlike a normal hammer, a hammer gun is approximately one and a half feet long and is used to drive nails into wood instantly with compressed air.

Non-power tools must use human power. One example, a hammer, is about one foot long and usually has a wooden handle. The head is located at the top of the handle and is used to drive a nail into an object by thrusting its flat end down onto the nail. It may take five or more blows to completely drive the nail into an object like wood. Another example of a non-power tool is a screwdriver, which can be anywhere from two inches to more than a foot long. A screwdriver has a handle at one end, and the other end either is flat or has a rounded point with four flanges that fit down inside the screw. A person uses this tool to drive screws into wood by putting the flat end or rounded point onto the screw and pressing down while turning it clockwise until the screw is driven all the way into the wood. Another tool is the socket wrench, which is used to screw nuts onto bolts and is usually about one foot long, although some are shorter and others can be more than two feet long. At one end of the wrench the socket can be connected, and at the other end a person holds it. The person places the socket end onto the right size nut, and then the wrench must be cranked clockwise until the nut tightens.

What would the world be like without tools? The world would be a completely different place because there wouldn't be any tools to construct things like buildings and vehicles.

Response to *Tools*

1. What organizing principle did Steven use to set up the two categories of tools?

_____

2. Do you think that there are enough examples of specific tools to give readers a clear understanding of each category? Why or why not?

_____

_____

3. The writer was careful to use the same kinds of details about each tool. Which characteristics did he include to describe each one?

_____

_____

Transitions for Classification

When you are writing a classification, transitional words and phrases can sometimes help you move smoothly from one category to the next or from one example to the next. For instance, the writer of *Tools* used these transitions to introduce some of his examples:

> *One example* is . . .
>
> *Another* power tool is . . .
>
> *Next* . . .
>
> *Another example* of a non-power tool is . . .

These transitional words helped introduce additional examples smoothly and effectively.

The writer of *Learning Styles* also used transitional words or phrases to introduce the three categories:

> *The first group*, visual learners, . . .
>
> Auditory learners, *on the other hand*, . . .
>
> *Unlike* visual and auditory learners, kinesthetic learners . . .

Notice that *unlike* and *on the other hand* both emphasize a contrast between the categories. Some other transitional words that could be used to emphasize a contrast are *however* and *in contrast*.

Ending Effectively

To end your classification effectively, you can review the categories, say something about the significance of the classification, or make some other appropriate closing comment. Let's take a look at how the writers in this chapter ended their classifications.

1. *Variations:* Many students consistently dress in the same style every day to express their identity. However, others dress in one style one day and another style the next day, depending on their personality, their mood, and their feelings about the different styles of dress.

2. *Learning Styles:* Understanding whether your learning style is visual, auditory, kinesthetic, or some combination of these styles can help you find ways to learn more effectively.

3. *Lineup:* When a lineup is constructed in the proper way, a team can find itself winning many ball games and may even find itself enjoying the sights of the playoffs at the end of the season.

4. *Tools:* What would the world be like without tools? The world would be a completely different place because there wouldn't be any tools to construct things like buildings and vehicles.

Which of these conclusions say something about the significance of the classification or the topic?

_____

By reminding us that the order of the players in a baseball lineup can help a team win more games, the writer of *Lineup* is letting us know that this classification is important to anyone interested in baseball. The conclusion for *Learning Styles* also stresses the importance of the classification by pointing out that understanding your learning style can help you learn better. In the conclusion for *Tools,* the writer emphasizes the significance of the topic by commenting on what the world would be like without tools. Therefore, all three of these conclusions, in one way or another, say something about why the classification or the topic is significant.

The first conclusion, for *Variations,* is the only one that does not focus on the significance of the classification or the topic. Instead, the writer wanted to add the comment that some people change their style of dress from day to day, so they do not always fit into the same category. This too is an effective conclusion because it gives us a better understanding of the classification.

As you read the following classification about three types of music that were originated by African Americans, notice how the conclusion ties everything together and makes the paper seem complete.

African American Music
by Tiffany Turner

Three popular types of music that were originated by African Americans are jazz, rhythm and blues, and soul. Although individual performers have different styles, each type of music has its own distinctive sounds that appeal to a wide variety of listeners.

Jazz is a "laid back" type of music that you can relax to. After a long day of work and school, I like to come home and relax with the rhythmic beats of jazz. There are many different styles of jazz that you can listen to, and jazz players like to create their own spontaneous rhythms and melodies. Jazz started to appear around 1900, based mainly on African American folk music and West African rhythms. Early jazz innovators who helped to establish jazz as a distinct type of music include Louis Armstrong, Duke Ellington, and Dizzy Gillespie.

Rhythm and blues is a special freestyle type of music. In order to listen to rhythm and blues, you have to be in a rhythm and blues mood. This music you pour your broken heart and soul into. Many people sing the blues when they break up with their boyfriend or lose their job because it is a very expressive type of music. The blues style of singing was originally developed in the late nineteenth century and came from African American slave songs about life's hardships. In the 1940s and 1950s, performers like Ray Charles and Fats Domino helped to popularize rhythm and blues.

Soul is the up-beat dance music. It is easy to sing and dance to. The coordinated tones, rhythms, and syncopated beats create this modern music sound. Lyrics make up a big part of soul songs. The lyrics tell the story instead of the music. Soul music is what is on the radio. It began in the 1950s as a combination of rhythm and blues and gospel music. Early soul artists include Otis Redding and Stevie Wonder.

Jazz, rhythm and blues, and soul each offer us something different to suit our different moods. These three types of music have been historically popular, and all originated with my people.

Response to *African American Music*

1. Which details are based on Tiffany's own personal experiences with the three different kinds of music?

   _____

   _____

   _____

2. Why is a little bit about the history of each kind of music also included?

   _____

   _____

3. In addition to reviewing the three categories, what does the conclusion tell us that we didn't already know?

   _____

   Do you like this conclusion? Why or why not?

   _____

Now look at your own rough draft and make sure that it has an effective ending. You may want to mention the names of your categories again, or you may want to focus on how your classification could be helpful to someone. Try to think of a final comment that will make your paper seem complete.

As you do Section Two, Sentence and Grammar Skills, you will learn more about sentence patterns and subject–verb agreement. The skills that you learn in Section Two can help you edit and revise your rough draft. At the end of Section Two, there is a checklist to help you make sure that you haven't forgotten anything in your classification.

SECTION TWO:
Sentence and Grammar Skills

Goals

In this section of the chapter, you will learn how to do the following:

- Recognize sentences that have more than two SVs
- Use Group A, B, and C connectors, relative connectors, and semicolons to write sentences with more than two SVs
- Connect SVs correctly in a series
- Avoid problems with subject–verb agreement

Learning about Longer Sentences

In Chapters 1 through 5 you learned that in a sentence with two SVs, each SV must be connected correctly with the SV that comes before or after it. In this chapter you will practice using the same connectors (Group A, B, and C connectors, relative connectors, and semicolons) to write sentences with three or more clauses, like this:

SV   connector   SV   connector   SV.

You will also learn a new way of connecting SVs in longer sentences. Then in Chapter 7 you will learn other ways to connect three or more clauses: with the Group B connector first, and with the relative clause in the middle of the main clause.

Here are some examples of sentences with three or more SVs:

                        S   V   Group B   S   V   , Group A
EXAMPLE 1 ➤ Brenda listened *as* her professor presented the lecture, *and* then
                        S   V
she asked a question about the new material.

The first clause is connected to the second one by the Group B connector *as.* The second clause is connected to the third one by a comma and the Group A connector *and.* This is a good sentence because it sounds natural, the meaning is clear, the ideas are connected logically, and the punctuation is correct.

                        S   V   Group B   S   V   ;
EXAMPLE 2 ➤ Tyler mixed the cement *while* Daniel finished the wooden forms;
                        S   V
afterward they worked together to pour the foundation.

In this sentence, the first SV is joined to the second one with a Group B connector, and the second SV is connected to the third one by a semicolon. Again, it is a good sentence. Remember that a semicolon can be used to connect two clauses that are closely related in meaning.

Here are some more examples:

EXAMPLE 3 ➤   Mr. and Mrs. Watanabe were very particular about the plans for their new house, so the architect needed to make several revisions before they were satisfied.

What are the connectors in this sentence?

A. Between the first and second SVs? _____

B. Between the second and third SVs? _____

Does this sentence sound natural? Are both connections appropriate for the meaning of the sentence? Is the punctuation correct for each connector? If so, then it is a good sentence.

The structure of this sentence can be shown like this:

SV   **, Group A**   SV   **Group B**   SV.

EXAMPLE 4 ➤   Archeologists recently discovered a cache of more than 900 jade artifacts in Mexico; in fact, this is the largest single collection of Mayan artifacts that anyone has discovered.

What are the connectors in this sentence?

A. Between the first and second SVs? _____

B. Between the second and third SVs? _____

This is a good sentence because it sounds natural, uses appropriate connectors, and is correctly punctuated.

The structure of Example 4 can be shown like this:

SV   **; Group C,**   SV   **relative**   SV.

EXAMPLE 5 ➤   *More than Three SVs:*
Many people in America today do not have the traditional family, community, and church involvement that our ancestors often had in the past; instead, we are turning to groups that offer help for specific problems, like Overeaters Anonymous, women's and men's support groups, and MADD—Mothers Against Drunk Driving.

What are the connectors in this sentence?

A. Between the first and second SVs? _____

B. Between the second and third SVs? _____

C. Between the third and fourth SVs? _____

Are all of the connectors appropriate in meaning, and is the punctuation correct for each connector?

The structure of Example 5 can be shown like this:

SV **relative** SV **; Group C ,** SV **relative**=S V.

The most important thing to remember about writing sentences with three or more SVs is to join each SV to the next one with a correct connector. The diagram below shows how each SV can be joined to the next one with any of the connectors listed. Just be sure that the sentence sounds natural and that the meaning is appropriate. Then check to see that the punctuation is correct for each connector, as shown below:

	, Group A connector		**, Group A connector**	
	Group B connector		**Group B connector**	
SV	**Relative**	**SV**	**Relative**	**SV**
	; Group C connector,		**; Group C connector**	
	;		**;**	

You can write a sentence that has several SVs by using any of these connections.

■ **CLASS PRACTICE**

Analyzing Longer Sentences in a Paper

Directions: First read the following classification paper for the meaning. Then mark the subjects and verbs in each sentence, and count the clauses. Write the number of clauses in the blank at the beginning of each sentence.

Two Types of Thinkers

1.____ My friend and co-author Anna Ingalls once told me that she admired the way that I could do more than one thing at a time. 2.____ I promptly replied that I admired how she could do only one thing at a time and get it done! 3.____ By working on this textbook together, we have gained a real understanding of each other's way of thinking, and we have come to the conclusion that there are two basic types of thinkers: linear thinkers and mosaic thinkers. 4.____ Each type of thinker can do some things better than the other type of thinker can.

5.____ Linear thinkers usually do one thing at a time, in a very logical step-by-step order, until they finish what they are doing. 6.____ For example, many linear thinkers prefer to start with the introduction of the paper they* are writing, and then they proceed in order to the body and finally the conclusion. 7.____ Linear thinkers prefer to give and receive information in a very organized manner, with one piece of information building to the next. 8.____ Sometimes linear thinkers are uncomfortable with a teacher who moves all over the book, teaching part of one chapter and then part of another chapter.

9.____ On the other hand, mosaic thinkers are perfectly happy to get bits of information that eventually make a picture, in the same way that bits of tile or glass come together to make a mosaic, but they have a harder time concentrating on just one thing, and they often have many unfinished projects going at the same time. 10.____ Mosaic thinkers often begin writing somewhere in the body of the paper; then they write the introduction and conclusion. 11.____ In general, they write in chunks that they must assemble or put in order later. 12.____ A good point of mosaic thinkers is that they can often see a pattern after seeing just a few pieces of information, and they don't worry if they don't know where each piece of information fits. 13.____ They are confident that each piece of information will fit in later, like putting a puzzle together.

14.____ You may be a linear thinker like Anna, or a mosaic thinker like me, but no matter which type of thinker you are, there are some things that you will be good at.

---

*The connecting word *that* is omitted here. In Chapter 4, you saw that sometimes the relative pronoun *that* is omitted if the meaning of the sentence is clear without it.

■ CLASS
PRACTICE **2**

Combining Short Sentences to Make Longer Sentences

Directions: Combine the following short sentences with appropriate connectors to make sentences with three or more SVs. Use a variety of Group A, B, and C connectors, relative connectors, and semicolons. Try to make your sentences sound natural, and don't use the words *and* and *but* in all of them.

EXAMPLE ➤   Roses are harder to grow than many other flowers. Many people grow them anyway. They are beautiful to look at. They smell wonderful too.

Answer: *Roses are harder to grow than many other flowers, but many people grow them anyway because they are beautiful to look at, and they smell wonderful too.*

1. Traveling is educational. You can see new things. You never knew about the new things before.

   _____

   _____

   _____

2. Hamad bought a bicycle. He can ride to the university. He wants to be more ecological. He wants to get more exercise.

   _____

   _____

   _____

3. The Hawaiian Islands have one of the best climates in the world. There are many cultural and historical things to see. A lot of tourists take vacations there every year.

   _____

   _____

   _____

4. The United States has a larger population than Canada. The United States has a gentler climate than Canada. Much of Canada lies north of the Arctic Circle.

_____

_____

_____

5. Racquetball and tennis are both played with a racquet. A tennis racquet is larger than a racquetball racquet. Racquetball is played indoors. Tennis is played outdoors.

_____

_____

_____

6. Macintosh computers are no longer so different from IBM-style computers. They are much more similar to each other than they used to be. It doesn't matter as much anymore which kind you buy.

_____

_____

_____

Clauses in a Series: A New Way of Connecting SVs in a Longer Sentence

The following example shows another way of connecting clauses when there are three or more clauses in a sentence.

EXAMPLE ➤ *Clauses in a Series*

$$S \qquad V \qquad , \quad S \qquad V$$
Last summer Margarita visited Mexico, Cristina went to

$$, and \quad S \qquad V$$
Australia, and Pat relaxed at her home in rural Jamul.

In this sentence there is a comma between the first and second SVs. The final SV in the series is connected by the word *and* and a comma. This pattern can be shown like this:

SV ,   SV ,   **and**   SV.

This is the only new way of connecting three or more SVs in a sentence that will be presented in this chapter. The other ways use the same connectors and patterns that you have studied in previous chapters to connect two SVs.

Try writing an original sentence with three clauses in a series, and check it with other students:

_____

_____

_____

■ **CLASS PRACTICE** **3**

Writing Sentences with Three or More Clauses

Directions: Write some original sentences using three or more SVs. Use *Group A, B,* or *C* connectors, relative connectors, or semicolons between the clauses. Try to use a variety of different connecting words, and try writing one with SVs in a series.

1. _____

   _____

2. _____

   _____

3. _____

   _____

4. _____

   _____

5. _____

   _____

When you are finished, ask another student to check that each connecting word is used correctly and that each sentence sounds natural.

Combining Sentences in a Short Paper

Directions: The following passage contains fragments and short sentences, most of which have just one clause each. Connect the fragments and some of the short sentences to make longer sentences of two, three, or four clauses. There is more than one possible correct answer in many cases.

Types of Driving Vacations

When you were growing up. Did your family go on vacations? Or did you ever take a trip with a group of friends? Many families or groups of friends travel to visit relatives, to see the country, or just to get away from the stress of everyday life for a little while. There are basically two types of driving vacations: touring vacations and stay-in-one-spot vacations.

Touring vacations involve a lot of traveling. People who take this kind of vacation. They will spend a lot of time in the car driving from one interesting or scenic place to another. The goal is to see as much as can possibly be seen in the allotted amount of time. Children can easily get bored and tired. When they are sitting in the car for a long time. If you plan this type of vacation. Be sure to have a good supply of nutritious snacks, books, games, and maybe even stereo headphones for each child. When I graduated, I took a touring vacation. I went with some friends. We traveled all over California in two weeks.

When people go on a stay-in-one-spot vacation. They drive to one place and spend their whole vacation there. There are several possible reasons for taking this type of vacation: relaxing, getting to know an area in depth. Or visiting family or friends. Children can get bored. On this type of vacation too. Especially if adults spend a lot of time talking to each other. If you take this type of vacation. Be sure to plan interesting activities that will appeal to all members of the group. When I lived with my parents we used to go on this type of vacation every year. We usually went to Sequoia National Park.

Both touring vacations and stay-in-one-spot vacations are good. They offer families and friends an opportunity to spend time together. And strengthen their relationships.

Avoiding Sentence Structure Errors in Longer Sentences

In earlier chapters you learned about avoiding run-ons and comma splices in sentences with two clauses. The same principles apply in sentences with three or more clauses. Remember that a run-on has no connector between the clauses, and a comma splice uses only a comma, which isn't a legitimate connector, between the clauses. In this part of Chapter 6 you will practice recognizing and correcting run-ons, comma splices, and other incorrect punctuation in sentences with three or more SVs.

Here are some examples of common sentence structure errors in longer sentences:

INCORRECT EXAMPLE 1 ➤
$$\overset{S}{} \overset{V}{}$$
One lone adventurer paddled his kayak in toward shore Filipino

$$\overset{S}{} \overset{V}{} \qquad , \overset{S}{} \overset{V}{}$$
fishermen surf-fished for halibut, cyclists rode by on the nearby highway.

How are the first two SVs joined together? There is no connector, so it is a run-on. How are the second and third SVs connected? There is only a comma, so it is a comma splice. All of these clauses are connected incorrectly.

Here are some possible corrections:

SV   Group B   SV   , Group A   SV.

One lone adventurer paddled his kayak in toward shore *while* Filipino fishermen surf-fished for halibut, *and* cyclists rode by on the nearby highway.

Each clause is correctly connected to the next clause using some of the connectors you have studied in previous chapters.

or

SV   , Group A   SV   Group B   SV.

One lone adventurer surfed his kayak in toward shore, *and* Filipino fishermen surf-fished for halibut *while* cyclists rode by on the nearby highway.

This is also correct.

or

SV   ,   SV   , and   SV.

One lone adventurer surfed his kayak in toward shore, Filipino fishermen surf-fished for halibut, *and* cyclists rode by on the nearby highway.

This sentence connects the three clauses in a series. Many times you will have a choice of more than one correct way of connecting clauses. Choose whichever way sounds best to you.

INCORRECT EXAMPLE 2 ➤   The U.S.A. has a three-part government, *because* the authors of the constitution wanted some limits on the power of government, *however* a stronger government wouldn't be so slow to respond to new situations.

This sentence is incorrect because it is not punctuated correctly. Here is the same sentence, correctly punctuated:

> The U.S.A. has a three-part government *because* the authors of the constitution wanted some limits on the power of government; *however,* a stronger government wouldn't be so slow to respond to new situations.

Be sure to use the correct punctuation for the connectors you are using. By checking for run-ons, comma splices, and incorrect punctuation, you can avoid most sentence structure errors in longer sentences.

■ **CLASS PRACTICE** **5**

Proofreading for Sentence Structure Errors

Directions: Correct all comma splices, run-ons, fragments, and punctuation errors. Use any of the correct sentence patterns you have studied.

Types of Bicycles

In my recent hunt for a bicycle, I learned that in today's marketplace there are many more options than there were in the 1970s. When I bought my Schwinn ten-speed. At that time there were basically only two choices: whether or not to get fenders and whether to get upright or dropped handle-bars. Today there is a bewildering number of choices to make, however the most important choice is whether to buy a road bike, a mountain bike, or a hybrid bicycle.

Road bikes are the most similar to the old ten-speed bikes but most of them have at least twelve speeds now some of them have 21 or even 24 speeds! As you might suspect these bicycles are best suited for riding on paved roads. They have narrow tires and a low-slung frame, there are two sub-categories of road bikes: racing bikes and touring bikes. Racing bikes have shorter frames from front to back, they are a little stiffer; so that, every ounce of power exerted on the pedals is transmitted to forward motion rather than absorbed by the bicycle frame. While touring bikes are generally longer and somewhat heavier to give a smooth ride and to carry camping and personal gear for long distances.

Hybrid bicycles are just what their name states: a cross between road bikes and mountain bikes. These bicycles are somewhat sturdier than road bikes, therefore they are better for gravel roads and small potholes but they still roll easily; they are not too much heavier than road bikes, so they also work well for smooth roads. The handlebars are straight across rather than curved down for a more comfortable upright riding position but, this also means that riders are limited to fewer riding positions and experience more wind drag.

Mountain bikes are the new 'in' thing their popularity continues to increase in recent years. As more and more people learn about them and come to appreciate their advantages. Mountain bikes are nearly indestructible. They are designed for getting over, through, and around trail obstacles such as rocks, logs, debris, sand, mud, and potholes. In order to accomplish this, they have a higher bottom bracket; consequently, there is more clearance for obstacles. They also have heavier and sturdier frames, a more upright riding position, and large knobby tires for good traction.

Bicycling is a healthy sport that's good for you, so whichever type of bike suits your needs. I hope you get plenty of chances to enjoy riding it!

■ **CLASS**
PRACTICE **6**

Writing with Sentences of Three or More Clauses

PART A. Looking at Writing from an Example Paper

Directions: Look at the following sentences from *African American Music*, by Tiffany Turner, on pages 289–290. Highlight or underline the sentences that have more than two clauses.

Three popular types of music that were originated by African Americans are jazz, rhythm and blues, and soul. Although individual performers have different styles, each type of music has its own distinctive sounds that appeal to a wide variety of listeners.

Jazz is a "laid back" type of music that you can relax to. After a long day of work and school, I like to come home and relax with the rhythmic beats of jazz. There are many different styles of jazz that you can listen to, and jazz players like to create their own spontaneous rhythms and melodies. Jazz started to appear around 1900, based mainly on African American folk music and West African rhythms. Early jazz innovators who helped to establish jazz as a distinct type of music include Louis Armstrong, Duke Ellington, and Dizzy Gillespie.

Rhythm and blues is a special freestyle type of music. In order to listen to rhythm and blues, you have to be in a rhythm and blues mood. This music you pour your broken heart and soul into. Many people sing the blues when they break up with their boyfriend or lose their job because it is a very expressive type of music. The blues style of singing was originally developed in the late nineteenth century and came from African American slave songs about life's hardships. In the 1940s and 1950s, performers like Ray Charles and Fats Domino helped to popularize rhythm and blues.

PART B: Looking at Your Own Writing

Directions: Find one or two sentences with at least three SVs in your own *Classification* rough draft and write them below. If you don't have any of these sentences, you may want to combine some of your shorter sentences to achieve greater sentence variety. Write your sentences in the blanks below.

1. _____

   _____

   _____

2. _____

   _____

   _____

Now check your sentences by marking the subjects and verbs and circling the connectors you used to join the clauses together. Make sure that they sound natural, the meaning is clear, and the punctuation is correct.

Classification Sentence Combining Paragraph

Directions: Sentences may be combined in any way that is effective. Try to write at least two or three sentences that have more than two SVs.

You Are What You Eat

1.1 There are eaters.
1.2 There are four different kinds.

2.1 Each group has preferences.
2.2 The preferences are its own.
2.3 The preferences are for certain kinds of food.

3.1 Some people are junk-food junkies.
3.2 They crave potato chips and candy bars.
3.3 They crave other fattening snacks.
3.4 Junk-food junkies don't take time for regular meals.
3.5 They like to make a quick stop at a fast-food place.

4.1 Fatty-food fiends are another group of eaters.
4.2 Their diet is also unhealthful.

5.1 They love fried chicken.
5.2 They love french fries.
5.3 They love other fried foods.
5.4 They can't resist pizzas.
5.5 The pizzas have lots of pepperoni and sausage.
5.6 The pizzas have lots of cheese.

6.1 Fatty-food fiends can't resist desserts.
6.2 The desserts are rich.
6.3 The desserts are loaded with calories.

7.1 People who are vegetarians do not eat meat.
7.2 They do not eat meat products.
7.3 Their diet includes many vegetables.
7.4 Their diet includes fruits.
7.5 Their diet includes carbohydrates.

8.1 Vegetarians still need protein in their diet.
8.2 They must find other sources of protein.
8.3 The sources include lima beans.
8.4 The sources include nuts.

9.1 The fourth group of people eat a greater variety of foods.
9.2 The foods are nutritious.
9.3 The foods are healthful.
9.4 Therefore, we can call them healthy eaters.

10.1 They eat fruits and vegetables.
10.2 They eat complex carbohydrates.
10.3 They eat moderate servings of meat.
10.4 Healthy eaters don't eat a lot of junk food.
10.5 They don't "pig out" on rich desserts.

11.1 These eaters are usually health-conscious.
11.2 They plan meals.
11.3 The meals include all of the food groups.

12.1 You are a junk-food junkie or a fatty-food fiend.
12.2 Consider changing to an eating style.
12.3 This style is more healthful.

Avoiding Problems with Subject–Verb Agreement

In Chapter 1 we looked at basic subject–verb agreement, and you learned that most verbs have two forms in the present tense. When the subject is *he, she,* or *it,* the verb ends in *-s.* (See Chapter 1 if you need a review.)

In this chapter you will learn about some special words and problem situations with subject–verb agreement. These include singular words that refer to a group of people or things, singular words that look plural, plural words that look singular, nouns that are separated from the verb by another noun, and words that can be either singular or plural depending on what follows them.

Category One: Collective Nouns

Collective nouns are those words that refer to a group of people or things collectively, such as *audience, band, class, collection, committee, faculty, family, group, jury, tribe,* and *team*. In American English, these are almost always used as singular nouns.

EXAMPLES ➤ 1. The family *is* large.

2. The jury *has decided* on a verdict.

3. A large collection of Matisse paintings *is* on display at the Museum of Art.

Category Two: Singular Nouns That End with -s

A second category of tricky singular nouns is made up of those words that end with *-s* but are treated as singular nouns: *politics, news, mathematics, civics, physics* (and certain other fields of study).

EXAMPLES ➤ 4. Politics *is* a rough game.

5. The news *wasn't* all bad.

6. Physics *requires* some knowledge of math.

Category Three: Indefinite Pronouns

A third area of problem words includes the indefinite pronouns *anybody, anyone, each, every, everybody, everyone,* and *everything*. These words are always singular, even though they may refer to more than one person or thing.

EXAMPLES ➤ 7. Each of the tests *was* harder than the previous one.

8. Every diplomat in the room *is* accredited to the United Nations.

Category Four: One, Another, Either, and Neither

Another problem category includes singular words that are sometimes separated from the verb by a plural noun, such as *one, another, either,* and *neither.* The verb must agree with the singular word.

EXAMPLES ➤   **9.** *One* of the best vacation destinations *is* San Diego.

           10. *Another* of the federal agents *was* missing.

Category Five: Plural Nouns That Don't End with -s

These potentially difficult nouns don't appear to be plural because they don't have a plural -*s* ending. Examples are *the Spanish, the Japanese, the Masai* (and other tribes or nationalities whose plural form doesn't end in -*s*), *the police, men, women, children, feet, octopi, geese, deer, sheep, mice,* and others. Be sure to use plural forms with these nouns. The expression *a number of* is always plural too.

EXAMPLES ➤   **11.** The Spanish *seem* proud of the new Olympic facilities in Barcelona.

           12. Some famous mice *are* Mickey Mouse, the three blind mice, and the mouse that took the thorn out of the lion's paw.

           13. A number of students from the engineering class *are planning* to promote their program next week.

Category Six: Words That Can Be either Singular or Plural

In addition to the tricky singular and plural nouns, there is a category of words that can be either singular or plural depending on the noun that follows, even if it's in a prepositional phrase. These words include *all, any, more, most, some,* and *a lot of.*

EXAMPLES ➤   **14.** All of the assignments *were* difficult.

              (The word *all* refers to the plural word *assignments,* so the verb must be plural.)

           15. All of the pizza *was* eaten.

              (The word *all* refers to the singular word *pizza,* so the verb must be singular.)

           16. Some students *learn* best by seeing something.

              (The verb agrees with the word *students,* which is plural.)

17. Some protein *is* necessary for good health.
(The word *protein* is singular.)

18. Most of the students *have* finished the assignment.
(*Students*, the noun that follows *most*, is plural.)

19. Most of the board *was* covered with examples.
(The word *board* is singular, so a singular verb is needed.)

■ **CLASS PRACTICE** **7** — **Subject–Verb Agreement Problems**

Directions: Circle the correct form of the verb.

EXAMPLE ➤ Every college student (needs, need) to dedicate time for studying.
In this example, the verb must agree with the word *every*, which is singular, so circle *needs*.

1. The Senate ethics committee (investigates, investigate) morals charges.

2. Most of the project (has, have) been completed.

3. Our women's volleyball team (is, are) considered to be the best in the nation.

4. Some of the contestants (has, have) come from as far as Philadelphia.

5. One of our most dignified scientists (loves, love) rollerblading.

6. The French (is, are) famous for their love of good food and wine.

7. Each of the presentations (was, were) great.

8. Physics (requires, require) a lot of math.

9. Everything often (seems, seem) better after a good night of sleep.

10. A large number of community college instructors (has, have) master's degrees.

■ **CLASS**
PRACTICE **8**

Proofreading for Subject–Verb Agreement

Directions: Carefully read the passage below, checking for correct subject–verb agreement. Make corrections as necessary.

Theme Cruises of the Caribbean

Not all Caribbean cruises are created equal. Theme cruises are those cruises where everything about the cruise revolve around one central idea, or theme. In recent years, mystery cruises have become very popular. Astronomy, football and baseball, and many other areas of popular interest have also had cruises designed for them. Often a professional team even send players to mingle with the passengers! On some cruises, politics serve as the unifying theme. One country music theme tour of Caribbean islands uses country music props throughout the ship. Most of the public areas of the ship, from the pool to the dining room to the casino, is decorated with hay, western hats, cowboy boots, and lots of horsey and country-type things. Men and women goes all-out on these trips; each of the passengers dress up as a famous country music singer like Dolly Parton or Garth Brooks. So if you ever get a chance to take a cruise, make sure that you choose a cruise that is interesting to you. Remember that every cruise is unique!

Classification Sentence Combining Paragraph

Directions: Be sure that all of your sentence combinations use correct subject–verb agreement. You may use Group A, B, or C connectors, relative connectors, or any other effective way to combine sentences. Some of your sentences will have more than two clauses.

Dilemma

1.1 You are writing a business letter.
1.2 The letter is to a woman.
1.3 You have to decide something.
1.4 The decision is how to address her.

2.1   *Mrs.* is a title for women.

2.2   *Miss* is a title for women.

2.3   *Ms.* is a title for women.

3.1   All of these titles are appropriate.

3.2   It's difficult to decide which one to use.

4.1   Many women prefer the title *Ms.*

4.2   *Ms.* is neutral.

4.3   *Ms.* says nothing about marital status.

5.1   A married woman can be addressed as *Ms.*

5.2   An unmarried woman can be addressed as *Ms.*

6.1   However, some women don't like *Ms.*

6.2   They think it sounds too impersonal.

6.3   They think it sounds phony.

7.1   For example, my grandmother doesn't like *Ms.*

7.2   My anthropology professor doesn't like *Ms.*

7.3   My piano teacher doesn't like *Ms.*

8.1   My grandmother wants to be called *Mrs.*

8.2   My anthropology teacher wants to be called *Mrs.*

8.3   They were both married for many years.

9.1   My piano teacher wants to be called *Miss.*

9.2   She wants people to know something.

9.3   They know that she is single.

10.1   *Mrs.* is a traditional title.

10.2   *Miss* is a traditional title.

10.3   Many people are accustomed to these titles.

11.1   You don't want to use the wrong title in your letter.

11.2   You might offend someone.

12.1   The problem is that you don't know everything.

12.2   You don't know the woman's marital status.

12.3   You don't know which title she prefers.

13.1   Sometimes you can solve the problem.

13.2   Solve it by using a job-related title.

13.3   There are job-related titles such as Dr. Dorn, Director Stevens, or Professor Tuyay.

13.4   Or you can call the person's office.

13.5   You can ask which title she prefers.

14.1   It is easier to address a letter to a man.

14.2   A man can always be called *Mr.*

Putting the Finishing Touches On Your Writing

Before you turn in your completed classification paper, read through it once more to be sure that you have done the best job you can. Think about the structure of the paper, paying special attention to the topic sentence and organization of your categories, and make sure that the categories are clearly defined. Take another look at your sentences as well. You should probably have some sentences with three or more clauses, without run-ons, comma splices, or fragments.

Use the following classification writing checklist when you are proofreading your final draft before you turn it in.

Classification Writing Checklist

Content and Organization

_____ 1. Does my topic sentence identify the categories?

_____ 2. Are my categories clear and well-defined, without overlapping?

_____ 3. Is my classification effectively organized?

_____ 4. Do I have roughly the same amount of information about each category?

_____ 5. Have I included enough details and information to explain the categories?

_____ 6. Is it easy to see where one category ends and another begins?

_____ 7. Does the conclusion make the paper seem complete?

Sentence Structure and Grammar

_____ 1. Have I avoided run-ons, comma splices, and fragments?

_____ 2. Have I used connecting words correctly, especially in sentences with three or more clauses?

_____ 3. Have I used a variety of sentence connectors?

_____ 4. Have I checked for problems with subject-verb agreement?

_____ 5. Did I check for spelling and grammar errors?

ENRICHMENT SECTION:
Conducting a Survey

Goals

In the enrichment section of this chapter, you will learn how to do the following:

■ Find out other people's opinions by taking a survey

■ Use classification to sort survey responses

■ Present the results of your survey

One way to find out what other people think about something is to take a survey. Surveys are often used to learn about public opinion on political or social issues, such as which candidate the public likes or whether people are in favor of something, such as health-care reform. If the results of a survey show that many people share a certain viewpoint, it may even be helpful in persuading or convincing others. Sometimes taking a survey can also help you research a topic that you want to report on or write about for one of your classes.

Taking a survey involves three main steps: preparing good questions, asking the questions, and writing up the results. In order to present the results effectively, you will need to sort people's responses into categories by using the classification methods that you have studied in this chapter. You can do your own survey and write it up by yourself, or you can work with a group of classmates.

First, you need to decide on a topic for the survey. Is there something that you would like to ask students at your school or college? For example, what do they think about a proposed change in the school calendar? Why don't more students attend football games and support the team? How many people experience test anxiety and what do they do about it? Is there a school service or program that you would like to get opinions about, such as a tutorial center, financial aid, or counseling? Or perhaps there is some controversial issue of general interest that you would like to survey people about. For example, you could design a survey to find out about people's views on immigration, abortion, or some other current topic that interests you.

Next you will need to decide on a few questions to ask about your topic. Try to keep your survey short, with five or six questions at the most. If your survey is too long or too complicated, it may be difficult to find people who will take the time to answer your questions. Instead of asking general questions like "How do you feel about crime?" make your questions more specific. Questions like "Are you in favor of capital punishment?" or "Are you in favor of a three strikes law?" are better because they ask specifically about one issue.

If possible, set up categories for the answers to most questions so that people can simply choose an answer and mark it. This will also make it easier for you to report the results. For example, suppose you are taking a survey about the food at the cafeteria or Student Union. You might begin with this question:

1. How often do you eat at the school cafeteria?
   _____ 5 or more times per week
   _____ 3–4 times per week
   _____ 1–2 times per week
   _____ less than 1 time per week

Some of your other questions could include categories for rating the food, like this:

2. How would you rate the quality and taste of the cafeteria food?
   _____ excellent   _____ fair
   _____ good   _____ poor

If you use categories similar to these, it will be easy to count the number of people who mark each answer. If you don't set up categories for the answers, you will probably need to sort the answers into categories after you gather the information.

You may also want to give people an opportunity to express their opinion in their own words. If so, include one question that asks for comments. For example, if your survey is designed to find out how people feel about campus safety and security, one of your questions might be, "What suggestions do you have for improving campus safety and security?" When you write up the results of your survey, you might want to quote some of the comments. If similar suggestions are made by more than one person, you might also want to sort the comments into different categories.

The form on page 313 was used to survey freshman composition students at Southwestern College. The people who wrote the survey questions wanted to find out whether students felt that the computer writing lab met their writing needs, or whether they thought it was overcrowded. Therefore, they decided to survey the freshman composition students who used the lab. The survey questions focused on whether students used the lab to write papers for other classes and whether they felt that more lab hours were needed. Notice that most of the questions have categories already set up so that the results of the survey will be easy to analyze. Only the last question asks for comments.

When you have figured out the questions that you want to ask, type or print them neatly on one sheet of paper, like the survey form on the following page. Then you will need to have copies made so that you can distribute the survey forms. You should plan to survey at least fifteen people. If you are working on the survey as a group project, however, you will probably be able to survey a larger number of people. The Computer Writing Lab Survey, for example, was conducted by several people working together, so it was possible to survey more than three hundred students. In general,

Computer Writing Lab Survey

1. Did you use the computer lab to write papers for other classes (besides English composition) this semester?

    YES _____   NO _____

2. If your answer to question 1 is YES, how many other assignments did you write in the lab?

    _____ One Assignment   _____ Three to Five Assignments

    _____ Two Assignments   _____ Six to Ten Assignments

    For which classes?

    _____ Art   _____ History

    _____ Biology   _____ Political Science

    _____ Business   _____ Psychology

    _____ Economics   _____ Speech

    _____ English (other courses)   _____ Other: _____

3. Do you think that more open lab hours are needed?

    YES _____   NO _____

4. If your answer to question 3 is YES, when should more open lab hours be offered?

    _____ Mornings   _____ Evenings

    _____ Afternoons   _____ Saturdays

5. Do you plan to use the computer lab to write assignments for other classes next semester?

    YES _____   NO _____

6. Comments about the computer lab:

the larger the number of people included in a survey, the more valid the results are.

Also think about who you should ask to fill out the survey forms. In many cases, a *random survey* is the best. A *random survey* means that you can ask anyone you happen to see *at random* to answer the questions. However, for some topics, you may want to ask only certain people to complete the survey. The Computer Writing Lab Survey on the previous page, for instance, was passed out only to students in freshman composition classes who used the writing lab.

After the survey questionnaires have been completed and returned to you, you need to analyze the results. Begin by counting the number of responses in each category. When you have all of the totals, write them on one of your blank survey forms. At the top of the page, write the total number of people that you surveyed.

The Computer Writing Lab Survey form is shown again on page 316, with all of the totals reported. Although 335 students were surveyed, some did not answer all of the questions, so the total responses for some questions do not add up to 335.

The final step is to write a paragraph or short paper about the results of the survey. In order to write a good paper, you should look over the totals and think about what the figures show. Try to decide what you really learned from the survey. Are you surprised by any of the responses, or did people answer more or less the way you expected them to? What conclusions, if any, can you make based on the results of the survey?

At the beginning of your paragraph, you should include a little bit of background information, such as why you took the survey and how you selected people to fill out the questionnaires. This will be the introduction. Then your topic sentence should focus on the most important information that you gained from the survey. In the body of your paper, briefly discuss the answers to all of the questions. If you wish, you may convert the most important numbers to percentages or fractions to emphasize important points. For example, instead of saying that 201 out of 335 students surveyed wrote papers for other classes in the lab, we could say that 60% of the students surveyed, or nearly two thirds, wrote papers for other classes. If one of your questions asked for comments, select some of the best ones and include them at the end of your paper or on a separate sheet.

The following paragraph about the Computer Writing Lab Survey shows how the results can be written up effectively.

Results of Computer Writing Lab Survey

In order to find out if the computer writing lab meets students' needs, we surveyed 335 freshman composition students who use the lab. Although comments about the lab were mostly favorable, our survey indicates that students need more open hours available in order to write papers for a variety of classes. According to our survey, many students use the computer lab for other classes besides freshman composition. 60% of the students in the survey reported writing papers for other classes, especially Speech, History, Psychology, and Biology. Furthermore, 70% plan to use the computer lab to write papers for other classes next semester, which means that the lab will become even busier. Responses to question 2 indicate that 70% of the students surveyed also think that more open lab hours are needed. Mornings and evenings were the top choices of times for additional open lab hours, although afternoons and Saturdays were almost as much in demand. Since there are classes and open hours presently scheduled in the lab from 7:00 a.m. to 9:00 p.m. Monday through Thursday and 7:00 a.m. to 4:00 p.m. on Fridays, as well as some hours on Saturdays, arranging more open lab hours will not be easy. In our opinion, it may be necessary to add another writing lab in the near future so that students' needs will be met.

Many people responded to question 6 with comments about the helpfulness of the lab or the need for more computers. Here are a few of their comments:

"Very helpful—easy computer to operate and very diversified."

"I feel that the lab gets overcrowded sometimes. Increasing the number of computers and expanding the lab space are ideas that should be looked into."

"It is a fantastic tool."

"Not enough computers."

"I felt the lab was not very helpful since it couldn't be used whenever I needed it."

"The computer lab was extremely helpful when I was doing my assignments. I've learned a lot about the Macintosh computers, and they make everything easier."

"It makes assignments easier to do. I'm so glad they had something like this for me."

"Perhaps, if funds were available, the lab could be expanded in the future. That way more computers would be available for the long list of students waiting to use the current lab."

"The lab really helped me this semester—not just in English but in all my classes."

"The lab is fine—the open lab hours are not. The hours are simply not accessible!"

Computer Writing Lab Survey
(335 people surveyed)

1. Did you use the computer lab to write papers for other classes (besides English composition) this semester?

    YES _201_   NO _134_

2. If your answer to question 1 is YES, how many other assignments did you write in the lab?

    _44_ One Assignment   _44_ Three to Five Assignments

    _40_ Two Assignments   _26_ Six to Ten Assignments

    For which classes?

    _7_ Art   _19_ History

    _12_ Biology   _4_ Political Science

    _11_ Business   _12_ Psychology

    _4_ Economics   _31_ Speech

    _16_ English (other courses)   _77_ Other: *Philosophy, Journalism, etc.*

3. Do you think that more open lab hours are needed?

    YES _236_   NO _86_

4. If your answer to question 3 is YES, when should more open lab hours be offered?

    _102_ Mornings   _103_ Evenings

    _92_ Afternoons   _94_ Saturdays

5. Do you plan to use the computer lab to write assignments for other classes next semester?

    YES _236_   NO _99_

6. Comments about the computer lab:

    See separate sheet for some of the comments made by students.

Writing That Analyzes Why and How

SECTION ONE:
The Writing Process for Cause and Effect Analysis

Goals

In this section of the chapter, you will learn how to do the following:

- Identify and analyze causes and effects
- Use branching to discover details
- Write a clear topic sentence and introduction for a cause and effect analysis
- Plan and write a cause and effect analysis
- Use clear, logical reasoning about causes and effects

Learning about Cause and Effect Analysis

What Is Cause and Effect Analysis?

Writing that explains *what happens as a result of certain events* or *why certain events occur* is called *cause and effect analysis*. From the time we are children, all of us ask questions about why and how things happen: Why is the sky blue? What makes planes fly? Why are vegetables good for us? Why do the seasons change? What causes earthquakes? What makes the waves on the ocean? Even after we have grown up, we never completely lose our sense of curiosity about why and how things happen. We continue to wonder about what causes things to happen the way they do and how certain things affect our lives. Whenever we try to figure out and explain the causes of something or the effects of something, we are using cause and effect analysis.

Writing Objective: Analyzing Causes or Effects

Your objective for this chapter is to write a paragraph or short paper that analyzes the causes of something or the effects of something. You may write about a personal topic, such as how being in the military service or winning an award affected you, or why you made a certain decision; or you may want to choose a more objective, informative topic, such as the effects of acid rain or the causes of the American Civil War. Informative topics may relate to history, economics, psychology, geology, nutrition, or any other area of knowledge that you are interested in. You may want to consider topics like the effects of a certain chemical or nutrient, the causes of a physical or mental disease, or the effects of an economic recession. With this kind of topic, it may be helpful to look up some information in a reference book or magazine article to be sure that your facts are accurate.

Prewriting Activities

Exploring Topics for Cause and Effect Analysis

The first step in the writing process is to think of some interesting topic ideas. On the *Exploring Topics Worksheet,* under *Option 1: Starting with a Cause,* you will try to identify people, events, situations, or conditions that cause certain effects to occur. This is one way to begin a cause and effect analysis. *Option 2: Starting with an Effect,* suggests an alternative approach. On this part of the worksheet, you will explore a variety of situations or problems that you could write about by analyzing their causes. Do both parts of the worksheet before you make your decision about which kind of topic to use.

■ **WORKSHEET I**

Exploring Topics for Cause and Effect Analysis

Option 1: Starting with a Cause

Directions: Try to think of at least one person, event, situation, or condition for each kind of topic listed below.

1. A person, event, or experience that has strongly affected your life

2. Something that affected you as you were growing up, such as a school, a place where you lived, or a group that you belonged to

3. A natural disaster such as earthquake, tornado, hurricane, tropical storm, forest fire, etc., especially if you experienced it yourself

4. Something that you do (or would like to do) that has beneficial effects—for example, exercise, meditation, physical therapy, following a special diet, etc.

5. A disability, handicap, or problem that affects you or someone you know, such as an eating disorder, an addiction, an injury, etc.

6. A historical event or current event that caused other things to occur

7. Anything else that *causes* certain effects to occur

Option 2: Starting with an Effect

Directions: Write down some problems or situations that you might want to analyze the causes of.

1. A personal or family problem that you would like to analyze

2. Something that didn't turn out the way you expected it to or wanted it to

3. A problem that someone you know has experienced

4. A current problem at your college or in your community

5. A national or international situation that is of interest to you

6. A natural occurrence that has explainable causes such as earthquakes, thunderstorms, ocean tides, etc.

7. Any other problem or situation that you would like to analyze the causes of

Discovering Details 1:
Asking and Answering Questions—
What? How? Why?

First look over the possible topics that you listed on your *Exploring Topics Worksheet* under *Option 1: Starting with a Cause* or *Option 2: Starting with an Effect* and choose one that you would like to talk about for this activity. You and a partner will ask each other questions in order to discover details about as many causes or effects as you can think of for your topics. If you start with a cause (Option 1), you will be looking for effects, and if you start with an effect (Option 2), you will be looking for causes.

Option 1: Starting with a Cause

If you select a topic under *Option 1: Starting with a Cause* (on page 318), the topic that you wrote on the worksheet is the *cause,* and you will be trying to identify and explain the *effects* that it has on you, other people, or society in general. Your objective in this prewriting activity is to discover as many *effects* as you can, as well as to explain how and why they happen. You will need to find a partner in the class to do this activity with you.

When it is your turn, begin by telling your partner a little bit about your topic, including any effects that you have already thought of. Then have your partner ask you the following questions orally, putting your topic in the blank in each question. For example, if your topic is self-hypnosis, your partner would ask you, "How did ___self-hypnosis___ affect you in the past?" Although some questions may not apply to your particular topic, answer as many as you can, giving details and explanations whenever possible. Your partner may also ask additional questions to help you identify and explain the effects.

After you have finished answering all of the following questions and any additional questions that your partner asked, change roles and repeat the same activity with your partner's topic.

- How did _____ affect you in the past?
- How does _____ affect you now?
- In what ways does _____ affect other people?
- Why does each of these effects occur?
- What things have changed in your life or someone else's life because of _____ ?
- What things have happened because of _____ ?
- Are there any other effects that you can think of?
- Which effects do you think are the most significant? Why?

(Notice the two different words, *affect* and *effect,* used in some of these questions. The difference is that *affect* is a verb, as in the first three questions, and *effect* is a noun. Be careful to use the correct spelling when you are writing your own paper.)

Option 2: Starting with an Effect

If you selected a topic under *Option 2: Starting with an Effect*, you have already identified an effect, so your objective is to figure out how and why this effect occurs. In some cases, there may be just one main cause or explanation; in other cases, there may be several reasons that the effect occurs.

Find a partner to work with, and begin by telling your partner some background information about your topic, including any causes that you have already thought of. Then your partner should ask you *How* and *Why* questions to help you figure out more about the causes. Of course, if more information is needed, your partner may also ask other questions.

Some general questions to help you get started are listed below. Your partner should put your topic in the blanks when asking you the questions. If necessary, the wording of the questions can be changed to make them more appropriate for a particular topic. When you have finished answering questions about your topic, change roles and ask your partner questions, putting your partner's topic in the blanks.

- Why do you think _____ happens (or happened)?
- Are other people or circumstances partly responsible for _____ ?
- Are there causes of _____ that are beyond your/our control?
- Is there an objective, scientific explanation for _____ ?
- What other problems or factors, if any, may contribute to _____ ?
- Are there any other causes that you can think of?

It isn't necessary to know all the answers yet, so don't worry if you aren't sure about some of the causes at this point. You may be able to make some reasonable guesses about the causes and then investigate further before you write your paper.

Follow-up

If the topic that you selected didn't work very well, go back to your *Exploring Topics Worksheet* and choose another topic. Then have a partner ask you questions about your new topic to help you discover details about the causes or the effects. If you wish, you may want to write down some of your ideas after you have completed this activity so that you will remember them when you write your rough draft.

Discovering Details 2: Branching

A good way to figure out the causes or the effects of something is to begin by writing your topic in the center of a piece of paper and then let your ideas branch out in different directions. This prewriting technique is called *branching* because you can connect your ideas with lines in any direction, like branches on a tree.

Look at the example of branching in Figure 7.1 to see how it works. The writer's topic was the effects of music, so she began by writing the word *music* in a circle in the middle of the page. Then she concentrated on the various ways that music affects people. She drew a line (or branch) out from the center for each idea that she thought of and then wrote her ideas at the ends of the lines. When she wanted to add other related details to these ideas, she drew more branches out from the words she had already written.

Figure 7.1 **Branching Example**

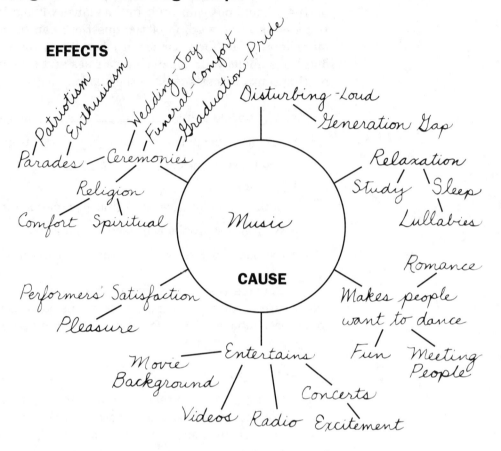

If a topic that you used for the previous oral prewriting activity worked well for you, you can use the same topic for branching. However, if you want to try a different topic, select another one from your *Exploring Topics Worksheet*. Begin branching by writing your topic in the circle on one of the two *Branching Worksheets* that follow. If your topic comes from *Option 1: Starting with a Cause*, use *Branching Worksheet Option 1*. Since this kind of topic begins with a *cause* (like *music* in the example), the word *CAUSE* is written in the circle, and you will write *effects* on the branches. If you choose a topic from *Option 2: Starting with an Effect*, use *Branching Worksheet Option 2*, which has the word *EFFECT* written in the circle. On this worksheet, you will be writing *causes* on the branches. If you have any doubt about which worksheet you should use for your topic, ask your instructor before starting to do branching.

It doesn't matter which directions your branches go in. Just take whichever direction feels right for each idea, and let the branches take whatever form and size seem to work best for your topic. If one branch gives you more ideas than the others and grows much larger, that's fine.

Occasionally your ideas on a branch may start to go in a direction that doesn't relate to causes or effects. If that happens, you can either discontinue the branch or add something that makes the ideas relate to causes or effects. For instance, in the branching example, the writer put "ceremonies" on one branch, which does not sound like an effect. However, she was thinking about the effects of music used in ceremonies, so she clarified this point by adding some smaller branches about the moods and feelings music may cause during different kinds of ceremonies.

Although there are six branches drawn on the worksheet, it is not necessary to use all six. However, if six branches are not enough, go ahead and add more.

■ **WORKSHEET II**

Branching

Option 1: Starting with a Cause

Directions: Write a cause in the circle and then think of effects to put on the branches.

EFFECTS

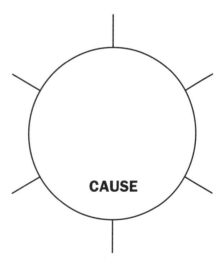

CAUSE

■ **WORSHEET III** | # Branching

Option 2: Starting with an Effect

Directions: Write an effect in the circle and then think of causes to put on the branches.

CAUSES

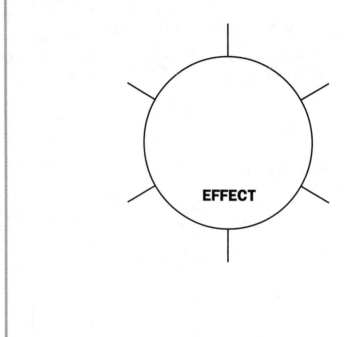

EFFECT

Writing a Rough Draft

Learning about Topic Sentences for Cause and Effect Analysis

The topic sentence (or main idea statement) for a cause and effect analysis should state your topic and the causes or effects that you are going to write about. If your paper will focus on the *effects* of something (an *Option 1 Topic*), your topic sentence should identify the kinds of effects that you will explain. If you intend to explain the *causes* of something (an *Option 2 Topic*), your topic sentence should identify the causes.

For example, one writer wanted to explain the effects that being an only child had on her (an *Option 1 Topic*). Therefore, her topic sentence needed to identify the kinds of effects that she planned to write about. The oral prewriting activity and the *Branching Worksheet* had helped her come up with several ideas:

Effects of Being an Only Child:

no brothers or sisters to play with
no one to argue with
lonely, quiet home life
somewhat spoiled—material things, privileges
close relationship with parents
poor social skills

In order to write a good topic sentence, she needed to decide which of these effects she wanted to write about. Since several of the effects seemed to be related to loneliness, she decided to focus on loneliness in her topic sentence. This was the first topic sentence that she tried:

TOPIC SENTENCE (DRAFT #1):

Because I was an only child, I was often lonely.

With this topic sentence, she could write about not having anyone to play with or argue with and having a quiet home life. However, it didn't include some of her other ideas, such as being spoiled and lacking social skills. She wanted to write about these effects too, so she decided it would be a good idea to include them in her topic sentence as well. Here is her revised topic sentence:

TOPIC SENTENCE (DRAFT #2):

Because I was an only child, I was often lonely, my social skills were slow to develop, and sometimes my parents spoiled me.

With this topic sentence, the writer has identified three main effects that she will discuss in her cause and effect analysis. As she explains and gives details about each of these points, she will also be able to mention other effects that she listed. For example, having a close relationship with her parents is related to being spoiled, so it could be included as part of that main point.

A diagram of her paper would look something like this, with one cause leading to three effects:

           ➡   EFFECT 1

CAUSE ➡   EFFECT 2

           ➡   EFFECT 3

Of course, the number of effects that you decide to write about will depend on your topic. In some cases, there may be only one or two important effects, and in other cases there may be more than three effects.

If you selected a topic from *Option 2: Starting with an Effect,* your paper should explain and analyze one or more causes that have made the effect happen. Therefore, your topic sentence needs to briefly identify the causes that your paper will be about.

Here is one writer's topic sentence about the causes of headaches:

TOPIC SENTENCE (DRAFT #1):

Most headaches are caused by stress.

When she showed this topic sentence to members of her workshop group, they asked her if she was going to write her entire paper about how stress causes headaches. She realized that with this topic sentence, she wouldn't be able to include any other causes besides stress. After discussing what she wanted to write about with her workshop group, she decided that she could write a more effective paper if she included other causes too, so she tried this topic sentence:

TOPIC SENTENCE (DRAFT #2):

Headaches have a variety of different causes, including stress.

Her workshop group liked this topic sentence a little better because it mentioned other causes. However, it did not actually identify any of the causes except stress, so she decided to revise it again. This is the topic sentence that she used to write her paper:

TOPIC SENTENCE (DRAFT #3):

Headaches have a variety of different causes, including stress, various physical problems, and certain foods or drinks.

With this topic sentence, her paper would be much more informative because she could write about three main kinds of causes. When she showed the third draft of her topic sentence to her workshop group, they agreed that it was more effective than her other two topic sentences.

A diagram for her paper about the causes of headaches would look like this:

CAUSE 1 ➡

CAUSE 2 ➡ EFFECT

CAUSE 3 ➡

As this diagram shows, the paper would explain three different causes that lead to the same effect, headaches.

If you are writing about a personal topic, such as how being an only child affected you, you are probably the best judge of which causes or effects are accurate. However, when you are writing about an informative topic, such as causes of headaches, you may need to check the accuracy of your information before deciding what to include in your topic sentence. If not, your topic sentence may be faulty. For instance, one writer who wanted to investigate and explain the causes of tidal waves came up with these two different topic sentences based on what he had heard about tidal waves. Do you think that either one of them accurately identifies the cause of tidal waves?

TOPIC SENTENCE (DRAFT #1):

Tidal waves are caused by exceptionally high tides.

TOPIC SENTENCE (DRAFT #2):

Tidal waves can be caused by storms at sea.

Since no one in his workshop group knew any more about the causes of tidal waves than he did, they advised him to research his topic a little before deciding on a topic sentence. By doing some reading, he found out that his first topic sentence was not true at all. Tidal waves are not related to normal ocean tides. However, he verified that Draft #2 of his topic sentence was partially true, since tidal waves are sometimes caused by hurricanes at sea. In addition, he learned about another cause of tidal waves—underwater earthquakes. Then he was able to write an accurate topic sentence to use in his paper:

TOPIC SENTENCE (DRAFT #3):

Tidal waves are caused by underwater earthquakes or hurricanes out at sea.

By reading about tidal waves, not only did he have a good topic sentence, but he had also learned enough about each of the causes to write an interesting, detailed paper.

Before you write your own topic sentence, do the following activity, *Evaluating Topic Sentences for Cause and Effect Analysis*. Remember that a good topic sentence can either identify the *effects* that are caused by something or identify the *causes* of a certain effect.

Evaluating Topic Sentences for Cause and Effect Analysis

Directions: Write OK in the blank by each good topic sentence (or main idea statement) that clearly identifies causes or effects. Write NO by the ones that need revision. Be ready to explain your answers.

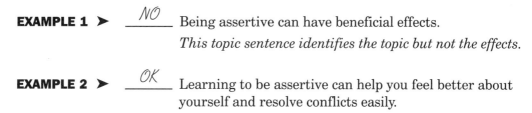

EXAMPLE 1 ➤ _____*NO*_____ Being assertive can have beneficial effects.

This topic sentence identifies the topic but not the effects.

EXAMPLE 2 ➤ _____*OK*_____ Learning to be assertive can help you feel better about yourself and resolve conflicts easily.

_____ 1. Current economic conditions have affected many people's way of life.

_____ 2. I used to think I was dumb until I found out that my problems with reading and writing are caused by a learning disability.

_____ 3. If the residents of North Lake have to pay for an expensive new sewer system, many people will be forced to sell their homes and move.

_____ 4. There are many reasons why some people are afraid to make commitments.

_____ 5. Nightmares are usually caused by fears or problems that you may be afraid to face when you are awake.

_____ 6. A well-balanced diet is good for you.

_____ 7. A low-fat diet can help you lose weight and lower your risk of heart disease.

_____ 8. There are good reasons for taking general education courses.

_____ 9. Credit cards are dangerous to use.

_____ 10. The Christmas holiday has become so commercialized that many people forget about its religious significance.

Writing Your Own Topic Sentence

Before you can write an effective topic sentence (or main idea statement), you need to decide which ideas from the _Branching Worksheet_ you want to use in your paper. Look over what you wrote on the worksheet and select the most important causes (if you wrote causes on the branches) or the most important effects (if you wrote effects on the branches). Some of the things that you wrote on your worksheet may turn out to be less important than the others, so it is not necessary to include all of the ideas in your paper—only the best ones. Also check to see if there are related ideas on two different branches that should be combined.

Some of the ideas that you thought of during the oral prewriting activity may also be helpful. Try to recall the causes or effects that you discussed with your partner. Although most of them are probably on your _Branching Worksheet_ as well, there may be some additional ideas that you would like to include in your paper.

After reviewing your prewriting ideas, make a list on the lines below of the causes or effects that seem to be the most important. List at least two or three ideas but not more than five or six. Remember that if you used an _Option 1 Topic_ and the branching worksheet where you wrote effects on the branches, you should make a list of effects. If you used an _Option 2 Topic_ and the branching worksheet where you wrote causes on the branches, you should make a list of causes. Write your list under Option 1 or Option 2, depending on your topic.

- *Option 1 Topic:* _____

  List of Effects:

  _____

  _____

  _____

  _____

  _____

  _____

- *Option 2 Topic:* _____

  List of Causes:

  _____

  _____

  _____

  _____

  _____

  _____

Now look over the list that you just wrote. Do you want to write your paper about all of the effects or causes that you listed, or do you think that some are more important than others? Which ones would be the most interesting or most informative for readers? Which ones could you most easily explain? When you have decided which ideas you want to write about in your paper, try writing a topic sentence. Remember to identify your topic as well as the causes or effects that you are going to write about.

TOPIC SENTENCE (DRAFT #1):

_____

_____

Now have your workshop group read your topic sentence, and ask for their suggestions. For most topics, you should make sure that the topic sentence identifies at least two effects (if you started with a cause) or two causes (if you started with an effect). If a topic sentence identifies only one cause or effect, think about whether there are any others that should be included. Also make sure that the causes or effects are based on accurate information, especially for an informative topic.

If you decide to revise your topic sentence to make it more accurate or more complete, write your new topic sentence here:

TOPIC SENTENCE (DRAFT #1):

_____

_____

Having a good topic sentence will make it easier to write the first draft of your cause and effect analysis. If you would like to get readers more interested or give them a little background information about your topic, you may also want to add another introductory sentence or two, especially if your paper is going to be more than one paragraph long. In that case, the topic sentence should usually be the last sentence of the introduction.

From Topic Sentence to First Draft

Read about Option 1 or Option 2 below to help you plan and develop your first draft. Option 1 explains how to work with topics that begin with a cause, which means that your paper will examine the effects. Option 2 is for topics that begin with an effect, so you will focus on analyzing the causes.

Option 1: *Starting with a Cause and Analyzing Effects*

If your topic started with a cause from Option 1 on the *Exploring Topics Worksheet*, remember that your paper should explain the effects resulting from that cause, as this diagram shows:

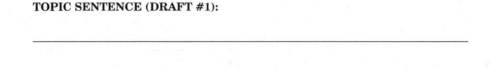

In this diagram, one cause leads to four different effects. However, depending on your topic, you may want to write about only two or three effects or, in some cases, perhaps only one effect. It is even possible to include more than four effects, although you might need to write a longer paper in order to explain each one.

Use your topic sentence (or main idea statement) as a guideline for planning your first draft. First check to make sure that your topic sentence clearly identifies both the cause and the kinds of effects that you plan to write about. Your topic sentence may be the first sentence of your paper, or you may begin with one or more additional introductory sentences before the topic sentence. For a longer paper, the introduction should be a separate paragraph.

In the body of your paper, explain the effects one at a time. The same order used to name the effects in your topic sentence is generally the most effective. Plan to write at least a few sentences about each effect, explaining with enough details so that readers will understand exactly what happened. In a short paper, all of the effects can be included in one paragraph. However, the body of a longer paper usually has one paragraph about each effect.

If possible, you should explain how and why the effects occur. For example, if you are writing about the effects of television on our society, one effect might be that television can interfere with family relationships, but if you don't explain *how* television interferes with family relationships, readers may not understand what you mean. Therefore, it's important to include details like these that show specifically how families are affected by television:

> Families often sit and watch television rather than communicating with each other. Although family members may be in the same room, they are all focused on the TV rather than sharing their feelings or ideas with each other. In some homes, they may even be in different rooms watching separate TV sets.

With an explanation like this, readers would understand clearly how television interferes with family relationships.

Read the first draft of *Effects of Dyslexia* that follows and think about whether or not the writer has followed all of the instructions for writing his first draft. Look for the introduction and topic sentence. Then check the body of the paper to see if the writer has discussed all of the effects that he identified in the topic sentence and if he has included enough details.

First Draft

Effects of Dyslexia

Many people have a learning disability known as dyslexia, which interferes with their perception of letters, words, and symbols. Dyslexia affects a person's ability to read and write, performance in school, and self-esteem. A dyslexic person has trouble reading because letters often appear to be reversed, scrambled, or even upside down. For example, a word like *sang* may look like *snag* or *sagn*. The word *body* may look like *doby*, with the *b* and *d* reversed. To someone who has severe dyslexia, letters may even appear to jump around on the page. The same types of problems occur when a dyslexic person tries to write. Even simple words are often misspelled, and a dyslexic person's handwriting is usually poor. In spite of their difficulties with learning, dyslexics generally have average or above average intelligence. However, teachers and parents may think that a child who has so much trouble learning to read and write has low intelligence, so he or she may mistakenly be put with a group of slow learners in school. Although dyslexia can't be cured, there are ways to help dyslexics overcome some of their problems with reading and writing. It is important to identify dyslexia early and to get the right kind of help.

Response to *Effects of Dyslexia*

1. Which sentence do you think is the writer's topic sentence?

   _____

2. List all of the effects of dyslexia that the writer identifies in his introduction and topic sentence:

   _____

   _____

   _____

   _____

3. Are all of these effects explained in the body of the paper? If not, which one(s) did the writer forget to include?

   _____

   _____

As you read the next cause and effect analysis, *Going to College* by Mary Miller, look for details about the three ways in which the writer's life has changed since she started attending college. Although she does not identify each way specifically in her topic sentence, she states her main idea that going to college has changed her life.

Going to College
by Mary Miller

My life has changed in three ways since I started going to Cuyamaca College. Throughout the semester, I have discovered that my leisure time has become limited. Since I now study an average of eight hours and attend class for four hours a week, rarely do I have the opportunity to spend time with my friends or family. Whereas I used to exercise at the gym four times a week, I now work out only twice a week. Not only has my time become a limited commodity, but my budget has also decreased. Before returning to college, I worked an average of 25–32 hours every week. Because I now work an average of only 18–25 hours a week, my monthly income has been reduced by about four hundred dollars. Furthermore, I have acquired the additional expense of my education. Perhaps the most critical change in my life is that my self-esteem has dramatically improved. It seemed that my life had little purpose or direction when my only goal was to make it through another boring day. Now I aspire to become a drug and alcohol counselor. Where there was little challenge, I now feel a sense of pride and accomplishment, especially when I receive the highest of grades (an "A") in my courses. Even though I have had to make sacrifices in continuing my education, the benefits I have gained through this experience are truly immeasurable.

Response to *Going to College*

1. In what three ways has going to college changed the writer's life?

    _____   _____

    _____

    _____

2. By including several details about each point, the writer shows us how these effects have occurred. Which details do you think are the most interesting and effective?

    _____

    _____

    _____

If your cause and effect analysis is going to explain the effects of something, like *Effects of Dyslexia* or *Going to College*, you should start working on your first draft now. Next you will learn how to write a paper that analyzes the causes of something (Option 2).

Option 2: Starting with an Effect and Analyzing Causes

If you select a topic from *Option 2* of your *Exploring Topics Worksheet*, remember that your paper must examine the causes of the problem, situation, or condition that you have chosen as your topic. For example, you could be writing about the causes of stress, the causes of the Civil War, the causes of low self-esteem, the causes of the deterioration of the ozone layer, or any other topic that focuses on the causes of something.

If you have already written a good topic sentence that identifies the causes of something, it will help you get started. Check your topic sentence to make sure that it identifies one or more causes that you intend to explain in the body of your paper. The diagram below represents a cause and effect analysis with four causes leading to one effect:

    CAUSE 1   ➡

    CAUSE 2   ➡   EFFECT

    CAUSE 3   ➡

    CAUSE 4   ➡

Of course, it is possible to write about any number of causes. However, if you try to write about more than four causes, your paper will probably have to be fairly long in order to explain each one well. On the other hand, if you write about only one cause, you will need to have a lot of information about it in order to write an interesting paper.

Before you begin writing your first draft, it is a good idea to look over the ideas that you wrote on your *Branching Worksheet*. It may also be helpful to think about the details that you discussed with your partner during the oral prewriting activity. Then you can begin with your topic sentence, or you may want to have a short introduction first to tell readers something about the topic before stating the topic sentence. For a longer paper, the introduction should be a separate paragraph.

In the body of the paper, you should explain each cause that you identified in your topic sentence. Whenever possible, remember to include details about *how* each cause leads to the effect. Try to give the reader a clear picture of exactly what happens (or happened) and why. It is usually best to discuss the causes in the same order that they are named in your topic sentence so that your paper will be clearly organized. You may want to include everything in one full paragraph, or you may want to divide the body into separate paragraphs, with one paragraph explaining each cause.

As you read the following paper, *Causes of Anxiety* by Joy Snyder, notice that the topic sentence identifies several factors that can contribute to anxiety. Although some of these factors, such as poor diet and lack of exercise, are not likely to cause anxiety by themselves, when combined with other factors, they may contribute to an anxiety attack. Therefore, it is appropriate to include them in the cause and effect analysis.

Causes of Anxiety
by Joy Snyder

Anxiety is a feeling of excessive anxiousness and irrational worrying, which most of us experience at some time in our lives. The main factors that contribute to anxiety are stressful situations, earlier traumatic experiences, negative attitudes, poor diet, and lack of exercise. At one time or another, each of us encounters high pressure situations that create anxiety. We get a breathless feeling, knots in our stomach, or the shakes. Some common situations which may bring on anxiety are speaking in public, first dates, dental checkups, birthdays, and weddings. Some anxiety disorders may be a result of traumatic experiences during childhood. An unresolved event from a person's past may interfere with a situation in the present, thus creating a feeling of anxiety. Attitude also has a great deal to do with anxiety. If our inner voice is telling us that we are going to fail or that something horrible is going to happen, our anxiety will definitely increase. The increased anxiety will take away energy, confidence, and creativity as well. Because we require more nutrients when we're under stress, it is especially important to eat three balanced meals a day during times of stress. Those who consume a lot of junk food and frequently skip meals are weakening the body's natural resistance to anxiety. It is also a good idea to get plenty of aerobic exercise in order to prevent anxiety, especially when you are feeling stressed. Raising your pulse rate to between sixty and eighty percent of your maximum heart rate for fifteen to twenty minutes can alleviate shallow breathing and lightheadedness, which often are symptoms of anxiety. There are several effective methods for relieving anxiety, such as relaxation, meditation, and even laughter. It just takes time and practice in order to figure out which method works best for you so that you can avoid anxiety attacks.

Response to *Causes of Anxiety*

1. Which sentence do you think is the topic sentence?

_____

List all of the causes of anxiety that the writer identifies in her topic sentence:

_____

_____

_____

_____

_____

Are all of these causes discussed in the body of the paper?

_____

2. Which details do you think are the most interesting or informative?

_____

_____

3. Have you ever experienced anxiety for any of the reasons explained in this paper? If so, briefly describe your own experience.

_____

_____

If you are going to write a paper about the causes of something, like *Causes of Anxiety,* you should write your first draft now.

Rough Draft Workshop

After you have completed the rough draft of your cause and effect analysis, show it to your workshop group. You can help each other by working together to spot problems and making constructive suggestions. Use the questions below as guidelines for discussing your rough draft. The questions can be applied to both types of papers—a paper about the effects of something (Option 1) or a paper about the causes of something (Option 2).

Rough Draft Workshop Questions

1. Does the topic sentence identify the kinds of causes or effects that the paper is about?

2. Does the paper clearly explain each of these causes or effects?

3. Has the writer developed each point with enough explanations and details? If not, where should more details be added?

4. Whenever possible, has the writer explained *how* causes lead to effects?

5. Is the organization of the paper clear and logical?

Using Clear Logic

It is important to present accurate, logical information about causes and effects. Don't make the mistake of automatically assuming that the first in a sequence of events caused the events that happened afterward. In order to prove that there is actually a cause and effect relationship between two events, you must have some facts or other evidence to show how and why the first event caused the second one to happen. Sometimes it may be just a coincidence that one event happened before another, and you will find that the second event was actually caused by something else.

For instance, suppose that someone you know breaks up with his girlfriend, and a few hours later he is seriously injured when his car goes off the road. Did breaking up with his girlfriend *cause* him to lose control and wreck his car? It's possible that being upset about the breakup distracted him from his driving, thus causing him to go off the road and into a ditch. However, it's also possible that the accident was caused by a mechanical failure, a person or animal unexpectedly crossing the road, or an oncoming car that made him swerve off the road. Unless you talk to your friend and find out that his mind was on breaking up instead of on driving, you can't say for sure that breaking up with his girlfriend was one of the causes of the accident. It may be just a coincidence that one event happened shortly before the other.

Let's consider another example. Suppose that you study hard for the first test in your political science class but get a D. For the second test, you don't have a chance to study and you get a B. Can you conclude that you get better grades when you don't study for tests? Probably not. Maybe the second test was easier, maybe you were extremely nervous about the first test but not about the second one, or maybe you were absent a lot before the first test but attended every class meeting just before the second test. You need to consider all of these possible causes instead of jumping to the conclusion that lack of study leads to high grades.

Sometimes unreasonable opinions can also interfere with logical thinking. If a cause and effect statement is based on a prejudice or a bias toward someone or something, it will not be valid. For example, if someone said, "Today's music is rotting the minds of our teenagers," would this statement be reasonable? The speaker seems to be prejudiced; in other words, the opinion is based only on an emotional reaction, with no facts to support it. In order for this cause and effect statement to be valid, it would be necessary to prove that music can cause someone's mind to rot and that teenagers' minds are actually being affected. Therefore, the speaker's claim that today's music causes teenagers' minds to rot is invalid.

Think about this statement: "Tricia shouldn't take geometry because girls aren't good at math." Is this a logical cause and effect statement, or does it express an unreasonable opinion? Math may be difficult for a lot of people, and it may even be difficult for Tricia, but there is no evidence that women in general lack math skills. The statement clearly is based on a prejudice or bias regarding women, so it is illogical.

The following activity will give you more practice identifying errors in logical thinking.

Activity with Logical Thinking

Directions: Most of the following statements about causes and effects are based on faulty logic. Some incorrectly assume that an earlier event caused a later event. Others show a bias or prejudice toward some group of people. In the blank below each faulty statement, explain why the thinking is not logical. Write CORRECT after any statements that express a logical cause and effect relationship.

1. I got lost because a black cat crossed my path and brought me bad luck.

2. Television corrupts people's minds.

3. If that car wasn't made in the United States, it isn't any good.

4. Jack failed his math class last semester. That's why he's getting help from a tutor this semester.

5. Our basketball team is winning this year because most of the players are African Americans.

6. If you eat everything on your plate, you'll grow up to be strong and healthy.

7. One cause of low grades is drinking too much coffee while you're study-
    ing. I drank a lot of coffee while I was studying for the last two tests, and
    I got low grades on both of them.

8. One reason for illiteracy is that reading isn't necessary for people who
    have low-income jobs.

After you have figured out what's wrong with the reasoning in the
above statements, compare your answers with those of other class members. Then read through your own cause and effect paper again to check for
logical thinking. Be sure that you have not assumed one event caused another just because it happened first. Also make sure that none of your statements are based on an irrational prejudice or bias against any person or
group.

As you read the next cause and effect analysis, *Clean Water at Last* by
Zachary Reiff, notice that Zachary has given convincing reasons to explain
why he believes each effect will occur when the new sewage treatment plant
is completed. Although no one can predict the future with absolute cer-
tainty, by using clear logic and accurate information, a writer can analyze
effects that will probably occur.

Clean Water at Last
by Zachary J. Reiff

A new sewage treatment plant that is to become fully operational within
the next two years will have numerous positive effects in the South Bay area.
The first obvious benefits brought about by the plant would be its effects on
the city of Imperial Beach. The ocean water off Imperial Beach will be clean
year round for the first time in two decades. This will undoubtedly eliminate the
many cases of hepatitis caused by surfers or swimmers venturing into the
ocean even when the contaminated water signs are posted. The clean water
will also bring more business to the most southwesterly city in the continental
United States. For many years, investors have been skeptical about putting
their money into a place where the primary resources have been the neighboring ocean and the wonderful year-round weather. When the dilemma of raw
sewage spewing into the ocean has been rectified, money will flow through the
city of Imperial Beach like a freshly tapped keg of Budweiser flows through college students during "rush week" at a major university. Another certain benefit
will be the effect on the Tijuana Estuary, which is a National Wildlife Sanctuary.
The estuary contains birds on the endangered species list that may soon
flourish in a healthier environment. The treatment plant will also reduce, if not
eliminate, the "sewage flood" problems that have occurred in the Tijuana River
valley. These floods have caused the local residents much hardship and unfor-
tunate struggles, but, even more importantly, these floods have taken the lives
of many immigrants attempting to enter the United States by crossing the
Tijuana River. The new sewage treatment plant will solve many problems for
everyone.

Response to *Clean Water at Last*

1. After reading Zachary's paper, which effects do you think will definitely occur when the new sewage plant goes into operation?

_____

_____

_____

2. Sometimes one effect can also lead to other effects that a writer may want to include. For example, one effect of the sewage treatment plant will be clean ocean water. What two other effects does Zachary say will happen as a result of the ocean water off Imperial Beach being cleaner?

   A. _____

   B. _____

Transitions for Cause and Effect Analysis

In your cause and effect paper, you may want to use some transitional words that emphasize cause and effect, such as *as a result, because, because of, consequently, therefore,* or *thus.* For example, here are some sentences from *Going to College* and *Causes of Anxiety* that use *because* and *thus* to show a cause and effect relationship:

> **Because** I now work an average of only 18–25 hours a week, my monthly income has been reduced by about four hundred dollars.

> An unresolved event from a person's past may interfere with a situation in the present, **thus** creating a feeling of anxiety.

In the first sentence, *because* explains the connection between two ideas: the number of hours the writer works now that she is going to college, and her reduced monthly income. In the second sentence, *thus* helps to establish the cause and effect relationship between unresolved events from the past and feelings of anxiety.

Other kinds of transitional words, phrases, and sentences can also be very useful. For example, you may want to use some time-order transitions, such as clauses that begin with *when,* or transitions to add an additional point, such as *also, another, furthermore,* or *in addition.* Here is a sentence from *Clean Water at Last* that uses *another* to make a smooth transition from one effect to the next.

> **Another** certain benefit will be the effect on the Tijuana Estuary, which is a National Wildlife Sanctuary.

The following transitional sentence from *Going to College* by Mary Miller is also very effective. It links the previously discussed effect (limited time) with the next effect that the writer is starting to explain (budget problems):

Not only has my time become a limited commodity, but my budget has also decreased.

Another way to make smooth, natural transitions is to repeat key words from previous sentences so that the connections between ideas are clear. Writers sometimes prefer to connect their thoughts this way rather than adding other transitional words or phrases.

Let's take a look at a few sentences from *Causes of Anxiety* that illustrate this technique. In Sentence 1, the writer states that *stressful situations* are one of the main factors that contribute to anxiety. Then, in the following sentences, some of her words refer to the same idea again. As additional related ideas are introduced, the key words "anxiety" and "situations" are repeated in some of the other sentences in order to create continuity.

(1) The main factors that contribute to *anxiety* are *stressful situations,* earlier traumatic experiences, negative attitudes, poor diet, and lack of exercise.
(2) At one time or another, each of us encounters *high pressure situations that create anxiety.* (3) We get a breathless feeling, knots in our stomach, or the shakes. (4) *Some common situations which may bring on anxiety* are speaking in public, first dates, dental checkups, birthdays, and weddings.

Notice that the writer varied the wording a little in some of the sentences. Instead of saying "stressful situations" each time, she referred to them as "high pressure situations" and "some common situations." This made the sentences sound natural but still connected the ideas effectively. In Sentence 3, no key words needed to be repeated because it is already clear that the writer is describing symptoms of anxiety.

When you are using this technique for transitions, be careful not to repeat key words too many times, or your writing will sound wordy and repetitious. You should use transitions only when they help to connect your ideas smoothly and naturally.

In the following paper, Shawn McPherren examines why brushfires are a serious problem in Southern California. Notice that in many of his sentences, he uses references to previously mentioned key words or ideas in order to create good continuity. For example, at the beginning of the second sentence, "These fires" refers back to "Brushfires" in the first sentence, and in the second paragraph references to the warm weather and sunshine are repeated.

Brushfires in Southern California
by Shawn McPherren

Brushfires are a big problem in Southern California at certain times of the year. *These fires* range from relatively harmless field fires to raging community infernos. Hot, dry conditions and Santa Ana winds make it easy for fires to get started and difficult to keep them from spreading.

Southern California is known for its warm, sunny weather almost year round. While the warm weather makes for a great vacation spot, it also increases the danger of brushfires. Among the hills are tall weeds and a lot of brush and "scrub" that get bone dry as the hot summer sun bakes out their moisture. The arid semi-desert land becomes covered with dry, brittle kindling, which is highly combustible. Once a fire starts, it races quickly through the dry vegetation.

Most fires are started by unnatural causes: arson, cigarettes thrown from cars, kids playing with matches, and migrant workers' cooking fires. Only occasionally are fires started naturally, such as by lightning. No matter how a brushfire gets started, it must be attended to as soon as possible before it grows to be deadly. Once a fire gets large enough, it sucks up oxygen with increasing force, creating a vacuum that feeds the fire as it grows and grows. With fires of this size, conventional methods of firefighting can no longer be used. Helicopters with loads of water and big cargo planes with fire retardant are used to try to extinguish the blaze.

A local phenomenon that often makes a fire grow more rapidly is known as Santa Ana winds. These very hot and dry winds help to feed the fire with oxygen, spread the fire by blowing embers, and frighten firefighters with their unpredictable shifts of direction. When it's a Santa Ana day and there's a brushfire on the news, many locals pay close attention because we all know how deadly a mix those two are.

Southern Californians must learn to be very careful with fire, especially when weather conditions create ideal settings for large and dangerous fires. Safety measures about fire are taught to school children at a young age so that everyone will understand the serious dangers of fire and the need for fire prevention.

Response to *Brushfires in Southern California*

1. Although Shawn mentions several causes of fires, most of his paper actually explains two factors that cause brushfires to be especially dangerous in Southern California. What are these two factors?

   A. _____

   B. _____

2. Why do you think that Shawn divided his cause and effect paper into several paragraphs instead of putting everything into one long paragraph?

   _____

   _____

3. Look for references to key words or ideas that help create smooth transitions in the first three paragraphs of *Brushfires in Southern California*.

Underline all of the repeated words or ideas that you find, and then compare your answers with those of your classmates. Do you think this method of making transitions is effective? Why or why not?

_____

_____

_____

Now proofread your own rough draft again to see if all of the ideas are connected smoothly and clearly. If you find places where your ideas seem to change abruptly, you may want to add transitional words or phrases that are appropriate for the situation, or you may want to try the technique of repeating some key words as Shawn did in *Brushfires in Southern California.*

Ending Effectively

The conclusion for a cause and effect paper should leave readers with an important idea that you want them to remember about your topic. If you are writing about something that has positive or beneficial effects, one way to write an effective ending is to make a general statement about the effects. If your paper is about the causes of some problem (such as anxiety) or the negative effects of something (such as dyslexia), you may want to use the conclusion to suggest a solution or a way of coping with the problem.

Let's look at how the writers in this chapter ended their cause and effect papers effectively either by commenting on positive effects or by suggesting solutions to a problem.

1. *Effects of Dyslexia:* Although dyslexia can't be cured, there are ways to help dyslexics overcome some of their problems with reading and writing. It is important to identify dyslexia early and to get the right kind of help.

2. *Going to College:* Even though I have had to make sacrifices in continuing my education, the benefits I have gained through this experience are truly immeasurable.

3. *Causes of Anxiety:* There are several effective methods for relieving anxiety such as relaxation, meditation, and even laughter. It just takes time and practice in order to figure out which method works best for you so that you can avoid anxiety attacks.

4. *Clean Water at Last:* The new sewage treatment plant will solve many problems for everyone.

5. *Brushfires in Southern California*: Southern Californians must learn to be very careful with fire, especially when weather conditions create ideal settings for large and dangerous fires. Safety measures about fire are taught to school children at a young age so that everyone will understand the serious dangers of fire and the need for fire prevention.

Which of these conclusions suggest solutions to the problem that the paper was about?

_____

_____

Which of these conclusions make a general statement about beneficial effects that were explained in the paper?

_____

_____

Which conclusions do you think are the most effective? Why?

_____

_____

The type of conclusion that works best for a cause and effect analysis will depend on the topic of the paper. However, for most cause and effect topics, either suggesting a solution or commenting on the significance of the effects will probably be an effective ending.

As you are reading *Situations* by Nancy Gutierrez, think about what kind of conclusion you expect the paper to have. Since this paper is about a personal topic, the conclusion, like everything else, is based on the writer's personal experiences and feelings. You may be surprised at her final comments about being heavyset.

Situations
by Nancy Gutierrez

Ever since I was a small child, I have been heavyset. Because of this, many of my peers teased me, which made my self-esteem diminish as well as affecting my social life and the way I looked at others.

During my junior high years I felt the worst. I became a bully in order to have people notice me for something other than my weight. At that age I had so much rage that I took it out on whoever was closest to me. Because of this, I was always in trouble in school. I also remember a feeling of loneliness and not being wanted. Even my mother would tell me how fat I was and how no one would ever want me. I can still recall the nights I lay in bed crying, wishing I was dead or maybe just someone else.

My social life wasn't that great either. My mother usually had me busy around the house. When I did go out, I would go roller skating, to the movies, or to school functions. Hardly ever was I asked out by a boy. My main problem with boys was, instead of kissing them, I was beating them up. Sometimes I would daydream of being the most popular girl whom everyone liked and dating the most popular guy in school. In the end I would always return to reality, and my sad life (as I knew it) would continue. If it hadn't been for my friends who would give me their pep talks and cheer me up, I might have been a different person today.

Since then I've learned that you can't judge people by their appearance. Even the ugliest of people can find someone to love and care for. I've also learned to express my feelings and to show others the beauty I have on the inside. Because of all the put-downs and name calling, I've become a very shy person, as well as very judgmental about myself. I try my hardest not to judge other people for who they are on the outside, but what they are about. I think if more people were this way, there would be less hatred and criticism and more love and understanding for one another.

Maybe all of this has made me a better person; I don't know. What I do know is that life would be a whole lot easier if adults would show their kids that there is more to a person than size and shape. I am still a heavy person, but I no longer care about what people think. If they can't see me for who I am, then they are not worth knowing.

Response to *Situations*

1. What solution does Nancy suggest in the conclusion that would help to overcome the kinds of negative effects she wrote about?

    _____

    _____

2. Do you think this conclusion is effective? Why or why not?

    _____

    _____

3. Because this is a personal topic, the writer has included her feelings. What words can you find in the paper that express some of the writer's feelings?

    _____   _____

    _____   _____

    _____   _____

    Do these feelings help make the paper more effective? Why or why not?

    _____

    _____

Now write a conclusion to complete your own rough draft. If your paper is a page or less in length, one or two sentences will be enough for a conclusion. If your paper is a little longer, it is a good idea to write a longer conclusion, especially if you have divided the paper into three or more paragraphs. Use one of the suggestions below, depending on the topic of your paper:

- Is your paper about effects that are beneficial in some way? If so, try writing a conclusion that states the significance of the effects or some other general comments about them. Write the first draft of your conclusion here:

CONCLUSION (DRAFT #1):

_____

_____

- Is your paper about negative effects of something? If so, is there a way to prevent these effects, to make them less serious, or to solve the problem that causes them? Try writing a conclusion about preventing or solving the problem:

CONCLUSION (DRAFT #1):

_____

_____

- Is your paper about the causes of a problem? If so, you could propose a solution to the problem or a way of coping with the problem. Write your conclusion here:

CONCLUSION (DRAFT #1):

_____

_____

- Is your paper about causes of something else rather than a problem (like the causes of ocean tides, for example)? In this case, try a conclusion about why it's important for readers to understand the topic:

CONCLUSION (DRAFT #1):

_____

_____

Now add your conclusion to your rough draft and have your workshop group read the entire rough draft one more time to make sure that the conclusion is effective. If members of your group offer good suggestions, you may want to add some of their ideas to your conclusion.

Your instructor may ask you to turn in your rough draft at this time, or you may continue to revise and improve it while you are doing Section Two of this chapter, Sentence and Grammar Skills. In Section Two you will learn more about writing sentences that have three or more clauses, and you will sharpen your grammar skills by learning how to use pronouns correctly. The proofreading paragraphs in Class Practices 5 and 9 and the sentence combining paragraphs will give you more examples of cause and effect writing.

Be sure to do the *Cause and Effect Writing Checklist* at the end of the chapter before turning in the final copy of your cause and effect paper.

SECTION TWO:
Sentence and Grammar Skills

Goals

In this section of the chapter, you will learn how to do the following:

- Recognize and write longer sentences that use a Group B connector at the beginning to join two of the clauses

- Recognize and write longer sentences that have a relative clause in the middle of another clause

- Avoid errors with Group B connectors and relative clauses in longer sentences

- Use pronouns that correspond to the person, thing, or idea you are referring to

Learning about Different Sentence Types
That Have More than Two SVs

In Chapter 6 you learned to recognize and write longer sentences with two or more SVs that follow these two patterns:

SV   connector   SV   connector   SV.

SV,   SV,   and   SV.   (clauses in a series)

In this chapter you will learn to use two patterns that we haven't looked at before in longer sentences:

1. Sentences with a Group B connector at the beginning
2. Sentences that have a relative clause in the middle of another clause.

You have already used both of these constructions to connect two clauses. In Chapter 3 you learned about using Group B connectors at the beginning of a sentence to join two clauses, and in Chapter 4 you learned how to use a relative clause in the middle of another clause. Now you will learn how to use both of these constructions in sentences that have more than two clauses.

Using a Group B Connector First

The three sentences below, from pages 117 and 118 in Chapter 3, are examples of using a Group B connector first to join two clauses. They fit the following pattern:

| Group B connector | S | V | , | S | V. |

EXAMPLE 1 ➤ While Georgia took inventory of the stock, Ruben handled a customer complaint.

What if you want to add more information and make this a longer sentence? One way of doing this is by adding another clause (SV). Here are some possibilities:

       Group B   *S*   *V*   , *S*   *V*

EXAMPLE 1A ➤ While Georgia took inventory of the stock, Ruben handled a

                , *Group A*   *S*   *V*

customer complaint,   and   Margaret set up a new display.

In this longer sentence, the first two clauses are joined by a Group B connector at the beginning, and the second and third clauses are joined by a comma and the Group A connector *and*.

       Group B   *S*   *V*   *Rel = S* *V*

EXAMPLE 1B ➤ While Georgia took inventory of the stock that was going to be

          , *S*   *V*

marked down, Ruben handled a customer complaint.

In Example 1B, a relative clause containing more information about the stock has been added using the relative pronoun *that* as a connector as well as the subject of the new clause. As long as each clause is connected to the other clauses by a correct connector, the sentence is correct. Here is another example:

EXAMPLE 2 ➤ Although transactional analysis is not the only valid model, it is a useful method of examining interpersonal relationships.

What is the connector in this sentence? _____

What Group of connectors does it belong to? _____

Now let's add more information:

EXAMPLE 2A ➤ Although transactional analysis is not the only valid model, it is a useful method of examining interpersonal relationships, so it might be worth looking into.

What connector is used to add the new clause? _____

Is it a correct sentence? Why or why not? _____

EXAMPLE 2B ➤ Although transactional analysis is not the only valid model, it is a useful method of examining interpersonal relationships which might be worth looking into.

In Example 2B the relative pronoun *which* is used to add the final clause.

EXAMPLE 3 ➤ As the bride came down the aisle, everyone stood up.

Now let's add more information and make this a longer sentence:

Group B   *S*   *V*   *Group A*   *S*   *V*   ,
EXAMPLE 3A ➤ As the music started   and   the bride came down the aisle,

          S   *V*
          everyone stood up.

In this example we have added a short clause to the beginning of the sentence. In this case we don't need a comma with the Group A connector *and* because the Group B connector *as* joins both the first and second clauses with the third one. Many times when you are revising your sentences, you can change the structure of the original sentence to express the exact meaning you want.

Using a Relative Clause in the Middle of Another Clause

The following examples are from Chapter 4. They have a relative clause in the middle of another clause and fit the following pattern:

> **S**   Rel   S   V   **V.**

EXAMPLE 1 ➤   The class that you recommended taught me a lot.

If you want to add another clause to this sentence, you can choose from any of the correct ways of connecting clauses. Here are some possibilities:

> *S   Rel   S   V   V   ; S   V*

EXAMPLE 1A ➤   The class that you recommended taught me a lot; I should ask for your advice more often.

You can see that the new clause has been connected with a semicolon. Here is another possibility:

EXAMPLE 1B ➤   The class that you recommended taught me a lot, so I should ask for your advice more often.

In this case we used a Group A connector to add the new clause. Finally, here's still another possibility that has both a Group B connector at the beginning and a relative clause in the middle of another clause:

EXAMPLE 1C ➤   Because the class that you recommended taught me a lot, I should ask for your advice more often.

What is the Group B connector that adds the new clause? _____

Is Example 1C a correct sentence? Why or why not? _____

These two ways of adding another SV to a sentence, along with the patterns that you learned and practiced in previous chapters, are tools you can choose from to express your ideas skillfully and in a way that will interest your reader. In Chapter 8 you will practice using these patterns to give your writing a rich texture with an interesting variety of sentence lengths and constructions.

■ **CLASS** **Analyzing Longer Sentences**
PRACTICE **1** **from Example Papers**

Directions: The following sentences are from cause and effect papers in this chapter. Mark the subjects, verbs, and all connectors. Circle the Group B connectors used at the beginning, and then underline any relative clauses that are in the middle of another clause.

From *Causes of Anxiety*, by Joy Snyder, on page 334:

1. Because we require more nutrients when we're under stress, it is especially important to eat three balanced meals a day during times of stress.

From *Brushfires in Southern California*, by Shawn McPherren, on page 340:

2. When it's a Santa Ana day and there's a brushfire on the news, many locals pay close attention because we all know how deadly a mix those two are.

From *Situations*, by Nancy Gutierrez, on pages 343–344:

3. When I was asked out, I wouldn't tell my mother, mainly because of the criticism she would give me.*

4. If it hadn't been for my friends who would give me their pep talks and cheer me up, I might have been a different person today.

5. I think if more people were this way, there would be less hatred and criticism and more love and understanding for one another.†

From *Effects of Dyslexia*, on page 331:

6. However, teachers and parents may think that a child who has so much trouble learning to read and write has low intelligence, so he or she may mistakenly be put with a group of slow learners in school.

   (*Notice that the first word,* however, *does not connect the clauses within this sentence. It connected this sentence logically with the preceding sentence in the paragraph.*)

---

*The connecting word *that,* joining the second clause with the third one, has been omitted from this sentence.

†This is another sentence where the connecting word *that* has been omitted.

■ **CLASS PRACTICE** **2** **Combining Short Sentences to Make Longer Sentences**

Directions: Combine the following sentences using appropriate connectors to make sentences with three or more SVs. Use a *Group B* connector first in some of them, a relative clause in the middle of another clause in others, and a variety of other connectors.

EXAMPLE ➤ I was growing up in Spring Valley. It was much more rural than it is today. There were no freeways. Quite a few people had horses.

Possible Answer: When I was growing up in Spring Valley, it was much more rural than it is today; there were no freeways, and quite a few people had horses.

1. We knew that the water was swift and deep. We wouldn't let the children go near the stream.

2. The suit that looked best on me was too expensive for my budget. I kept looking until I found it on sale.

3. Sometimes life isn't easy. Pressures mount, and it feels as if you can't cope with everything. When this happens, turn to someone for help.

4. Before the storm struck, there was a beautiful 70-foot cypress in front of the house. Afterwards it was just a pile of brush and wood.

5. There is more rain in California in some years. There is an *El Niño* weather pattern. It is characterized by higher water temperatures in the Pacific Ocean. It changes the direction of the storm track.

_____

_____

6. You have access to a computer and a modem. You can experience the joys of the information highway. It is not really a highway. It is a network of computers. The public can access them for free.

_____

_____

■ **CLASS PRACTICE** **3**

Using a Variety of Connectors to Write Sentences with Three or More Clauses

Directions: Now write some original sentences using three or more SVs. Write at least two that use a Group B connector at the beginning, and at least two that have a relative clause in the middle of another clause.

1. _____

_____

2. _____

_____

3. _____

_____

4. _____

_____

5. _____

_____

When you are finished, ask another student to check that each connector is used correctly and that each sentence sounds natural.

Combining Sentences in a Paragraph

Directions: In the following paragraph, connect the fragments and some of the short sentences to make longer sentences. Some of your sentences should use a Group B connector first or a relative clause in the middle of another clause.

Regular Exercise

Regular exercise for at least 40 minutes four times a week can help you live longer and enjoy your life more. When you elevate your heart rate even a little for the whole 40 minutes. There are many benefits. The first and probably most important effect of regular exercise is on the cardiovascular system. Because the increased heart size and lung capacity that exercise provides. Will enable your muscles to burn more oxygen. You will have more endurance. You will be able to maintain a higher level of activity in your regular activities and sports. You will feel better and live longer too. Another important benefit is that you will look better. If you think you are too skinny. You will be happy to see your muscles toning up and becoming more defined. You will probably gain in muscle mass too. If you think you are overweight. You will be happy to learn that exercise serves as an appetite suppressant. It helps to regulate your 'appestat' and aids you in controlling your calories. Moreover, the exercise itself burns calories. In addition, muscle, which is heavier than fat, will make you look slimmer. Because it replaces bulkier fat. Finally, regular exercise can help you feel better mentally and emotionally. Exercise causes your body to produce higher levels of endorphins and hormones. They serve as mood regulators, reduce your body's reaction to stress, make you more alert, and help you feel happier in general. These effects of regular exercise should make you want to get started on an easy but consistent exercise program right away!

Avoiding Errors with Group B Connectors and Relative Clauses in Longer Sentences

In Chapter 6 you practiced correcting run-ons, comma splices, and punctuation errors in longer sentences. In this chapter we will focus on avoiding some other types of errors in longer sentences that use Group B connectors and relative clauses. Here are some examples of common errors:

EXAMPLE 1 ➤ *Too Many Connectors*

Group B   *S*   *V*
Because the Chargers had just won the AFC division

                            , Group A *S* *V*   , *Group A*
championship,   and   they were going to the Superbowl,   so

        S   *V.*
the crowd went wild.

This sentence is incorrect because there are too many connectors. The Group B connector *because* is enough to join the first clause to the second one, so *and* is not needed. Here are some possible corrections:

> *Correct:*   Because the Chargers had just won the AFC division championship, they were going to the Superbowl, so the crowd went wild.
>
> or
>
> *Correct:*   The Chargers had won the AFC division championship, and they were going to the Superbowl, so the crowd went wild.

EXAMPLE 2 ➤ *Incorrect Punctuation*

> Indianapolis which is the capital city of Indiana hosts a famous race every year, and race enthusiasts come from all over the world to see it.

In this sentence the relative clause is incorrectly punctuated because it isn't needed to identify Indianapolis, so it should be set off by commas. Here is the corrected sentence:

> *Correct:*   Indianapolis, which is the capital city of Indiana, hosts a famous race every year, and race enthusiasts come from all over the world to see it.

Remember that all of the punctuation rules for different kinds of connectors still apply to longer sentences with three or more clauses (SVs). Relative clauses should be set off by commas when they are not necessary to identify someone or something, as in the sentence above. (See Chapter 4 to review punctuation of relative clauses.) Group A connectors, such as *and*, *but*, and *so*, should be preceded by a comma when they join two clauses (see Chapter 2), and clauses beginning with Group B connectors, such as *because*, *if*, and *when*, need to be followed by a comma when they are at the beginning of a sentence (see Chapter 3).

EXAMPLE 3 ➤ *Incorrect Placement of Relative Clause*

> Ruth and Rickey publish a science fiction newsletter whom I met at a gaming convention.

In this incorrect example the relative clause is in the wrong place. The sentence should be:

> ***Correct:***   Ruth and Rickey, whom I met at a gaming convention, publish a science fiction newsletter.

Remember that in most cases the relative clause should directly follow the noun it modifies.

■ **CLASS**
PRACTICE **5**

Proofreading Paragraph:
Errors in Longer Sentences

Directions: Check the sentences in the following paragraph. Look for sentences with too many connectors, punctuation errors, and errors with relative clauses, as well as other sentence structure errors. Then correct them using what you know about correct sentence structure and punctuation.

The Mountain Lions Are Coming!

Several states, which lie west of the Mississippi River, have recently experienced a dramatic surge in mountain lion attacks, and a few people have even been killed. Because there is not just one simple reason for these attacks; instead, there are several factors, that contribute to the increased danger. For one thing, because more people are now spending time hiking, fishing, and driving in areas that were previously wilderness, and there is a greater chance of meeting up with wild animals of all kinds another factor is an increase in the mountain lion population in the national parks, which has contributed to this problem. Human hunters have greatly reduced the number of deer outside of the national parks, because deer herds are protected from hunting in the parks, so they tend to stay there, and mountain lions are drawn by the abundant supply of meat-on-the-hoof. Finally, due to the same ban on hunting, a whole generation of mountain lions which has grown up in the national parks with no fear of man. While no single factor is responsible for the increased number of terrifying encounters, it is certainly possible for park visitors to minimize their risk.

Writing with Sentences of Three or More Clauses

PART A: Looking at Writing from an Example Paper

Directions: Look at the following selection from *Going to College,* by Mary Miller, on pages 332–333. Highlight or underline the sentences that have three or more clauses, and circle the connectors. Notice that some of the longer sentences begin with a Group B connector or have a relative clause in the middle of another clause.

> Perhaps the most critical change in my life is that my self-esteem has dramatically improved. It seemed that my life had little purpose or direction when my only goal was to make it through another boring day. Now I aspire to become a drug and alcohol counselor. Where there was little challenge, I now feel a sense of pride and accomplishment, especially when I receive the highest of grades (an "A") in my courses. Even though I have had to make sacrifices in continuing my education, the benefits I have gained through this experience are truly immeasurable.

PART B: Looking at Your Own Writing

Directions: Find one or two sentences with at least three SVs in your own *Cause and Effect* rough draft and write them below. Is there one with the Group B connector first or with a relative clause in the middle of another clause? If you don't have any of these sentences, you may want to add one for greater variety. Write your new sentence in the blanks below.

1. _____

   _____

   _____

2. _____

   _____

   _____

Now check your sentences by marking the subjects and verbs in each sentence and circling the connectors you used to join the clauses together. Make sure that your sentences sound natural, the meaning is clear, and the punctuation is correct.

Cause and Effect
Sentence Combining Paragraph

Directions: Most of the sentences will have two or three clauses (SVs) when they are combined. You may use any connectors that join the clauses effectively, but try to write at least one sentence with a Group B connector first and one sentence that has a relative clause in the middle of another clause.

Laughter

1.1 Laughter has many effects.
1.2 The effects are beneficial to our physical health.
1.3 The effects are beneficial to our mental health.

2.1 Laughter is like exercise in some ways.
2.2 Its effects on the body are similar.

3.1 For example, you are laughing.
3.2 The level of adrenaline in your body increases.
3.3 Your pulse rate becomes higher.

4.1 Laughter also increases the blood flow to the brain.
4.2 Laughter gives your heart and lungs a workout.
4.3 Laughter relieves stress.

5.1 You have high blood pressure.
5.2 You can lower it by laughing.
5.3 You can strengthen your immune system.

6.1 You can even tone your muscles by laughing.
6.2 Laughter makes your muscles contract.

7.1 The effort is not necessary.
7.2 The effort is required by physical exercise.
7.3 You can achieve some of the same benefits.

8.1 There are also emotional benefits.
8.2 These occur if you laugh.
8.3 You must laugh frequently.

9.1 Your outlook on life becomes more positive.
9.2 Your problems seem less serious.

10.1 Natural chemicals alter your mood.
10.2 The chemicals are released into the bloodstream during laughter.
10.3 The chemicals cause these changes.

11.1 Laughter is something.
11.2 We take it for granted.
11.3 Without it, we might be depressed.
11.4 We might be unhappy.

12.1   You are feeling down.
12.2   Remember that giggling is good for you.
12.3   Chuckling can cheer you up.
12.4   Roaring with laughter will revitalize you.

13.1   Try it.
13.2   You'll discover something.
13.3   Laughter really is medicine.
13.4   The medicine is the best.

Learning about Pronouns

In the early chapters of this book you learned about nouns, verbs, adjectives, and adverbs. In this chapter we will look at another part of speech: pronouns. A pronoun is a word that is used to represent a noun. It is important to use pronouns appropriately because if we had to repeat the same nouns over and over again, our writing would probably be boring and choppy. Notice the pronouns in bold print in the following paragraph.

A few hours after the car had been rear-ended, Carol Lee began to experience pain in **her** neck and back. Then **she** began to feel a little dizzy. **Her** husband Joey was concerned, so **he** took **her** to the emergency room. **She** wanted to drive **herself,** but **he** wouldn't let **her. He** was afraid that **his** wife was suffering from whiplash and maybe a mild concussion. Less than a year ago **he** had experienced the same kinds of problems **himself** after a minor accident. **He** hoped that the other driver's insurance would pay for Carol Lee's treatment because **they** were on a limited budget, and **their** budget didn't include any extra money for emergencies.

Some of these pronouns refer to Carol Lee, a woman. These pronouns are *she, her,* and *herself.* Others refer to Joey, a man: *he, his,* and *himself.* Two pronouns in this selection refer to both of them: *they* and *their.* We use different pronouns depending on what noun we are referring to, what function the pronoun has in the sentence, and whether it represents a singular or a plural noun. Table 7.1 is a chart of personal pronouns.

Subject Pronouns

The subject of a sentence is usually the person, place, thing, or idea that produces the action of the sentence. When a pronoun is used as the subject of a clause or sentence, it has to be a subject pronoun. These pronouns are *I, we, you, he, she, it,* and *they.* Check your pronouns carefully, especially when you have a compound subject, and be sure not to use object pronouns as the subject of a sentence. Here is an example of incorrect usage when the wrong pronoun is substituted for one of the nouns in the following sentence:

Table 7.1   Pronoun Chart

| Subject Pronouns | Object Pronouns | Possessives | | Reflexive Pronouns |
		Possessive Adjectives	Possessive Pronouns	
I	me	my	mine	myself
we	us	our	ours	ourselves
you	you	your	yours	yourself yourselves
he	him	his	his	himself
she	her	her	hers	herself
it	it	its	——	itself
they	them	their	theirs	themselves

(Mark and two of his friends transferred to the Massachusetts Institute of Technology.)

Him and two of his friends transferred to the Massachusetts Institute of Technology.

In this sentence, *him* is an object pronoun and cannot be used as a subject. One easy way to check sentences with compound subjects like this example is to try the same sentence with only one pronoun at a time to decide whether the pronouns are correct. When we try this with the example, we end up with the following sentences:

Him transferred to the Massachusetts Institute of Technology. (Incorrect)

Two of his friends transferred to the Massachusetts Institute of Technology.

The first sentence obviously sounds wrong. Here is the corrected sentence using the subject pronoun *he*:

He and two of his friends transferred to the Massachusetts Institute of Technology.

Object Pronouns

In grammar, the term *object* usually refers to the noun or pronoun that receives the action of the verb or that follows a preposition, whether it's a person, place, thing, or idea. (Notice that this term has a different meaning than the common word *object,* which means a thing.) Here are some examples of nouns and pronouns used as objects:

> ***Using nouns:***   Yolanda read the article to her blind grandfather.

> ***Using pronouns:***   She enjoyed reading it to him.

In the first sentence above, *the article* and *her blind grandfather* are objects. The second sentence uses the object pronouns *it* and *him* in place of these nouns.

Be sure not to use subject pronouns when you need object pronouns. Here is an example of a pronoun error when the wrong pronoun is substituted for one of the nouns in the sentence below:

> (The financial counselor advised my sister and her husband to draw up a will.)

> The financial counselor advised my sister and *he* to draw up a will. (Incorrect)

In this sentence, *counselor* is the subject, and *my sister* and *her husband* are objects. Therefore, we need to use an object pronoun if we replace *my sister* or *her husband* in this sentence. Here is the corrected sentence:

> The financial counselor advised my sister and *him* to draw up a will.

Another way to correct this one is to use the plural pronoun *them* instead, like this:

> The financial counselor advised *them* to draw up a will.

Possessive Adjectives and Possessive Pronouns

There are two types of possessives, and both of them are technically pronouns. However, in this book we will use the term *possessive adjectives* to refer to those possessives that need to have the noun stated, and *possessive pronouns* for the possessives that are used without a stated noun.

Possessive Adjectives

Possessive adjectives are used with a noun to show who or what the noun belongs to. It is always necessary to state the noun when we use possessive adjectives. Here are a couple of examples:

> Maria let Henry borrow *her* pen.

> Will and Jezzyda used *their* acting talent to get parts in the play.

In the first sentence above, *her* is used with *pen* to show that it belongs to Maria. In the second sentence, *their* is used with *acting talent* to show that both Will and Jezzyda have acting talent.

Possessive Pronouns

Unlike possessive adjectives, possessive pronouns are used alone, without the noun, to show what belongs to whom. Here are some examples:

> Henry forgot to bring a pen, so Maria let him borrow *hers*.

> The actors trying out for the play had to perform different skits. When Will and Jezzyda performed *theirs*, they were immediately given parts in the play.

Be sure to use possessive pronouns only in place of the noun and not with the noun.

Reflexive (or Emphatic) Pronouns

When the same noun is both the subject and an object in a sentence, reflexive pronouns are often used. Here is an example:

> Nina looked at *herself* in a mirror as she finished getting ready to go out.

Reflexive pronouns are also used to stress, or emphasize, the noun they are referring to. Here is an example of this usage:

> The millionaire playboy always washes his car *himself*.

The reader might think that a millionaire would pay somebody to wash his car, so the pronoun *himself* is used to emphasize that it really is the millionaire who washes the car.

Unless the subject and the object are the same person or thing, be sure not to use reflexive pronouns as objects even when you are referring to yourself, as in the following incorrect example:

> ***Incorrect:*** Barry made charcoal drawings for Lydia and *myself*.
>
> ***Correct:*** Barry made charcoal drawings for Lydia and *me*.

Also remember that reflexive pronouns cannot be used as subjects:

> ***Incorrect:*** Megan and *myself* took the ferry to Staten Island.
>
> ***Correct:*** Megan and *I* took the ferry to Staten Island.

Another common error is using the wrong form for some of these pronouns. For example, be sure to use *himself* and not "hisself." Don't use "theirselves" instead of *themselves*. And be sure to use *yourself* when you are talking to one person, but *yourselves* when you are talking to more than one person. You can use the pronoun chart to check your pronouns and make sure that they are correct.

■ **CLASS PRACTICE** ## Practice with Pronouns

Directions: Look for pronoun mistakes in the following sentences. Cross out any mistakes you find and write in the correct pronoun. If the sentence is correct, write CORRECT instead.

1. I am pleased to announce that Karla and me already finished our class project.

2. When Norman visits the prisoners, he doesn't mind helping them write theirs letters.

3. I need a receipt from both you and he for the work you did at the rental property.

4. The judges thought that mine was the best painting in the exhibition.

5. I hope that you and your wife are planning to reserve some time for yourself.

6. The UPS delivery person said that his trainee and himself had a hard time finding our house.

7. Zona's supervisor and her have mutual respect for each other.

8. Judith and Rob wanted to buy a new car for themselves.

Pronoun Reference and Agreement

In formal writing, each pronoun normally refers to a specific noun that has been named earlier in the paper. This noun is called the *antecedent*. With a few exceptions, the antecedent is usually in the previous sentence or clause. In any case, the antecedent must always be recent enough that the meaning (or reference) is clear. When you use a pronoun, that pronoun must be appropriate for the noun it refers to; in other words, the pronoun must *agree* with its antecedent. Two common pronoun errors to avoid are *unclear pronoun reference* and *faulty pronoun agreement*.

Unclear Pronoun Reference

When you use a pronoun, make sure the reader can clearly understand what noun it refers to. Look at the following sentence:

> ***Incorrect:*** When Ross Perot and George Bush debated, *he* made a rude comment.

In this sentence, we don't know which of the two politicians made the rude comment or whether someone else did. It is not clear which noun the pronoun refers to. We call this type of error *unclear pronoun reference*. Be sure that each pronoun you use clearly refers to a specific noun. Written like this, the sentence would be clear:

> ***Correct:*** When Ross Perot and George Bush debated, *Phil* made a rude comment.

Here is another incorrect sentence:

> ***Incorrect:*** Elvira usually makes photocopies in the afternoon because they are not as busy then.

In this sentence, the reader doesn't know who is meant by *they*. The sentence would be clearer like this:

> ***Correct:*** Elvira usually makes photocopies in the afternoon because the copiers are not as busy then.

Another common error of this type occurs when the pronoun *it* doesn't clearly refer to one person or thing.

> ***Incorrect:*** When Eduardo and Kevin started attending the men's support group, we thought *it* was great.

In this sentence we don't know if *it* refers to the men's group or to the fact that Eduardo and Kevin started attending the men's group. Depending on the meaning, the sentence would be written in one of these two ways:

Correct: When Eduardo and Kevin started attending the men's support group, we thought the group was great.

or:

Correct: We thought it was great that Eduardo and Kevin started attending the men's support group.

Faulty Pronoun Agreement

Be sure to choose the correct pronoun for the noun that it refers to. Be especially careful when you use the following words:

one, no one, nobody
anyone, anybody
someone, somebody
every, everyone, everybody
either, neither
each

These words are called *indefinite pronouns,* and they are always singular. When you use any of these words, use singular pronouns to refer to them.

EXAMPLES ➤   **1.** *Each* of the brothers has *his* own strengths.

   2. *Neither* the salon manager nor the assistant manager had brought *her* keys with *her*.

One common mistake with some of these words is to use a plural pronoun. Look at the following incorrect sentence:

Incorrect: *Each* boy scout should bring *their* own water on the hike.

What noun does the possessive pronoun *their* refer to? It refers to *each boy scout*, that is, *each individual person*, so a singular pronoun should be used. The sentence could be corrected like this:

Correct: Each boy scout should bring *his* own water on the hike.

Notice that in this case we are only talking about males, so the use of the pronoun *his* is acceptable and correct.

Point of View

When you are writing a paragraph or paper, you should avoid shifting your point of view unnecessarily. For example, if you are speaking from your own experience, use the pronoun *I* or *we,* and try not to switch to *you* or *they* unless it is necessary. Here is a sentence that is faulty because the point of view shifts unnecessarily:

> ***Incorrect:***   We kept hiking even though we were lost, but you would have a better chance of being found if you stayed in one place.

This sentence should be:

> ***Correct:***   We kept hiking even though we were lost, but *we* would have had a better chance of being found if *we* had stayed in one place.

Gender Issues

Traditionally, English writers have used the male pronouns *he, him, his,* and *himself* in situations where the gender of the person isn't specified. Here is an example of this situation:

> Each college student must take it upon *himself* to keep up with *his* homework.

This sentence is grammatically correct, but it seems to create the impression that all college students are males. Unfortunately, there is no easy alternative that is widely accepted. One possibility is to use *himself or herself,* and *his or her,* as in the following example:

> Each college student must take it upon *himself or herself* to keep up with *his or her* homework.

While this takes care of the problem of gender, the sentence has become awkward. In an effort to avoid this problem, some writers have tried alternating pronouns, using male pronouns in one sentence and female pronouns in the following sentence. This solution can be very confusing. Another technique is to avoid male and female pronouns by making the nouns and pronouns plural:

> All college students must take it upon *themselves* to keep up with *their* homework.

Still another technique that can sometimes be used is to avoid using a personal pronoun at all. The example above could also be corrected like this:

> All college students must take it upon *themselves* to keep up with *the* homework.

Many writers consider these last two solutions to be very effective because the sentences sound natural and are fair to everyone. You may want to experiment with one or more of these techniques, and you can be guided by the advice of your instructor in this area.

More Practice with Pronouns

Directions: The following sentences contain unclear pronoun references, faulty pronoun agreement errors, and gender problems. Cross out the problem words and write the corrections above the sentence.

1. When each student is finished, he or she should turn in his or her paper to their teacher.

2. Everyone who was at the picnic hoped that she would win the raffle.

3. Both tractors had their motors running. They were inside having coffee.

4. Sarah and myself went for a walk around the neighborhood.

5. When Mariana and Felicia worked in the Adult Literacy Program, we thought it was great.

6. Anyone who has a problem with being violent should ask themselves if they should get help.

7. When students were protesting the Vietnam War in the 1960s, you were cool if you wore your hair long.

8. I took a trip to Atlanta, where the economy is booming and you can find many new businesses starting up.

9. Gary asked Tony if he had received a raise.

10. No one was willing to admit that they were wrong.

■ **CLASS PRACTICE** **9**

Proofreading for Pronoun Errors

Directions: The following selection contains several errors with pronouns. Cross out the incorrect forms and write in the correction above the error. When you change pronouns from singular to plural or from plural to singular, you may also need to change the verbs to agree with their new subjects.

Eating Disorders

Many young people today suffer from an eating disorder. The three most common eating disorders are anorexia nervosa, bulimia, and food addiction. Anorexia nervosa, or self-imposed starvation, and bulimia, which involves vomiting after eating, have some things in common. Anorexia nervosa affects more young women than any other group, and they can have devastating effects on the individual and their family. In addition, anorexia and bulimia have some common psychological or emotional causes. Every young person wants to feel loved and accepted by their friends and family, and when a young person doesn't feel that they are giving them enough attention, or they feel unworthy of receiving love from the people around them, you can start to feel desperate and develop a distorted and repugnant view of your own body. A young person often believes that he or she is extremely fat when in fact that is not true at all. As a result you starve yourself or eat and purge in an effort to become thinner.

The third disorder, food addiction, is similar in many ways to alcoholism. Someone who suffers from food addiction is unable to control their eating, so you overeat and it makes you gain too much weight. There are emotional and psychological roots to this addiction as well, and it can affect yourself in many ways.

Anorexia, bulimia, and addictive overeating can cause dangerous health problems. It can even be life-threatening. If you or anyone you know suffers from one of these eating disorders, don't be afraid to get help. It is much more dangerous than it might seem.

Cause and Effect Sentence Combining Paragraph

Directions: To combine the following sentences, you may use any connectors that join the clauses effectively. Notice that many of the sentences use personal pronouns.

Why TV?

1.1   There are many different reasons.
1.2   Millions of people watch TV.
1.3   This happens every day.

2.1   Some people watch TV to learn things.
2.2   Some people wouldn't learn these things otherwise.

3.1   Informative programs appeal to some people.
3.2   Informative programs are offered on the Discovery channel.
3.3   Informative programs are offered on public broadcasting channels.

4.1   TV allows them to follow stock market reports.
4.2   TV allows them to watch extensive news coverage.
4.3   TV allows them to get current information on a variety of topics.
4.4   They can do this while relaxing in their living room.

5.1   Parents often turn on the TV.
5.2   They do this because the TV will entertain their small children.
5.3   Some programs will help preschoolers learn to read and count.

6.1   The children watch because special shows appeal to them.
6.2   Special shows have lively music.
6.3   Special shows have imaginative characters
6.4   Special shows have stories with lots of action.

7.1   For adult viewers, TV also provides entertainment.
7.2   There are many different kinds of entertainment.

8.1   People watch situation comedies to experience laughter.
8.2   People watch dramas to experience intense emotions.
8.3   These include anger, sadness, and fear.

9.1   Some viewers like to watch movies.
9.2   Viewers can see the movies that they missed at the theaters.
9.3   Viewers can also see new movies that were made especially for TV.

10.1   Sports enthusiasts get so involved in baseball, football, or basketball.
10.2   They forget about everything else while they are watching.

11.1   Soap opera fans like to observe other people's lives.
11.2   Soap opera fans can forget about their own problems for awhile.
11.3   They worry about their favorite characters' problems instead.

12.1 For some viewers, TV programs are a way to escape.
12.2 They can escape their daily lives.
12.3 Their daily lives may be dull or boring.

13.1 People watch TV for all these reasons and more.
13.2 It's no wonder there's a TV set in every home.

Putting the Finishing Touches on Your Writing

Before you turn in your completed cause and effect paper, read it again and see if you have made it as good as it can be. Check the paragraph structure and make sure that the body of your paper supports your topic sentence. Check your sentences too. If you used structures that were presented in this chapter, you will have some sentences with three or more clauses that have a relative clause in the middle or that begin with a Group B connector. Be sure that these sentences are correctly written and punctuated. Also be sure that you have used correct pronouns consistently in the paper.

Finally, use the cause and effect writing checklist below to make sure that your paper is well-organized and that your sentence structure and grammar are correct.

Cause and Effect Writing Checklist

Content and Organization

_____ 1. Does the topic sentence identify the causes or the effects?

_____ 2. Are these causes or effects clearly and logically explained in the paper?

_____ 3. Have I included enough details to make all of the points clear?

_____ 4. Are transitions used smoothly and effectively?

_____ 5. Does the conclusion suggest a solution, comment on the significance of the effects, or in some way make the paper feel finished?

Sentence Structure and Grammar

_____ 1. Have I used a variety of sentence connectors?

_____ 2. Have I used some longer sentences with Group B connectors and relative clauses?

_____ 3. Have I used connectors correctly, especially in sentences with three or more clauses?

_____ 4. Do all the pronouns agree with the noun they refer to, and are they clear?

ENRICHMENT SECTION:
A Cause and Effect Experiment

Goals

In the enrichment section of this chapter, you will learn how to do the following:

- Conduct an experiment in human behavior
- Observe people's reactions
- Write about the results of your experiment

If you enjoy observing other people, you will probably have fun with this experiment in human behavior. The experiment involves doing something unusual or out of the ordinary, observing how your actions affect other people, and writing about your observations. For example, if you wore your shirt backwards, how would people react? Would they stare at you? Would anyone tell you about it? What if you took your dog, cat, hamster, or pet mouse along with you on a date? Would your date be enthusiastic about your pet or annoyed? How would having an animal along affect the evening? By using your imagination, try to think of some unusual behavior that is sure to have an effect on other people. You may plan your own individual experiment, or, if you wish, you may plan an experiment together with a group of your classmates.

Here is a list of some possible experiments that you may want to consider:

> wear clothes backwards
> wear a strange outfit
> wear a wild wig
> wear long, artificial fingernails
> wear a false nose or a pig nose
> take a pet with you on a date
> sit someplace other than your usual seat in class
> yawn or hum repeatedly during a conversation
> laugh at everything, even if it isn't funny
> say nothing but one phrase over and over during a conversation, such as "No way, man," "I don't know," or "Who cares?"
> secretly move furniture or other items
> hide things so someone can't find them, or move things to different places

When you have decided what you want to do for your experiment, plan where and when to do it and whose reactions you want to observe. If you walk around your school campus dressed strangely, you will be seen by a lot of people whose reactions you can observe and write about. On the other hand, if you do an experiment at home, such as secretly moving things to new locations, you will be observing only your family members. If you plan an experiment that involves only one other person, such as yawning all the time while someone is talking, you will probably want to try it with a few different individuals so that you will be able to observe a variety of reactions. Keep in mind that your objective is not to make people angry, only to observe how they react to something out of the ordinary.

In some cases, you will probably have an idea already about how people will react to your experiment. However, you may be surprised. Try to keep an open mind and just observe people's reactions, without letting them know that you are conducting an experiment. Notice their facial expressions, gestures, and other non-verbal communication, as well as what they say to you. Pay special attention to any feelings that they express or that they seem to be experiencing. After you have completed your observations, you may want to tell them about the experiment. (This is especially important if you think someone may resent your strange behavior!) If you do, it is all right to ask them how they were feeling during the experiment, and you may include some of their comments in your writeup if you want to.

Afterward, you will need to write about the experiment and your observations. First, describe your experiment in a few sentences, or perhaps in a paragraph. Give specific details about what you did, such as how you dressed, what you changed, how you acted, and/or what you said. Then write one or more paragraphs about the results. Include all of your observations about other people's reactions. Finally, comment on anything that you learned about human behavior by doing this experiment. For example, did you learn something about how people who look or act different are treated by others? Or did you learn something about how a change in the environment or a change in the usual routine affects people?

The paper that follows is about an experiment that the writer did along with other members of her Disability and Society class. They all dressed strangely, wore a sign that said "I am different," and walked around the San Diego State University campus to see how other people would react. Part of their assignment was to see how people who are noticeably different (like people with disabilities) are treated by others, so the writer commented on this aspect of the experiment in her paper.

Reactions to Difference
by Joy Snyder

The Experiment:

My costume for the experiment consisted of a white blouse with black polka dots, black and white striped baggy pants, a black and white beanie, and Budweiser boxer shorts that I wore *over* the pants. I also had black sandals, one red sock, and a pair of rebellious black shades. Two other members of our group were dressed like bums, but the other three weren't brave enough to wear costumes. We all wore signs that said "I am different" and walked around the SDSU campus for about twenty minutes.

The Results:

As I was walking to class dressed something like a jailmate, rebel, or freak, I received many reactions. Some people stared or glared at me, some laughed aloud, and some pretended they didn't notice. I received much less reaction while walking around with a group from class. First we went to the cafeteria. As I expected, people gawked at our group. Some stopped eating and stared at us, and some laughed. Others just took a look and then turned away as if they didn't care. They probably assumed it was a class project because we were in a group. Next we went to Monty's Den (where there are various restaurants and a bar) and sat down for awhile. The reactions were similar: people stopped eating, stopped talking, and stared. Nobody said anything to us the entire time.

During the experiment, I observed that people have a tendency to react differently to those who are other than their idea of normal. If the "I am different" sign were permanently attached or I had a visual exceptionality, I would feel somewhat isolated and alone for being so different. I might feel uncomfortable and embarrassed too, and at times maybe even a bit ashamed that I am exceptional and not like the majority.

....8

Writing Short Essays

SECTION ONE:
The Writing Process for Short Essays

Goals

In this section of the chapter, you will learn how to do the following:

- Select appropriate types of writing for specific topics
- Combine different types of writing to communicate your message
- Develop a thesis statement for a short essay
- Write an effective introductory paragraph and a concluding paragraph for a short essay
- Organize and develop one or more body paragraphs, each dealing with one aspect or part of the topic
- Use transitions to connect ideas and to maintain continuity between paragraphs

Learning about Short Essays

What Is a Short Essay?

In the first few chapters of this book, we focused mainly on paragraph-length writing assignments, although some papers that were longer than one paragraph were also included. Beginning with Chapter 5, there has been more emphasis on planning and developing longer papers consisting of three or more paragraphs, and you may have discovered that one paragraph was often not long enough to express all of your ideas about some topics. Therefore, at this point, most of you have probably already written at least one paper longer than a single paragraph, especially for comparison/contrast, classification, or cause and effect writing. Informative papers like these that consist of three or more paragraphs can also be called *short essays*.

373

It may be helpful to think of writing a short essay as simply expanding a one-paragraph paper by adding more details, examples, and explanations. A short essay is very similar to a one-paragraph paper except that a short essay is longer and is divided into three or more paragraphs. The introduction and the conclusion for a short essay are both separate paragraphs instead of just a sentence or two. At the end of the introduction, there is a main idea statement, or *thesis statement,* for the entire paper, which works the same way that a topic sentence does for a one-paragraph paper. The middle section of a short essay, which is called the *body,* usually consists of one to four paragraphs (or sometimes more). Each paragraph in the body presents and develops one aspect or one part of the topic.

All of the types of writing that we have studied so far can be used in writing short essays: narration, instructions, description, comparison/contrast, classification, and cause and effect analysis. Short essays are often developed by using one of these techniques. The writer can choose whichever type of writing is most appropriate for the specific topic or assignment. However, many short essays use a combination of two or three different writing techniques. For example, if you are writing about the historic events of D-Day, June 6, 1944, when Allied forces landed in Normandy, France, you might want to begin by *narrating* what happened, including the almost overwhelming obstacles that the Allies faced and the heavy casualties on both sides. Then you could explain the significant *effects* of D-Day, for it was the first step in the liberation of France and the defeat of Germany, leading to the end of World War II in Europe. Your paper would seem incomplete if you told only what happened and didn't explain the importance of the events. Therefore, combining narration and cause and effect analysis would help to make the essay effective.

Writing Objective: Writing a Short Essay

Your objective for this chapter is to write a short essay that is three or more paragraphs long. It must have an introductory paragraph, enough body paragraphs to develop the topic effectively, and a concluding paragraph. At the end of the introduction, you should have a clear main idea statement, or *thesis statement,* that tells readers the topic and purpose of your paper, similar to the topic sentence for a paragraph. (Thesis statements will be explained in more detail later in this chapter.)

You may write about any topic that you are interested in. You may want to write about something related to one of your other classes, such as history, art, or political science, or you may choose a current topic that you would like to investigate and learn more about, such as a proposition on the ballot in an upcoming election or a career choice that you are considering. It is also possible to choose a more personal topic, such as your favorite hobby or sport, or any other special interest that you would like to write about.

Your short essay should use one or more of the types of writing that we have studied: narration, instructions, description, comparison/contrast, classification, or cause and effect analysis. The type or types of writing that you decide to use will depend on the topic that you want to write about. With some topics, one type of writing may be the most logical choice. For example, if you want to write about your two favorite musical groups, comparison/contrast would probably be the most effective.

However, with many topics, you may be able to write a better paper by combining different types of writing. For instance, let's say that a person wants to write about his job as a teacher's aide. This topic does not automatically suggest one particular type of writing, so the writer might consider some combinations, such as how to be a good teacher's aide (instructions) combined with the positive effects that a good teacher's aide can have on the children. This would be a particularly good choice if the writer's audience consists of people who are interested in becoming teacher's aides. If the writer wants to focus mainly on the children, another option might be to classify them into categories (such as leaders, followers, and loners) and tell some stories about them (narration) as he explains each group. Another option might be comparing and contrasting his job as a teacher's aide with his previous job, including how both jobs affected him personally (cause and effect).

If you decide to combine two or more kinds of writing, you must be sure that the combination will work together smoothly and logically. The result must be one integrated paper, not two short papers that don't really belong together.

The prewriting activities that follow will help you find a topic and decide which types of writing you want to use for your short essay.

Prewriting Activities

Even if you already have a topic in mind that you might like to write about, it is always a good idea to consider several options. Therefore, whether or not you already have an idea for a topic, you should complete the *Exploring Topics Worksheet*. Try to think of things that you are interested in and would enjoy writing about, as well as things that other people would really like to read about. You are also free to use other topics that are not on the worksheet if your instructor approves.

■ **WORKSHEET I**   ## Exploring Topics for Short Essays

Directions: Write down as many possible topic ideas as you can think of.

1. What activities or special projects do you spend a lot of time doing?

2. What social issues are important to you?
   (Examples: issues related to education, health care reform, assisted suicide, gang violence)

3. What personal or spiritual topics are you interested in? (Examples: self-confidence, assertiveness, spiritual healing, personal goals)

4. Are you facing a major decision or dealing with a major change in your life? If so, what is it?

5. What interesting things have you recently learned or read about?

6. What issues, problems, or situations make you angry?

7. Is there some aspect of your career (past, present, or future) that you would like to write about?

8. What events have had a major impact on your life?

9. If you could write about anything that you want to, what would you choose?

Discovering Details 1: Brainstorming

Brainstorming literally means creating a "storm" of ideas in your brain. Like freewriting (Chapter 2) and listing (Chapter 3), brainstorming is based on expressing whatever comes to your mind about a possible topic. The differences are that brainstorming can be either oral or written, and it does not have to be in any particular form. For written brainstorming, you may write things in a list, in sentences, or even on different parts of the page if you wish. Just let the brainstorming take any form that works. For oral brainstorming, it is usually best to work with at least one other person in order to share ideas. You and your partner (or partners) should each say whatever you think of about a particular topic, trying to discover as many ideas as possible.

First choose one of your most interesting topic ideas from the *Exploring Topics Worksheet*. At this point, it is only a general idea, and you will need to figure out some more specific aspects of the topic to write about. For example, suppose you have decided to write about the general topic of sexual harassment. There are many different aspects of this topic that you could focus on, such as the effects of sexual harassment in the workplace, sexual harassment lawsuits, how to avoid sexual harassment, and so on. Brainstorming could help you come up with several ideas about sexual harassment that you might want to use in your paper, such as the following:

Ideas from Brainstorming:

effects of sexual harassment in the workplace
a woman's perspective on sexual harassment
a man's perspective on sexual harassment
how to avoid sexual harassment
sexual equality in employment
attitude changes about sexual harassment in the last twenty years
how to handle sexual harassment if it happens to you
legal definition of sexual harassment
sexual harassment lawsuits and their results
personal experiences (yourself or others)

With your partner or partners, try to come up with as many ideas as you can about your topic. If no ideas occur to you right away, simply start talking about the topic in order to discover some. This type of brainstorming is primarily an oral activity, so it is not necessary to write everything down. However, you will probably find it helpful to make a list of some of your best ideas. You can do this while you are brainstorming with your partner or afterward. Write your list of ideas here:

Ideas from Brainstorming:

_____

_____

_____

_____

_____

_____

_____

_____

Discovering Details 2:
Clustering

Clustering is another good prewriting technique to use when you are still trying to decide which aspects of a general topic you want to write about. Clustering is simply a way of putting related ideas together into groups or "clusters." It is similar to branching, which was introduced in Chapter 7, except that clusters may be developed in any pattern or direction.

Clustering begins with your general topic idea written in a circle somewhere in the middle of a blank page. Then draw lines out from this circle to add other related ideas. Circle each idea that you add, and then continue drawing lines and circles to add more ideas. Don't try to control the kinds of information that you cluster or the form that your clustering takes. Simply write down whatever ideas come to mind, as you did with other prewriting activities in earlier chapters, such as freewriting and listing.

Your clusters may go in any direction from the idea that you started with, or you may decide to concentrate on one of the other ideas that appear instead of your original idea. Don't worry if you seem to be straying from your original topic sometimes. You may discover that you actually would rather write about a different topic that shows up while you are clustering.

To see how clustering works, look at Figure 8.1. The writer started with the word *adoption* because she wanted to write about the general topic of adoption. However, she didn't know exactly what aspects of adoption she wanted to write about, so she just started putting down key words and ideas that she thought of. As the clusters began to take shape, she realized that there were a number of interesting writing topics related to adoption, such as rights of birth mothers, adoption as a solution for childless couples, and the issue of whether gay couples should be allowed to adopt. This is what her clustering looked like:

Figure 8.1   Clustering Example

Now try clustering with one of your own topic ideas from the *Exploring Topics Worksheet*. Use the *Clustering Worksheet* that follows. Remember that there aren't any "right" or "wrong" ways to develop the clusters. Even if several people began clustering with the same topic idea in the circle, their clustering would look very different because everyone's thought patterns and word associations are not the same.

■ **WORKSHEET II** | ## Clustering

Directions: First write your topic idea in the middle of the page. Then draw lines in any direction to attach ideas that are related to your topic. Circle these ideas as you attach them, and then draw more lines to attach additional ideas. Let the clusters of ideas take whatever form works best.

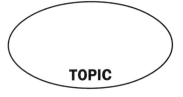

TOPIC

After you have finished clustering, look over the ideas on your *Clustering Worksheet* and consider which ones you would like to write about. Some of them may be the same ideas that you came up with while brainstorming, but there will probably be some new ones as well. The writer of the clustering example on adoption, for instance, found some ideas that she had not considered before, such as fertility treatments and "Black Market" babies. By starting with the general topic of adoption and clustering, she discovered a lot of related topic ideas to choose from.

If brainstorming and clustering did not produce any specific topic ideas that you would like to write about, you may want to select another topic from your *Exploring Topics Worksheet* and try these prewriting techniques with your new topic. If you wish, you may also use some of the other prewriting techniques that have been helpful for you in previous chapters, such as freewriting or visualizing. By visualizing scenes related to your topic, such as a couple going through the process of adopting a child or a young woman giving up her child for adoption, you may discover additional topic ideas.

Writing a Rough Draft

Narrowing Your Topic

If you take a general topic directly from the *Exploring Topics Worksheet* and just start writing, the topic will probably be very broad and thus difficult to write about effectively. For example, one writer chose his favorite activity, snowboarding, as his topic. He thought that he could easily cover everything about snowboarding in one short essay, so he began writing about the equipment needed, snowboarding versus skiing, basic techniques for snowboarding, the best places to go snowboarding, and some of his personal experiences. Soon he realized that his paper was getting longer and longer, but it seemed disorganized, and he still hadn't covered everything. Finally, he solved his problem by narrowing his topic to snowboarding versus skiing. Selecting this specific topic made it easier to organize his short essay and to complete it in a couple of pages. By setting up the paper as a Point-by-Point comparison/contrast, he could include some of his other ideas too, such as contrasting equipment and techniques for snowboarding with equipment and techniques for skiing.

Looking at the list of ideas that you came up with during brainstorming and the ideas that you discovered through clustering will help you narrow your general topic to a specific topic before you begin writing your paper. For example, here are some ways that the general topic of sexual harassment could be narrowed down:

General Topic: sexual harassment

Specific Topic: how to handle sexual harassment if it happens to you

General Topic: sexual harassment

Specific Topic: effects of sexual harassment in the workplace

Either of these specific topics would be appropriate for a short essay. Of course, there are additional topics related to sexual harassment that would also work, such as others on the brainstorming list for this topic (page 377). As the writer, you can choose the specific topic that appeals to you the most or that you could write about the most easily.

Here are some good choices for the topic of adoption, which was the general topic in the clustering example:

> *General Topic:* adoption
>
> *Specific Topic:* rights of gays and lesbians to adopt
>
> *General Topic:* adoption
>
> *Specific Topic:* adoption procedures

Now try narrowing down some other general topics. For each general topic listed, try to think of at least one specific topic that would work for a short essay:

1. *General Topic:* education

   Specific Topic: _____

   _____

2. *General Topic:* pollution

   Specific Topic: _____

   _____

3. *General Topic:* television

   Specific Topic: _____

   _____

Now share some of these specific topic ideas with other members of your class. Do you have a variety of different ideas? Which ones do you like best? Why?

If you have not already selected a general topic for your own short essay, you should do so now and write it on page 382 on the line that says *General Topic*. Be sure to do the two prewriting activities in this chapter, brainstorming and clustering, to help you discover various aspects of the topic that you might want to write about. Then look over your completed brainstorming list and your *Clustering Worksheet* to figure out which ideas you like best. After that, try narrowing down your general topic to two or three specific topics that you might like to write about, and write them on the lines below labeled *Specific Topic*:

General Topic: _____

Specific Topic #1: _____

_____

Specific Topic #2: _____

_____

Specific Topic #3: _____

_____

Now discuss your specific topics with members of your workshop group and tell them a little bit about what you could write in a short essay for each one. With the help of your workshop group, select the one that you think will work best for you. If none of your specific topics seem to be satisfactory, have your workshop group look over your clustering worksheet with you for some additional ideas. You may even want to brainstorm again with your workshop group before you decide which specific topic to use.

Now read the short essay that follows about flamenco dancing, which is one of the writer's favorite activities. When Rosa was trying to narrow down the general topic of flamenco dancing, she decided that her personal experience and feelings about dancing would be a better specific topic to write about than other possibilities such as the history of flamenco dancing, flamenco music, famous flamenco dancers, or flamenco dance steps. Notice that she tells about her early dancing experiences and what happens when she is dancing as if she is telling a story. She also emphasizes the effects that flamenco dancing has on her.

Flamenco
by Rosa Hammar

To be a flamenco dancer is to have another persona, other passions, and other desires. It is a different way of seeing the world, with music in one's nerves, a fierce pride, happiness mingled with tears, and the translation of life into an art of caprices and of freedom.

I began with flamenco seeking to better express myself with music and dance. When I was a little girl, I remember my father playing the guitar and listening to Spanish music. Since then I've wanted to be a flamenco dancer. I had put that off because I was raising a family and attending school part-time. Now that my children are adults, I've pursued my long-time ambition. I began taking classes in 1989 and had my first performance at Southwestern College that same year. I learned a lot, and it gave me an insight into the theater, expression with the body, walking in silence, playing the castanets, and performing with a guitarist. I learned technique, but I soon realized that you can't learn the ability to make your feelings appear on your face, hands, and body.

First you have to feel, to live deeply what you are doing. Then you must open yourself to express that inner world and transfer it to your body. This is why in flamenco music the guitarist follows the dancer, because the dancer creates the intensity and the fury of the dance. This happens when the dancer feels and expresses the emotions and the fire waiting to release itself through controlled or released energy.

When I dance, I am in a pleasant state of being where I feel no obstacles, and I dance freely with no sensation of body weight. I'm in a state of harmony so great that I begin to create a thousand new things, and I can dance all night without stopping. As my body floats, my hands and arms move by themselves. I'm aware of nothing but the music and the vocalist, and fusing with them to the extent that I am unaware of my own existence. At that moment I identify myself so strongly with the dance that I *am* the dance and the music. To achieve this, I break myself down inside and empty myself of everything else. Once I reach this point, a surge of energy will come forth and release itself. Sometimes it comes with no effort when I'm lifting my arms with a special sweetness. Once I have it, I don't want it to ever end.

Through flamenco dancing, I experience a marvelous inner harmony that I can find nowhere else away from the stage.

Response to *Flamenco*

1. Rosa's main purpose in writing this was to share her special feelings about flamenco dancing. Find at least five phrases that express some of the feelings she experiences while dancing.

_____

_____

_____

_____

_____

2. Which parts of this short essay use narration (storytelling)?

_____

_____

Choosing Which Writing Techniques to Use

Any of the types of writing that we have studied—*narration, description, instructions, comparison/contrast, classification,* or *cause and effect analysis*—can be used to write a short essay. With some topics, you may want to use only one of these writing techniques. For example, if your general topic is the Great Lakes, and you narrow it down to recreation on the Great Lakes, you could organize your entire essay as a classification of the various types of recreation. However, depending on your topic, your essay may be more effective if you combine two or more writing techniques. The writer of *Flamenco,* for instance, used narration to tell the story of her life-long interest in flamenco dancing. Then she added a little bit of instructions, as well as cause and effect analysis, to write about what happens and how she feels while dancing.

In addition to the major writing techniques that we have studied, there are a few other types of writing that may also be useful for short essays. One of these is *definition,* which was explained briefly in Chapter 6. Another is *exemplification,* or giving examples, which you may have used in some of the earlier chapters along with the major type of writing. For some essays, you may also want to use *process* writing, which is similar to instructions. The difference is that process writing explains the steps of a process without actually telling the reader how to do it. If you are writing about a controversial issue, you will probably want to use *argument* to present your point of view effectively. Later in this chapter you will read a short essay that uses argument and learn some argumentative writing techniques. There may also be parts of an essay that are just explanatory or informative, without necessarily fitting into any particular category of writing.

Sometimes combinations of different writing techniques happen naturally in the process of expressing your ideas. However, it is often helpful to plan combinations of different types of writing ahead of time. In order to choose writing techniques that will be effective for your topic, you should consider different ways that you might present the information. For example, if you wanted to write about the value of exercise, your choices could include any of the following: explaining how regular exercise is good for the body and mind (*cause and effect*), *classifying* different types of exercise, giving *instructions* for starting an exercise program, *contrasting* the health and fitness of someone who exercises and someone who doesn't, and/or telling the story of how exercise has helped you personally (*narration*). After considering these options, you might want to combine two or more of them. For instance, you could combine *instructions* for an exercise program with the *effects* of regular exercise on the body and mind. Whenever you combine two or more writing techniques in this way, remember that they must work together logically and naturally.

The next writer, Danny Banda, wanted to describe the island of Iwo Jima as it looked when he visited it a few years ago and tell the story of his trip. He also wanted to include some historical facts, as well as his opinions about what took place on Iwo Jima during World War II. To do this, he combined narration and description. These two types of writing are often combined because they work together very naturally and effectively. As you read Danny's essay, try to picture what he saw on the island and what it was like during World War II. Since his paper includes a lot of details, it is somewhat longer than most short essays.

Iwo Jima
by Danny Banda

The island of Iwo Jima, which is located 700 miles south of Japan in the Pacific Ocean, is only three miles long and one mile wide. Presently the island houses a few Japanese soldiers who take care of it. In 1989, about 100 Marines were chosen for a trip to Iwo Jima to learn about military tactics, and I was one of the lucky ones. The most exciting experience in my life was walking over this piece of land that once was a bloody battlefield and imagining what it must have been like.

When we got off the plane, we were put in groups of six to explore the island. The old airfield from World War II was now covered with heavy, tall vegetation. Above the airfield remained the caves and tunnels where the Japanese pilots were housed during World War II. When we went into the underground tunnels, the entrances were very small, so we had to crawl to get inside. Inside there were big rats, old Japanese uniforms, cups, plates, bottles of saki, old rusted machine guns, and rifles. There were well over one hundred caves and underground tunnels. They varied in size, and some of them had held several hundred men. On the north side of the island we found about seven to ten Japanese ships that had been sunk on the shoreline off the beach to be used as a pier for unloading other ships. Most of the ships had only their stacks showing above the water. Inland, to the west of the ships, we found an active volcano. It was spitting hot gray lava, and around the crater was sulfuric acid. We got a headache from the smell of the acid, so we left the area immediately.

Afterward we walked to the west end of the island to Mt. Suribachi. I climbed Mt. Suribachi, and it was such a thrill standing at the top. I tried to imagine how the Japanese from Mt. Suribachi, which is only 550 feet in elevation, were able to kill 6,821 Marines as they hit the beach. This thought made me sad and angry. The beach directly below and to the east of Mt. Suribachi where the landing was made is deep volcanic sand, and if you walk on it, you will sink halfway up to your knees. Because it was very difficult to traverse the volcanic sand by foot or vehicle, the Marines couldn't move fast enough. They ended up getting pinned down, and many lives were lost. Although Iwo Jima received the longest and most intensive pre-invasion bombardment of any campaign in the Pacific, we did not destroy the island's defenses because all that bombardment did was cause the Japanese to dig deeper into the underground tunnels. Because of these well-fortified tunnels and caves, Marines found very strong resistance during the battle and sometimes were able to advance only seventy yards a day. From the top of Mt. Suribachi, I could see the whole island, and it was very clear that the Japanese had the terrain advantage. While on top of Mt. Suribachi, we took a picture symbolizing the original flag raising.

Next we went to see a bottomless pit that was used after the war to dispose of captured enemy weapons and other military equipment. To the south of the island we toured a tar pit. I was scared because we were walking on top of the tar and it felt like walking on a waterbed. I kept thinking we were going to sink and drown as if we were in quicksand. A few feet from the tar pit heading north, we went into a cave and discovered a natural sauna that had benches carved from the volcanic rock to sit along one side of the wall. The farther we went inside, the hotter it got, and it was well over 200 degrees. I had to get out because I was suffocating from the heat. Also on the south end of the island we went into the underground tunnel that once housed the Japanese general and his staff. This headquarters was able to house up to 1500 men. It was just like a two-story building with the stairs carved out from volcanic rock and walls five feet thick. It had a large room, a clinic, a communications center, a conference room, a mess hall, etc. Inside in some of the tunnels, the walls still had original holes from hand grenades where the Japanese soldiers had committed suicide instead of surrendering. The Japanese were seldom seen dead or alive, and when they would retreat they would take their dead and wounded with them through the underground channels. For two days we searched for as many underground tunnels as we could find, for we were hoping to find some of the Japanese soldiers who are still unaccounted for.

The conquest of Iwo Jima was a costly one for both sides. Even though this island could have been bypassed, the losses of the Marines were justified in the end because 2,251 B-29 bombers carrying a total of 24,761 crew members made emergency landings on Iwo Jima, including the *Enola Gay* after it dropped the atomic bomb on Nagasaki. The savings in men and planes and the effect on morale were very significant, and for the United States military, dropping the bomb was considered an essential step to end World War II. However, it seems ironic now that after all that blood was shed in capturing a strategic point, we ended up giving it back to the Japanese.

Visiting and walking over the battlefield of Iwo Jima drew me closer to those forgotten Marines who gave their lives for a cause. I know they fought for what they believed in and for preserving freedom. A part of me will always be with those Marines who did not come back alive from that shore, and to those Marines I acknowledge an everlasting debt that neither I nor any other American can ever repay, and that is living in FREEDOM.

Response to *Iwo Jima*

1. Which descriptive details do you think are the most interesting?

_____

_____

_____

2. What did you learn about events on Iwo Jima during World War II from reading this essay?

_____

_____

_____

3. Do you agree with the writer's choice to include both description and narration in the same essay? Why or why not?

_____

_____

_____

Learning about Thesis Statements

A *thesis statement* serves the same purpose as a topic sentence does for a paragraph or short paper: it tells the reader your topic and your main idea about it. Usually a thesis statement works best at the end of a one-paragraph introduction. At this point, it establishes where the essay is going, so it can help both the writer and the reader stay focused on the main idea.

All of the suggestions for writing topic sentences in Chapters 2 through 7 can also apply to writing a thesis statement for a short essay. For example, the writer's thesis statement for *Iwo Jima* is just like a topic sentence for a narration paragraph. It focuses on the most significant thing about his experience:

> The most exciting experience in my life was walking over this piece of land that once was a bloody battlefield and imagining what it must have been like.

To help you write an effective thesis statement, you may want to review topic sentences for the types of writing that you plan to use in your essay.

No matter what kinds of writing you use in your short essay, the most important thing to remember about a thesis statement is that it should state the main idea of your paper. One way to write a good thesis statement is to pretend that you can use only one sentence to tell readers about your topic. Therefore, you need to make sure that your sentence expresses the most important thing about your topic. Occasionally, if one sentence doesn't seem to be enough, writers may use two sentences for their thesis statement. However, it is usually a good idea to express the main idea in just one sentence if possible.

Let's look at a few thesis statements to see what makes some more effective than others. One writer began with this statement about the Bermuda Triangle:

DRAFT #1:

The Bermuda Triangle is a mysterious place.

Although this statement contains an idea about the Bermuda Triangle (it's mysterious), it doesn't really say much. A good thesis statement should tell more about the topic. His second draft was better:

DRAFT #2:

Many ships and planes have mysteriously disappeared in the area known as the Bermuda Triangle.

This thesis statement was effective for his short essay because it focused on what he wanted to write about—stories about some of the planes and ships that have disappeared with no explanation.

What about these thesis statements? Which one do you think is the best?

A. This paper is going to be about the uses of herbs.

B. Many herbs can be used as home remedies for common illnesses.

C. Here are some surprising remedies for common illnesses.

Did you choose thesis statement B as the best one? It clearly identifies the writer's topic and states the main idea of the essay, that herbs can be used as home remedies. Even though statement C may sound interesting, neither statement A nor statement C contains enough information. Statement A doesn't mention remedies for illnesses, and C doesn't mention herbs. There is also another problem with statement A. It begins with "This paper is going to be about . . ." This type of phrase should not be used to introduce a thesis statement. Your thesis statement should concentrate on the topic and the main idea, without making references to the paper itself or to your plans, such as "I'd like to write about . . ." or "My topic is . . ."

Now do the next activity, *Evaluating Thesis Statement*s, to get more practice before writing your own.

Evaluating Thesis Statements for Short Essays

Directions: Write OK in the blank by each effective thesis statement. Write NO by the ones that need revision. Be ready to explain your answers.

EXAMPLE 1 ➤   _*NO*_   Couples should communicate with each other.

This thesis statement is too general. Why is it important for couples to communicate?

EXAMPLE 2 ➤   _*OK*_   Relationships often fail because of lack of communication and inadequate problem-solving skills.

_____ 1. Regular exercise activity, such as jogging, swimming, bicycling, or aerobics, will help you look better and feel better about yourself.

_____ 2. Recycling is a good idea.

_____ 3. I'm going to write about drug problems among teenagers.

_____ 4. Affirmative action guidelines help to ensure that minorities have equal employment opportunities.

_____ 5. Because of changing values and health concerns, casual sex is no longer as popular as it used to be.

_____ 6. Something should be done about the homeless.

_____ 7. Having a pet can help a child learn about responsibility, as well as love and affection.

_____ 8. In this paper I will discuss how to improve your self-confidence and become more assertive.

_____ 9. Each year the summer concert program in the park features several different types of music.

_____ 10. Although nursing homes help to relieve the burden of home care for the elderly, they often do not provide a quality living environment.

Writing Your Own Thesis Statement

If you have narrowed down your general topic and decided which writing techniques you intend to use in your short essay, the next step is to write your thesis statement. Although the thesis statement usually comes at the end of the introduction, it will probably be easier to write the thesis statement first and then decide how to lead up to it with an interesting introduction.

Begin by writing your general topic, your specific topic, and the types of writing you plan to use on the lines below. (Types of writing can include narration, description, instructions, comparison/contrast, classification, cause and effect, definition, exemplification, process, and argument.) If you're not sure yet which types of writing will work best for your topic, leave those lines blank for the time being. Once you have decided on your thesis statement, it may be easier to figure out which types of writing to use.

General Topic: _____

Specific Topic: _____

Types of Writing: _____

Now think about the main things that you are going to write in your short essay, and fill in the blanks that follow the questions below.

> ***Question 1:*** Is there a main point that you want to make in your short essay, such as a point of view on some issue? Or is there one idea about your topic that is more important than anything else?

> _____

> _____

> ***Question 2:*** What will readers learn from your essay? Will they gain some insight or understand something better than they did before?

> _____

> _____

> ***Question 3:*** Does the topic have some special significance for you personally? If so, what is its significance?

> _____

> _____

> ***Question 4:*** If you could use only one or two sentences to tell readers about your topic, what would you say?

> _____

> _____

Use your answer to Question 4 as the first draft of your thesis statement, and look over your answers to Questions 1–3 to see if there are some other ideas that should be added. Then write a revised version of your thesis statement here:

THESIS STATEMENT (DRAFT #2):

_____

_____

_____

At this point it will be helpful to have members of your workshop group read your thesis statement. Check to make sure that everyone's thesis statement clearly expresses a significant idea about the topic. It should be something that can be developed and explained in a few paragraphs. If your workshop group has some suggestions, incorporate them into your thesis statement and write a third draft:

THESIS STATEMENT (DRAFT #3):

_____

_____

_____

Writing an Introduction

Usually an introduction begins with fairly general information related to the topic of the essay. This may include background information or something else to familiarize readers with the situation or idea that you are going to write about. The introduction should lead up to the thesis statement, which is usually the last sentence (or last two sentences) of the introductory paragraph. For example, read the introduction to *Iwo Jima* again and notice how Danny Banda started with general information about the island and a little bit of background about his trip so that his thesis statement at the end of the introduction would be clear to the reader:

> The island of Iwo Jima, which is located 700 miles south of Japan in the Pacific Ocean, is only three miles long and one mile wide. Presently the island houses a few Japanese soldiers who take care of it. In 1989, about 100 Marines were chosen for a trip to Iwo Jima to learn about military tactics, and I was one of the lucky ones. *The most exciting experience in my life was walking over this piece of land that once was a bloody battlefield and imagining what it must have been like.*

Another way to write an interesting introduction is to begin with something that will capture the reader's attention, such as a brief story or a description of something that relates to your topic. For example, here is an introduction that Trent Parker used to begin a short essay about the death of one of his friends:

> A group of young teens ready for a little harmless mischief gather at the local after-school hangout. "Hey, Ethan," I say, "I dare you to pull down your shorts and moon that car full of chicks stopped at the light." "You're on," he says with a mischievous little grin. Sure enough he struts over to the car with his unforgettable walk and casually moons the carload of girls. We laugh until we're all blue in the face. This and hundreds of other ludicrous pranks are all I have to remember one of my good friends by. *Ethan John Edmonds was shot and killed at the age of twenty. I never wanted to think of such a horrible thought as what if one of my bro's were to die, but suddenly he's gone, and I am stripped of one of my good friends.*

This brief story is an effective introduction because it makes Trent's friend seem real and interesting to the reader. It also makes us want to read the rest of the essay and find out what happened. (The entire essay is included later in this chapter on page 400.)

Now try writing your own introduction. Begin with something general, such as background information about your topic, or something else that can lead up to your thesis statement. If there is an interesting story or description that would be effective as an introduction, you may want to try that instead. Or you may have another idea for an introduction that would work well for your topic. Include your thesis statement as the last sentence or two of the introduction. If necessary, you may want to change the wording of your thesis statement a little so that it follows smoothly after the first part of the introduction.

Introduction:

_____

_____

_____

_____

_____

(Thesis Statement):_____

_____

_____

Show this introduction to your workshop group and ask for comments and suggestions. You need to make sure that it begins your short essay effectively by starting with something general or something attention-getting and that it leads into your thesis statement smoothly. When you are more or less satisfied with the introduction, you can begin writing the body of your paper. However, remember that this introduction is only a first draft, so if you decide to change it later, you can.

Sometimes writers have trouble doing the introduction before they have written the rest of the paper, so don't worry if you get stuck on it temporarily. The best solution is to go ahead with the body of the paper. Writing the body of the paper will probably help you come up with some good ideas for the introduction, and you can come back to it when you are ready.

From Thesis Statement to First Draft

Just as a topic sentence can serve as a guideline for developing a paragraph, your thesis statement should be a guideline for writing the body of your short essay. Each paragraph in the body of the essay must be about one part or one aspect of the thesis statement, or one point that will help support your thesis statement.

Before you begin writing the first draft, it is a good idea to plan how many paragraphs will be in the body of the paper and what each paragraph will be about. Some thesis statements seem to already divide the topic into two or more distinct parts. For instance, the following thesis statement automatically suggests a logical division of the topic into two parts:

> ***Thesis Statement:***   Relationships often fail because of lack of communication and inadequate problem-solving skills.

The two parts of the topic identified in this statement are *lack of communication* and *inadequate problem-solving skills*. Two body paragraphs, one that explains and supports each of these ideas, would be an appropriate way to develop a short essay on this topic.

Here's another thesis statement that makes it relatively easy to identify a different part of the topic to be developed in each body paragraph:

> ***Thesis Statement:***   A regular exercise activity, such as jogging, swimming, bicycling, or aerobics, will help you look better and feel better about yourself.

The writer could explain in one paragraph how exercise can make a person look and feel better, followed by one paragraph about each of the four activities that are mentioned. If the writer wants to include only a few sentences about each activity, another option would be to combine all of the activities in one paragraph.

Other types of thesis statements do not necessarily indicate any divisions of the topic, so the writer must figure out a logical plan for the body paragraphs. This thesis statement, for example, does not suggest specific parts of the topic to be developed in separate paragraphs:

> ***Thesis Statement:***   Many ships and planes have mysteriously disappeared in the area known as the Bermuda Triangle.

Probably the writer would want to include a few examples of some of the ships and planes that have disappeared in the Bermuda Triangle. Two major examples with a story about each incident could make up two body paragraphs. To make the essay more complete, the writer might also want to include other supporting information, such as a paragraph (or more) about theories and possible explanations of the disappearances. This would make three paragraphs in the body of the essay, plus an introductory paragraph and a concluding paragraph. The introductory paragraph would probably present general information about the location of the Bermuda Triangle and the number of ships and planes that have vanished there over the years. Although there are probably numerous other ways to develop the topic, this plan would be one way to organize an effective essay.

Try to make a tentative plan like this so that you will know where your short essay is going before you begin writing. However, keep in mind that writing is a creative process, so you may come up with some new ideas while you are writing and decide to make some changes in your plan. If this happens, be sure that everything you decide to write about relates to your thesis statement and that the divisions of the body paragraphs are logical and well-organized. If you make major changes in the content, you may even want to consider revising your thesis statement to make it express the main point of your essay better.

If you are writing about a controversial issue or a certain point of view that others might not agree with, you should also read the following section, *Using Argumentative Techniques*, to help you plan and develop your first draft.

Using Argumentative Techniques

Many short essays deal with controversial issues or advocate a certain point of view. When you are writing this type of essay, it is especially important to consider your audience. In order to convince readers that your opinion is valid, your arguments must be reasonable and logical. If you insult readers who disagree with you or accuse them of not thinking clearly, they will not be interested in your opinion. However, if you present evidence objectively, they will at least think seriously about what you are saying. You may even be able to persuade some of them to your point of view if your argument is effective.

To show that you have considered opposing arguments, it is a good idea to discuss both sides of the issue somewhere in your essay. By including some of the arguments on the opposing side, you can show that you are being fair and impartial. Your own side of the issue, of course, should always come out on top. Be sure to point out any flaws in the opposition's thinking, and explain why the arguments on your side are stronger or make more sense.

For example, suppose someone is writing about women in the military, and his thesis statement is, "Women should be allowed to serve in the same military positions as men." This is a controversial issue, so the writer must consider how to present his argument effectively. In order to show that he has thought about both sides of the issue, he should briefly mention some of the arguments on the other side, followed by more convincing arguments that support his point of view. The following paragraph shows how he might state one of the opposition's points in the body of his essay and then present a stronger counterargument in support of his thesis statement:

Some people think that women should not serve in combat positions because they are not as strong as men. While it is generally true that men tend to be stronger than women, in this age of advanced technology, winning a war is not based on the physical strength of a nation's military forces. Someone who is stronger is not necessarily a better pilot, a better navigator, a better radar or sonar operator, a better marksman (or markswoman), or a better commander. Most military jobs require other types of training and skills, not exceptional strength. However, for those situations where strength would be an asset, such as hand-to-hand combat, minimum standards could be established that both men and women would be required to meet. This would give everyone an equal opportunity, and some men might be surprised to find that a number of women are as qualified as they are in every respect.

Although the paragraph begins by agreeing that men tend to be stronger than women, the argument used to counter it is very convincing: exceptional strength is not required for all combat positions. Thus, both sides of the argument are included, but the writer's side comes out ahead. Even if you do not agree with this writer's viewpoint, you can see that presenting both sides of the issue can be an effective technique.

In the short argumentative essay that follows, *Dead-Beat Dads,* Angelique St. Jacques uses this technique in the second and sixth paragraphs. Notice that at first she seems to be on the other side of the issue when she mentions the advantages of being a single parent in the second paragraph and an irresponsible father's attitude in paragraph six, but in both cases she shows that there are stronger arguments to support her side of the issue. Although many argumentative essays do not include personal information, the writer's own experience is effective in this paper because it provides an example that helps to prove her point.

Dead-Beat Dads
by Angelique St. Jacques

The number of single parents in this country is continuing to grow, especially the number of single mothers. Whether they are divorced or were never married, these women are left almost entirely on their own to care for themselves and their children because our government makes it easy for men to escape their responsibilities as fathers.

I too have the privilege of being a single parent and all that implies. Being a single parent is not without advantages. Without a second party, there are no arguments about the subject of childrearing. In my case, I believe my children and I have a closer relationship because they have no father figure in their lives. Unfortunately, because of the outdated laws that govern this situation and lack of enforcement of the laws, the disadvantages far outweigh any possible perks.

Being a single parent is all about sacrifices, usually the mother's sacrifices. I am currently receiving financial aid from the government only in the form of food stamps. The amount of child support I receive from my ex-husband just tips the scale to make me ineligible for a cash grant. My family is living below poverty level. Being a full-time student makes it difficult to get a job. It's not impossible; I just have to prioritize and decide what is most important to me and my family. My children come first. The amount of time I spend with them cannot be sacrificed. If I were to continue to attend school and to work also, who would care for my kids? Should I quit school in order to work at a minimum wage job, just to increase our financial position slightly? Or should I suffer the humiliation of receiving food stamps a while longer so I can continue going to school, in the hopes of being able to provide a better future for my family?

While we live below the average standard of living, my daughter's father earns over $100,000.00 a year. According to the laws in California, the absent parents are to pay 1% of their annual income per month toward child support. He pays $240.00 a month, and my calculations show he should be paying $1000.00 a month! I want to know what kind of sacrifices he has had to make.

What kind of help is available to people in my position? I have the District Attorney's office in my corner. Some consolation. I have been trying to get an increase in child support for two years and still have not seen anything that resembles a resolution. People at the DA's office tell me I have to be patient; they have many cases they are working on. I might be mistaken, but I thought the whole idea was to get as many families off welfare as possible. Why do I still have to be supported by the system? If I had been receiving the correct amount of child support, my family wouldn't have had to make so many sacrifices.

Many men feel that it is the woman's choice to have the baby, so shouldn't she take care of it? While I recognize the ultimate decision to have a child lies with the woman, it still takes two people to make one. All a man has to say is, "I don't want it," and the burden of responsibility is miraculously lifted from his shoulders. Our society still treats single mothers as if they were promiscuous and punishes them by making them solely responsible for the actions of two. Men are held blameless; therefore, they feel no remorse. They are free to populate the countryside with their offspring without having to support them.

I believe if men were held at least financially responsible for the children they produce, the number of unplanned pregnancies would drop dramatically. If they believed they were to be held accountable for their actions, men would look at birth control in a whole new light. It is simply not acceptable to let innocent children suffer because of irresponsible fathers and the apathy of government on this issue.

Response to *Dead-Beat Dads*

1. Do you agree with the writer's point of view on this issue? Why or why not?

2. Which sentence in the introductory paragraph is the writer's thesis statement?

_____

_____

3. Which parts of this argumentative essay do you think are the most convincing?

_____

_____

_____

Using Transitions between Body Paragraphs

In addition to connecting the ideas smoothly and clearly within each paragraph of a short essay, it is also important to begin every paragraph with a sentence that ties it to the previous paragraph or shows how it relates to the essay as a whole. To make clear transitions between paragraphs, writers often use the same kinds of transitional words and phrases that were suggested for different types of writing in Chapters 2 through 7. For example, look at some of the transitional sentences from *Iwo Jima*. Since one of the main types of writing used in this essay is narration, these sentences use transitional words that refer to the time order of the events:

> *When we got off the plane,* we were put in groups of six to explore the island.

> *Afterward* we walked to the west end of the island to Mt. Suribachi.

> *Next* we went to see a bottomless pit that was used after the war to dispose of captured enemy weapons and other military equipment.

Sometimes writers like to use the transitional sentence at the beginning of each body paragraph as a topic sentence for the paragraph too. In other words, the transitional sentence states the point or the part of the main idea that will be developed in that paragraph, as well as connecting the content of the paragraph to the rest of the essay. Here is a transitional sentence from *Flamenco* that also serves as a topic sentence for the paragraph that follows:

> When I dance, I am in a pleasant state of being where I feel no obstacles . . . .

The rest of the paragraph that begins with this sentence goes into detail about how the writer feels when she is dancing.

Other transitional sentences introduce the point to be covered but are not actually topic sentences. Instead, they link the idea to be developed in the new paragraph to ideas that were previously mentioned. (This is similar to the technique of repeating key words and ideas that you learned for transitions in Chapter 7.) In this case, words and ideas in the last sentence of the previous paragraph are also important in making a smooth transition. For example, notice the transition between the third and fourth paragraphs of *Dead-Beat Dads*. The sentence at the beginning of the fourth paragraph mentions living "below the average standard of living," which ties in with the idea of receiving food stamps in the last sentence of the third paragraph:

END OF PARAGRAPH 3:

Or should I suffer the humiliation of receiving food stamps a while longer so I can continue going to school, in the hopes of being able to provide a better future for my family?

BEGINNING OF PARAGRAPH 4:

While we live below the average standard of living, my daughter's father earns over $100,000.00 a year.

The transition between the sixth and seventh paragraphs of *Dead-Beat Dads* is similar. At the end of paragraph six, the writer is talking about the attitude of irresponsible fathers. Then she begins paragraph seven with the opposite side of this issue—the idea that men should be held financially responsible:

END OF PARAGRAPH 6:

Men are held blameless; therefore, they feel no remorse. They are free to populate the countryside with their offspring without having to support them.

BEGINNING OF PARAGRAPH 7:

I believe if men were held at least financially responsible for the children they produce, the number of unplanned pregnancies would drop dramatically.

As you write your own rough draft, pay particular attention to the first sentence of each paragraph in order to make a smooth transition from the ideas discussed in the previous paragraph.

Ending Effectively

The conclusion for a short essay is just like the conclusion for a paragraph, except that the conclusion for an essay is generally a little longer and is written as a separate paragraph. The purpose of a conclusion is to make the paper seem finished and complete. In addition, a good conclusion often leaves the reader with something to think about.

The suggestions for *Ending Effectively* at the end of Chapters 2 through 7 can also apply to short essays, so you may want to review these suggestions for the main types of writing that you have used. In general, most conclusions either review and reinforce the main points discussed in the essay or explain some insight or understanding to be gained from the essay.

Let's take a look at the conclusions for the three essays in this chapter so far:

FLAMENCO:

> Through flamenco dancing, I experience a marvelous inner harmony that I can find nowhere else away from the stage.

Although this conclusion is rather short, it effectively reminds the reader of the writer's main idea about her topic.

IWO JIMA:

> Visiting and walking over the battlefield of Iwo Jima drew me closer to those forgotten Marines who gave their lives for a cause. I know they fought for what they believed in and for preserving freedom. A part of me will always be with those Marines who did not come back alive from that shore, and to those Marines I acknowledge an everlasting debt that neither I nor any other American can ever repay, and that is living in FREEDOM.

The conclusion for *Iwo Jima* expresses the writer's insight into the situation. As a result of his experiences, he gained a new understanding and appreciation of the sacrifices made by men who gave their lives during World War II, which he decided to share with readers in the conclusion. This makes an effective ending for his essay.

DEAD-BEAT DADS:

> I believe if men were held at least financially responsible for the children they produce, the number of unplanned pregnancies would drop dramatically. If they believed they were to be held accountable for their actions, men would look at birth control in a whole new light. It is simply not acceptable to let innocent children suffer because of irresponsible fathers and the apathy of government on this issue.

Since *Dead-Beat Dads* was about a controversial issue, it was important for the writer to restate and reinforce her point of view in the conclusion. In addition, the conclusion makes us think about the solution that she is proposing.

In the conclusion of the following essay, *Tears in Heaven*, the writer reviews some of his main points and also shares the understanding he has gained about the death of his friend. As you read the essay, notice how narration, classification, and cause and effect analysis are effectively combined.

Tears in Heaven
by Trent Parker

A group of young teens ready for a little harmless mischief gather at the local after-school hangout. "Hey, Ethan," I say, "I dare you to pull down your shorts and moon that car full of chicks stopped at the light." "You're on," he says with a mischievous little grin. Sure enough, he struts over to the car with his unforgettable walk and casually moons the carload of girls. We laugh until we're all blue in the face. This and hundreds of other ludicrous pranks are all I have to remember one of my good friends by. Ethan John Edmonds was shot and killed at the age of twenty. I never wanted to think of such a horrible thought as what if one of my bro's were to die, but suddenly he's gone.

When a loved one dies, a person undergoes different stages of grief, which occur according to time. First is shock: "No, this did not really happen," or "It can't be true." Second is an overwhelming feeling of anger and hatred, and third is revenge. Eventually, though, one comes to accept that a loved one is gone. These stages of grief are the hardest concepts in life to understand. Sometimes I think about what happened and try to understand the emotions that I felt during these different stages.

Tuesday, July 28, started out like any other summer day. I woke up early and went surfing for a few hours. When I came in, I saw my friend Dylan, who was going to work. He said, "Hey, I'm sorry to tell you this, but Ethan was shot and died last night." My first reaction was, "That's not even funny. You're kidding, right?" But I looked into his eyes and I knew he wasn't. I just stood there while my mind and body went into shock. The tears didn't come until I was driving home. This is what I call the initial shock, which lasts a few hours after hearing any traumatic news about death. I don't remember much, just a bunch of phone calls with mindless conversations. My body almost became numb with emotions. On Friday, July 31, it was time for another type of shock, the shock of saying goodbye to someone for the last time. As I approached his open casket for one last goodbye, I shed a final tear. The shock was over. Now his spirit was free to go to Heaven.

The days to follow became ones of anger and outrage. I needed to understand why someone would kill one of my friends. I was told the story firsthand by a person who was there on the night of the shooting. A simple fight over trash cans being knocked over was the cause of my friend's death. What it comes down to is a thirty-year-old homeowner's word against the word of a group of teenagers who were attending a party. The guy who shot Ethan spent only one night in jail and was released the next day. Apparently it was too complex a case and not a guaranteed verdict, so the district attorney shoved it under the carpet and it disappeared. Revenge was all I thought about the first week after this happened. Everywhere I went, something reminded me of Ethan. Some vandalism was done to the man's house, like broken windows and gunfire. I probably would have vandalized his house too except that at the funeral Ethan's mother had pleaded for no revenge or bloodshed. I can see why people did it, but it's not the right action to take. Revenge is a hard emotion to overcome, but just like all emotions, it takes time to heal.

Now there is an acceptance that Ethan is gone, and he will always have a place in my heart. Ethan can now rest in Heaven. When my day comes, I know I will see him and he'll show me the way. But for now, the memories will last. Losing a loved one brings forth the most overwhelming rush of emotions I will ever encounter. The stages of grief are how the body and mind react to such a trauma: shock, sorrow, then revenge or anger, and finally acceptance. The better I understand these emotions that I experienced, the easier it will be to cope with the loss of a loved one.

Response to *Tears in Heaven*

1. Do you think the conclusion is effective? Why or why not?

_____

_____

_____

2. How has the writer used classification in this essay?

_____

_____

3. What parts of the essay use narration?

_____

_____

4. What parts of the essay use cause and effect analysis?

_____

_____

Keep in mind that conclusions for short essays will vary, depending on the kind of topic that the essay is about. However, answering the following questions about your paper will probably help you come up with some ideas for ending it effectively:

Question 1: What do you want the reader to remember the most about your paper?

_____

_____

Question 2:   What are the most important points that you made?

_____

_____

Question 3:   Have you gained any special insight or understanding that you want to share with the reader?

_____

_____

Question 4:   If your essay was about a problem or issue of some kind, are there some solutions that you would like to suggest in the conclusion?

_____

_____

Question 5:   Is there anything else you would like to tell the reader?

_____

_____

Using some of the ideas that you wrote in your answers to questions 1–5, write a concluding paragraph for your short essay.

Then get together with members of your workshop group and read each other's rough drafts. Answer the following Rough Draft Workshop Questions about each person's paper, and try to help each other by suggesting revisions.

Rough Draft Workshop Questions

1. Does the thesis statement express an important idea about the writer's specific topic?
2. Are appropriate types of writing used to develop the topic effectively?
3. Is there an interesting introduction?
4. Does each body paragraph develop one part or aspect of the topic?
5. Are the paragraphs connected smoothly by transitional sentences?
6. Does the conclusion make the paper seem complete and leave the reader with something to think about?

If you think that some of your workshop group's suggestions would make your essay more effective, you will probably want to make a few revisions before turning in your final draft. Section Two of this chapter explains sentence variety, several tenses and forms of verbs, and punctuation rules, all of which will help you with proofreading and correcting your final draft. Use the *Short Essay Writing Checklist* on page 436 to make sure that your essay has followed all of the guidelines for good writing in this chapter.

SECTION TWO:
Sentence and Grammar Skills

Goals

In this section of the chapter, you will learn how to do the following:

- Use a variety of sentence types to add interest to your writing
- Make your writing effective by using sentences of various lengths
- Use regular and irregular past participles in perfect tenses
- Decide when to use the active voice and the passive voice
- Use commas, colons, semicolons, and dashes correctly

Using a Variety of Sentences
to Make Your Writing More Interesting

By now you know how to write a wide range of types of sentences by choosing from many different connecting words. Each type of connector—Group A, B, and C connectors, Relatives, and semicolons—has its own use, its own flavor or precise shade of meaning, and each one gives a particular feel to any sentence that it's used in. These connectors are like tools that you have learned how to use to help construct a well-written paragraph or short paper. In this part of the chapter, you will focus on your paper as a whole, instead of on each individual sentence, to see that your writing reflects this knowledge of different sentence types. The objective is to make your writing interesting and effective.

Take a look at the words that connect the SVs in the sentences of the following Class Practice exercise: *and, so,* and *but.* Only Group A connectors are used. The topic may be an interesting one, but when you rewrite this story using a better variety of connecting words, the sentences will help make it good reading as well.

■ CLASS PRACTICE ▮1▮ Variety of Sentence Types

Directions: Rewrite the following paragraph and make the sentences more interesting by using a variety of connecting words. In some sentences you may be able to just replace a Group A connector with a different type of connector, but in other sentences you will probably need to change the order of the clauses.

A Norwegian Community in Iowa

My grandmother's aunt grew up in a Norwegian area of Iowa around 1900, *and* only Norwegians lived there. One year a Swedish family had lived there, *but* they weren't made to feel welcome. I asked her about their treatment of the Swedish family, *so* she told me the story. Swedes talked funny, she said, *and* they drank an awful lot of coffee. To me, Swedish and Norwegian accents sound very similar, *and* my Norwegian relatives drank a lot of coffee too, *so* I scratched my head and said as much to my aunt. "Oh, my, no," she said, "Swedes drink much more coffee than Norwegians, *and* they have such a funny accent." I asked her how much coffee Swedes drank, *and* she said, "They might drink eight or nine cups of coffee a day." I asked her, "How much coffee do Norwegians drink?" *and* she replied, "Oh, we only drink six or seven cups a day." These differences were very real to my first-generation aunt, *but* to a quarter-Norwegian third-generation American, Swedes and Norwegians seemed very much alike.

Rewrite:

_____

_____

_____

_____

_____

_____

_____

_____

_____

_____

Using a Variety of Sentence Lengths

Another way to make your papers more interesting is to vary the length of your sentences. A good mix of sentence lengths and types is one sign of good writing ability that is sometimes used by colleges to determine what writing class a student should take. Sentences of different lengths often convey different shades of meaning. A short sentence may be used for emphasis—to make a dramatic point or to underscore an important or unexpected twist in your paper. Still, if you use only short sentences, the paper will seem choppy. Longer sentences give the paper a feeling of flow and movement. These longer sentences may include more than two SVs, introductory elements, many descriptive words, or other elements. In order for your essay to sound smooth, natural, and effective, you need a good mix of various sentence lengths.

The following paragraph shows what happens when all the sentences are the same length.

■ **CLASS PRACTICE 2**

Variety of Sentence Lengths

Directions: Rewrite the following paragraph using a variety of sentence lengths. Try to keep some short sentences, but write some that have three or more SVs. You may also add prepositional phrases or other elements where appropriate. Use your own paper for this exercise.

Steps in Manufacturing Woolen Cloth

There are eight steps in manufacturing woolen fabric. These are grading and sorting, scouring, lanolin recovery, dyeing, carding, spinning, weaving, and finishing. The first step is grading and sorting. Different grades of wool are blended to assure a consistent fiber mix. The next process is scouring, or cleaning. Lanolin is also removed during this process. Wool can be dyed after this step or later. Carding is the process of pulling the wool fibers in the same direction. The wool is also divided into equal strands called roving. The next step is spinning. Yarn is formed by twisting and pulling the strands of roving. Yarn is then woven on a loom to make unfinished cloth. Finally, the cloth is finished. During the finishing process it is subjected to heat, moisture, friction, and pressure. This step makes it softer and more compact. Now the wool is ready to make clothes and blankets.

■ CLASS
PRACTICE **3**

Looking at Your Own Writing

Directions: Now look at your own paper to see if you have a good variety of sentence lengths. First, count how many SVs there are in each sentence of your first two paragraphs and list them below. You may add more blanks if you need them.

1. ___ 2. ___ 3. ___ 4. ___ 5. ___ 6. ___

7. ___ 8. ___ 9. ___ 10. ___ 11. ___ 12. ___

13. ___ 14. ___ 15. ___

Is there a good variety of shorter and longer sentences? If not, you will probably want to change some of the sentences in your paper to achieve a better mix of sentence lengths.

Sentence Combining Activity

Directions: Try to use a variety of different sentence structures and lengths. You may use any connectors that we have studied throughout the book to join the clauses effectively.

Dreams

1.1 Some people think that they never dream.
1.2 They don't remember their dreams.
1.3 Researchers have proven that all of us have dreams.
1.4 This happens every night.

2.1 Other mammals have dreams too.
2.2 You may see your cat twitching his tail.
2.3 You may hear your cat growling.
2.4 He is asleep.

3.1 He may be catching a mouse.
3.2 He may be chasing a bird.
3.3 He may be doing this in his dream.

4.1 Only about one third of our dreams are pleasant.
4.2 The rest are unpleasant.
4.3 The rest are sometimes frightening.

5.1 For example, many people dream of falling.
5.2 Another dream is being chased.

6.1   These dreams may seem very real.

6.2   They do not mean that the person is in danger in real life.

7.1   The meaning of dreams is not always the same.

7.2   Dreams relate to individuals' lives in different ways.

7.3   Dreams should not be interpreted according to standard symbols.

8.1   For example, a cat does not necessarily symbolize death.

8.2   A snake does not always mean you are thinking about sex.

9.1   A snake could represent a person who has certain qualities.

9.2   These are qualities like a snake.

9.3   Perhaps someone speaks with a forked tongue.

9.4   A snake could just be a snake.

10.1   Some people believe that what we eat can cause bad dreams.

10.2   This is a myth.

11.1   You eat pickles and sausage at bedtime.

11.2   Your stomach may be upset.

11.3   It won't cause nightmares.

12.1   Dreams can help us learn about ourselves.

12.2   Dreams can help us discover our inner feelings.

12.3   Dreams can help us deal with our anxieties.

13.1   We can even learn to control our dreams.

13.2   We can defeat our dream-enemies.

14.1   To do this, we have to create a version of the dream.

14.2   This version is different.

14.3   This version ends happily.

15.1   Learning to control our dreams can make us feel better.

15.2   This happens when we wake up.

15.3   Learning to control our dreams can reduce depression.

16.1   Dreams may be a window to our subconscious.

16.2   We should pay attention to them.

Learning about Perfect Tenses and Other Uses of the Past Participle

In Chapter 2 we looked at the simple past tense, which we use to talk about an action that happened at a definite time in the past or about an action that is already finished. In this chapter we will focus on some other tenses that can be used to show an action that happened in the past. The most common of these tenses is the *present perfect* tense.

Learning about the Present Perfect Tense

The *present perfect* tense has two main uses. We often use this tense to talk about something that has happened at an indefinite time in the past. Some of the examples listed below show this meaning. Another use of the present perfect tense is to show an action that began in the past and is still happening. Here are some examples of the present perfect tense from the short essays in this chapter:

From *Flamenco*, by Rosa Hammar, page 382

EXAMPLE 1 ➤ When I was a little girl, I remember my father playing the guitar and listening to Spanish music. Since then *I've wanted* to be a flamenco dancer.

In this example, Rosa tells how she wanted to be a flamenco dancer, beginning when she was a little girl and continuing until now. When we want to show that an action began in the past and continues until the present, the present perfect tense is usually the best choice.

EXAMPLE 2 ➤ Now that my children are adults, *I've pursued* my life-long ambition.

Example 2 shows a similar situation. Beginning sometime before now, Rosa has continued to pursue her ambition of learning to dance flamenco. Her use of the present perfect tense emphasizes that she is still involved in this activity.

From *Dead-Beat Dads*, by Angelique St. Jacques, page 396

EXAMPLE 3 ➤ I want to know what kind of sacrifices he *has had* to make.

This third example illustrates the other common use of the present perfect tense. Angelique is asking what sacrifices her daughter's absent father has made, at any time in the past. When the specific time of an action doesn't matter, the present perfect tense is often used. This is called using the present perfect to show *indefinite time*. We use it when we don't know what time something happened, or we don't care, or we don't want to say.

The Structure of the Present Perfect Tense

Unlike the past tense, the present perfect doesn't have a one-word form. Instead, the present perfect tense uses the present tense of the verb *to have* along with a form of the main verb that we call the *past participle*. The verbs in the above examples, (I)*'ve wanted*, (I)*'ve pursued*, (he) *has had*, show that the helping verb can be either *have* or *has* to agree with the subject of the sentence. Notice that some of the past participles are the same as the simple past tense: *wanted*, *pursued*, and *had*. However, other verbs have past participles, such as *been* and *seen*, that are quite different from the past tense.

The following exercise will help you learn to recognize both the helping verb and the past participle.

■ **CLASS PRACTICE** **4**

Identifying Present Perfect Verbs

Directions: Look at these examples of present perfect verbs taken from sentences in example papers in this book, and identify the helping verb and the past participle in the spaces provided.

EXAMPLE 1 ➤ I *have* never *heard* anything like that howl again. (*The Howl*, by Mark Field)

Helping verb: ____*have*____   Past Participle: ____*heard*____

EXAMPLE 2 ➤ The sun *has slipped* down past the horizon. (*Horsethief Canyon*, by Shawn McPherren)

Helping verb: ____*has*____   Past Participle: ____*slipped*____

I *'ve seen* programs about mental illness on TV, and I *'ve heard* about it from people. (*A Lost Friend*, Todd Louis)

1. Helping verb: _____   Past participle: _____

2. Helping verb: _____   Past participle: _____

Students in college have already developed their idea of who they want to be. (*Variations*, by Cynthia Uribe)

3. Helping verb: _____   Past participle: _____

Although I have climbed a tree, . . . I've taken this wondrous woody plant for granted. (*A Tree Like Me*, by Aurora Alvarez)

4. Helping verb: _____   Past participle: _____

5. Helping verb: _____   Past participle: _____

I have discovered that my leisure time has become limited. (*Going to College*, by Mary Miller)

6. Helping verb: _____   Past participle: _____

7. Helping verb: _____   Past participle: _____

My self-esteem has dramatically improved. (*Going to College*, by Mary Miller)

8. Helping verb: _____   Past participle: _____

These floods have taken the lives of many immigrants . . . . (*Clean Water at Last*, by Zachary J. Reiff)

9. Helping verb: _____   Past participle: _____

I . . . still have not seen anything that resembles a resolution. (*Dead-Beat Dads*, by Angelique St. Jacques)

10. Helping verb: _____   Past participle: _____

Irregular Past Participles

When you are writing your own paragraphs and short essays, you will need to use the correct form of the past participle of each verb whenever you use the present perfect tense. Regular verbs are easy—the past tense form and the past participle both end in *-ed*. Just remember to check the past tense spelling rules covered in Chapter 2 and listed in Appendix IV.

On the other hand, irregular verbs, those verbs that don't end in *-ed* in the past tense, are more difficult because they must be memorized. Fortunately, most irregular verbs fall into several categories, based on how they are formed, that might help you memorize them. Here are some of the major categories:

I. Verbs that are the same in the simple form, the past, and the past participle

EXAMPLES ➤	*Simple Form*	*Simple Past Form*	*Past Participle*
	bet	bet	bet
	burst	burst	burst
	cut	cut	cut
	fit	fit	fit
	hit	hit	hit
	hurt	hurt	hurt
	let	let	let
	put	put	put
	quit	quit	quit
	rid	rid	rid
	set	set	set
	shut	shut	shut
	slit	slit	slit
	spread	spread	spread

II. Verbs whose past participles end in *-n*, *-en*, or *-ne*

EXAMPLES ➤	*Simple Form*	*Simple Past Form*	*Past Participle*
	beat	beat	beaten
	bite	bit	bitten
	blow	blew	blown
	break	broke	broken
	choose	chose	chosen
	do	did	done
	draw	drew	drawn
	drive	drove	driven
	eat	ate	eaten
	fall	fell	fallen
	fly	flew	flown
	forget	forgot	forgotten
	forgive	forgave	forgiven
	freeze	froze	frozen
	get	got	gotten
	give	gave	given
	go	went	gone
	grow	grew	grown
	hide	hid	hidden
	know	knew	known
	ride	rode	ridden
	see	saw	seen
	shake	shook	shaken
	speak	spoke	spoken
	steal	stole	stolen
	swear	swore	sworn
	take	took	taken
	tear	tore	torn
	throw	threw	thrown
	wake	woke	woken
	write	wrote	written

III. Verbs that end with *-d* and change to *-t*

EXAMPLES ➤	*Simple Form*	*Simple Past Form*	*Past Participle*
	bend	bent	bent
	build	built	built
	lend	lent	lent
	send	sent	sent
	spend	spent	spent

IV. Verbs that have the same form for the past participle and simple form but a different form for the past tense

EXAMPLES ➤	*Simple Form*	*Simple Past Form*	*Past Participle*
	become	became	become
	come	came	come
	run	ran	run

V. Verbs that have a vowel change and use the same form for the past tense and the past participle

EXAMPLES ➤

Simple Form	Simple Past Form	Past Participle
bleed	bled	bled
dig	dug	dug
feed	fed	fed
find	found	found
fight	fought	fought
grind	ground	ground
hang	hung	hung
hold	held	held
lead	led	led
meet	met	met
read	read	read*
shoot	shot	shot
sit	sat	sat
slide	slid	slid
spin	spun	spun
stand	stood	stood
stick	stuck	stuck
swing	swung	swung
win	won	won

VI. Verbs with vowel changes from *i* to *a* to *u*

EXAMPLES ➤

Simple Form	Simple Past Form	Past Participle
begin	began	begun
drink	drank	drunk
ring	rang	rung
sing	sang	sung
sink	sank	sunk
swim	swam	swum

VII. Verbs that end in *-ought* or *-aught* in the past form and past participle.

EXAMPLES ➤

Simple Form	Simple Past Form	Past Participle
bring	brought	brought
buy	bought	bought
catch	caught	caught†
teach	taught	taught
think	thought	thought

There are many other irregular verbs that haven't been listed above, and some of them don't fit any of the patterns very well. A more complete list of irregular verbs is in Appendix III.

*The spelling of the past form and the past participle of the verb *read* is the same as the simple form, but the vowel sound changes.

†Notice that all of these verbs end in *-ought* unless the simple form has the letter *a* in it. Then they end in *-aught*.

Avoiding a Common Error

It's important to avoid making the common error of using the past participle alone, without the helping verb *have*, as in this incorrect example:

INCORRECT EXAMPLE 1 ➤   Both students already *done* their homework.

If you find this type of error in your own writing, you can correct it either by using the simple past tense or by adding the correct form of the auxiliary verb *to have*. The example sentence could be corrected in either of the following ways, depending on the emphasis you want:

> Both students already *did* their homework.
>
> *or*
>
> Both students *have* already *done* their homework.

■ **CLASS PRACTICE** **5**

Irregular Past Participles

Directions: Fill in the blanks with the correct form of the helping verb *to have* and the correct past participle. Remember that past participles of regular verbs end in *-ed*.

Online Services and The Internet

In the last couple of years, the Internet (go) _____ _____ from being an unknown communication system for scientists and the military to an information and communications superhighway that many people (begin) _____ _____ to use in the comfort of their own homes. Technically, it's not really a thing—it's a pathway through millions of separate computers that users (connect) _____ _____ together in order to send messages and requests from computer to computer until they reach their intended destination. A computer owner in Seattle, Washington, USA, can reach someone in Europe, Latin America, Asia, Africa, the Middle East, or the Pacific Rim area cheaply and easily by sending the message through the Internet.

Many new users (access) _____ _____ the Internet through on-line services. Some of the most popular are America Online, Compuserve, and Prodigy, but there are many more. These services make it easy to use the Internet, although some of them _____ not (offer) _____ full access to all Internet features yet. Each of these services (try) _____ _____ to attract a loyal and growing clientele by offering much more than just access to the Internet. Some of them (provide) _____ _____ everything from free homework help to special interest groups on almost any subject imaginable. Many newspapers and magazines are also available online, and recently some of the most popular features (be) _____ _____ the chat rooms, where subscribers can meet 'face to face' and chat via their keyboards and monitors, or screens.

The potential of the Internet and online services _____ hardly (begin) _____ to be tapped. In recent months, hundreds of thousands of ordinary people (be) _____ _____ able to buy and sell items, do research, visit an online library, talk with experts, use specialized software or games programs that reside on other computers, or just chat with other users that share the same interests. Predicting what new features will be available via the Internet and online services in the future is not easy, but there is no doubt that the new offerings will continue to amaze us.

Other Perfect Tenses

Tenses that are formed by the auxiliary verb *to have* and the past participle of the main verb are called *perfect tenses*. We have already looked at the present perfect tense, which uses the present tense of the verb to have: *have* or *has*. In this part of Section 2 you will learn about the *present perfect continuous* tense, the *past perfect* tense, and perfect tenses with modal verbs.

Present Perfect Continuous

The present perfect continuous tense is formed with *have* or *has,* the past participle *been,* and the *-ing* form of the main verb. Here is an example from a student paper in this chapter:

> *I have been trying* to get an increase in child support for two years . . . . (*Dead-Beat Dads*, by Angelique St. Jacques)

In this sentence, Angelique uses a form of the present perfect tense, *have been trying*, to show that she began trying to get an increase sometime in the past, before now, and that she is still trying. The continuous form emphasizes that the action is very definitely still continuing. Use this tense when you want to emphasize that the action or condition is still happening.

Past Perfect

The past perfect tense is formed with *had* plus the past participle of the main verb. It shows an action that happened before another action in the past. In the following example, Mark uses the past perfect to show that packing the parachute took place sometime *before* everyone asked him about it.

EXAMPLE 1 ➤   Everyone asked me how I *had packed* my chute so quickly. (*Sky Diving*, by Mark Albarran)

Here are a few more examples taken from student papers in this book:

EXAMPLE 2 ➤   I *had put* that off because I was raising a family and attending school part-time. (*Flamenco*, by Rosa Hammar)

EXAMPLE 3 ➤   When my mom reached my room, the earthquake *had calmed down* a little, but it *had not stopped* completely. (*Earthquake*, by Deanna Hernandez)

Use the past perfect tense to show that the action you are describing happened before another action or time in the past.

Perfect Tenses with Modal Verbs

It's possible to use modal auxiliary verbs like *could, might, must, should,* and *would* with a perfect tense. In Chapter 1 you learned that *modal auxiliaries* add other meanings to the main verb, such as possibility or obligation. Another meaning is to speculate about past actions that didn't really happen. Look at the following student examples:

EXAMPLE 1 ➤   The most exciting experience in my life was walking over this piece of land that once was a bloody battlefield and imagining what it *must have been* like. (*Iwo Jima*, by Danny Banda)

EXAMPLE 2 ➤   I *wouldn't have had* time to pull the reserve. (*Sky Diving*, by Mark Albarran)

EXAMPLE 3 ➤   *Could* it *have been* a dog? (*The Howl*, by Mark Field)

EXAMPLE 4 ➤   I used to wonder why she *couldn't have said* that in a nicer way. (*Japanese and American Customs*, by Toshiko Williams)

EXAMPLE 5 ➤   If I had been receiving the correct amount of child support, my family *wouldn't have had* to make so many sacrifices. (*Dead-Beat Dads*, by Angelique St. Jacques)

To write a modal auxiliary with a perfect tense, use the *modal*, the simple form of the verb *have*, and the *past participle* of the main verb.

Other Common Errors to Avoid

Spoken English is often less formal than written English, and short forms of verbs, or contractions, are often used. One common contraction often used with *would, could, should,* and some of the other modals is the form *'ve* for *have*. Be sure not to make the common error of using *of* instead of *have*, as in this incorrect example:

INCORRECT EXAMPLE 1 ➤ I *would of* applied to Ohio State if you had told me about the basketball program there.

The correct sentence should be: I *would have* (or *would've*) applied to Ohio State if you had told me about the basketball program there.

Other common errors include spelling contractions wrong, such as *hasen't* instead of the correct spelling *hasn't*, and leaving out the apostrophe or putting it in the wrong place, like *havent* or *hav'ent* instead of *haven't*. The following exercise will give you practice recognizing common errors with perfect tenses and past participles.

■ **CLASS PRACTICE 6**

Proofreading for Errors with Perfect Tenses

Directions: The following selection contains ten errors with perfect tenses and past participles. Cross out each incorrect form and write in the correct form above the error.

My College Experience

Looking back at my many years of college, I realize that it have been worthwhile, although it certainly hasn't been easy. When I graduated from high school, I started going to Grossmont College, where I done most of my general education classes before I transferred to San Diego State University. At that time the country had just came through the Vietnam War, and protest was still in the air. In fact, even before I first signed up for college, I had already decided that a degree wasn't important—it was only a piece of paper. If I could of seen the future then, I would of known that that little piece of paper would be worth a lot, not only in terms of money, but more importantly, in the choice of jobs it would give me.

After I met my wife-to-be, I realized that I would need a job that I could support a family with, so I got busy, hit the books, and graduated from SDSU with a bachelor's degree just 8 years after I had began. By then I have decided to go on and get a Master's degree in my chosen field, teaching English as a Second Language (ESL). I have never regret that decision, although while I was working part-time in two or three different schools, I came close. Now I been a teacher with a full-time contract for almost nine years, and if I could do it over, I would make the exact same decisions again.

Passive Voice

English sentences can be either active or passive. No matter what tense we use for the verb, if the subject of the sentences produces the action, we say that the sentence is in the *active voice*. But if the subject of the sentence receives the action, or is acted upon by something or someone else, we say that the sentence uses the *passive voice*. The passive voice has two parts: (1) a form of the auxiliary verb *to be* and (2) the past participle of the main verb. Here are some examples of active and passive verbs taken from sentences in student papers in this book:

EXAMPLE 1 ➤ Defensive players *are put* in the lineup for their defensive skills rather than their offensive ones. (*The Lineup*, by Richard D. Munholland)

The action in this sentence is expressed by the verb *are put*. The subject of this sentence is *defensive players*. Do the defensive players put themselves in the lineup? No, someone else puts them in the lineup. You can see that they receive the action of being put in the lineup, and that the verb consists of *are* plus the past participle *put*. Therefore, this is an example of the passive voice.

EXAMPLE 2 ➤ Sometimes they *wear* baggy pants so low at the waist that their belly buttons *can be seen*. (*Variations*, by Cynthia Uribe)

The first part of this sentence is *active* because the subject (*they*) is doing the action—wearing baggy pants. The second part of this sentence is passive because the subject (*their belly buttons*) is not what is able to see. Instead, the subject is being seen by someone else.

EXAMPLE 3 ➤ The blues style of singing *was* originally *developed* in the late 19th century and came from African American slave songs about life's hardships. (*African American Music*, by Tiffany Turner)

The verb in Example 3, *was developed*, shows that the passive voice can be used in the past tense. In fact, the passive voice can be used with any appropriate tense.

Uses of the Passive Voice

The passive voice can be used when the writer wants to emphasize the recipient of the action rather than the person or thing that produces the action. We also use the passive voice when we don't know who or what produced the action, or when we don't care, or when we don't want to say. Here are a few examples that illustrate these uses:

EXAMPLE 1 ➤ He*'s been busted* for shoplifting, drugs, reckless driving, speeding, and being truant. (*Spoiled Rotten*, by Trent Parker)

In Example 1, we don't care who arrested the subject—the important thing is that it happened.

EXAMPLE 2 ➤ Have you ever seen somebody who *was given* too much love [by his parents]? (*Spoiled Rotten*, by Trent Parker)

This sentence uses the passive voice to emphasize the recipient of the action rather than the giver. Notice that the preposition *by* can be used to show who or what produces the action.

EXAMPLE 3 ➤ As sunlight fades, the fiery sky calms down and *is replaced* with a deep azure. (*Horsethief Canyon*, by Shawn McPherren)

Example 3 uses the passive voice because it really isn't possible to say who replaced the fiery colors of the sunset without making a religious statement or an involved scientific explanation.

EXAMPLE 4 ➤ Teachers and parents may think that a child who has so much trouble learning to read and write has low intelligence, so he or she *may* mistakenly *be put* with a group of slow learners in school. (*Effects of Dyslexia,* page 331)

In this example the passive voice puts the emphasis on the child rather than on the parents, the school, or the teacher. It also illustrates a situation where the writer may not want to say who did the action in order to avoid accusing the parents, the school, or the teachers.

When you come to a place in your writing where you want to emphasize the recipient of the action rather than the person or thing that performs the action, consider using the passive voice.

Choosing Active or Passive Voice

As a general rule, active-voice sentences are considered to be more interesting than passive-voice sentences, so it's important to use a lot of active-voice sentences in your writing. If you use the passive voice only where you really need it, your papers will seem more lively and interesting.

Using Past Participles as Adjectives

Past participles can also be used as adjectives. Here are some examples of this use:

EXAMPLE 1 ➤ Mickey is probably one of the most *spoiled* kids in the United States. (*Spoiled Rotten*, by Trent Parker)

EXAMPLE 2 ➤ It is much easier to get the opponent in a *controlled* hold for 30 seconds than to try to get both of the opponent's shoulders to touch the mat. (*Judo Versus Wrestling*, by Ray Jensen)

EXAMPLE 3 ➤ The scoring system in wrestling is more *complicated* than in judo. (*Judo Versus Wrestling*, by Ray Jensen)

EXAMPLE 4 ➤ A lot of the skills [for paramedics] are the same as the skills that an EMT has to learn, with *advanced* components added. (*Becoming an EMT or a Paramedic*, by Damon Aikens)

When the past participle is used as an adjective, it often looks similar to the passive voice. This is especially true when it follows a form of the verb *to be*, like *is* in Example 3 above. The meaning is often similar also. Using a past participle as an adjective usually shows that an action has been performed on the noun it affects. We know that someone *spoiled* Mickey in Example 1, someone is *controlling* the wrestling or judo hold in Example 2, and the scoring system in Example 3 didn't just *complicate* itself.

Using past participles as adjectives is just one more way of making your writing more interesting to add to the other ways you have already learned.

■ **CLASS PRACTICE** **7**

Practice with Active and Passive Voice

Directions: Rewrite the following sentences to make all of the passive verbs active, and make the two active verbs passive.

EXAMPLE ➤ The Iditarod dogsled race was won by a woman.

A woman won the Iditarod dogsled race.

1. *Lady and the Tramp*, a famous children's animated movie, was produced by Walt Disney.

_____

_____

2. The bicycling class coach was assisted by veteran bicyclists from the South Bay Slow Spokes.

_____

_____

3. The Student Center was designed and constructed by students from the architecture and engineering classes.

_____

_____

4. The previous world record for the 440 relay had been set by a local swimmer.

   _____

   _____

5. Harvard University accepted 27 students from the local area.

   _____

   _____

6. The French President and the Chilean ambassador to the United States were introduced by President Clinton.

   _____

   _____

7. Another fundraiser was scheduled by the organizing committee.

   _____

   _____

8. "The Rose" was performed by Bette Midler.

   _____

   _____

9. *Pooh and Piglet Nearly Catch a Woozle* will be presented by the Marie Hitchcock Puppet Theater.

   _____

   _____

10. Someone named Washington, D.C., in honor of the first president.

    _____

    _____

Learning about Punctuation

As different sentence patterns have been presented, we have also looked at the correct punctuation for each pattern, so you have already practiced some of the rules for correct use of commas and semicolons. In this chapter, you will learn four basic comma rules that cover almost every situation you will encounter in your writing. Then we will look at how to use semicolons, colons, and dashes for greater variety in your writing, as well as how to punctuate quotations.

Commas

Placing commas correctly helps to make your writing clear and easy to understand. If commas appear in the wrong places, they can make sentences confusing for readers and may sometimes even change the meaning. Some people try to place commas according to where there are natural pauses, but this method is not very reliable. It's true that when we are reading, we often pause where there are commas. However, commas are actually intended to correspond with different elements of sentence structure and grammar, not necessarily with pauses.

There are four main comma rules that every writer should learn. These four rules cover almost all of the situations where commas are needed in written English.

Comma Rule #1

Use a comma before a Group A connector (and, but, or, for, nor, so, yet) used to join two clauses.

Do not use a comma when one of these words joins only two words or phrases.

The first part of Comma Rule #1 may look familiar because it was introduced in Chapter 2 when you studied compound sentences. To see how this rule applies, let's look at some examples:

$$S \qquad V$$

EXAMPLE 1 ➤ Dwayne failed the math competency test the first time, *but*

$$S \quad V$$

he passed it the second time.

In this sentence, *but* connects two clauses (two SVs), so a comma is necessary. However, notice that if the sentence is rewritten without the subject *he* in the second clause, a comma should not be used:

S   *V*

EXAMPLE 2 ➤ Dwayne failed the math competency test the first time but

V

passed it the second time.

S   *V*

EXAMPLE 3 ➤ Many psychotherapists use dream analysis as a form of therapy,

S   *V*

for they believe that dreams can help people understand themselves better.

S   *V*

EXAMPLE 4 ➤ The band played a few classical pieces and a medley of songs from *The Music Man.*

The sentence in Example 3 needs a comma before the Group A connector *for* because *for* is used to connect the first two clauses. However, in Example 4, *and* does not require a comma because it does not connect two clauses. Instead, *and* connects the two kinds of music: *a few classical pieces* **and** *a medley of songs from The Music Man.* Like *and*, the connecting words *but, or, nor,* and *yet* are sometimes used to join two words or phrases rather than two clauses. Remember that in these cases a comma should not be used.

At this point, you may want to do Sentences 1–4 in Class Practice 8 on page 427. These sentences will help you check your understanding of Comma Rule #1.

Comma Rule #2

Use a comma to separate items in a series.

A series is like a list of three or more different words or phrases that form part of a sentence. There is usually an *and* (or occasionally *or*) before the last item in the series. Here are some examples of sentences that contain a series of items separated by commas:

EXAMPLE 1 ➤ You can take deductions for *medical expenses, property taxes, mortgage interest, donations, and certain job-related expenses* on Schedule A.

(Notice that there is no comma after the last item, *job-related expenses.*)

EXAMPLE 2 ➤ Each applicant must *fill out a job application, submit a resumé, and come in for an interview.*

Sometimes the items in a series contain only one or two words each, like most of the items in Example 1. However, various kinds of longer phrases can also be written in a series. In Example 2, there are three verb phrases in the series: *fill out a job application, submit a resumé,* and *come in for an interview*. Sometimes a series may even consist of three clauses (a sentence pattern that was presented in Chapter 7):

EXAMPLE 3 ➤   The lawyers argued the point, the judge took the matter under advisement, and a ruling is expected tomorrow.

Some books suggest that the last comma in a series, the one just before *and*, is optional. However, in this book, we have included the last comma as part of the series rule because sometimes the meaning can be confusing without it.

Remember that a series must consist of three or more items, which can be words, phrases, or clauses. If there are only two items joined by *and*, no comma is needed, as in this example:

EXAMPLE 4 ➤   Wildflowers along the parkway include Queen Anne's lace and lupine.

In this sentence, a comma before *and* would be incorrect because there are only two items named, so it is not a series.

However, there is one situation in which two items sometimes function like a series and require a comma: two separate adjectives that precede a noun. If the adjectives function independently of each other to describe the noun, then we use a comma between them, as in this example:

EXAMPLE 5 ➤   What we need is a *quiet, comfortable* place to study.

In order to determine whether the two adjectives are really functioning independently and require a comma, check to see if the order of the adjectives can be reversed. It would be equally correct to say a "comfortable, quiet place" instead of a "quiet, comfortable place." Because the adjectives are reversible, this means that the adjectives are independent of each other, so a comma is appropriate. Another test is to try *and* between the adjectives. If *and* sounds correct (quiet and comfortable), this also indicates that the adjectives are independent and require a comma.

Sentences 5–8 in Class Practice 8 relate to Comma Rule #2. You may want to do these sentences now before going on to the next comma rule.

Comma Rule #3

A. Use a comma after an introductory group of words at the beginning of a sentence.

B. Use a comma before a group of words placed at the end of a sentence as an addition or afterthought.

Comma Rule #3 applies to groups of words added before or after the main clause. A comma should be used to separate these kinds of word groups from the rest of the sentence. In order to apply Comma Rule #3, it is not necessary to identify the specific kind of phrase or clause used at the beginning or the end of the sentence. You only need to recognize it as something introductory or as an afterthought in order to know that it needs a comma.

Most writers use introductory phrases of various kinds as well as introductory subordinate clauses. Let's look at some examples:

EXAMPLE 1 ➤ *Because of the baseball strike,* there were no more games for the rest of the season.

EXAMPLE 2 ➤ *Accompanied by his guide dog,* Don goes everywhere on campus and around town.

EXAMPLE 3 ➤ *After the keel had snapped off,* the French yacht capsized.

All of these sentences have an introductory element. In Example 1, there is an introductory prepositional phrase. In Example 2, the introductory phrase begins with a past participle. Example 3 has a subordinate clause at the beginning of the sentence, a sentence pattern that we looked at in Chapter 3 with Group B connectors.

A pattern that we looked at in Chapter 5 with Group C connectors also comes under this rule:

EXAMPLE 4 ➤ *Therefore,* anti-lock brakes will reduce the number of accidents.

In this sentence, *therefore* acts as an introductory word and requires a comma. A Group C connector at the beginning of a sentence or at the beginning of a clause almost always needs to be followed by a comma.

However, exceptions to Comma Rule #3 are often made with other single introductory words and short phrases of two or three words. If the introductory word or short phrase seems to flow smoothly into the main part of the sentence, writers often prefer to omit the comma, as in this example:

EXAMPLE 5 ➤ Last year the unemployment rate went down slightly.

The second part of Comma Rule #3, which applies to added phrases at the end of a sentence, is not used very often. Most phrases that follow the subject and verb are an essential part of the sentence, not an addition or an afterthought, so they do not need to be separated by a comma. Occasionally, though, an added phrase lacks direct continuity with the rest of the sentence and thus needs a comma before it. Here are a couple of examples:

EXAMPLE 6 ➤ A student may be suspended for plagiarism, *according to the student handbook.*

EXAMPLE 7 ➤ Emeralds are relatively soft stones, *not hard like diamonds.*

In Examples 6 and 7, the phrases *according to the student handbook* and *not hard like diamonds* need to be set off by commas because they are additions that do not have direct continuity with the rest of the sentence. For this part of Comma Rule #3, the natural pause before an addition is a fairly reliable signal that a comma is appropriate.

A subordinate clause at the end of a sentence, however, generally does not require a comma. The only exceptions are clauses that begin with certain Group B connectors that indicate a strong contrast such as *although, though,* and *even though.* Clauses that begin with *although, though,* or *even though* may be preceded by a comma if the writer wants to emphasize the contrast. Here are some examples of correctly punctuated sentences with a subordinate clause at the end:

EXAMPLE 8 ➤ Some people claim that affirmative action leads to reverse discrimination because white males have a harder time getting jobs. *(no commas)*

EXAMPLE 9 ➤ Good listening requires hearing others' words accurately, *although* the underlying feelings are even more important.

To check your understanding of Comma Rule #3, do Sentences 9–12 in Class Practice 8 before going on to the next rule.

Comma Rule #4

Place a pair of commas around any interrupting word, phrase, or clause inserted in a sentence.

Sometimes a word, phrase, or clause is inserted in the middle of a sentence, interrupting the sentence. To show that it is an interruption, it should be set off by a pair of commas. Here are some examples of sentences with an interrupting word, phrase, or clause:

EXAMPLE 1 ➤ The title of *Ms., however,* can apply to either a married woman or an unmarried woman.

In Example 1, *however* shows that this statement contrasts with something that the previous sentence said. Instead of being placed at the beginning of this sentence, it is in the middle for a variation in style. Commas are used before and after *however* to show that it is an interrupter.

EXAMPLE 2 ➤ The Dean of Student Activities, *in response to several complaints,* called a meeting of the Grievance Committee.

In this case, the phrase *in response to several complaints* comes between the subject and verb and interrupts the sentence. Therefore, it is set off by commas.

EXAMPLE 3 ➤   Dagmar, *who is a very talented actress,* plans to try out for the role of Lady Macbeth.

The relative clause *who is a very talented actress* gives additional information about the subject Dagmar, but this information is not necessary to identify the subject. Therefore, the relative clause is treated as an insertion in the middle of the sentence and should be set off by commas. As you learned in Chapter 4, this type of clause (sometimes called a *nonessential* or *nonrestrictive* clause) always needs commas. However, a relative clause that is necessary to identify the person or thing it refers to (an *essential* or *restrictive* clause) is not treated as an interrupter and should not be set off by commas:

EXAMPLE 4 ➤   The employees who failed the drug test were fired.
(no commas)

Before going on to read about special comma situations, you may want to do Sentences 13–16 in Class Practice 8 to make sure that you understand Comma Rule #4.

Special Comma Situations

The four comma rules that we have just examined will cover almost all types of sentences that you write. However, there are a few special situations that have their own rules, such as addresses and dates.

ADDRESSES:

When you write a letter or address an envelope, you should always put a comma between the city and the state, like this: *Wayne, Michigan.* Other items in an address are also separated by commas (almost like a series) when they are written on the same line or in a sentence.

DATES:

Whenever you write complete dates, there should be a comma before the year, like this: *September 6, 1996.*

If an address or date is included in a sentence, there is also a comma afterward to separate the address or date from the rest of the sentence, like these examples:

EXAMPLE 1 ➤   December 7, 1941, was the day that Pearl Harbor was attacked.

EXAMPLE 2 ➤   You can write to us at Southwestern College, 900 Otay Lakes Road, Chula Vista, California 91910, if you have any comments or questions.

As you can see, the correctly punctuated address in Example 2 looks like a series of items except that *and* is not used. Notice that there is no comma between the state and the zip code.

COMMAS FOR CLARITY OR EMPHASIS:

Occasionally writers choose to use a comma that does not follow the rules in order to improve clarity or add emphasis. For instance, the following sentence could be written with a comma, even though a comma is not required by the rules:

EXAMPLE 3 ➤ Effective discipline should be strict, but not harsh. *(comma for emphasis)*

Remember that Comma Rule #1 calls for a comma before *but* only when it connects two clauses, not when it connects two words or phrases. However, some writers might want to use a comma in this sentence to make the reader pause and notice the contrast between *strict* and *harsh*. In other words, this comma adds *emphasis*. If you come across special situations in your writing where you would like to use a comma for clarity or emphasis, it may be a good idea to consult with your instructor about them.

Until you have gained a considerable amount of writing experience with a wide variety of sentence structures, it is advisable to stick to the rules. If none of the rules apply to a given situation, then most likely a comma is not needed. By putting in commas only when the rules require them, you will be using punctuation effectively to enhance your writing.

■ **CLASS PRACTICE** **8**

Applying the Comma Rules

Directions: If the sentence is correct without adding any commas, write OK on the line. If commas are needed, add them in the appropriate places. At least one sentence in each group requires no commas.

Comma Rule #1:

_____ 1. It was impossible to determine whether the flying saucer in the photographs was the real thing or a clever hoax.

_____ 2. The cylindrical object appeared to hover above the trees for a few seconds and then it disappeared completely.

_____ 3. Some people claim to have seen extraterrestrials but there is no objective scientific evidence to back up their stories.

_____ 4. There has been more rain than usual this year so the hillsides are lush and green with vegetation.

Comma Rule #2:

_____ **5.** The workers are striking for higher wages better medical coverage and safer working conditions.

_____ **6.** Movies are generally rated R because of violence adult language or nudity.

_____ **7.** The weekend weather forecast includes high winds and heavy thunderstorms.

_____ **8.** JD wrote an exciting suspenseful short story about a lawman named Hollis.

Comma Rule #3:

_____ **9.** We have an average of five dreams every night according to dream researchers.

_____ **10.** At the graduation ceremony students can have their diplomas presented by the faculty member of their choice.

_____ **11.** Although he felt nervous Dan was able to answer all of the interviewers' questions effectively.

_____ **12.** The eagle represents wisdom in many Indian stories and legends.

Comma Rule #4:

_____ **13.** Morley who is the main character in the story is a Vietnam veteran.

_____ **14.** Flamingos in the wild unlike flamingos in the zoo can fly very gracefully.

_____ **15.** The rest of the lecture series however will continue as planned.

_____ **16.** Classrooms that are overcrowded do not provide a quality learning environment.

Using Commas Correctly in a Paragraph

Directions: Using the four comma rules, decide where to place commas in the following paragraph. If a comma is needed, write the comma in the blank. If no comma is needed, write O in the blank.

Transitions

Twenty or thirty years ago___(1) most young people expected to be on their own soon after they graduated from high school___(2) but today more___(3) and more young people continue to live with their parents___(4) until they are in their mid- or late-twenties. One reason for this change is today's high cost of living___(5) which makes it difficult___(6) for someone with a minimum-wage job to make it alone. The costs of rent___(7) utilities___(8) groceries___(9) and other living expenses are higher now than ever before. If a person doesn't have a job___(10) that pays well___(11) he or she simply can't afford a house or an apartment. One solution___(12) is to share a place with roommates. By sharing expenses___(13) two or three people can afford a modest___(14) comfortable apartment. Many other young people___(15) however___(16) continue living___(17) with their parents while they attend college. If they are lucky enough to find part-time jobs___(18) they will have some degree of financial freedom. They may contribute to household expenses___(19) but they have to pay much less___(20) than they would___(21) if they had their own place. Eventually___(22) of course___(23) most young people do move out of their parents' home___(24) and start life on their own. However___(25) in times of financial difficulty___(26) they are likely to return___(27) sometimes with a child or two. If they lose their job___(28) get divorced___(29) or are overwhelmed with debts___(30) their parents' home once more provides a temporary haven.

Other Punctuation

Some other punctuation marks that you may occasionally want to use in your writing are semicolons, colons, dashes, and quotation marks.

Semicolons

As you have seen in previous chapters, when a Group C connector (a conjunctive adverb like *therefore, however,* and *consequently*) is used to join two clauses, a semicolon is required, as in this sentence from the short essay *Dead-Beat Dads*:

EXAMPLE 1 ➤ Men are held blameless; *therefore,* they feel no remorse.

Remember that in this type of sentence there is usually a comma after the Group C connector. This comma follows Comma Rule #3 for introductory expressions since the Group C connector is introductory to the second clause.

A semicolon can also be used alone, without any connecting word, between two closely related clauses or sentences. Here are two sentences from the example essay *Iwo Jima* that could be written as one sentence by using a semicolon:

EXAMPLE 2 ➤ The old airfield from World War II was now covered with heavy, tall vegetation; above the airfield remained the caves and tunnels where the Japanese pilots were housed during World War II.

Of course, a period instead of a semicolon in Example 2 would also be correct. The difference is that the semicolon suggests a somewhat closer relationship between the two ideas. It's not a good idea to use a lot of sentences with semicolons because they may make your writing sound too formal; however, an occasional semicolon can be used quite effectively for sentence variety.

Colons

The main use of colons is to introduce an item or a list of items following a *complete sentence.* Here are two sentences with colons from example paragraphs in previous chapters:

EXAMPLE 3 ➤ A lineup consists of three types of players: power hitters, contact hitters, and those players who excel in defense but are usually weak hitters. (*Lineup,* by Richard D. Munholand)

EXAMPLE 4 ➤ Most fires are started by unnatural causes: arson, cigarettes thrown from cars, kids playing with matches, and migrant workers' cooking fires. (*Brushfires in Southern California,* by Shawn McPherren)

Notice that in both examples the words before the colon form complete sentences that could be written separately with periods at the end:

> ***Sentence:*** A lineup consists of three types of players.

> ***Sentence:*** Most fires are started by unnatural causes.

Colons can also be used to introduce certain kinds of examples or quotations. Perhaps you have noticed that many of the examples in this book are introduced with a colon. This is how we introduced the first two examples of colons:

EXAMPLE 5 ➤ Here are two topic sentences from previous chapters that used colons:

Dashes

Unlike other marks of punctuation, a dash is never mandatory. However, some writers like to use dashes occasionally to call attention to something. Usually a dash is used in a situation where just a comma would be correct, or occasionally where a semicolon or colon would be correct. By using a dash instead, the writer adds emphasis and causes the reader to pay more attention to the words that follow the dash. Here is a sentence from *Dead-Beat Dads* that could be written with a dash:

EXAMPLE 6 ➤ Being a single parent is all about sacrifices—usually the mother's sacrifices.

Although this sentence was originally written with a comma after *sacrifices* to set off the addition at the end of the sentence according to Comma Rule #3, the dash may be even more effective. It puts more emphasis on the fact that the mother is the one who makes the sacrifices.

Here is another sentence from the example essay *Tears in Heaven* that could be written very effectively with a dash instead of a comma:

EXAMPLE 7 ➤ On Friday, July 31, it was time for another type of shock—the shock of saying goodbye to someone for the last time.

When the phrase that you want to call attention to is in the middle of a sentence instead of at the end, a pair of dashes—one before the phrase and one after the phrase—can be used to get the right effect. If your typewriter or word processor does not have a dash, you can use two short lines (hyphens) instead- -a substitute for a dash.

Quotation Marks

If you use dialogue or quote a passage from a book or article, it is important to put quotation marks before and after the words you are quoting.

If there is a period, question mark, or exclamation mark at the end of the quoted words, it normally goes inside the quotation marks. When an introductory phrase such as *he said* is used at the beginning to identify the speaker, it must be followed by a comma. Here are some examples of dialogue from *Tears in Heaven* by Trent Parker. Notice the quotation marks, the commas after the introductory phrases, and the end punctuation of the sentences:

EXAMPLE 8 ➤ He said, "Hey, I'm sorry to tell you this, but Ethan was shot and died last night." My first reaction was, "That's not even funny. You're kidding, right?"

Occasionally the writer may want to identify the speaker somewhere in the middle of the dialogue instead of at the beginning. In this case, quotation marks go before and after the first part of the dialogue, then before and after the second part of the dialogue. Since the identification of the speaker interrupts the sentence, it must be set off by commas. Notice that the comma after the first part of the dialogue goes *inside* the quotation marks, as in the following example:

EXAMPLE 9 ➤ "Hey, Ethan," I say, "I dare you to pull down your shorts and moon that car full of chicks stopped at the light."

Ethan's response shows how to punctuate dialogue when the speaker is identified at the end. Here, too, the comma goes inside the quotation marks.

EXAMPLE 10 ➤ "You're on," he says with a mischievous little grin.

Although periods and commas always go inside the quotation marks when you are writing dialogue, question marks may go either inside or outside the quotation marks, depending on the meaning. If the quotation itself is a question, the question mark goes inside the quotation marks, as in Example 8. However, if the quotation is not a question but the rest of the sentence is, the question mark belongs outside the quotation marks, as in this example:

EXAMPLE 11 ➤ When was the last time you told somebody, "I love you"?

The same guidelines apply to exclamations. The exclamation mark goes outside the quotation marks if the main sentence is exclamatory. In other cases, when the dialogue is the exclamatory part, the exclamation mark goes inside the quotation marks, as in Example 12:

EXAMPLE 12 ➤ He screamed, "I can't believe I won the lottery!"

Using Correct Punctuation
in a Short Essay

Directions: The following short essay needs commas, as well as a few semicolons and colons. Write the correct punctuation in each blank. If no punctuation is needed, write O in the blank.

Magical Creatures

In most cultures___(1) there are stories and legends about imaginary beings___(2) that have magical powers. These imaginary beings include many different kinds of creatures___(3) elves___(4) faeries___(5) pixies___(6) genies___(7) leprechauns___(8) trolls___(9) banshees___(10) and gremlins___(11) to name just a few.

Generally these creatures resemble humans except___(12) that they are smaller___(13) in fact___(14) some are only a few inches high. For example___(15) leprechauns are tiny men___(16) dressed in green that live in Ireland. Pixies___(17) which are noted for their beauty___(18) are also very small. Trolls___(19) which are found___(20) in Scandinavian countries___(21) often look like short___(22) ugly men with humped backs.

Many___(23) magical creatures are helpful to humans___(24) or bring good luck. Elves may give a person pieces of gold if they like him___(25) the tooth fairy gives children money___(26) for their teeth. Certain types of magical creatures___(27) can even grant wishes. If an airy being comes out of a lamp or bottle and says___(28) "Your wish is my command___(29)" you have discovered a genie. Some faeries grant wishes too. Almost everyone has heard of Cinderella's fairy godmother___(30) who changed Cinderella's dirty___(31) ragged clothes into a beautiful gown___(32) so that she could attend the ball and meet Prince Charming.

However___(33) sometimes magical creatures cause problems___(34) for people or like to be mischievous. Gremlins___(35) for instance___(36) cause mechanical problems. They were first identified during World War I when pilots claimed that gremlins were responsible___(37) for engine failures___(38) fuel shortages___(39) and other difficulties. Some faeries are said to have stolen human babies and left changeling faerie babies in their place. According to Scottish legends___(40) if you hear a banshee wailing___(41) it means that someone___(42) in the family is going to die.

Faeries___(43) and other magical creatures___(44) can be found in many works of literature___(45) Sanskrit poetry___(46) Homer's epic tales___(47) some of Shakespeare's plays___(48) children's stories like *Peter Pan*___(49) and many books of faerie tales. They have appeared in folklore and legends for hundreds of years___(50) and are not likely to disappear.

Sentence Combining

Directions: Try to use a variety of different sentence connectors, and be sure to use correct punctuation in your sentence combinations. Notice that several of the verbs are in the present perfect tense, the past perfect tense, or the passive voice.

Elephants and Ivory

1.1   In 1979 there were about 1.3 million elephants in Africa.
1.2   By 1989 the number of elephants had been reduced to only about 625,000.

2.1   Many thousands of elephants have been illegally shot by poachers.
2.2   The poachers use automatic assault rifles.
2.3   They cut down entire herds of the huge animals.

3.1   The carcasses are left to rot.
3.2   Orphaned baby elephants are left to die.
3.3   They die of thirst or starvation.
3.4   An orphaned baby will not leave its dead mother.

4.1   The elephants have been killed for their tusks.
4.2   Their tusks have been carved into ivory statues.
4.3   Their tusks have been carved into ivory jewelry.
4.4   Their tusks have been carved into ivory trinkets.

5.1   Ivory is highly prized for its beauty.
5.2   Ivory is highly prized for its durability.
5.3   Unfortunately, elephants must die.
5.4   Ivory can be obtained.

6.1   We know that even the ancient Egyptians valued ivory.
6.2   Ivory artifacts have been found in Egyptian tombs.
6.3   King Solomon sat upon a throne.
6.4   It was said to be made of ivory.

7.1 Ivory has been used to make dice.
7.2 Ivory has been used to make rosary beads.
7.3 Ivory has been used to make pistol grips.
7.4 Ivory has been used to make toothpicks.
7.5 Ivory has been used to make mah-jongg tiles.
7.6 Ivory has been used to make chopsticks.
7.7 Ivory has been used to make many other items.

8.1 In the 1920s elephants were slaughtered to make 60,000 billiard balls per year.
8.2 This was in the United States alone.
8.3 Elephants were slaughtered to make hundreds of thousands of piano keys.

9.1 In the 1970s many people invested in ivory.
9.2 They did this instead of investing in gold or silver.
9.3 They were trying to guard against inflation.

10.1 Over the years, thousand of tons of ivory have been taken out of Africa.
10.2 The ivory has been imported into Hong Kong.
10.3 The ivory has been imported into other trade centers in the Far East.
10.4 Ivory traders have made huge profits.

11.1 Today most countries have agreed to ban the ivory trade.
11.2 These countries will not allow illegal ivory to be imported.
11.3 Fewer elephants are being killed.

12.1 Let's hope that these restrictions will save the African elephants.
12.2 The elephants are endangered.
12.3 They will be saved from extinction.

Putting the Finishing Touches on Your Writing

Now that you have completed the Sentence and Grammar Skills activities in this chapter, you should proofread your short essay one more time. Try to apply everything that you have learned in this chapter about sentence variety, verbs, and punctuation. If you discover that you do not have a variety of different sentence types and lengths, try using some different connectors for a few of your sentences. Make sure that all of your verbs are correctly written using a tense that is appropriate for the situation, and be especially careful with irregular verbs. Check the list of irregular verbs in Appendix III if you're not sure about the correct forms for some of the verbs. To make sure that your punctuation is correct, check each comma with the Comma Rules. If some of your commas do not seem to follow any of the rules, they probably should not be used. Check to make sure that you have used commas where they are needed with coordinating conjunctions, series, introductory elements, afterthoughts, and insertions, according to the Comma Rules.

You should also reread your short essay for content and organization. Remember that the introduction and conclusion should each be a separate short paragraph, and the introduction should contain a thesis statement. Make sure that the body of your paper gives the reader enough information about your topic. If you see places that need more details or explanations, add them on the final copy. Also check the paragraph divisions in the body of your paper. Remember that each paragraph should develop one main point or one part of the topic.

As you proofread your essay, use the Short Essay Writing Checklist below to make sure that you have not forgotten anything.

Short Essay Writing Checklist

Content and Organization

_____ 1. Does my paper have an interesting introduction and a clear thesis statement?

_____ 2. Are the types of writing that I have used appropriate for the topic?

_____ 3. Is my short essay organized effectively?

_____ 4. Do the body paragraphs each develop one point or one part of the topic?

_____ 5. Have I included enough details and explanations about each point?

_____ 6. Are the transitions between paragraphs smooth and effective?

_____ 7. Does my conclusion review the main points or leave the reader with something to think about?

Sentence Structure and Grammar

_____ 1. Have I used a variety of different sentence types and lengths?

_____ 2. Have I used my knowledge of correct sentence structure to avoid run-ons, comma splices, and fragments?

_____ 3. Are past participles used correctly where they appear in perfect tenses, in the passive voice, and/or as adjectives?

_____ 4. Are most of my verbs active rather than passive?

_____ 5. Have I checked all of the commas to be sure each comma follows one of the comma rules?

_____ 6. If there are any semicolons, colons, dashes, or quotation marks, are they used appropriately and correctly?

ENRICHMENT SECTION:
Writing a Book Review

Goals

In the enrichment section of this chapter, you will learn how to do the following:

- Understand the terms *novel, theme, character, conflict,* and *setting*
- Explain the main idea or theme of a novel
- Examine the conflicts or problems that the main character experiences
- Analyze the importance of the setting
- Select significant quotations
- Combine all of the above to write a book review

Although it is possible to write a review about any kind of book, the suggestions here apply to a fictional book, or *novel*. A *novel* is a book-length story about characters and events that are not real, even though they may seem very lifelike and believable. Some novels may include events that really happened or characters that are based on real people, but the author has added and changed things in order to create a fictional story. A book review of a novel usually analyzes and explains several different points about the book, such as the author's main point or main idea in the novel, the problems faced by the main characters, and the importance of the time period and the location where the novel takes place.

The first step in writing a book review is choosing a good book. You may want to ask your instructor or librarian for some suggestions before choosing the novel that you want to read. Your choice may be a classic (a novel that has achieved recognition over a long period of time), a current best-seller, or any novel that appeals to you. Whether you like fantasy, science fiction, mystery, adventure, realistic drama, or romance, you can find it in a novel. If the first novel that you choose doesn't turn out to be interesting, change to a different one that you will be able to enjoy reading.

While you are reading, it is a good idea to underline or highlight passages that seem especially significant. (If you are using a library book, you can mark pages with strips of paper or self-stick removable notes.) Look for sentences that express some special insight or interpretation, or that reveal something essential about the main character. If there are any parts that you don't understand, you should also mark them so that you can reread them later or ask someone else to help you interpret them. If other people in your class are reading the same book, you may want to get together in a discussion group to talk about your reactions and analyze the novel together.

After you have finished reading the book and are getting ready to write your review, begin by asking yourself what the novel was really about. Was the author trying to show readers something? Was there a reason for portraying certain types of characters or certain kinds of problems? Even though the people and events in a novel are not real, they are generally modeled after real people, so the author may be trying to show something about human nature or about situations that we may have to deal with in our own lives. Whatever the author is trying to show is the main idea or *theme* of the novel, and in some cases, a novel may have more than one important theme. You should try to explain all of the important themes in your book review.

It is not necessary to tell the whole story of the novel. You should give readers a general idea of what the book is about, but do not include a summary of all the events unless your instructor asks you to. You can mention a few crucial events that have an impact on the *main character* or that help to illustrate an important idea in the book, but you don't need to tell the reader everything that happens. If possible, focus on the challenges or obstacles faced by the main character (or characters). In most novels, the main character experiences problems or *conflicts* because of other people, events, or situations beyond his or her control. Characters can also experience *inner conflicts* such as doubt or uncertainty, just as real people do.

Another important element of most novels is the *setting*. *Setting* means the time period and the location where the novel takes place. Often the time period is important because it may affect how the characters think and act, as well as the kinds of problems that they face. For example, if a novel takes place during the Depression in the 1930's, characters will most likely be affected by the difficult economic times. If a novel takes place in a small rural village in Colombia, the people's outlook and values will be different than if the events take place in a large city like New York or Buenos Aires. In some novels, the setting is so important that the events could not even have happened in another time and place.

Since not all novels are alike, there may also be other points about your particular novel that seem important and that you want to include in your book review. For example, if there are two or three main characters instead of just one, you may want to write more about the characters and their interactions with each other. If the book is written in a special style or with an unusual approach, you could comment on how that contributes to the novel too. For instance, it might be written in the *first person,* as if one of the characters is telling the story, which would affect how everything is portrayed. Anything that helps to analyze or explain the book is appropriate to include in a book review.

Many writers like to include quotations from the book that express some of the author's main ideas or that relate to a key part of the story. A few appropriate quotations can give your readers more of a feel for the book and the characters. To find some good quotations, look again at the passages that you underlined or marked as you were reading. If any of them relate directly to what you are writing in your review, you may want to include one or more of them. Remember, if you use quotations from the book, be sure to put them in quotation marks and indicate the page numbers where the quotations appeared.

Like the paragraphs in a short essay, the paragraphs in the body of your book review should be organized according to the main points that you write about. For instance, a typical book review might have one paragraph about the main point of the book, one paragraph about the main character and the problems he or she has to deal with, and one paragraph about the significance of the setting. If your review includes different points about the book, just remember to use one body paragraph for each topic that you discuss.

A book review should also have an introduction and a conclusion. If you want to express some of your opinions and reactions to the book, the introduction or conclusion is the most appropriate place. What did you like best about this book? How did reading it affect you personally? Did you gain some insight or learn something that you didn't know before? Are there ways in which you think the book is particularly outstanding or impressive? Although it is not necessary to evaluate or critique the entire book, a few words of praise or criticism in the introduction or conclusion can help to give readers a clear overall picture.

As you read the following review of *The Bluest Eye,* a novel by Toni Morrison, notice that the writer, Ann E. Pietrzak, focuses on the main character and her problems, the setting, and a lesson about love. She uses quotations from the novel very effectively to help explain some of her comments.

Review of *The Bluest Eye*
by Ann E. Pietrzak

In the novel *The Bluest Eye,* Toni Morrison tells a gripping tale about one girl's traumatized life. She struggles through problems held within her, which relate to teenagers today and how often their emotions are like a roller coaster.

The main character, Pecola, yearns to be someone else, to have a new personality and especially a different exterior. She comes from an abusive family who regard her as ugly. She spends most of her time with two friends: Claudia, the narrator, and her sister, Frieda. They aid Pecola with her everyday shortcomings even though they cannot answer all of her questions, the most difficult of which is: "How do you do that? I mean, how do you get somebody to love you?" (29) This quote reveals how unloved Pecola truly is.

The setting is a crucial part of this novel because it takes place during the Depression. This circumstance helps to explain why Pecola's father doesn't care for his family. Factors such as unemployment and the overuse of alcohol lead him to abuse. Cholly is also very manipulative toward his daughter.

Pecola wishes to have blue eyes: ". . . if those eyes of hers were different, that is to say beautiful, she herself would be different" (40). She prays every night for blue eyes, and the perspective of the story begins to change more toward Pecola's feelings, not her social or economic status.

Later, Pecola is abused by Cholly and now must bear his child. At the young age of eleven, this is an overwhelming responsibility. She wants to be loved, not just used sexually. Love must be learned early in life. Self-love is also an important aspect of this lesson. Having seen the destructive effects of Cholly's kind of love and Pecola's inability to love herself, the narrator observes near the end of the novel, "Love is never any better than the lover. Wicked people love wickedly, violent people love violently, weak people weakly, stupid people love stupidly, but the love of a free man is never safe. The lover alone possesses his gift of love. The loved one is shorn, neutralized, frozen in the glare of the lover's inward eye" (159–160). The beauty of Pecola's bluest eyes may one day be found within when she learns to love another, and especially herself.

The Bluest Eye portrays a lesson unlearned by many teenagers. Pecola wanted to change the color of her skin and the color of her eyes, in the same way that some young people today conform to certain ways of life simply to be popular. This form of modeling others masks personality. The novel shows us that beauty is not only skin deep, and that true love is found within.

■ ■ ■ Reference Section

CONTENTS OF REFERENCE SECTION

APPENDIX I
Prewriting Worksheets

Additional prewriting worksheets are included here so that you can use one or more of them with any writing assignment, even if the chapter that you are working on uses a different prewriting technique. These worksheets are for the same prewriting techniques used in Chapters 2 through 8, although in some cases they have been changed slightly so that they can be used for various types of writing. The directions on each worksheet will tell you how to use it.

On the following pages, there is a worksheet for each of these prewriting techniques:

Freewriting (from Chapter 2)

Listing (from Chapter 3)

Visualizing (from Chapter 4)

Dividing and Listing (from Chapter 5)

Outlining (from Chapter 6)

Branching (from Chapter 7)

Clustering (from Chapter 8)

Freewriting Worksheet

Directions: Write whatever comes to mind about your topic without stopping to organize or edit.

Topic: _____

_____

_____

_____

_____

_____

_____

_____

_____

_____

_____

_____

_____

_____

_____

_____

_____

_____

_____

_____

Listing Worksheet

Directions: List all of the ideas that you can think of about your topic. It is not necessary to write complete sentences, and don't worry if some things are not in the right order.

Topic: _____

_____

_____

_____

_____

_____

_____

_____

_____

_____

_____

_____

_____

_____

_____

_____

_____

_____

Visualizing Worksheet

Directions: First close your eyes, relax, and spend some time visualizing the place, person, or event that you are writing about. Then answer whichever questions apply to your topic. Space is provided at the bottom of this workseet for additional observations.

Topic: _____

1. As you look all around you, what do you see? Include people, objects, and anything else that you remember.

   _____

   _____

   _____

2. As you visualize the scene, what is happening?

   _____

   _____

   _____

3. What sounds, smells, touch sensations, or tastes do you notice?

   _____

   _____

4. How do you feel while you are visualizing this place, person, or event? What makes you feel this way?

   _____

   _____

   _____

5. Other observations:

   _____

   _____

   _____

Outlining Worksheet

Directions: Write your main points after the Roman numerals. Then list two or more ideas or things that you want to say about each of your main points. There is extra space so that you can add more letters or numbers if you need to.

Topic: _____

    I. _____

        A. _____

        B. _____

        C. _____

    II. _____

        A. _____

        B. _____

        C. _____

    III. _____

        A. _____

        B. _____

        C. _____

    IV. _____

        A. _____

        B. _____

        C. _____

Dividing and Listing Worksheet

Directions: This worksheet can be used for a comparison/contrast topic or any other topic that has two parts. First write one part of the topic at the top of each column. Then list all the details that you can think of. Put related points side by side whenever possible, especially for a comparison/contrast.

TOPIC (Part 1):

_____

DETAILS:

TOPIC (Part 2):

_____

Branching Worksheet

Directions: For cause and effect analysis, write a cause in the circle and then think of effects to put on the branches, or write an effect in the circle and then think of causes to write on the branches. For other types of writing, put your topic in the circle and write the details about it on the branches. You may add more branches in any direction.

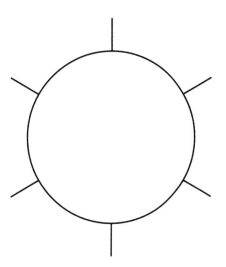

Clustering Worksheet

Directions: First write your topic idea in the middle of the page. Then draw lines in any direction to attach ideas that are related to your topic. Circle these ideas as you attach them, and then draw more lines to attach additional ideas. Let the clusters of ideas take whatever form works best.

TOPIC

APPENDIX II
Sentence Patterns

Pattern 1. SV.   SV.

One clause separated from the next by a period

$$S \quad V$$

EXAMPLE ➤   My name is Cassandra Dorsey.

Variations:

1a. The subject of a command isn't stated, but is understood to be
you.

$$[S = you] \quad V$$

EXAMPLE ➤   Lay the victim on his left side.

1b. After the words *there* and *here,* the true subject of the clause
follows the verb.

$$V \qquad\qquad S$$

EXAMPLE ➤   There are two final exams on Friday.

Pattern 2. SV ,   Group A   SV.

Clauses connected by a comma and a Group A word

$$S \qquad V \qquad\qquad , Group\ A \quad S \quad V$$

EXAMPLE ➤   Instantly the night became deathly quiet, *and* we froze like
rabbits.

Variations:

2a. Nor requires VS word order.

EXAMPLE ➤   No one answered our knock, *nor* had anyone gotten the mail.

2b. A comma is sometimes not used if the sentence is very short.

EXAMPLE ➤   Terry worked late *but* I went home.

Pattern 3. SV   Group B   SV.

Clauses connected by a Group B word with no comma

EXAMPLE ➤   He can call me *if* he wants to get together this week.

Variations:

3a. SV   Relative Pronoun   SV.

EXAMPLE ➤   Carl bought the toy *that* Aman wanted.

3b. SV   Relative Adverb   SV.

EXAMPLE ➤   Roy showed us the store *where* he found the amethyst ring.

3c. SV   Relative Pronoun (= S)   V.

EXAMPLE ➤   Marge knows an artist *who* paints trompe l'oeil walls.

3d. SV   (Relative Connector omitted)   SV.

EXAMPLE ➤   I learned a lot from the math class I took.

Pattern 4.   Group B   SV,   SV.

Clauses connected by a Group B word at the beginning and a comma before the second clause

EXAMPLE ➤   *When* you have time, I'd like to take you to lunch.

S

Pattern 5.   ⌈Group B   SV⌉   V.

Noun clause used as the subject of another clause

EXAMPLE ➤   *Whatever* you decide is fine with me.

Pattern 6.   S(,)   Relative Pronoun   SV(,)   V.

A relative clause in the middle of another clause with or without commas, depending on the meaning

EXAMPLE ➤   Tony Adderson, for *whom* we voted, won the election.

Variations:

6a. S   Relative Adverb   SV   V.

EXAMPLE ➤   The day *when* Kathleen said "Yes" was the best day of my life.

6b. S   Relative Pronoun (=) SV   V.

EXAMPLE ➤   Students *who* come late cannot take the test.

Pattern 7. SV ; Group C, SV.

Clauses connected by a semicolon, a Group C word, and a comma

EXAMPLE ➤ Writing is a complex process; however, it can be learned one step at a time.

Variation:

7a. SV . Group C, SV.

EXAMPLE ➤ Writing is a complex process. However, it can be learned one step at a time.

Pattern 8. SV ; SV.

Clauses connected by a semicolon alone

EXAMPLE ➤ The actors retired; the curtain descended.

Pattern 9. SV, SV, and SV.

Clauses in a series

EXAMPLE ➤ The red faded, the sun set, and the stars began to peek out.

APPENDIX III
Irregular Verbs

Simple Form	Simple Past	Past Participle
be	was/were	been
bear	bore	borne/born
beat	beat	beaten/beat
become	became	become
begin	began	begun
bend	bent	bent
bet	bet	bet
bid	bid	bid/bidden
bind	bound	bound
bite	bit	bitten
bleed	bled	bled
blow	blew	blown
break	broke	broken
breed	bred	bred
bring	brought	brought
broadcast	broadcast	broadcast
build	built	built
burn	burned/burnt	burned/burnt
burst	burst	burst
buy	bought	bought
cast	cast	cast
catch	caught	caught
choose	chose	chosen
cling	clung	clung
come	came	come
cost	cost	cost
creep	crept	crept
cut	cut	cut
deal	dealt	dealt
dig	dug	dug
dive	dived/dove	dived/dove
do	did	done
draw	drew	drawn
dream	dreamed/dreamt	dreamed/dreamt
drink	drank	drunk
drive	drove	driven
eat	ate	eaten
fall	fell	fallen
feed	fed	fed
feel	felt	felt
fight	fought	fought

Simple Form	*Simple Past*	*Past Participle*
find	found	found
fit	fit	fit
flee	fled	fled
fling	flung	flung
fly	flew	flown
forbid	forbade	forbidden
forecast	forecast	forecast
forget	forgot	forgotten
forgive	forgave	forgiven
freeze	froze	frozen
get	got	gotten/got*
give	gave	given
go	went	gone
grind	ground	ground
grow	grew	grown
hang	hanged/hung	hanged/hung†
have	had	had
hear	heard	heard
hide	hid	hidden
hit	hit	hit
hold	held	held
hurt	hurt	hurt
keep	kept	kept
kneel	kneeled/knelt	kneeled/knelt
know	knew	known
lay	laid	laid
lead	led	led
leap	leaped/leapt	leaped/leapt
leave	left	left
lend	lent	lent
let	let	let
lie	lay	lain
light	lighted/lit	lighted/lit
lose	lost	lost
make	made	made
mean	meant	meant
meet	met	met
mistake	mistook	mistaken
pay	paid	paid
prove	proved	proved/proven
put	put	put
quit	quit	quit

*American usage is *get, got, gotten*. British usage is *get, got, got*.

†Hanged is only used for death by *hanging;* all other uses are *hung.*

Simple Form	Simple Past	Past Participle
read	read	read*
rid	rid	rid
ride	rode	ridden
ring	rang	rung
rise	rose	risen
run	ran	run
say	said	said
see	saw	seen
seek	sought	sought
sell	sold	sold
send	sent	sent
set	set	set
sew	sewed	sewed/sewn
shake	shook	shaken
shed	shed	shed
shine	shined/shone	shined/shone†
shoot	shot	shot
show	showed	showed/shown
shrink	shrank/shrunk	shrunk/shrunken
shut	shut	shut
sing	sang	sung
sink	sank	sunk
sit	sat	sat
sleep	slept	slept
slide	slid	slid
slit	slit	slit
speak	spoke	spoken
speed	speeded/sped	speeded/sped
spend	spent	spent
spin	spun	spun
spit	spit/spat	spit/spat
split	split	split
spread	spread	spread
spring	sprang/sprung	sprung
stand	stood	stood
steal	stole	stolen
stick	stuck	stuck
sting	stung	stung
stink	stank/stunk	stunk
strike	struck	struck/stricken
string	strung	strung
strive	strived/strove	striven

*The pronunciation of the past tense and past participle sounds like the word *red*.

†*Shined* is used only when the verb is transitive, as in "I shined my shoes."

Simple Form	Simple Past	Past Participle
swear	swore	sworn
sweep	swept	swept
swell	swelled	swelled/swollen
swim	swam	swum
swing	swung	swung
take	took	taken
teach	taught	taught
tear	tore	torn
tell	told	told
think	thought	thought
throw	threw	thrown
thrust	thrust	thrust
understand	understood	understood
upset	upset	upset
wake	waked/woke	waked/woken
wear	wore	worn
weave	wove	woven
weep	wept	wept
win	won	won
wind	wound	wound
wring	wrung	wrung
write	wrote	written

APPENDIX IV
Spelling Rules for *-ed, -ing, -er,* and *-est* Endings

I. The Silent -e Rule:

If the word ends in a silent *-e,* drop the *-e.*

line–lined–lining,   nice–nicer–nicest

II. The Double Consonant Rule:

The double consonant rule applies to many words that end with a consonant, a vowel, and a consonant. It generally applies to all such one-syllable words. It also applies to those two-syllable words that have the stress on the second syllable.

If the word has one syllable and the last three letters are a consonant, a vowel, and a consonant, double the final consonant.

rip–ripped–ripping,   big–bigger–biggest

If the word is more than one syllable with the stress on the last syllable and the last three letters are a consonant, a vowel, and a consonant, double the final consonant.

admit–admitted–admitting

but

travel–traveled–traveling

Exceptions: Don't double a final h, w, x, or y.

mow–mowed–mowing,   wax–waxed–waxing

III. The -y to -i Rule:

For *-ed, -er,* and *-est* endings, if the word ends with a consonant plus *-y,* change the *-y* to *-i* and add the ending.

cry–cried–crying,   dry–drier–driest

but

play–played–playing,   gray–grayer–grayest

IV. The -ie to -y Rule:

For *-ing* endings, if the word ends with *-ie,* change the *-ie* to *-y* and add *-ing.*

die–dying,   lie–lying

▪ ▪ ▪ Index

NOTES

NOTES

NOTES

NOTES

NOTES